W9-CSX-093

HQ
1613
A735
2000

Allen, James Smith.
Poignant relations

12/00

Poignant Relations

James Smith Allen

Poignant Relations

➳ THREE MODERN FRENCH WOMEN

THE JOHNS HOPKINS UNIVERSITY PRESS · *Baltimore & London*

© 2000 The Johns Hopkins University Press
All rights reserved. Published 2000
Printed in the United States of America on acid-free paper

9 8 7 6 5 4 3 2 1

The Johns Hopkins University Press
2715 North Charles Street
Baltimore, Maryland 21218-4363
www.press.jhu.edu

Excerpts from *"In the Solitude of My Soul": The Diary of Geneviève Bréton, 1867–1871*, edited by James Smith Allen, © 1994 by the Board of Trustees, Southern Illinois University, reprinted by permission of the publisher.

Excerpts from *Worldmaking*, edited by William Pencak, © 1996 by Peter Lang Publishing, Inc., reprinted by permission of the publisher.

Library of Congress Cataloging-in-Publication Data will be found at the end of this book.

A catalog record for this book is available from the British Library.

ISBN 0-8018-6204-3

Für Anne

Wir leben wie Gott in Frankreich . . .

Contents

Illustrations

Acknowledgments

This book owes nearly everything to women—family members, dear friends, good students, and generous colleagues—all of whose help deserves recognition. So for the first but hardly the last time, the pronouns *I, she,* and their grammatical correlatives are invoked here to disarm, if not to charm the reader. The author's gratitude is no less sincere.

When my grandmother Louie Sutherland married in 1900, her mother kept a diary. It is curious how unimportant men were then to my great-grandmother, and I think it was deliberate. She apparently needed a private space of her own to cope with the changes in her family marked by the wedding of her youngest daughter. The diary's long lists of seemingly inconsequential details are poignant in their implicit expression of courage and regret. Clearly, writing helped its author to live with emotional loss; and her act of recollection suggested one major theme in my work: the consciousness of gender among the most unlikely of people.

It has been much the same with other women in my family. Each one of them remains an independent-minded individual of strength and dignity in spite, even because of, gendered constraints. My mother Marie-Louise valiantly nursed my father during a long, fatal illness; my sister Marie-Louise kept her promise, the first of many like it, to finish college; my sisters-in-law Frieda and Lori also balanced work and family wisely; and my wife's sister Jane has provided psychiatric care in several western U.S. towns. Like the saints and teachers among the "crazy" Wilsons who made life better in rural Oklahoma, their self-conscious efforts reveal the many ways that gender both poses problems and proposes solutions. For each of these women, consciousness and agency were more than mere words. They all assumed an identity suggested by my great-grandmother, at least discursively, to provide the original inspiration for this book.

Of more immediate assistance were the efforts of Daphné Doublet-Vaudoyer, who recalled details about her own grandmother Geneviève Bréton and her father Jean-Louis Vaudoyer. She graciously taught me the differences that culture as well as gender make in friendship and scholarship. Her kindness was perhaps matched by the consideration of Michèle Le Pavec at the Bibliothèque Nationale, who helped me with Geneviève's uncataloged diary and correspondence. I also appreciate the dispatch of the librarians responsible for the Marie Louise Bouglé papers at the Bibliothèque Historique de laVille de Paris and for the various archival dossiers at the Bibliothèque Marguerite Durand, both superb collections for research on the history of women. In Angers, Elisabeth Verry tracked down obscure public records, and Elisabeth Jessenne gladly took me to visit the gravesite and one of the homes belonging to Marie Leroyer.

Selfless colleagues listened to or read and critiqued my work at various stages of its development, and they deserve acknowledgment for their assistance in improving the final product, whether or not I took all their advice. Much of the good sense and none of the nonsense in this book can be attributed to the sharp insights of Jane Adams, Kay Carr, Michelle DenBeste-Barnett, Betsy George, Colette Hall, Joy Harvey, Robbie Lieberman, Joan McDermott (and the students in our course on the legal and social control of women), Marji Morgan, Jeannene Przyblyski, Minnie Sinha, Bonnie Smith, Tracy Thibodeau, and Clarisse Zimra (including her Theory Reading Group).

Rachel Stocking generously copyedited the entire manuscript and helped me to reorganize the text. Similarly, Hélène Lowe-Dupas checked all my translations and saved me from countless gaffes in both French and English. Laurel Petrich, my research assistant, competently managed the details of the book. All of these interventions have proved invaluable, like those of the students in my colloquium and seminar on European women's history in 1993–94, when this project first took shape.

I must thank four good and broad-minded men: Jules Jessenne of Angers told me much I needed to know about his distant neighbor Marie Leroyer; Tom Kselman provided maps of the town where she had lived; Jimmy Palmes shared with me his reflections on the art of writing and translating; and most important of all, Bob Nye read my manuscript with the same wisdom and perspicacity that he had brought to my previous work on the history of reading. I am particularly grateful to him once again.

Of course, I offer my appreciation to the institutions whose funding made this book possible: the Oklahoma Foundation for the Humanities (1991), the National Endowment for the Humanities (1991), the Office for Research Development and Administration, the College of Liberal Arts, and the office of the provost at Southern Illinois University, Carbondale (1992, 1996, 1997–99), and the American Bar Association (1996).

Just as Southern Illinois University Press permitted me to quote from *"In the Solitude of My Soul": The Diary of Geneviève Bréton, 1867–1871* (1994), the Bibliothèque Nationale de France, the Bibliothèque Historique de la Ville de Paris, the Musée des Beaux Arts d'Angers, the Musée Municipal de Château-Gontier, and the Musée Carnavalet granted me the rights to reproduce photographs of materials in their possession. Much of chapter 4 appeared in my contribution to Graham Falconer's collection of papers, *Autour d'un cabinet de lecture* (1999), published by the Centre des Etudes Romantiques Sablé at the University of Toronto. Portions of chapter 5 are taken from my essays on Céline Renooz in collections published by Peter Lang (*Worldmaking*, ed. William Pencak, 1996) and by the University of Massachusetts Press (*Making the News*, ed. Dean De la Motte and Jeannene Przyblyski, 1999), for whose permissions I am grateful.

Finally, I am deeply indebted to my wife Anne Winston, who taught an inveterate francophile, one displaced by a mere century, to love the German Middle Ages too. More to the point, her hard work, enduring affection, and profound generosity have shown me another side to feminist consciousness. What felicity there is in my scholarly endeavors comes from her. For these reasons and many more, this study is as much hers as it is mine. As I did with two earlier books that were much improved by her good counsel, I gratefully and joyfully dedicate my work to her.

Poignant Relations

✌ Introduction

> Writing is working; being worked; questioning (in) the between (letting one-
> self be questioned) of same *and of* other without which nothing lives; undoing
> death's work by willing the togetherness of one-another, infinitely charged
> with a ceaseless exchange of one with another—not knowing one another and
> beginning again only from what is most distant, from self, from other, from
> the other within. A course that multiplies transformations by the thousands.[1]

Less poetically but no less passionately, I want to explore what Hélène Cixous
suggests here. As a historian, I want to consider the discursive relations of
women to themselves, to others, and to the world, however grandiose such an
undertaking may seem. Although Cixous and her coauthor Catherine Clément develop other agendas besides that of *l'écriture féminine,* their insight into
writing as women's work charged with "ceaseless exchange" is profound and
well worth exploring historically.[2] Not just the historical but also the literary
sources of women's consciousness and of their relationships to self and other
define the themes and issues of my book, if only because, as Carolyn Heilbrun
has observed, "we live our lives through texts."[3] Simply put, the literate arts
of feminist consciousness in modern France give form to (and are informed
by) women's poignant relations both as texts and as experiences.

These matters are poignant, I think, because they touch us. In what Cixous
calls the "between . . . of same *and of* other without which nothing lives," who
can remain indifferent to the tales of triumph and tribulation that French
women have told of their lives, from medieval commentators like Christine
de Pisan to modern novelists like Marguerite Duras? Their affecting self-
narratives also differ from men's, as anyone alert to literary style and substance can readily attest.[4] Generally more sensitive to others, perhaps because
they have long been the Other, French women have crafted their personal

accounts with an eye to the impressions they make, to the postponement of closure especially, derived in part from sexual difference. Whether such writing concerns more the body than the mind or culture, I cannot say, but it can surely move the sympathetic intellect to serious reflection on the special nature of women's creative endeavor, by themselves and in their relations with others.

The operative words for me, however—arguably for Cixous and Clément as well—are *exchange, togetherness, self,* and *other,* all captured in the word *relations.*[5] This latter term has at least two meanings: narratives, stories, and accounts, on the one hand, and families, loves, and connections, on the other. Women wrote and continue to write both real and imagined tales about themselves, of course, but also, and just as telling, about relationships. Lovers and their troubles, for example, are related in novels, autobiographies, and similar *récits* by women and men alike. But like their lives with others (though not always with men), women have given voice to the pain of personal experience in words and a world not of their own making. To the extent that authors must also contend with an overpowering here-and-now, the reality of "patriarchy" and its dominant texts necessarily intrudes into women's writing.[6] In a historical context of subordination, even oppression, the written results of "undoing death's work" are pointedly personal; their relations in both senses of the word are poignant.

The Arts of Feminist Consciousness

The passage by Cixous thus raises the principal concerns that my book addresses, and one other. Writing of relationships, she states, "multiplies transformations by the thousands"—transformations of many different sorts but discursive ones above all. That is to say, writing is inherently textual, echoing the voices of other texts from which authors regularly draw their inspiration, resulting in what theorists call "intertextuality."[7] Women no less, maybe more than men borrow the language, as a grammar and as a vocabulary, that is available and most appropriate to them.[8] A writer's unacknowledged debt to someone else's work is one manifestation of this linguistic appropriation. But no matter what its source, authors must still craft their language; as human agents they create the literary texts that others read, interpret, and rewrite to make their own. Such deliberation within discourse I want to make explicit in this book on the arts of feminist consciousness.[9]

Historically these discursive arts have appeared in many different guises, but most obviously in women's personal writings, such as diaries, letters, and autobiographies. Some genres, certainly the most public of them like the autobiography, exist within well-established traditions defined by generations of mostly male but also many female writers.[10] Antoinette Bourignon (1683), Jeanne-Marie Guyon (1720), and the baronne de Staal de Launay (1755) were among the first French autobiographers published long before Jean-Jacques Rousseau's *Confessions* (1782–89). Other modes of women's self-expression appeared later. Eugénie de Guérin's diary (1862), for instance, was the first of its kind to be printed in France. As Gerda Lerner has argued, too little was known about the substantial tradition of women's published writing for others to draw on until the nineteenth century.[11] After 1870, thanks to circumstances making for a more pervasive feminist consciousness, women's contributions to the less personal fields of political polemic, literary criticism, cultural history, and scientific treatises became obvious. By then autobiographical genres were no longer considered their particular domain.

Not all women turned this craft to specifically feminist ends. Far from it. Writing's various manifestations are never as simple or as single-minded as that. Moreover, most women then and now have eschewed feminism's derogatory label, even if they have come to embrace many of its ideas. But because writing is an unusual, deliberative gesture—it is hard work, after all—I want to argue that the arts of women's literate expression are historical evidence of their self-consciousness. Implicitly at least, these sustained creative efforts fostered identity, a sense of agency in the world, a resistance to the very real constraints in women's lives. The author was alive to her subjectivity. By writing, she transgressed deliberately the patriarchal prohibitions against her intellectual life, at least until recently.[12] For this reason, all women writers in nineteenth-century France, whatever their purpose or ideology, expressed a feminist consciousness, in the very broadest definition of this term, that began in these acts of self-knowledge and self-assertion.[13]

The precise nature of this consciousness, to be sure, is difficult to define for such a large literate population. As most scholars ruefully acknowledge, each variety of feminism has its own definition.[14] But it is not difficult to find a common pattern to women's personal expression, which has historically tended to relationship, interdependence, and community. A dialogic identity has long come more easily for women than it has for men, plausibly because of both a gendered socialization process and a psychoanalytic dynamic priv-

ileging the mother-daughter bond.[15] Women have often developed fluid ego
boundaries, a fragmented, externally defined sense of self and otherness. Like
other marginal and subordinate social groups, they have acquired "this feeling of another reality," a double consciousness of their world apart from those
who dominate them.[16] Life in two worlds, their own and that of men, has
provided women a certain detachment from both. The profound connected-
ness of this view of themselves as the Other—a feeling apparent in much of
women's self-writing—must have contributed to the development of their
particular identity, agency, and resistance within subordination.[17] For individuals like Simone de Beauvoir, "one is not born, but becomes a woman."[18]
Ultimately, to write for oneself is to become, and to write for someone else
is to be.

French women were not unique in their poignant relations. What's so
special about this phenomenon in modern France? The answer, I think, lies in
the discursive forms this consciousness assumed—what Mona Ozouf terms
the "singularity" of their "words."[19] French feminist ideas, for example, were
more inspiring than effective; their realization was curiously elusive from the
very beginning.[20] With the revolution of 1789 and the industrial revolution
that followed, several prominent voices on behalf of women contended for
public attention. Flora Tristan, Maria Deraismes, and Hubertine Auclert, to
name only the better-known activists, actually inspired others to organize in
the defense of their civil and political rights. And however slowly and late,
reforms like the vote in 1944 did come. But most French women remained
indifferent if not openly hostile to these ideas; they declined to act in response
to feminist appeals.[21] As a consequence of this factor (among others), France
witnessed a far smaller and less influential women's movement than existed in
either England or the United States.

French feminism seems to have failed despite the very pervasiveness of its
language.[22] Throughout the nineteenth century, women's voices persisted
and developed within a truly revolutionary context. Although calls for wom-
en's rights encountered much more resistance after 1792, the political up-
heavals in 1830 and 1848 provided new opportunities that might never have
arisen otherwise. Moreover, after 1850 female literacy rates rose dramatically,
enabling women to experience a wider range of political views. In time many
more of them read and wrote about feminist ideals, however few were pre-
pared to act on them. Thus by 1870 no literate woman was altogether unaware
of her status as a legal minor under the Napoleonic Code.

Could it be then that Frenchwomen expressed and pursued their interests differently? Informed by a feminism distinctly their own, did they follow a historical course other than the one traced by English and American activists? Was gender equality configured and manifested singularly in France? Quite possibly. What French women wrote mattered to them. The arts of their feminist consciousness provide evidence that they addressed the issues in their own way, privately and discreetly, at a critical moment in the history of the women's-rights movement from 1848 to 1922. As historians know, the past follows no set formula, no more so for French women and their personal accounts than for other matters. The intense literary culture of France, with its Panthéon and many city streets dedicated to authors, fostered a profoundly literate awareness of women's issues.[23] This particular discursive practice in France is certainly worth exploring historically.

There are other reasons for studying French women's relations as literary texts and as historical realities. One major purpose of my work is readily appreciated; it is the satisfaction of a genuine curiosity about people and their past. In my research on a different project, I stumbled upon the papers of three people who were of inherent interest.[24] Their expression of personal pain, brave determination, and genuine pride in achievement moved me deeply. For the past seven years, their life writings—a mass of letters, notebooks, diaries, memoirs, and memorabilia—have claimed my sympathy and become my world. I have come to know these women, in their varied accounts of bitter trials and sweet triumphs, more directly than I have members of my own family. Their life and work constitute the principal sources for this book.

The first of these figures is Marie-Sophie Leroyer de Chantepie (1800–1888), novelist, literary critic, and frequent correspondent with the better-known authors George Sand and Gustave Flaubert (fig. 1).[25] She lived more than eighty years in Angers, a small town on the Maine River southwest of Paris, where she cared for a large retinue of relatives, friends, and dependents, though she never married. The descendant of a distinguished family in Anjou—hence her aristocratic name—Leroyer inherited enough property to devote her life to literature, writing four novels, three dozen short stories, a volume of criticism, and an incalculable number of letters. To the end of her life she remained a romantic idealist, whose politics favored the revolutionaries in 1848 and again in 1871. For Leroyer, writing defied all constraints, including time itself. Literary endeavor, she believed, was "clear evidence of the immortality inherent in [one's] indestructible being, because everything

Figure 1. Marie-Sophie Leroyer de Chantepie by D. Magu (1870). Oil on canvas (Musée Municipal de Château-Gontier)

that has ever existed can no longer cease to be."[26] In that firm faith, despite her many religious doubts, she was not alone.

The second woman here is Geneviève Bréton-Vaudoyer (1849–1918), indefatigable diarist and passionate correspondent with the promising young artist Henri Regnault and the aspiring author Jean-Louis Vaudoyer (fig. 2).[27] The daughter of a major publisher, living next to the Hachette bookstore on Paris's Boulevard Saint-Michel, Bréton turned her privileged leisure to writing, as much to survive as to defy. Her life was punctuated by profound

Figure 2. Geneviève Bréton-Vaudoyer (c. 1875). Photograph (private collection)

personal loss. Her beloved brother Antoine died when she was seventeen, and her fiancé Henri was killed during the Franco-Prussian War four years later. When she finally married in 1880, her husband, Alfred Vaudoyer, suffered from violent mood swings and serious bouts of paranoia. Her youngest son Michel died in the first weeks of World War I. To cope with these personal tragedies, Bréton kept a diary that soon seized control of her life. In the solitude of her soul, her writing became an emotional necessity, a "prison," as she put it more than once. She went on to write hundreds of letters, first to her

Figure 3. Céline Renooz-Muro (c. 1900). Lithograph from photograph (Document BHVP)

fiancé Henri and then to her son Jean-Louis, most often about their work. In time, however, through her extensive writing Bréton made their life and art very much her own source of creative liberation.

The last figure is Céline Renooz-Muro (1840–1928), scientist, historian, journalist, and polemicist on behalf of her utopian vision of society (fig. 3).[28] Born in Liège, Renooz moved to Paris in 1875 to escape an unhappy marriage and to satisfy a growing passion for natural history. Her unpublished memoirs and correspondence explain how Renooz's interests progressed from embryology, via religion, to women; her efforts resulted in more than a dozen published volumes and twenty boxes of personal papers. In spite of this enormous output, Renooz remained an intellectual pariah, ignored by scholars because of her unconventional epistemology and disdained by contemporaries because of her visionary arrogance. (She was nothing if not overbearing.) Consequently, Renooz saw her writing as a forum to relate both ideas and ideals, as much for their own sake as for posterity's, in her deliberate, often desperate efforts to construct a stable, reliable, discursive self. Like Leroyer and Bréton, Renooz considered her life and work inseparable, a destiny made manifest to one and all.

Leroyer, Bréton, and Renooz are remembered here, whether or not they ever achieve canonical status, because they illustrate well the arts of feminist consciousness in modern France. Their relative obscurity as "women on the margins," comparable to Natalie Zemon Davis's figures in an earlier period, actually makes their work and language revealing if not exemplary of discursive practices during the Third Republic.[29] Moreover, social historians and literary theorists know that such people and texts are well worth examining for what they tell us about the singularity of the French women's movement, but also about the substantial omissions from history books and literary classrooms today. Much of what women wrote is at long last being published and studied. For these reasons and more, the remarkable collection of letters, diaries, memoirs, and publications that Leroyer, Bréton, and Renooz left behind offer the historian a truly precious archive to explore; they document the private lives and words of the many women like them in the past two hundred years. There is much to learn from their hard, creative work.[30]

The Scholarly Conversation

These women's poignant relations touch on the concerns of recent historians and literary specialists. Gerda Lerner, for instance, is hardly alone in addressing the origins and development of feminist thought.[31] Women's history is among the fastest-growing fields in the historical discipline, especially in the United States, where scholars once took the lead in defining issues and themes for the history of women everywhere, including France.[32] Studies of French feminism, its forms and its influence on the women's movement, now share shelfspace with closely related work on women's social and economic conditions.[33] Similarly, the history of gender identity and gender relations—that is, how sexual differences are redefined by society and culture—has become increasingly prominent. Historians are exploring the ways in which the virtues and other values embodied by women have changed since the eighteenth century.[34] In this scholarly context, Leroyer, Bréton, and Renooz suggest just how widespread were feminism's various manifestations, under what historical conditions they evolved, and the extent to which the constructions of gender affected them.

This historical archive is also of interest to literary theorists and critics, feminists and nonfeminists alike.[35] For critics interested in remaking (or displacing) literary canons, the letters, diaries, memoirs, novels, criticism, and treatises here are works worth some analysis. The recovery of these texts returns them to the literary traditions where they belong.[36] For theorists more concerned with language, Leroyer, Bréton, and Renooz participated in the contending discourses of the nineteenth century. They shared in the discursive struggles of other marginalized voices in the past; a similar deliberative presence appears in the texts left by the impoverished, by the culturally outcast, and by the people of color and "different" sexual orientation.[37] Clearly the discursive dialectic, the progressive give-and-take of text and context, arose everywhere and not just among these women in modern France.[38] In this sense, the situations of Leroyer, Bréton, and Renooz were not unique.

No more unusual is my approach to their writing. Other studies privilege language as representation, both of itself and of the world, as a gesture somehow to someone about something.[39] For most scholars, discourse is not a closed, self-referential system; it relates (and relates to) human subjectivity and agency, however uncanny and complex those relations are. The Marxist critic and theorist Rosemary Hennessy, for one, thinks of language as more than an unchanging prison that holds us all captive within its ineffable structures.[40] As Max Weber once said of ideas, writing resembles more a railroad switchman controlling the direction, at least, "along which action has been pushed by the dynamic of interest."[41] Persuaded of language's referentiality and power, I have deliberately modeled my work on that of Richard Terdiman, James Scott, and Gerda Lerner. Although they represent very different disciplines, all three have elaborated on poststructuralism's tentative, somewhat belated sensitivity to the voluntarist elements in discursive practice.[42]

Terdiman the literary specialist, for example, has examined the conflicting ideological voices in nineteenth-century France. They are apparent in the dominant discourse of officialdom and the newspaper, on the one hand, and the counterdiscourse of social criticism and avant-garde literature, on the other. But there was overlap and appropriation on both sides. Balzac's apprenticeship novels, Marx's satirical journalism, Flaubert's parodic prose, and Mallarmé's symbolic poetry all "re/cite" or "de/cite," as the case may be, the dominant language for creative and polemical purposes of their own. And the official discourse did much the same to them; the press mimicked the better-known literati, and the state subvened their work. Even though Terdiman develops his dialectical analysis of clashing voices within a precise historical context, he omits serious consideration of the discursive dissonance introduced by women's writing in particular. Accordingly, I have attempted to address this omission.[43]

In a similar fashion, Scott the political scientist examines the active historical role of language. His book on domination and the arts of resistance focuses on how poor, landless peasants in Southeast Asia have managed to speak back to colonial authority since the nineteenth century. As a precondition for collective action, their revolutionary voices assumed different forms, from the barely perceptible gesture by an individual to the openly acknowledged manifesto on behalf of a community. Only in the latter stage, however, was the rebellious language sufficiently overt to require the organization and the mobilization of resources necessary for action. Until then, their discourse of political consciousness remained covert, in what Scott calls "hidden transcripts" in the subtitle to his book. An analogous analysis applies, I think, to the feminist consciousness expressed by Leroyer, Bréton, and Renooz in a comparable historical context, not of colonialism in the developing world but of patriarchal relations in modern France.[44]

More than either Terdiman or Scott, the historian Lerner places language at the heart of human consciousness and historical agency, but of the three authors only she attends specifically to feminist discourse. Her book ranges widely from the Middle Ages to 1870, in both Europe and the Americas, when women, one after another, tried to understand their subordination in patriarchy.[45] For Lerner, writers addressed feminist issues long before the women's movement organized in the nineteenth century. So why did it take them so long to act? Lerner's answer is that feminist consciousness could not be shared and mobilized until women were sufficiently aware of the large body of relevant work that already existed. Once many cultural restrictions on women's writing and publishing loosened after 1870, activists finally developed an audience sufficiently large enough to organize in pursuit of their common interests. Thus, like the approaches taken by Terdiman and Scott,

Lerner's treatment of a pervasive feminist consciousness prior to the women's movement invites analysis of the same phenomenon apparent in the lives and words of Leroyer, Bréton, and Renooz.

The organization of my book respects these issues, texts, and approaches. Chapter 1, "The Woman Question, Historically Speaking," examines the historical circumstances in which these particular women lived and wrote. The conditions specific to French women—their biological, familial, social, cultural, economic, legal, and political realities—engaged these writers in often predictable ways. As individuals, above all as authors, each of them assumed, modified, and opposed gender roles defined for them by their conflicted social and cultural world.[46] Auguste Comte, Jules Michelet, and Alexandre Dumas *fils* debated the woman question with the likes of Jenny d'Héricourt, George Sand, and Marguerite Durand, among others—such as less politically concerned writers from Claire de Rémusat to Colette—to create the contested climate of opinion concerning all women for the past two centuries.[47] Drawing on older generic conventions—the memoir and the letter especially—Leroyer, Bréton, and Renooz were also not alone in their creation of new, less personal modalities for women's self-expression in modern France.

Chapter 2, "Variations on the Feminine *I*," turns to the literary forms that feminist consciousness took in the writings of my three subjects. This attempt to classify their work is no idle academic exercise. For one thing, it is not altogether clear how to analyze their texts, much less what genres they represent for comparative purposes, so varied are the manifestations of the feminine voice here. Women's autobiographical writings take many different shapes in nineteenth- and twentieth-century France. To what extent are autobiography, memoir, diary, travelogue, correspondence, prose fiction, literary criticism, journalistic polemic, and scientific research expressions of a female self? How does the more or less explicit narrative in each one of these genres define women's personal identity, conscious agency, and discursive resistance? In answer to these important questions, the sizable corpus of theory and criticism devoted to the study of autobiographical writings, including those by women, deserves careful attention.[48]

The longest, most central chapters are devoted to Leroyer, Bréton, and Renooz. Their lives and writings interacted, much as they did with their historical moment, necessitating discussion of what these women said about themselves, who they thought they were, what they did, how, and why. In each case, the personal becomes discursive; family, marriage, religion, and politics are mediated by writing and its different manifestations. Their experiences are revealed in every genre, overtly autobiographical or not. Diaries, memoirs, letters, fiction, criticism, history, and science all expressed much of these women's historical and writerly transgression. How these poignant relations represented the arts of feminist consciousness is in fact the focus of the book. Consequently, readers who are more interested in women and biography than they are in history and theory should skip ahead to these discussions of Leroyer's devotions (chap. 3), Bréton's solitude (chap. 4), and Renooz's destiny (chap. 5). Their personal appeal is obvious and unavoidable.

Chapter 6, "The Traces of Feminist Consciousness," examines what these figures thought about women's issues. Each woman had decided views on marriage, religion, and the law that made them feminists in all but name, though they disdained the label and never organized with other women to address their subordination in French public life. Rather, theirs was a discreet, "relational" feminism, one they expressed as ever in their relationships to themselves and to others. For Leroyer, Bréton, and Renooz gender was manifested not solely in their dealings with men and their institutions, however important, but also in the context of their families, other women, and their writing especially. This awareness occurs at a precise historical moment with very specific implications for feminist literary theory and history.

Although these women and their writings obviously differ from one another—differences that merit consideration in the concluding chapter—their similarities are more important and receive closer study. The stories they tell, the issues they raise, the identities they frame, the assertion they express, and the defiance they make possible are appropriate to other French women writers like them in the same period. They thus establish a pattern of experiential and discursive relations that deserves historicization to be more fully understood. On such vital matters, notwithstanding the peculiarities of all case studies, the theorist has much to learn from the historian. Scholars are also, as Cixous suggests, "questioning (in) the between (letting oneself be questioned) of same *and of* other without which nothing lives."

In this way I affirm that women's writing, their autobiographical writing in particular, both requires and promotes self-consciousness, a sense of agency in the creation of identity and the possibility of resistance that constitutes a necessary precondition for a more fully engaged feminist politics. I do so for all the reasons suggested above: because women's writing is hard work, the deliberate and deliberative crafting of a product very often expressive of self, other, and their relationships; because the arts of autobiographical writing are so varied, assuming many different literary forms, wherever the feminine *I* appears in narrative (and nonnarrative) works; because feminist consciousness begins in such artful activities of self-knowledge and self-assertion, with telling implications for the women's movement during the French Third Republic; and because the passionate lives and literary texts of these three figures, but also of others like them in modern France, are fascinating and worth study in themselves and not just for what they tell us about important issues in women's history and literary theory.

There is another, ulterior, motive for this book. Although my work addresses an interdisciplinary audience of social historians, literary specialists, and others more generally interested in women's studies, I hope that it also will be of use to feminist theorists. At first blush, this expectation may seem presumptuous and naive. As a white, middle-aged, male academic, the product and beneficiary of the very system that feminists critique so shrewdly, I am surely not the person to take firm stands on controversial issues here. My experiential standpoint is privileged in all the wrong ways. But I must make clear the ideological assumptions at work in this study. These beliefs are derived from my political sympathies, of course, and from my professional interests in the history of women and their texts in modern France. To put the matter as forthrightly as Pascal Werner, "To write the history of women solely from the perspective of sexual oppression would be for them to lose their historical memory for the second time."[49]

In brief, I want to embrace the inherent dignity and integrity of the individual in her sexual difference. Whatever her personal views, however conflicted her self-conception, the human being always deserves our attention. Can feminism be anything less? In the context of our disagreements, how easy it is to forget the respect we owe to the person, the soul who experiences her joy and pain, with or without community, much like other subordinates. Neither all victims nor all victors, women live their questions endlessly, as both limitations and possibilities, alone and together with others. Accordingly, I think that constructive change becomes a necessary calling, because as self-conscious beings, ultimately as historical agents, women can and must act collectively, notwithstanding their deep divisions over theory and praxis.[50] The results are slow, fragile, and fragmentary, but all such important developments in history tend to be displaced, conflicted, and tenuous. As ever in struggles for liberation, to recall Cixous, the hope is in "willing the togetherness of one-another, . . . A course that multiplies transformations by the thousands."

In fact, Beauvoir's existentialist faith in the historical agency of self-conscious individualism, one defined in difference and in relationship, still has a place in contemporary feminist thought.[51] The failure and collapse of classical liberalism at the end of the nineteenth century did much to undermine ideas of self-sufficiency, and rightfully so. Within the structures of subordination, is anyone truly the captain of her destiny? But the opposite belief, that existentially speaking no one is free, defies historical precedent, perhaps, and philosophical reflection, for sure.[52] The bourgeoise is materially freer than her working-class sister; the liberation of white women in the industrialized West even depends in part upon the exploitation of nonwhite women in and from the developing countries of the world.[53] Moreover, as a host of post-Freudian theorists like Juliet Mitchell and Luce Irigaray have argued, pace Jacques Lacan, psychoanalysis need not repress women's psyches; the unconscious mind and its relations to woman's body are too complex to render women utterly speechless.[54] Surely no one is so vulnerable or so powerless where there is conscious, concerted, collective thought, exchange, and action.

Consequently, there must be an alternative to the dichotomous analysis of women's issues that ignores the related concerns of other subordinate groups; there must be an answer to the functionalist position that assumes a seamless web of oppression of women by a monolithic, omnipotent patriarchal system; finally there must be another way to frame the determinism at work in psychoanalytic essentialism that denies women conscious agency.[55] Cixous and Clément may have posited one such way out in *La Jeune née*, and other feminist theorists have explored related approaches to the politics of discourse and its practical implications.[56] But to borrow a telling phrase from the survivor of a Nazi concentration camp, as a historian "I would like to say how some people have lived captivity . . . as an initiation into liberty."[57] A comparable conviction in the face of oppression is surely worthy of women's long historical quest for a room of their own, a self-conscious space for them to relate to themselves and to others, often poignantly so.

Chapter one

❧ The Woman Question, Historically Speaking

> As women . . . we have our particular genius and we must take care to protect it, even to develop its original character, rather than attempting to conceal or to efface it. It is one more register in the grand instrument of nature's harmonies. So that it remains in tune with the universal concert, it should always keep its pitch and intonation. In short, we should differ in mind as much as in body; we should be in all things equal and analogous to man without ever making the concession of becoming the same as or identical to him.[1]

So spoke Clémence Royer, and women like her were not alone. They wrote in the moral presence of other people whose world they shared, for better or worse, every day from birth to death. Accordingly, Royer's ideas about equality in difference were widespread in modern France. Relations between men and women frequently and pervasively engendered similar texts, such as the letters, memoirs, and diaries by Marie Leroyer, Geneviève Bréton, and Céline Renooz. In their arts of feminist consciousness, that much will become obvious. But the specific ways in which all women's autobiographical writings sustained their authors' experience with others is very difficult to describe and even more difficult to analyze. The "questions-in-relation" are many.

To what extent was women's language their own? How much of it was borrowed from men and how much from other women? In what circumstances did they work, and what place did those circumstances have in their writing? Was their intellectual environment conducive or obstructive to their efforts? How so? Even without satisfactory answers to these questions, the existence of other people suggests that politics, society, culture, and the economy, at least indirectly, shared in women's lives and texts. As with Clémence

Royer, her contemporaries Leroyer, Bréton, and Renooz played very familiar roles in nineteenth-century France.[2] In effect, these women negotiated with their historical moment for the space they needed to create.

It was in a pervasive context that these figures related. But it was also in a discursive milieu that others like them debated the place of women in French society, a debate with consequences for the ways they wrote. "The woman question" is as old as patriarchy itself and can be traced from the earliest religious and legal texts, from the Garden of Eden in Genesis and the Code of Hammurabi onward.[3] Its modern French version entailed many more women and had a more complex impact on their lives than had earlier manifestations of the problem, such as the controversy elicited in the fourteenth century by Christine de Pisan and in the seventeenth century by the "précieuses."[4] Following the rationalist tradition of François Poullain de la Barre, French women contended for and eventually secured for themselves new public responsibilities. They did so in evolving but widely practiced discourses with serious implications for the literate efforts of Leroyer, Bréton, and Renooz.

Women's Place

According to historians like Dena Goodman and Margaret Jacob, women in the Old Regime fundamentally recast discussion over their place in intellectual life.[5] The Enlightenment was partly their creation. As salonkeepers, women were arbiters of new ideas; and they were as powerful as printers and booksellers in the eighteenth century—and maybe more so, because *salonnières* were not subject to the same governmental censorship and guild control as the book trade. Mesdames du Deffand, Geoffrin, and de Tencin, for example, determined the guest lists and guided the discussions of authorial activities, both personal and professional, at the heart of French culture. Salonwomen "functioned as adjuncts of a system of advancement for merit," Joan Landes has argued.[6] But the prominence of women in the Enlightenment was subject to adverse comment and continuous challenge. Jean-Jacques Rousseau expressed a growing concern to redefine "corrupt" gender relations. J. H. Bernardin de Saint-Pierre and the comte de Buffon, among others, also gave new life to the cultural construction of women's "true" nature limited to familial duties. "The moral sex" was losing its brief but active participation in the elite world of Western ideas, a participation that had been discussed since the ancient Greeks.[7] The terms had changed, but the denigration persisted.

With the outbreak of revolution in 1789, conflict over women in civic life intensified.[8] Politics exercised the hearts and minds of everyone, male and female alike, in momentous *journées,* innumerable pamphlets, and political clubs. In 1791, Olympe de Gouges proclaimed the rights of women in France a full year before Mary Wollstonecraft did so in England.[9] As the revolution shifted the boundaries between public and private activities, women at first gained and then lost the possibility of new roles. The Committee of Public Safety closed women's political clubs and sent de Gouges to the guillotine in 1793, the same year as Marie Antoinette. The new revolutionary order finally relegated women to the legal status of minors, leading to the inscription of gender inequality by the Napoleonic Code in 1804.[10] It was as if one element in the progress of the human mind, as discerned by the marquis de Condorcet in 1793, had resulted only in the domestic moral virtue imposed on women during the First French Republic (1792–1804). Not even the likes of Mesdames Récamier and de Staël could forestall the new republican responsibility of valiant mothers to remain at home that was reinforced during the First Empire (1804–14).[11] As Lynn Hunt described the revolution's impact, "Women became the figure of fragility who had to be protected from the outside world."[12]

The Bourbon Restoration (1815–30) failed to restore the Old Regime, including the intellectual life of the Enlightenment.[13] Women suffered still more than men the intense boredom of the salons portrayed so incisively in Stendhal's *Le Rouge et le noir* (1830). The 1830 revolution and the Orleanist regime that followed (1830–48) did little to change the situation. But the woman question reappeared elsewhere, in the so-called *cénacles* of romanticism and the utopian communities of socialism.[14] As the poet Marceline Desbordes-Valmore suggested in her luscious lyrics and mystical melancholy, romantic creative genius knew no sex, however reluctant the likes of Alphonse de Lamartine and Alfred de Musset were to recognize that truism. The inspired followers of the comte de Saint-Simon, Pierre Enfantin especially, tried more systematically to elevate the place of women in their new order and recruited them to join their experimental communities. The results of Saint-Simonian efforts also proved a mixed blessing, as Claire Goldberg Moses and other historians have pointed out.[15] Despite the support of women like Suzanne Voilquin, the editor of *La Tribune des femmes,* Enfantin's search for the female messiah in the Egyptian deserts was doomed from the start; in time, his feminist vision became increasingly paternalistic and ultimately patronizing.[16]

The early socialist failure to promote gender equality did not deter women from voicing their own views on the issue. The most directly influenced writers, Claire Démar, Elisa Lemonnier, and Voilquin spoke eloquently on behalf of the subordinate female and the oppressed worker.[17] "Yes," proclaimed Démar, "*the emancipation of the proletariat, of the poorest and most numerous class,* is possible only through *the emancipation of our sex.*"[18] Not just the revolution but industrialization forced women to face new challenges to their place outside the home.[19] The economic exploitation of working women, often paid at half the wages of men and sometimes forced into prostitution to make ends meet, paralleled the political exclusion and legal disability of their propertied sisters in the bourgeoisie.[20] The result was obvious to the many thousands of poor abandoned mothers and the children they had to relinquish for others to support.

These new historical forces combined to complicate the lives of females in all social classes. Especially among *ouvrières,* the alliance between feminism and socialism never succeeded.[21] Flora Tristan's *L'Union ouvrière* (1846), for example, convinced few people of the common fortunes of women and workers.[22] Consequently, a more conservative perspective on gender issues arose in the revolutionary political tradition of republicanism in 1848 and again in 1871. Pauline Roland enjoyed some leadership in the Second Republic similar to Louise Michel in the Paris Commune.[23] For both of them, however different their temperament and comportment, political not social or economic equality promised women a firm claim on civic life. Liberal republicanism seemed to offer more than radical socialism. As Maria Deraismes declared forthrightly, "Democracy, representing the interests of everyone, should logically favor a more equitable distribution of the fruits of everyone's labor."[24]

The politicization of the woman question developed in the multiple responses to the republican regimes since 1792.[25] The Second Empire (1852–70), for instance, nearly succeeded in suppressing all female voices of opposition. Moreover, Jules Michelet's remarkably popular books, *L'Amour* (1858) and *La Femme* (1860), lent both scientific and lyrical prestige to Rousseau's relegation of women to their natural functions within the home. In *La Femme affranchie* (1860), Jenny d'Héricourt answered capably Michelet's hostility, one shared by Pierre-Joseph Proudhon and Auguste Comte, to women's public responsibilities.[26] But she was overwhelmed by the still more potent Roman Catholic reaction to all forms of modernism that Pius IX's Syllabus of Errors identified in 1864. This religious admonition against women's interests outside the domestic sphere was conjoined by contemporary trends in medicine and science. As Jan Goldstein has argued, French psychiatry and republican anticlericalism also emphasized the physical and moral weakness of women and underscored the social dangers that these creatures posed by their independence.[27] Long before the concerns about French decadence in the fin de siècle, politicians, doctors, and scientists joined priests in blaming women for not living up to men's ideals of dutiful daughters, subservient wives, and nurturing mothers.[28]

The social and political context of the Third Republic (1870–1940), however, made possible the New Woman, a historical figure so very much like Leroyer, Bréton, and Renooz.[29] Educational opportunities from elementary school to the university provided more women with the literate skills necessary to support themselves in the rapidly growing service sector of an industrializing economy.[30] "The desire to do better induces effort," observed Dr. Madeleine Pelletier, who knew firsthand what opportunities schooling made possible for girls.[31] Maria Deraismes and Léon Richer had reinvigorated the women's-rights movement during the Second Empire, but with the end of press censorship in 1881, new voices appeared in print advocating the emancipation of women: Alfred Naquet promoted a law reestablishing divorce in 1884, and for the rest of the Third Republic Hubertine Auclert argued vigorously for female suffrage. In 1897 Frenchwomen would have their own daily newspaper, *La Fronde*, edited by Marguerite Durand, which joined the host of leagues, alliances, and congresses organized by and for women on the eve of World War I. The woman question had changed. Even though the gendered reality of women's lives had changed very little, its terms were no longer defined exclusively by men—hence perhaps the curious conversion of some voices like Alexandre Dumas *fils* and the overt hostility of others like Théodore Joran.

The woman question was indeed hotly debated from the revolution to the world wars.[32] Passionate voices on all sides hardly made it a coherent discussion of the issues. But most participants, Karen Offen writes, focused on the possibilities and the problems of equality in difference: "It may surprise contemporary readers to learn that, historically speaking, a case for women's rights could be predicated on sexual distinctions, family centeredness, and a sharp sexual division of labor not only in the family but in society as well."[33] Clémence Royer had said as much in her introduction to the philosophy of women. This peculiar feminist consensus for much of the nineteenth century accommodated widely accepted norms about the nature of women and their relations with men: the family was the most basic unit of society, the biological destiny of women determined their place in the home, and the brute public world of men required the countervailing force of feminine virtues and sensibilities. These social values were themselves reinforced by political and religious ideas that profoundly altered the development of all liberal reforms in the nineteenth century for both men and women, including Leroyer, Bréton, and Renooz.

These premises pervaded the views of feminists as diverse as Germaine de Staël during the First Empire, Jeanne Deroin during the revolution of 1848, and Nelly Roussel in the first decades of the Third Republic.[34] Despite their different perspectives—the first emphasizing emotional liberty, the second political engagement, and the last birth control—all three of them recognized the special nature of women underlying certain responsibilities to the family and society that men did not have. In the twentieth century, however, new values gave more weight to the individual woman's quest for autonomy as well as equality with men *tout court*. This shift occurred most visibly during the interwar period, in a civilization without sexes as Mary Louise Roberts characterizes it, even though this position was never as strong in France as it was in England and the United States.[35] It would take the existential revolution marked by Simone de Beauvoir's *Le Deuxième Sexe* (1949) to define a more liberal position in the French women's movement. To the *Psychanalyse et Politique* group, for example, sexual difference complements individual fulfillment, a major feminist theme for only the last fifty years.[36]

Nineteenth-century French critics of women's rights also emphasized sexual difference, but they did so in the name of social stability. Advocates of the patriarchal status quo feared change of any sort, thanks primarily to the apparent consequences of revolution. The suspicious calculus of misogyny regarded the biological nature of women as inherently immoral and dangerous to order, which required on the one hand the repression of women's personal interests and on the other the celebration of women's self-sacrifice to the needs of fathers, husbands, and children. "A bronze pedestal for the Goddess Woman" guaranteed her the visibility essential to both admiration and admonishment.[37] Tied to established institutions like the church and its critical view of women, the conservatives' response to feminist calls for reform was fear for the delicate balance of gender roles in the home. Changes in property rights, divorce law, child guardianship, girls' education, and universal suffrage were thus all bitterly contested, from Joseph de Maistre to Charles Maurras, as matters of principle rather than of discussion and negotiation.[38]

In 1922, when the senate rejected unrestricted female suffrage, the French women's movement carried on.[39] Perhaps too much had been staked on the vote in the expectation that it would ultimately resolve legal oppression and political subordination at the ballot box. Neither participation in the war effort, nor political polemic, nor selective civil disobedience was enough to overcome by rational means irrational fears and vested interests. Moreover, as Louise Tilly has remarked, "Suffrage interested few French women; but the vote [was] only one of the ways in which people [acted] collectively on their interests, as French women most assuredly did."[40] The ridicule heaped on publicly assertive activists, besides the undue influence of the Roman Catholic Church, provided excuses for excluding women from politics until World War II. Only then, after many more, less-vocal women had valiantly joined the war effort on the home front for the second time, thereby demonstrating their public and private responsibility, was the vote granted by the provisional government of Charles de Gaulle in 1944. However ironically, the movement prevailed.[41]

In the meantime, the woman question remained, in part because gender inequality remained the law.[42] The Napoleonic Code was only slowly amended to recognize the independent status of women. Despite the Code's provision for marriage as a contract—itself a major change from the Old Regime's religious sacrament—the texts of 1803 codified the asymmetry in the relations between men and women. For example, "The husband owes protection to his wife, the wife owes obedience to her husband" (art. 213); just as "the wife, even if not married with a communal estate settlement, cannot give, dispose of, mortgage, [or] acquire . . . [property] without [his] consent" (art. 217). Before 1884, in the case of adultery, a woman could sue for divorce only if her husband actually brought a concubine into the home (art. 230). It was not until 1938 that "the married woman [had] the full exercise of her civil capacity" (art. 215). Even with the vote, however, legal change remained elusive. Only in 1970 did women finally win the right to practice a profession without their husband's permission (art. 223).[43]

Modern French law enforced the domestication of women's lives.[44] In the eighteenth century, before industrialization and the revolution, women of every social class had assumed various responsibilities outside the home, working in the fields, selling and buying at the market, overseeing employees and domestic servants, keeping accounts of business receipts and household expenses, and challenging authors and public officials, albeit in a formally circumscribed corporate society. Reproduction went hand in hand with production within what social historians generally call "the family economy."[45] The participation of women in the revolutionary *journées* came as no real surprise to anyone, certainly not to the women who adapted their activities to the changing public sphere they shared with men, at least until the republican regime of virtue initiated the restrictions that would endure in one form or another into the twentieth century. Each new regime from the First Republic to the Third fostered efforts to contain women's extradomestic interests, ostensibly to maintain order in an increasingly open society.

By 1900 the convenient link between reproduction and production had broken for most working women.[46] As migration off the farm into the cities increased and as work shifted out of the home to the mill, babies and bosses created new problems for wives and mothers trying to do two jobs, to be in two places at the same time. With women forced to work for wages substantially lower than men's, the labor movement encouraged the same domestic ideology that bourgeois families had already established as the norm: mothers stayed home to nurture children while fathers ventured out to work for the entire family's support. Nothing could be more "natural" than this division of labor in a differentiated industrializing society. Hence Proudhon's insistence that women make a choice between being housewives in the closed, private sphere of the family or becoming harlots in the open, public world of the marketplace. Of course, this choice was a simplistic falsehood. The development of employment opportunities in the service sector, especially evident during the second wave of industrialization before World War I, eventually pulled more women out of the home, if not the family. As Michelle Perrot has observed, wage work served "as a lever for women's independence and in time for their integration into public life."[47]

Demographic trends facilitated this change in modern French gender roles.[48] During the Old Regime, high rates of fertility—anywhere between thirty and forty newborns per thousand population annually—kept married women extremely busy at home. Families would have been even larger than they were if there had not been dramatically high rates of infant mortality—as high as one-fourth of all infants before their first birthday. The average preindustrial family rarely numbered more than seven; many of the surviving children were apprenticed or farmed out as field hands or domestic servants by age eight.[49] But before the nineteenth century, many middle-class couples were already controlling their fertility in order to ensure still smaller families. This trend would reach the rest of French society by 1890, so much so that public officials worried about the long-term consequences of negative population growth.[50] By the twentieth century, better nutrition and sanitation, both the by-products of higher material standards of living, created the conditions for the demographic transition to lower rates of mortality as well as lower rates of fertility (fewer than fifteen per thousand population annually). The average family size in the interwar period—two parents and two children— was less than half of what it had been only two hundred years earlier, and less than what was necessary to maintain a constant national population of just more than 41 million.[51]

With fewer children and new employment opportunities, Frenchwomen were the apparent beneficiaries of social and economic developments by 1940.[52] The lives of a growing class of bourgeoises were materially easier, but their legal and political status remained subordinate to men's and their public lives continued to be constrained by social and cultural expectations of proper ladies from *soi-disant* good families. As Adeline Daumard has noted, "For a long time customs imposed on women a proper restraint that resulted in a certain self-effacement, despite the worldly aura that salon life gave to some women and despite the prestige others drew from their status as mothers."[53] Young women's education still focused on domestic training essential to a successful marriage rather than on a professional preparation for employment outside the home.[54] Despite the rise in affective expectations of marital bonds, many wealthy young women suffered husbands chosen for them by their families, who were more interested in dowries than they were in the emotional happiness of their wives. The resistance of unmarried women to such a regime was often labeled hysteria or some other female malady by a nearly all-male medical community that prescribed a cure of complete passivity in order to restore the compliant fertility of the patient.[55] In this way modern science was enlisted in the support of rigid social convention to constrain young middle-class women in well-defined and enduring gender roles.[56]

The development of the paternalistic welfare state in France was a comparable mixed blessing.[57] At the beginning of the nineteenth century, the poor turned to the inadequate resources of private charity. The Société de Saint François Régis, the Société de Charité Maternelle, and the Société de Saint Vincent de Paul, for instance, provided deserving women some assistance in desperate times. But these moralizing institutions failed to address pressing social problems, and the state eventually displaced the church as an intimate companion to impoverished women. Hygiene instead of morality finally determined public policy. As Rachel Fuchs has described the process, "Nationalism inspired legislators to provide aid, rather than sermons, for the poor and pregnant, not to please God, but to save France" from all threats to its national security.[58] By the outbreak of World War I, France had laid the foundations for *l'état providence* that saved many families from misery, but at the expense of poor women's relative autonomy in their private lives.[59]

A host of women's organizations arose to promote such well-meaning intrusions only to complicate matters for mothers struggling to support their families. In 1901, for example, Blanche Edwards-Pilliet and Augusta Moll-Weiss founded the Ligue des Mères de Famille to bring home help and advice to working-class women. These efforts to subsidize motherhood went hand in hand with those to frame protective legislation, however uncomfortable this development made women's-rights activists like Maria Pognon, who defended women's interests to work when and how they wished. "Wherever the night work is well paid," complained Pognon in 1899, "someone has found it too tiring for women, or unhygienic, or even dangerous!"[60] Such currents and countercurrents presumably on behalf of women also appeared in the establishment of government medals for successful motherhood the same year as the enactment of draconian measures against contraception and abortion (1920). State intervention and its advocates remain an ambivalent if not ambiguous benefit.

Women's Words

Against this historical backdrop then, from the fires of revolution to the age of total war, lived and wrote my three subjects: Marie Leroyer, Geneviève Bréton, and Céline Renooz. To the extent that these women's choices were constrained in ways that men's were not—or more to the point, to the extent that their lives were determined for them by social structures and systems that privileged men's interests—one can speak of patriarchy in modern France. Certainly for 125 years after 1800, the preponderance of French laws, institutions, and ideas discouraged if not prohibited Leroyer, Bréton, and Renooz from assuming most public responsibilities in politics, religion, business, and traditional professions like medicine and the law; political suffrage, religious

ordination, business management, and the university faculties were all reserved for men. Whether or not women resisted this reality, it was perfectly
evident to them. At times their homes were virtual prisons.

On the other hand, patriarchal subordination changed dramatically in
Leroyer, Bréton, and Renooz's lifetimes (1800–1928). Increasingly literate
women turned their education to exploring new genres of personal expression; intellectually they were less subject to their husband's control. They
came to expect greater symmetry in their marital relations, as romantic literary ideals fostered new emotional space at home for personal growth. Accordingly, they were in a better position to learn from other women's experiences and, if they wished, to act both individually and collectively to protect
their interests. Also like many women in the nineteenth and early twentieth
centuries, they acquired and disposed more of their own property and earn-
ings; and with generally higher material standards of living and the tendency
of the middle classes to limit their fertility, their families were smaller, better
nourished, and healthier. Public life became a possibility, especially in the
marketplace, charitable activity, religious observance, and cultural expression, even if social convention strictly limited its range. In short, their circumstances were a curiously colored fabric with many folds, holes, and patterns
that permitted certain liberties and opportunities, which were not always
apparent to all observers.

Perhaps the most telling feature of this complex situation was discursive.
By the time Leroyer, Bréton, and Renooz put pen to paper, autobiography, for
example, was already a well-established male tradition.[61] Saint Augustine was
as revered as Rousseau was reviled, even though they both called their work
"confessions" in a gesture of atonement for their professed honesty. But for
women in nineteenth-century France, neither of these texts was an appropriate model for their efforts at self-writing, primarily because their own lives
and circumstances as women were so different. The memoirs of notable public
figures, such as Germaine de Staël's *Dix années d'exil* (1810) and Claire de la
Clairon's *Réflexions sur l'art dramatique* (1799), served these purposes better.
Even if the intentions of such memoirists were not necessarily more modest,
the nature and scope of their revelations were certainly more discrete (and
discreet). Thus the excuses of the memoir, not the apologies of the confession,
provided Frenchwomen the most widely read and imitated examples of autobiographical writing before the twentieth century.[62]

The published results are impressive achievements.[63] Besides the many accounts of religious faith in the manner of Jeanne-Marie Guyon, French-women left versions of themselves in relation to important events. Louise-Elisabeth Vigée-Lebrun (1835–37), for example, detailed her life with the royalty she painted before and after the French Revolution. In sharp contrast with the turbulent life and times of Mme Roland (1789–93), the comtesse de Rémusat wrote of her political experiences in Napoleonic Paris (1801–8). In time, these writers were joined by the best-known women memoirists in the nineteenth century: the duchesse d'Abrantès (1836), Daniel Stern (Marie d'Agoult, 1833–54), and Hortense Allart (1872–74). But as French society and politics eventually became more open, the memoirs of famous women gave way to the autobiographies of more plebeian if no less extraordinary individuals like Flora Tristan (1838), Suzanne Voilquin (1866), and Louise Michel (1886), all prominent figures of various political movements on the left. It took the talent of George Sand, however, to define autobiography as a genre of particular interest and relevance to Frenchwomen.[64] Even though Bréton and Renooz did not actually discuss Sand's *Histoire de ma vie* (1854–55)—unlike Leroyer, who wrote a long letter about it[65]—the tradition of women's memoir and autobiography that her work represents also informs their writing.

In a literary tradition even longer than the autobiography, the personal letter was a widespread practice in nineteenth-century France. Until the invention of the telephone, correspondence was the most common form of expression adopted by literate Frenchwomen, thereby "recreating the conditions of speech in written conversations," according to Elizabeth Goldsmith.[66] The published exchanges of Héloïse with Abélard (1687), Mme de Sévigné with her daughter (1726), and the eighteenth-century *salonnières* with the *philosophes* engaged as many imaginations as the comtesse du Barry (1779), Mme de Châteauroux (1807), and Hortense de Beauharnais (1835) did with their various royal and aristocratic interlocutors. But because their letters were usually edited by men for other purposes, these women expressed themselves in the shadows of their male correspondents; the published spaces for women's autobiographical revelations remained limited until their lives became as important as their notoriety.[67] After 1850 the personal letters of less socially exalted but accomplished women like Eugénie de Guérin (1865), Sophie Arnould (1877), and Marceline Desbordes-Valmore (1896) appeared in print. In their own correspondence, Leroyer, Bréton, and Renooz adopted the prose, if not all the purposes, of this developing literary form.[68]

The diary was another genre important to women in nineteenth-century France.[69] It may have taken longer to develop, but it ultimately became far more widely practiced than autobiography. Unlike the Anglo-American confessional, the personal journal in France was rarely devoted solely to matters of religious faith. Rather, this literary form evolved out of more secular interests in recording and accounting for events and impressions, concerns driven largely by the romantic movement's celebration of the self and its inner life. Guérin's diary (1862) exemplifies this tendency that was shared by Pauline de La Ferronnays (1866), Marie-Edmée Pau (1876), Marie Bashkirtseff (1887), and thousands of young women whose personal writings never reached a larger audience. By 1900 the journal was an established genre apparently of women's own making. Colette (1941), Simone Weil (1951), Marie Bonaparte (1939–51), and Simone de Beauvoir (1990), for instance, only expanded on a literate habit that is evident in the growing list of women's diaries discovered and published just in the past fifteen years.[70]

Despite its bewildering variety and rich history, the diary was initially an attempt to control adolescent women, who, it was believed, required more careful supervision than young men. Educators and mothers often imposed these exercises of self-examination on girls in order to monitor their intellectual, emotional, and moral development. Philippe Lejeune writes, "The diary [was] an educational tool among others."[71] Guidebooks similar to those for letters helped define this rite of passage to mature gender roles. Of course, writing is not so easily controlled, as the recent publication of Frenchwomen's diaries amply suggests; it appears that the deliberate efforts to appropriate this genre for another purpose failed. Young women, like Isabelle Eberhardt as well as Geneviève Bréton, welcomed the deeply subversive possibilities of their personal journals.[72]

As a literary form, the diary owes much to memoir and autobiography, its retrospective narrative of the self in particular.[73] But the intimate, more or less spontaneous account written soon after the event is a feature common to both the journal and the letter, distinguishing them from the autobiography, which is often carefully composed long after the fact. Letters and diaries also endeavor to circumscribe their audience as much as possible. Unlike the autobiography, the diary is intended for no one but the writer, and the letter for no one but the recipient(s). Naturally their audience changes when these forms are published, but the authors' original intentions clearly affect the way they are written.[74] The result makes the diary a hybrid genre that borrows from

longer and better-established literary traditions, especially from the autobiography and the letter. In developing such a new mode of expression in the
nineteenth century, Frenchwomen perhaps synthesized more than they actually created.[75]

Another discursive form of self-expression for women was the novel. Like
the diary, prose fiction in the eighteenth and nineteenth centuries was regarded as a genre by and for women, and perhaps for good reason: by then,
many novelists and their readers were female. As Joan DeJean has put it, "In
France the novel was a feminist creation."[76] Mesdames de Scudéry, de Lafayette, de Graffigny, de Staël, de Genlis, and de Charrière—to mention
only the more prominent of those distinguished by an aristocratic particle—
created a distinct generic interest well before the nineteenth century. Women
like Marie-Jeanne Riccoboni specialized in moralizing narratives, while others like Ann Radcliffe in translation developed the gothic novel. Possibly
because the letter was one of the few forms that women were allowed to
practice, their efforts were even more of an impetus behind the epistolary
novel than Rousseau's better-known *Julie, ou La Nouvelle Héloïse* (1761). This
outlet provided women their most widely published and most lucrative opportunity to define themselves and to share that identity, albeit in a much
disparaged fictional code, with others like Leroyer, Bréton, and Renooz.[77]

In the nineteenth century, prose fiction became many women's entrée into
French intellectual life. As the Enlightenment's faith in human reason, natural
law, and cultural progress foundered in the violence of revolution and empire,
romanticism created greater space for a wider variety of expression, including
the novel, for women to explore more fully. The creative excesses of the
romantics in their turn became painfully obvious to the scientifically inclined
positivists after 1848, precisely when more and more women were taking up
new literate activities. In this way their writing participated in the cultural
movements that continued to preoccupy French intellectuals well into the
twentieth century. At the same time, however, women offered a critique of
their own to the development of French culture. They added, implicitly at
least, a gendered perspective, one that appears in the work by the three
women under study here.

Marie Leroyer, for one, was perhaps most fully aware of her contemporaries' reassessment of the eighteenth-century Enlightenment's gendered
ideals in rationality and empiricism. The pervasive privileging of these values, she believed, deprived sensitive women like her of emotional expression.

In her personal correspondence, Leroyer confessed sympathy for the conflicted plight of George Sand's romantic alter ego, the principal character in Sand's novel *Lélia* (1833). "What on earth is this soul you have given me?" asks Lélia of God. "Is this what's called a poet's soul? More flickering than light and more changeable than wind, always avid, always restless, always breathless, always searching outside of itself for the nourishment it needs to exist and devouring everything before even having tasted anything!"[78] Here Leroyer's favorite novel expressed her profound affinity for this mysterious, visionary figure in dialogue with her unresolvable contradictions—nihilism at odds with creation, sin with expiation, doubt with superstition, otherworldliness with passion, ambition with resignation, and the angelic with the demonic. Ultimately, Leroyer's Lélia symbolized the female romantic in opposition to the male philosophe.

Geneviève Bréton recognized her place within a similar reassessment. Rather than the Enlightenment, Bréton's moment engaged the gendered implications of romanticism itself, especially as they appeared in academic art. After the 1848 revolution, cultural attitudes hardened, and Bréton was drawn into this new creative toughness. As a young woman she had been attracted to the expressive possibilities explored by her fiancé Henri Regnault, whose formal training at the Ecole des Beaux Arts in Paris and the Villa Medici in Rome favored traditional male historical subjects, but in exotic locales and in dramatic situations. The Orient fascinated him. But Regnault's death during the Franco-Prussian War released Bréton from such formal romanticizing, and grief led her to a more detached personal expression in her diary and later in the correspondence with her son Jean-Louis Vaudoyer. She deliberately encouraged Vaudoyer's elegant precision and attention to subtleties in his travelogues and prose fiction. In her creative interests and endeavors, despite lingering romantic elements in her own work, Bréton replayed her contemporaries' cultural realism as a self-conscious woman.

Finally, Céline Renooz shared in a comparable contextual revaluation, another one of special significance to the arts of feminist consciousness in modern France. Where Leroyer and Bréton challenged the prevailing values of the Enlightenment and romanticism, respectively, Renooz took on the equally gendered features of positivism. By 1900 the epistemology of the scientific method had received institutional sanction in the various university faculties that were dominated by men. The disciplines, in the natural and social sciences particularly but not exclusively, however, encountered serious resistance to their philosophical foundations in empiricism. Like Henri Bergson, for example, though with far less intellectual precision or public success, Renooz urged a reconsideration of scientific knowledge not solely for its epistemological limitations, but also for its exclusion of women's distinct manner of knowing. She firmly believed that women need not recognize any of the disciplinary boundaries established at the end of the nineteenth century. Feminist ideas, it would seem, arose in science as well as other empirical spheres of intellectual life. Renooz's contested historical moment thus also limited and expanded creative engagement by similar women.

Just how these historical developments and personal involvements played out in the lives and writings of Leroyer, Bréton, and Renooz provide the focus for the rest of my book. Each woman saw herself very curiously at odds and yet in concert with the historical circumstances they endured. As writers they did so in relationship with themselves, and as women they did so in their relations with others. Their personal accounts—in autobiography, memoir, diary, letter, fiction, and much else—suggest the many manifestations of this historical and discursive dialogue between self and other. It makes sense now to delve into their private literate world to see more precisely the ways in which they developed an identity, a sense of agency, and the possibility of resistance within these special historical circumstances. Such were the expressions of a feminist consciousness, historically speaking, at the heart of the woman question and its many relations in modern France.

Chapter two

❧ Variations on the Feminine *I*

"Can my story—or yours—ever be more than that: a dialogue with other selves?"[1] asked Nancy K. Miller, the literary theorist and critic, in 1996. Earlier, in 1988, Miller had emphasized this dialogic tendency in feminine writing generally.

> At the first level . . . feminist writing articulates as and in discourse a self-consciousness about women's identity. I mean by this both an inherited cultural fiction and a process of social construction. Second, feminist writing makes a claim for the heroine's singularity by staging the difficulty of her relation as a woman in fiction to Woman [as gender]. Third, it contests the available plots of female development or *Bildung* and embodies dissent from the dominant tradition in a certain number of recurrent narrative gestures, especially in the modalities of closure. . . . Finally, through an insistence on singularity, feminist writing figures the existence of other subjective economies, other styles of identity.[2]

It is no accident that each feature of feminism in literature, as Miller describes it here, also applies to the texts examined in this book. Here, too, literary language embodies a self-conscious identity in relationship with others, a singular female character at odds with social norms, a challenge to men's generic conventions, and a propensity for different discursive practices. As a prolegomenon to the study of modern French feminist consciousness, this chapter will consider the implications of Miller's prescriptions for women's autobiographical writings in general, and for those by Marie Leroyer, Geneviève Bréton, and Céline Renooz in particular. Like many other theorists and critics besides Miller, I want to address the narrative manifestations and historical agency of women's personal voices.

Specifically this chapter will elaborate two of Miller's points. First, the feminine *I* is manifested historically as a discursive practice that ignores generic boundaries.[3] The text of the female self appears wherever women write as subjects in their own right, whatever ideology they espouse, whatever the literary form they choose to explore. Those genres expressive of the female self include autobiography, of course, but also the diary, the letter, the novel, even literary criticism, polemical journalism, and history, all forms that open textual spaces for women to express, to define, to create a narrative identity. Like at least one other student of autobiography, Georges May, I believe the narrative needs to be conceived broadly to allow for its appearance within a variety of literary genres.[4]

Second, with Miller this chapter contends that the very diversity of these historical and literary manifestations of the feminine *I* shapes their narrative strategies as well as the self-definitions of their authors.[5] The autobiographical *récit* clearly incorporates nonautobiographical gestures, including the expansive, the nonlinear, and the arational, which George Sand's *Histoire de ma vie* (1848–54) exemplifies in nineteenth-century French literature.[6] At the same time, this intertextuality, subject to individual agency, owes much to its patriarchal context as women struggled with the double bind of authorship and social norms that actively discouraged it. Thus women's narrative identities are also the apparent products of nonnarrative strategies and the experiential moment that frames them. This dialogue between the literary and the historical is fully evident in the textual forms that female authors read and practice.

Practice

These claims are based on an acquaintance with recent studies of autobiography as a genre, a rapidly growing field today.[7] Within this large body of scholarly and theoretical work, there are several discernible trends in ideas about the complex nature of the gendered narrative *I*. Some consideration here of the issues relevant to women's personal narratives is therefore in order. But this discussion of genre and gender also rests on work with the autobiographical texts left by Leroyer, Bréton, and Renooz. In the light of recent literary theories, an initial reading of the writings by these three figures supports the position that this chapter takes: the generic diversity and the dialogic relation between the textual and the experiential in women's personal writings created the conditions for a distinct and active feminine subjectivity.[8] From this perspective, much like Miller's own autobiography, one can make sense of the historical clash of discourses by and about women in nineteenth- and twentieth-century France.

The narrative elements evident in the personal papers left by Leroyer, Bréton, and Renooz are both familiar and manifold. It is the intertextual character of their many and varied self-narrations that illustrates well the indeterminacy of their form. All three women left extensive accounts of their lives, only one of which might qualify as an autobiography—Renooz's unpublished memoirs. The other personal narratives appear in Leroyer's autobiographical fiction, literary criticism, and correspondence with George Sand, Gustave Flaubert, and Jules Michelet; in Bréton's diary and correspondence with Henri Regnault and Jean-Louis Vaudoyer; and in Renooz's self-revealing correspondence, scientific treatises, histories of Western religions, and journalistic advocacy. In each instance the writer's life story was incorporated, quite intentionally, into different textual forms; and each story itself incorporated, also quite intentionally, nonnarrative elements from still other genres. Political polemic and philosophical analysis, for example, were deliberately woven into their accounts. All their personal writings were creatively idiosyncratic in their generic transgressions, in their discursive practices, in what one may call their literary *assemblages.* Their work reveals an obvious textuality in these writers' active quest to define a self in and out of narrative.

Leroyer's correspondence is an excellent example of these various voices at work.[9] Despite their other intentions and features, Leroyer's missives provide detailed, retrospective accounts of her life. Their first-person narratives, chapterlike in their continuity from letter to letter, resemble autobiography in every way but its comprehensive design. Over the course of her extended exchanges with prominent contemporaries, Leroyer recounts her conflicted religious convictions, her repressive education in a provincial town, her troubled relationships with men, her serious efforts to establish a writing career, and her changing familial and social circumstances in light of these earlier experiences.

Almost invariably the motive behind these extended revelations was Leroyer's identification with the authors of similar personal narratives. "In reading your life," she wrote to Sand on 3 January 1856, "I have seen how you suffered. I have understood, shared, suffered your sorrows; I have found and taken hold of you entirely in these true, simple, eloquent, and immortal pages. Now I, too, have lived and suffered all my life with you. In a word, it seems to me that there is something of you in me and that at the same time the best part of my soul also lives in you."[10] The parallels of other lives with hers induced her to narrate, to explain, and to justify herself to others whose texts became her own—hence Leroyer's identification with Sand's autobiographical self, Flaubert's Madame Bovary, and Michelet's revolutionary women.[11] Her letters borrow the texts of other literary lives in order to create her own narrative identity.

Leroyer adopts a similar discursive strategy when she turns her attention to other genres.[12] Like her correspondence, her fiction is frequently and obviously autobiographical, even though she never wrote any novels entirely in the first person.[13] Rather, Leroyer distanced herself from the principal characters in the *Mémoires d'une provinciale* (1880), a fictional re-creation of her life as suggested by the title. From its opening sentence, she highlights her frustrations with the monotony, calumny, and hypocrisy of Angers, where she spent nearly her entire life: "Provincial life is deadly to true intelligence. . . . All superiority is condemned to ostracism, and genius itself is obliged to bow before the egalitarian force of mediocrity."[14] Accordingly, one of Leroyer's alter egos in the novel, Valérie de Stenneville, suffers the same miseries that the author describes in such haunting detail in her correspondence. Here the personal narrative is transformed, subsumed within an explicitly nonautobiographical genre, almost perfectly. Despite its status as fiction, this novel is the fullest extant account of Leroyer's personal and discursive identity. But the narrative self is borrowed from the well-established conventions of literary romance, the textual model for the author's displaced feminine *I*.

Leroyer adapts the romance form to specific autobiographical purposes. In nearly every one of her long novels, for example, she incorporates brief first-person narratives by the characters who most resemble her. The life story told by Rosine Bellerive and the long letters exchanged by Valérie de Stenneville and Marcie de Villermès in the *Mémoires d'une provinciale* are not unique. Cécile de Monthierry and Julia O'Flaerthy also write revealing missives in *Cécile* (c. 1840), Leroyer's only novella narrated largely in the first person, a long tale told by another anguished surrogate soul, Cécile's cousin Arthur. And the title character of *Angélique Lagier* (1851) uses the mail to justify her life in a sad farewell before her execution for a crime that she did not commit.[15] Epistolary elements of the romance allow fictional characters to speak in a voice resembling Leroyer's, one well skilled in letter writing; for more than twenty-eight years she maintained her correspondence with Sand, and in 1856 she won a prize for her entry in a competition organized by the *Courrier de la mode.*[16]

A similar autobiographical transcription appears in Leroyer's literary criticism and essays. Narratives of her life intrude into these texts, as well. For instance, her collection of chronicles and legends is frankly motivated by a need to recapture her childhood. "In deciding to publish this little volume," she writes, "I had no other wish than to prove to my compatriots the profound affection I still have for Château-Gontier, my birthplace."[17] The very first "chronique" is Leroyer's account of returning to her home town for the first time in more than twenty years, a story completed by the third chronicle about the now-deserted house where she was born. The historical legends are all of her own making, based on her life but registered in another genre appropriated for autobiographical purposes. She repeats this practice in her reviews of books collected in *Souvenirs et impressions littéraires* (1892). Again the title reveals the author's mixing of literary form and intention; in good romantic tradition if not good generic convention, her life and identity are inseparable from the texts she discusses and creates.

Geneviève Bréton's personal narratives are certainly less varied than Leroyer's, but they follow the same intertextual pattern of literary transcription and appropriation, the same quest for identity in and out of the texts she created.[18] In thirty-three notebooks written over the course of forty-one years (1867–1908), Bréton kept a scrupulous account of her daily activities, often modeled deliberately on the many books she read. Like Leroyer, Bréton was an omnivorous reader; and elements of Chateaubriand's *Mémoires d'outre-tombe* (1820–48), Staël's *De l'Allemagne* (1810), and novels by Rousseau, Stendhal, Hugo, and Sand, among others, all appeared in her diary and shaped its rhetorical devices and ultimately its narrative strategies. At one point, she sees herself as Mathilde de la Mole in Stendhal's *Le Rouge et le noir* (1830): "This bored and rich, depraved and guilty girl is in every respect unpleasant, but I certainly resemble her."[19] So when her fiancé dies in the Franco-Prussian War, she reenacts Mathilde's fascination with the corpse of her beloved; she imagines and writes about her wedding with the dead man in his crypt.[20] Here as elsewhere in her diary, Bréton's self-conscious pose is based on extensive literary as well as tragic personal experience. Her autobiographical voice both mimics and speaks in its own right.

Another kind of textual interchange occurs in Bréton's self narratives.

Because she anticipated publishing her diary—leaving explicit instructions to this effect just before she died—Bréton included much of the correspondence she sent and received in her lifetime. She often copied the letters directly into the notebooks and tailored her text to accord with the events they concern.[21] The fit between letter and diary entry is, of course, a natural one, even if this public documentation impedes the progress of an intimate story. But Bréton's careful editing of the diary and selective rewriting of whole entries minimize these intrusions in her very personal accounts. In this way the letters become an integral part of the narratives; the author simply adapted the conventions of two different literary forms to suit her purpose. Perhaps if Bréton had not sought a larger readership, this intertextual feature to her diary would never have occurred. And yet all such narratives, no matter how private, allow for such contingencies; why else would Bréton tear out entire signatures, rewrite them, and then reinsert them back into her notebooks? Whether she anticipated an audience of one or a million, she clearly required another text from the one she originally wrote.

Bréton adopts a similar strategy of generic transgression in the letters she sent to her son Jean-Louis Vaudoyer. This extensive correspondence, or what is left of it, spans more than eighteen years, from 1896 to 1914, when Vaudoyer was just developing his own identity as a writer. Although her letters are not unusual in their expression of familial concerns, they assume a self-consciously writerly quality; they discuss important literary issues and texts; but more important they actually replace the diary that Bréton neglects in this period. In time, the correspondence fulfills the same literary function as her personal journal to record immediate impressions on a regular basis, to develop self-knowledge and self-assertion in the face of adversity, and to live vicariously through the writings of her son that she critiques so shrewdly. In guiding his career, step by step, text by text, through her letters to Jean-Louis, Bréton assumes her son's publications as her own.

That the last figure, Céline Renooz, adopted intertextual narrative strategies very similar to those employed by Leroyer and Bréton should come as no surprise.[22] For example, she, too, included private correspondence in her unpublished memoirs, often pinning it to the paper and then writing around the intruding document. What correspondence she did not include in her autobiography Renooz kept in a dozen large boxes, annexes to the actual account that explains and justifies her life's work in embryology and natural history. But as the only actual autobiographer of the three writers under consideration here, Renooz felt compelled to follow more closely the conventions of this literary genre. Consequently she cites in her work, as a matter of public record, copies of newspaper articles by and about her.

The most important of these documents was the piece she wrote recounting the revelation that began her scientific career. Both in her memoirs and in the article itself, Renooz details her epiphany in the Bibliothèque Nationale one morning in June 1878: "During this fleeting moment, I began to see all the importance of my discovery, the immensity of its practical effects. I found myself actually growing larger morally-speaking, and the idea that I had an enormous mission to accomplish overcame me."[23] This idea becomes the organizing theme for the rest of her memoirs, a blend of autobiographical chronicle, personal correspondence, scientific theory, journalistic polemic, feminist vision, and self-justification.

Renooz's memoirs only appear to follow the generic norms of autobiography. While she apparently develops a traditional narrative from childhood onward, detailing the events of her life in proper chronological order, her writing is no different from the rest of her personal papers and published work. The title suggests the intertextual features of Renooz's achievement; "Prédestinée: L'Autobiographie de la femme cachée" does not specify a particular individual but a destiny that the author feels compelled to reveal. The narrative gives way to revelation, demonstration, exposition, and argumentation, so much so that the chronology of her life becomes intertwined with the missionary role she wants to play in scientific inquiry, historical research, and feminist activity. "It is not enough for me to show what I have done," she writes, "I also want to say who I am"—that is, to establish an identity.[24] The result is of a piece with her entire life's work (especially as her memoirs evolve into a chronicle of her public appearances), with her various publications, but above all with her letters, which form more than half of the archive.

Renooz's correspondence also tends to the autobiographical. In each appeal to a public official to promote her vision of a better society, in each invitation to attend one of her conferences on women's issues, in each attempt to interest a publisher in her scientific and historical research, Renooz invariably provided her correspondents important details about herself and her work. This habit became a necessity whenever she wrote people for the first time to explain why she was approaching them. Though apparently none of them ever responded, Georges Clemenceau, Henri Bergson, Alfred Dreyfus,

Raymond Poincaré, and a host of other French notables received at least one of her intrusively revealing letters, often accompanied by an offprint or brochure summarizing her concerns of the moment. At times Renooz's correspondence offers a more accurate and detailed account of her life and work than her memoirs. Letters are another form of Renooz's self-writing, whether or not she recomposed them from memory long after having sent the originals. Her correspondence is a necessary complement to her autobiography.

Another of Renooz's multiple intertexts appears in her published work, especially her six-volume history of religion *Ere de vérité* (1921–33). Here and elsewhere, the feminine *I* is transposed into a feminist *we* to refigure the text's personal, unconventional features for one audience in particular: the members of the Société Néosophique, who underwrote many of her publication expenses, including the last volume, which appeared posthumously. This final work, however, summarizes the ideas that in Renooz's mind have become virtually indistinguishable from her self, her identity as activist, scholar, and visionary. At the end of this passionate synthesis, written shortly before her death, Renooz states, "In order to complete our historical work, we must therefore write the history of this Renaissance whose . . . first stages are already completed. The last alone remains to be realized. It is much awaited, and its author will be the True Messiah of the new era, the *new teacher* of humanity."[25] No further separation exists between her ideas, her mission, and her existence as feminist, messiah, and writer. Conventional generic and existential distinctions disappear. Fact and fiction, induction and deduction, reason and intuition, self and world, language and form—all seem to devolve into a single discourse. Even her closest associates could not criticize this work without criticizing its author. In effect, Renooz becomes her own self-aggrandizing text.

From the perspective suggested by these authors, then, the personal narrative of the feminine *I* knows no generic boundaries. It appears in and borrows from various literary forms that the women used to establish an identity in and out of their texts. It is as if the self-in-creation here were more important than the genre it assumes. All texts are implicated as the narrative self artfully draws on both language and experience for its development. In defining a distinct and active feminine subjectivity, the intimate account thrives on generic intertextuality, at least for Leroyer, Bréton, and Renooz, whose relative obscurity makes them reasonably typical women writers. Their personal papers and publications represent the culmination of a long, historical evolution, one explored recently by Gerda Lerner's *The Creation of Feminist Consciousness*, based on the work of many, much better-known women writers.[26] The various manifestations of the feminine *I* are in effect a historical phenomenon, one defining both genre and identity in women's texts nearly everywhere in the West for the past thousand years. Clearly they all merit closer study by historians and literary specialists alike for what they tell us about the arts of feminist consciousness.

These personal narratives, regardless of their literary form, are theoretically interesting for at least two other reasons. First, they demonstrate how extremely porous are the boundaries marking all women's writing, though their discursive practices are not all simply personal.[27] Because of their particular self-conception in sexual difference, these women figured their literary identity differently from men if only to distinguish the grammatical gender of the first-person pronoun. And second, the issues concerning the narration of the female self, especially its ontology in and out of the text, arise wherever the feminine *I* appears.[28] That is, in such a complex relation, the first-person pronoun here actually refers to itself as well as to someone in the world. For both of these reasons, then, the autobiographical writing of Leroyer, Bréton, and Renooz in particular, but also women's autobiography in general, is a moot genre;[29] despite their best efforts to define the form, literary historians and critics have failed to discern these discursive complexities.

Theory

Philippe Lejeune has posited that all autobiography is "the retrospective prose narrative that someone makes of his own existence, when he places the principal emphasis on his particular life, especially on the history of his personality."[30] Although Lejeune has gone on to develop another, more flexible position based on the writer's "pact" with the reader, he identifies here several distinct elements that seem appropriate to the genre—namely, the retrospective narration in prose; the focus on the history of a personality; the identity of author, narrator, and character; and (later in his study) the publication of the text.[31] Unfortunately, few female autobiographical voices fit this narrow definition, and for good reason: Lejeune's examples are nearly all written by men.[32]

Sexual difference precludes such critical enclosure. In writing personal narratives, women such as Leroyer, Bréton, and Renooz have been disadvantaged several times over by the "heteroglosia" of their discourses, by the fragmentation of their personalities, by the discrepancy between their selves and their texts, and by the paucity of opportunities to publish their work.[33] But similar problems arise in other genres that women have explored, particularly the novel and children's literature that obviously suit their authors' personal experiences. Consequently, like Lejeune's otherwise important work on auto-biography, traditional approaches to literature's techniques, origins, inten-tions, and creators tend to exclude women's texts from serious study, in part at least because their critical assumptions are more appropriate to men than they are to women.[34] The tight generic boundaries prescribed by literary history and the old New Criticism, resulting in a nearly all-male canon, seem arbi-trary (and political).

Sexual difference apparently also limits referentiality in women's texts.[35] Shari Benstock and Shoshana Felman, among others, have focused on the problematic relationship between the female self and the feminine *I*. For scholars such as Lejeune and Georges Gusdorf who circumscribe the personal narrative to little more than a historical document, writes Benstock, "auto-biography 'is the mirror in which the individual reflects his own image'; in such a mirror the 'self' and the 'reflection' coincide. But this definition of autobiography overlooks what might be the most interesting aspect of the autobiographical: the measure to which 'self' and 'self-image' might not coincide, can never coincide in language."[36] As is true for much recent femi-nist thinking indebted to Jacques Derrida, Benstock's position is anchored in poststructuralist literary theories that privilege the slippage between signs and their referents. The discrepancy between the *I* and its reference to the author's self in women's autobiographical writings suggests the autonomy of language—what Roland Barthes termed "the death of the author"—to deny the existence, much less the efficacy, of the Cartesian self behind all discursive practices.[37] In this way the study of feminine discourse is freed from the dominant tradition of a rationalism centered on the male ego, a tradition that has long objectified women and thereby subordinated them in the logos.

According to poststructuralist feminist theorists, then, the conscious fe-male self behind women's texts disappears; its discourse is all that matters.[38] The advantage of such a strategy is significant: women have a language of their own whose world is worth study in and for itself. But the disadvantages of this theory are equally evident: the feminine *I* refers only to its textuality; it relates no experience in the world; it becomes a semiotic automaton, an autograph without a life.[39] Women writers thus lose their historical agency as conscious actors responsible to themselves and to others in their work. For this reason, among others, Miller has argued for another style of reading women's literature, spiderlike in the web of their texts, "to discover the embodiment in writing of a gendered subjectivity, to recover within representation the emblems of its construction."[40] Otherwise, as Sidonie Smith poignantly asks, "where in the maze of proliferating definitions and theories, in the articulation of teleologies and epistemologies, in the tension between poetics and historiography, in the placement and displacement of the 'self' is there any consideration of woman's *bios,* woman's *aute,* woman's *graphia,* or woman's hermeneutics?"[41]

The answer to that question ultimately lies, I believe, in the dialectics of the existential self and its various literary manifestations. A textual identity must exist in the synthesis of the differences between the self as experience and the self as language.[42] The feminine *I* is neither conscious existence in the world nor mere discursive practice, but an entity unto itself, with features clearly derived from both. Although some theorists like Joan Wallach Scott have questioned the authenticity of experience, it is no more subject to challenge than the epistemological basis of the discursive self.[43] It is fair to say, however, that so long as the analytical categories used are properly historicized—that is, so long as they are seen as subject to cultural construction over time—the existence of the self in and out of texts can be posited and contextualized. And this practice is apparent in the writings by Leroyer, Bréton, and Renooz, and more, in the theory and practice of autobiography as a genre.

Though they do not discuss the specific ontology of the female autobiographical self in a patriarchal context, Paul John Eakin and James Olney take a similar approach to personal narratives. These critics would return conscious agency and subjectivity to the *I* as it is represented in texts. On this point Olney asserts that "the self expresses itself by the metaphors it creates and projects, and we know it by those metaphors; but it did not exist as it now does and as it now is before creating its metaphors. We do not see or touch the self, but we do see and touch its metaphors; and thus we 'know' the self, activity or agent, represented in the metaphor and the metaphorizing."[44] Referentiality in autobiographical texts is mediated by its literary figures, but it does not disappear altogether. Or as Eakin puts it more succinctly, "the self and language are mutually implicated in a single, interdependent system of symbolic behavior."[45]

This position is based on the neo-Kantian faith in the inherent cultural meaning of symbols. Ernst Cassirer, for example, claimed that the acquisition of a symbolic system "transforms the whole of human life" and makes possible society's dramatically enlarged control of its world in a way that no group of nonhumans can.[46] Subject to withering challenge in the modern era, the knowing self is here defended and its use of language as the ultimate symbolic function explored. Although structural linguistics since Ferdinand de Saussure has shown how little correspondence there is between *langue* and *parole*— that is, between grammatical and logical forms in language—the ability to assign meaning to particular signs remains essential to human life in the objective world. "The function of a name," Cassirer asserts, "is always limited to emphasizing a particular aspect of a thing, and it is precisely this restriction and limitation upon which the value of the name depends."[47] On these assumptions, then, Cassirer's student Susanne K. Langer developed her "philosophy in a new key" to study the symbolisms at work in reason, rite, and art, whose subjective criticism accepts language as "the means and agency of our characteristic human awareness."[48]

More recently and much more rigorously, this view is defended by Paul Ricoeur's hermeneutics of the self. In his *Oneself as Another* (1992), this philosopher maps an existential and ontological space between the radically antithetical positions on language and meaning taken by the Cartesian (and logocentric) cogito and the Nietzschian (and postmodernist) anticogito. In fact, Ricoeur argues, the very existence of self depends upon language to express it, in much the same way that the definition of self depends upon differences both within and outside its being. The self stands exclusively neither before nor in the text, but out from the interaction between these locations. It is a situation, if you will, that requires a measure of referentiality in language, on the one hand, and a measure of textuality in the world, on the other. Writing is therefore not entirely an autonomous linguistic system; it also expresses the writer's relationship to herself and her context if she is to have any existence and meaning at all.[49]

More concretely, what this work suggests for reading Leroyer's, Bréton's, and Renooz's autobiographical accounts are important distinctions between *I* and self, between self and other, as they all appear and interact in the text's metaphorical representation of identity, as they are represented in the feminine *I*. In this way these women's agency and subjectivity, women as historical actors as well as writers, are recalled and vigorously defended from the gendered bias of traditional literary history and criticism. These authors have created a body of texts worth study; it just assumes forms that differ from the norms established by men practicing the old New Criticism. But this position also disavows a feminist essentialism that would make of these textual females helpless victims, unconscious objects, of a seemingly monolithic patriarchal hegemony. Such discursive functionalism precludes a more pragmatic constructivism in critical practice; it forecloses the literary possibility, much less the historical existence, of their often subtle, sometimes overt resistance to subordination and oppression. For obvious political reasons, then, feminist theorists of autobiography like Miller and Smith have long recognized the problems both with the male canon and with postmodern theorists.[50]

Given the importance of the issues, other critical approaches to Leroyer, Bréton, and Renooz are worth considering, such as those in the work of Elizabeth Bruss, Bella Brodzki, and Celeste Schenk. Bruss, for example, argues for autobiography not as an unauthored discourse, but as a deliberate "illocutionary" act. All writers make choices in their rhetorical strategies, thematic subjects, and literary forms, choices that often pose problems whose resolution is part of the creative process. Self-writing as a range of related genres is especially rich in such activity, with fundamental implications for the reader trying to make sense of the artful author crafting her life with the plastic materials at her disposal. Language is therefore a well-practiced gesture as well as a system of signs.[51] Here writing becomes a self-directed activity in the world, a potential strategy for establishing identity both inside and outside of the text, that assumes the character of a determined social and political consciousness.

Such is also the argument that Brodzki and Schenk make for a feminist criticism sensitive to autobiographical voices seeking to establish an alternative cultural identity in language. "We strongly believe," they write, "that the duplicitous and complicitous relationship of 'life' and 'art' in autobiographical modes is precisely the point. To elide it in the name of eliminating the 'facile assumption of referentiality' is dangerously to ignore the crucial referentiality of [gender], class, race, and sexual orientation; it is to beg serious political questions."[52] In power relations, self-effacing language is a tactic fraught with failure, a self-defeating move in a game with very real consequences that no writer and her audience can easily ignore. It is these repercussions that all writing women need to consider.

The study of selfhood and identity in Leroyer, Bréton, and Renooz thus requires attention to more than the textuality of the feminine *I* in their auto-biographical writing. Indeed, the self-referentiality of the gendered text is not everything there is to autobiography, no more so than this genre in particular is everything there is to women's personal narratives. Selfhood and identity, as these authors have represented them metaphorically, appear in various literary forms, in every text where these writers have chosen consciously to redefine their world. Regardless of genre, the narrative *I* serves the same purpose and function in this linguistic act of self-assertion. Consequently, historians are interested in women's personal writings of all sorts: memoirs, diaries, personal letters, and wherever else the self and its narrative intrude into the text, including fiction, criticism, and exposition. Historically, the autobiographical act may not matter more than its textuality, but actually the specific form that such an act assumes does not matter any more than its textuality, either.[53]

Autobiographical writings by Leroyer, Bréton, and Renooz also provide an occasion to examine the relationship of women's narrative identity to their historical agency and discursive resistance. Although a related problem has attracted considerable attention from philosophers like Ricoeur, as noted above, it has been more of a concern, albeit an antithetical one, for theorists like Mikhail Bakhtin and Michel Foucault.[54] And like other scholars indebted to them—Richard Terdiman, James Scott, and Gerda Lerner especially—their work is more immediately relevant here. In Bahktin's historical concept of the dialogic imagination, for example, the discursive sources of opposition to social control have always been diverse, heterogeneous, even cacophonous in their unintelligibility to the dominant. Occasionally they are transposed into a more understandable code, as in Rabelais's work in the sixteenth century; otherwise, as a plebeian folk culture throughout the early modern period, they remain marginal and impotent in the Western literary canon, notwithstanding the powerfully disruptive forces of the carnivalesque. But as this book will attempt to show, a similar destabilizing code appears in Leroyer's, Bréton's, and Renooz's writings four hundred years later, not as a popular discourse but as a feminist one.

Foucault's later analysis of power assigns more discursive sites to re-sistance. This historical phenomenon is most forthrightly stated in his account of sexuality and the conflicted practices it has elicited in the West. Historically, Foucault came to believe, language's folds offered innumerable spaces for marginal voices, like women's personal narratives, to contest the language of power. "There is no single locus of great Refusal, no soul of revolt, source of all rebellions, or pure law of the revolutionary. Instead, there is a plurality of resistances, each of them a special case."[55] The multiplicity of the private thus becomes an advantage rather than a disadvantage in the public sphere. This approach makes the feminine *I* in women's autobiographical writings, whatever form they take, much more significant in their quest to establish personal identity as a historical act of self-assertion, often by confounding and dissolving the apparent separation between public and private. In language, such a divide simply does not exist.

Recent historical scholarship has substantially widened this opening for agency in poststructuralist theory.[56] Women's historians, for example, are redefining, if not avoiding altogether, the term *patriarchy,* primarily because, like the category *women,* it is too broad to be a useful analytical tool. Much more to the point, I think, is the promising range of possibilities in the notion of gender as a cultural construction, in which both social organization and self-concept play active roles. This field of inquiry lends itself to rigorous study. Consequently, scholars in literature and history like Nancy K. Miller and Michelle Perrot have turned to texts as language and idea, as writing and action, in effect as *langue* and *parole* in a subtle negotiation of mutual influence of one upon the other. Such an approach authorizes the study of other voices besides women's—people of different color, class, ethnicity, and sexual orientation. They are receiving increased attention not merely out of political sympathy, but for what they tell us about the dialogue between the linguistic moment and its historical context.

Nowhere is this development more obvious than in the work on the social margins. In light of the new texts now worthy of examination, a historical anthropology of discursive practices makes sense. Here the work by Tyler Stovall on the African American experience in Paris, by Vernon Rosario on the French world of alternative eroticisms, and Jann Matlock on the uncontained seductions of Parisian prostitutes, for instance, suggest well the historical logic of neglected voices. In the history of gender and its manifestations, these efforts shed light on the similarities expressed by subordinates, subalterns of many different sorts, whose writings have functioned within the same system of power relations. Frenchwomen were not alone in their recourse to writing for identity and agency. Nor are they unique in the scholarly attention that their selves, language, and circumstance have elicited. This historical phenomenon is remarkably general across groups, periods, and places.[57]

The personal texts by Leroyer, Bréton, and Renooz are therefore excellent illustrations of the politics of discursive practice. As objects of study and as subjects in their own right, these women and their writing suggest how similar figures maneuvered in spaces once thought closed to the inscriptions of mere individuals. Rather, it is apparent that within a complex dialogue between the experiential and the discursive, the generic diversity and inter-textuality evident in their expression of the self and its relation to others fostered a real historical agency. Each woman in her own way serves as a protean source of self-definition and empowerment in a world otherwise alien, indeed hostile, to such independent intention. As the next three chapters will show in more detail, these figures had the resources necessary to create literate spaces of some moment — Leroyer in her provincial devotions, Bréton in the solitude of her soul, and Renooz in her contrary destiny made manifest.[58]

Chapter three

❧ A Provincial's Devotions: Marie Leroyer

What Marie Leroyer (fig. 4) wrote about the protagonist in her novel *Angèle* (1860) also applies to herself: "So it is that youth, beauty, fortune, and fame all fade and disappear into eternal oblivion. Only good deeds for humanity remain and survive their author. Happy therefore are those who while here on earth leave the marks of their good works! Happy too are those who following Angèle's example live and die solely for their deeds of virtue and devotion."[1] Self-sacrifice was truly the central feature of Leroyer's conscious life and work, an attachment that was the expression of both her profound religious convictions and her equally profound commitments to other people. In part because of her Roman Catholic faith, in part because of her own misfortunes, Leroyer felt a strong sympathy for the oppressed and suffering. Like the characters in her fiction, she identified with troubled souls, very often women, in an alien and hostile world. She felt a moral obligation to her family, of course, but oftentimes even more to the unhappy people she encountered in her home town of Angers, in the novels she read, and in those she wrote herself. Again and again Leroyer gave voice to these romantic ideals whose pantheistic quality suggests just how important religion was for the many self-conscious women like her in nineteenth-century France.

The story of the adolescent Angèle de Chavigny, "simple, good, loving, devoted," certainly emphasizes Leroyer's own generous commitments.[2] The girl single-handedly saves her entire family from disgrace, including their exile from France and the loss of their estate. Thanks to her love for both her parents and her faith in God, she undertakes a dangerous journey from Saint-Louis in Senegal all the way to Paris in order to make a personal appeal to King Louis XIII; only he could undo the injustice committed against her

Figure 4. Marie-Sophie Leroyer de Chantepie by D. Magu (1855). Oil on canvas (Cliché Musées d'Angers)

father. En route up the Loire River valley from Nantes, Angers, Tours, and Orléans to Paris, she survives shipwreck, thieves, and faithless friends, finally eliciting the sympathy of the nuns and the powerful benefactor of their cloister who make her project possible. Joyously reunited with her parents on their property in France, their fortune and good name restored, Angèle and family live happily ever after in the religious faith and personal devotion that had overcome all obstacles. "She understood the infinite happiness of existing in and for God," writes Leroyer of the girl. "She felt that attachment to her parents and charity for the poor should be the guiding principles of her conduct"—and ultimately of every romantic feature of the author's long life.[3]

In writing that verges insistently on the personal, especially in its generous descriptions of familiar people and places, Leroyer defines a specific set of moral relationships to herself, to others, and to God. Her personal sacrifices appear in the deeply conflicted self-writing of her fiction, as well as in her correspondence with George Sand and Gustave Flaubert, her two most patient interlocutors for twenty years or more. For eighty years in a small provincial town, she remained paradoxically at odds with herself, society, and the church, all the while she gave voice to her many sympathies and unshakable commitments. In short, Leroyer expressed a distinct feminist consciousness as a romantic idealist and devoted provincial.

The Setting

On the Grande rue in Château-Gontier, a small town north of Angers, Marie-Sophie Leroyer de Chantepie was born at 11 A.M. on Friday, 31 October 1800 (known then as 9 Brumaire in the year 9 of the French revolutionary calendar). Her father was Robert-Pierre Leroyer, an inspector of public schools. For whatever reason, he did not claim the rest of his aristocratic name, de Chantepie, on the birth certificate. Either he or the local clerk must have acceded to the egalitarian spirit of the revolutionary First Republic, for which both men worked three full years before Napoléon Bonaparte proclaimed the First Empire. The mother, Marie-Catherine-Renée Dupouet, had no such political or practical scruples to observe. A pious woman much younger than her husband, she was undoubtedly more concerned about the forthcoming baptism in the parish church of Saint Jean than she was about the formality of names in the civil register.[4]

Marie Leroyer was this couple's only child. From previous marriages, both parents already had children, all of them much older than she.[5] Her father had been widowed, her mother divorced. A revolutionary law authorizing divorce in 1792 had made their union possible, but the law was much modified in 1803 under the authoritarian Consulate and then revoked in 1816 during the conservative Bourbon Restoration.[6] Consequently, a long shadow was cast over their daughter's legitimacy; she became the object of petty public disparagement in rural Anjou, where the church's influence had survived the revolution: "My birth brought with it the reproach that the children of divorced women represented then, this was my first misery," she confessed to Sand in 1849.[7] But Leroyer also saw in her parents the institutional evils of marriage up close. "I had before me the sad spectacle of the pain that came with the inequality of rights and duties in marriage," she continued in the same letter to Sand. "My father was a good man in every conceivable way, my mother was an angel from heaven, they loved each other and yet I could see that she was more miserable, more dependent, more subjected than the least of servant girls."[8]

Marie Leroyer's mother was her principal familial relationship. Long after she died on 10 August 1835, in fact throughout Leroyer's life, she remained a powerful sentimental force. Leroyer's correspondence is replete with regret on nearly every occasion that evoked her memory, such as each anniversary of her death on 10 August or the passing of Flaubert's own mother thirty-seven years later.[9] Ailing and dependent upon Leroyer long after her husband's death in 1815, she embodied the closest, most enduring bond in her daughter's life: "She was both my mother and my child," Leroyer assured Flaubert in 1872.[10] "No one has ever replaced her in my affections."[11] The lingering presence of her mother provided Leroyer emotional consolation for the many disappointing relationships she had with other members of her actual and surrogate family.[12] It also deepened Leroyer's religious faith. To Sand in 1856 she wrote, "Everything that belonged to my mother is sacred to me," such that Leroyer came to believe that her mother's soul lived on within her.[13] Despite what must have been heavy demands of time and attention during her prolonged illness, the only criticism that Leroyer ever made of her mother was the occasional lament of an impoverished childhood: "My childhood was very unhappy. Our home resembled the one that Balzac depicted so well in *Eugénie Grandet*," she wrote, referring to her mother's valiant efforts to help Pierre-Robert restore the family estate.[14]

Leroyer's father had descended from a family distinguished by its loyal service to the king (fig. 5). From the sixteenth century onward, this Angevin *noblesse de robe* acquired substantial public offices and with them various properties until the revolution of 1789. Then their fortunes changed dramatically. What remained in family hands were little more than the stories, portraits, and genealogies of illustrious ancestors who had earned their titles as seigneurs and *lieutenants-généraux* in the annals of local history.[15] But under the revolutionary regime, Robert-Pierre worked hard to acquire new properties. Thanks to these efforts, though not as prominent as earlier genera-

Figure 5. Robert-Pierre Leroyer de Chantepie by unknown artist (c. 1780). Oil on canvas (Cliché Musées d'Angers)

tions of Leroyers de Chantepie, Marie was able to support a large retinue of extended family and friends for most of her adult life and still bequeath a substantial estate upon her death.[16] She may have adored her mother and written copiously about her, but she also admired her father and his family. After a nostalgic visit to Château-Gontier in 1869, Marie returned to her family "maison déserte," where she recognized her father's features in the seventeenth-century portrait of Madeleine Leroyer hanging in the room where he had died; despite Madeleine's formal hair *à la Sévigné,* here was the one relative most like Leroyer.[17]

The daughter's memories of her childhood in Château-Gontier were very selective. She remembered playing with her beloved nurse Modeste (Anne Michel), attending with her mother a Te Deum performed in Saint Rémi to celebrate an unspecified Napoleonic victory, and then reading in the library on the rue du Musée.[18] In 1807 the family moved to Angers, a much larger town forty-five kilometers away, where Marie lived the rest of her life, leaving for only two years to be with relatives in Tours (1830–32). Despite numerous invitations to visit Paris and several enjoyable summer months in Nantes in the 1860s, her physical and emotional attachment to Angers remained very strong. Leroyer found it virtually impossible to leave her home in Anjou. Notwithstanding her professed aversion to provincial society, Leroyer's sense of place appeared frequently in her lush descriptions of the countryside and in her need to write a chronicle of the region, a labor of love, late in life, that she completed in only episodic form as *Chroniques et légendes* (1870) and *Figures historiques et légendaires* (n.d.).[19]

Leroyer's selective appreciation of Anjou's most prominent historical features is remarkable. Nowhere in her writings, for example, appear the dramatic moments of the "Angevin Peril" in the twelfth century, when Eleanor of Aquitaine's marriage to Henry II of England placed nearly all of western France under the control of Louis the Pious's archenemy.[20] Nor does she take any satisfaction from Angers's celebrated medieval achievements—the fortified château built by Blanche of Castille, the romanesque church of Saint Martin, the gothic cathedral of Saint Maurice, or the recently restored tapestry of the Apocalypse.[21] Modern events of note, like the local resistance to the Jacobean revolution in 1793 and the inauguration of the first railway link to Paris in 1849, seem too mundane to merit the narrative attention she gives to the lives and loves of romanticized characters. As Leroyer states in rewriting Adenet le Roi's *Li Roumains de Berte aus grains piés* (c. 1285) based on the life of Charlemagne's mother, she deliberately confused Queen Berthe with her own mother, the one historical, the other personal.[22] A mythical rather than an actual past is celebrated here, despite the author's firm grasp of more recent history, the immediate past of republican politics and the revolutionaries of 1848.[23]

Leroyer was profoundly ambivalent about her quiet world in western France. "What a frightful emptiness surrounds me!" she sighed to Flaubert, a lament reiterated in nearly all her writing.[24] The town of Angers, she felt, was nothing less than a sepulcher, the most backward of cities, in a region given over to darkness, superstition, constraint, and ignorance.[25] She said the same in her many letters to Sand and in her fictional memoirs: "Bigotry and stupidity keep company there," she wrote on the very first page of her last novel.[26] On the other hand, Leroyer recalled some very good moments on trips to Tours and Château-Gontier, "this little piece of ground where I passed the only happy time of my life."[27] Anjou meant more to her than did Angers, perhaps because she knew the area only in passing and the town all too well. The older she grew, however, the greater became her need to define more precisely her debt to home. In time, Leroyer realized, "the grave returns to the cradle" in only one place in the world, whether or not she found happiness there.[28]

Leroyer owned three houses and several farms.[29] Her first home was located in the area curiously known as La Doutre, suggestive of doubt and distance, but actually just on the other side of the river from the center of town. The house itself was situated opposite a local cemetery whose church had been burned by the Normans in the tenth century; Saint Laurent still lay in ruins on a slight rise, providing Leroyer's quaint address, 20 tertre Saint Laurent, now 3 rue Belle-Poignée. In 1859, however, Leroyer reacquired and moved into the "little old house . . . belonging to my father," with its majestic chestnut tree in the garden and the portrait-lined room in which her many relatives had once lived and died.[30] The deserted house still protected the dahlias that had been planted when Leroyer's mother passed away in 1835.[31] Not long after its repurchase, she wrote Jules Michelet, "So sad and somber as it is, this house is not without poetry," obviously because it evoked various family memories.[32] Here on the east side of the river at 16 boulevard des Lices, now 24 boulevard du Roi-René, Leroyer lived until she died in 1888. A third house, La Licorne, lay in the countryside: "There's a large garden that I have saved for myself, a meadow of fields which make up the farm. The air is healthful, the view of the Maine River superb," she wrote serenely to Michelet.[33] Now on the west of town at 30 rue de la Barre, this rural retreat served Leroyer well whenever she needed to escape from intrusive neighbors (fig. 6).

The remaining properties had little sentimental value. At least five local farms were hers to manage after 1835, and probably earlier because of her mother's debilitating illness. The estimated return of at least 10,000 francs a year was indeed a proper provincial middle-class income.[34] The operations themselves ranged widely in size, from less than three to more than a hundred acres, but whose total of 125 hectares or 308 acres made Leroyer a wealthy landowner. For example, she sold two properties, one for 38,000 francs in

Figure 6. La Licorne, 30, rue de la Barre, Angers (1998). Photograph (private collection)

1881 and another for 110,000 francs and a 500-franc annuity in 1886, to support her comfortably in old age. Such wealth placed her easily among the wealthiest 4 percent of the French population.[35] Even though Leroyer occasionally worried about money matters, usually because of her large household of dependents, they were never serious problems, and seemed troublesome only to an impulsively generous spirit like hers.

Leroyer's problems, however, seemed real enough to her. All her life she endured considerable emotional and physical pain. At age thirteen Leroyer nearly died from an unspecified childhood disease; although she miraculously recovered, the ignorant doctor had ruined her health for years thereafter.[36] As for her nervous disposition and excessive sensibility, she apparently inherited them from her mother, whose unnerving experiences during the revolution Leroyer recalled from family stories and from the history Michelet wrote of the revolutionary women like her.[37] As a girl, Leroyer was too impressionable to read Rousseau, and she first suffered the miseries of a deep religious crisis that would plague her for decades.[38] "Already in my childhood, my religious scruples almost drove me mad," she told Michelet.[39] They would eventually be displaced by concern about her failing eyesight, compounded by bouts of conjunctivitis, which for long periods prevented her from reading and writing.[40]

A major factor in Leroyer's moral life was her education. Her later religious doubts arose at least in part from the efforts of two fanatics, a woman
and a priest, who instilled in her as a child both a love for literate activity and
a hatred of doctrinal bigotry.[41] These two impulses remained at odds in
Leroyer's sensitive nature. In 1849 she wrote Sand, "Thanks to this dreadful
dual influence, my religious soul and my rational mind contested vainly with
each other, I nearly lost both life and reason, and since then I have endured
innumerable anxieties, innumerable moral qualms unknown to others."[42]
Leroyer suffered, she felt, from the severe limitations of her education in just
one language, French, unlike most middle-class schoolboys who also learned
Greek and Latin, the languages of God in the Roman Catholic tradition. "My
ignorance of the things of this world," she wrote Flaubert, "is an extreme
personal embarrassment," spiritually as well as intellectually.[43]

Her situation was complicated by her literate habits. An autodidact, Leroyer was an omnivorous reader of contemporary literature and thought in
no particular system or logical order. Besides works by Sand, Flaubert, and
Michelet, she tackled texts by a heterogenous collection of authors: Jacques
Arago, Germaine de Staël, Alphonse Karr, Auguste Lafontaine, Jean Rey-
baud, Félicité de Lamennais, Pierre Leroux, Lord Byron, Alphonse de Lamartine, and Victor Hugo.[44] Moreover, she was a regular subscriber to the Mangin
brothers' *Le Phare de la Loire*. On at least one occasion, Leroyer lamented that
her education prevented her from undertaking work in more serious genres
than that of prose fiction.[45] She remarked to Flaubert wistfully, "I would like
some knowledge and power!" in a notable underestimation of the critical
abilities evident in her many shrewd readings of literary texts.[46] A lifetime of
criticism and creative writing hardly seemed accomplishment enough for so
conflicted and insecure an intellectual.

In some ways Leroyer's problematic devotions are suggested in her 1870
portrait (see fig. 1). Although she commissioned the painting at age seventy,
her image is that of a prim, much-younger woman with deep, dark eyes, her
brown hair in ringlets fashionable thirty years earlier, her family coat of arms
neatly inscribed in the canvas's upper-right corner. In one hand she is holding
a quill, in the other a large piece of paper that reads, "She lived, she suffered,
her life and her memory are shrouded in oblivion."[47] The contradictions
between youth and maturity, between image and reality, between fame and
neglect are equally at work in her life, her writing, and the faith that ruled and
nearly ruined her.

Truer perhaps to what Leroyer actually looked like is another portrait by the same artist fifteen years earlier (see fig. 4).[48] This second image suggests the same admixture of determination and doubt that plagued her for years. The inscription in the painting asserts a blind faith in God and the immortality of the soul that required more emotional stability than she could manage.[49] Despite a clear identity and sense of agency in the world, Leroyer sent a lithographic copy of her portrait to Flaubert in 1857, declaring herself already an old woman.[50] This inner conflict was owed to much more than the illnesses and boredom that she experienced in provincial Angers.

Leroyer was all too aware of her ambivalences. In the letters to Flaubert and Sand, she described herself as torn and passionate, "a romanesque character," because "the most gifted suffer the most," though this self-assurance was uncharacteristic of her.[51] Like the character Elisa de Senneville in Leroyer's posthumous collection of novellas and short stories, *Récits d'amour* (1890), she felt keenly the loss of "her idealism, this wing of the soul rising up to God."[52] The clash of Leroyer's ideals with the demands of the mundane, including her own, underlay much of this inner discord. It was a major theme of her autobiographical writings.

Such a sensibility had its own special affinity with nature, whose subtle changes loomed large in Leroyer's emotional landscape. The passing seasons of the year, for instance, had a dramatic effect on her mood, which in its turn affected Leroyer's fulsome descriptions of the natural world.[53] Seemingly at one with her immediate surroundings, Leroyer would regularly appropriate them as extensions of herself in typical romantic fashion. The pathetic fallacy laced her prose, where all living creatures, however mute, felt her joy and her grief.[54] "There exists for [whoever] understands them secret sympathies between the human soul and external nature," she once stated emphatically, like the many female characters in her fiction who repeatedly expressed this sentiment.[55] The special love for nature, however, did not always console the restlessness within her.

Leroyer had remarkable powers of empathy. It was easy for her to develop an affinity with Sand's apparent persona in *Lélia,* a tortured romantic par excellence. From the evidence of her correspondence, no other novel preoccupied Leroyer for so many years.[56] "My entire soul sees itself there, like the features of a face found in a mirror. . . . This book is my whole self."[57] Leroyer repeatedly referred to this enigmatic figure as herself, though without ever specifying the features they had in common. She made a similar identification with Michelet's revolutionary women and Flaubert's Emma Bovary, who seemed no less misunderstood than Lélia.[58] Rereading *Madame Bovary* actually made her ill, "as if I had just seen this drama occur right before my eyes!"[59] Such tender-heartedness verged on obsession, like Leroyer's nursing a dying pet dog for six long months.[60] Her family's ingratitude for Leroyer's constant solicitude did not deter her, it only made her complain: "Here I have done well by one and all, and [yet] I have created an enemy with each obligation," she confided to Flaubert in one of her many moments of self-pity that came to annoy others much more than they did the novelist.[61] As Mona Ozouf once remarked, Leroyer expressed all too little predisposition to happiness.[62]

Happy or not, Leroyer had a passionate need for commitment. Its object, a person or an activity, mattered less to her than its intention—that is, as an ideal. Her remark to Flaubert in 1860 was typical: "I have never been able to live except in idealism."[63] Literature and, more, religion served this purpose, hence Leroyer's literary and religious passions. "Already dead to this world," she told Michelet in an exaggerated mood, "I have tried to place my hope in the other."[64] Even in the midst of a prolonged spiritual crisis when she denied herself the church's sacraments, Leroyer still aspired, still yearned for something more. "Perhaps in such matters only doubt is more hideous than certitude," she informed Michelet a couple of weeks later.[65] Despite or perhaps because of what she called moral hallucinations, Leroyer gave voice to her continuing desire for a family of like-minded free-spirits who shared her visions of the (im)possible. When she felt most alone in her idealism, she firmly believed herself tortured by a cruelly sick soul.[66] "The greatest [pain] is the absence of a strong passion, of a love, of an admiration without limits for some one or some thing."[67] With or without a community of kindred souls, she must strive toward a goal; she must have an end to work for.[68]

Leroyer's quests could be quite practical. At the head of a large household, this woman had to address the pressing problems of other people. Who was to nurse the sick members of her extended family, if not Leroyer? Who was to find her godson a job, to provide her stepniece a home, or to keep the manager of her farms sober? These were more than mundane matters; they were the activities that ensured Leroyer's sanity: "Inaction and boredom just add to my misery," she told her friend Victor Mangin in 1867.[69] However bad her health, she could not stand to be idle.[70] Leroyer knew how to get things done, arranging for a house to rent in Nantes, publishing her own books, buying and selling property, all to give substance to her dreams. Moreover, she offered the Mangin brothers advice on financing a newspaper when one of their partners died, and she elicited Flaubert's assistance to rebuild the theater in Angers after it had burned to the ground in 1868.[71] In her activities on behalf of others, Leroyer had a presence of mind worthy of her more exalted devotions.

If there is one consistent theme to Leroyer's long life and varied writing, it was this personal dedication. In the simplest sense, it was an elaboration of her feeling of responsibility for others. "There is something more powerful than the interest in the existence even of reason, and it is the accomplishment of [one's] duty! When it becomes impossible, there is nothing more left but the deepest despair."[72] Consequently Leroyer's way of coping in the face of loneliness and inner conflict was to throw herself passionately into some purposeful activity. Her life was given over to continuous sacrifice, because it was so necessary to her emotional and moral survival in a conflicted internal world all her own.[73] Her family and friends provided no help when they pursued different passions: "I love all those who surround me and yet they are strangers to me, I remain apart even in the midst of them," was her constant lament.[74] To Leroyer nothing seemed more cruel, "like the feeling of abandonment," than to be alone in one's idealism.[75]

Leroyer's devotion to her family, to her faith, above all to her writing was deliberate and enduring. Her passion for art was a moral salvation: "It's like the presence of a loved one who conjures away suffering and death," she declared to Flaubert. "Whatever the passion—a strong feeling for art, for literature, or for other things—is that not life itself? And how can one exist otherwise?"[76] In this principle, Leroyer was perfectly consistent. Ten years earlier she had written to Sand in nearly identical terms: "And yet I have the wish and the will to live, yes, I can feel it, if I could only find a reason for being, a love, a [horizon], a purpose beyond all I have loved, and [only] then will I live."[77] A true romantic, Leroyer's passionate engagement was the chief aesthetic criterion by which she judged the literary works of other writers.[78] What better way is there, then, to frame the experiential and discursive nature of Leroyer's own personal attachments?

Relationships

Leroyer's living arrangements were cause for gossip, if not scandal, in provincial Angers. True to her many sympathies for others less fortunate than she, her houses were filled with as many as eighteen family members, friends, and servants; all of them were dependent upon her largesse.[79] Because she never married, this mixed company attracted the neighbors' attention, from which there was no escape, not even to La Licorne, just outside of town, where she occasionally retreated to be alone. "It constitutes a phalanstery, a kind of community, to which I dispense what I possess, always counting myself last."[80] She obviously could not live without personal attachments, without the opportunity to help others, however unworthy they may have been. "I would like to be able to give others a little of the happiness that I never had," she explained to Flaubert in 1857.[81] "In effect my vocation for sacrifice and devotion marks my place in [charge of] a hospital," with an unambiguous purposefulness that this situation necessarily entailed for so romantic an ideal.[82]

As passionate as she was compassionate, Leroyer was often drawn into complicated relationships. Her first love was, as one would expect, another incurable idealist. In 1824 a handsome and talented actor, Eugène André, worked at the Angers theater where Leroyer the drama enthusiast was often in attendance. Years later Leroyer remarked to Sand how "this truly ideal love, the poem of my life" had literally swept her off her feet, and could be recognized and relived in Sand's own *Léone Léonie* (1834).[83] But Leroyer's mother strongly disapproved of the man's profession; and rather than see her daughter ruined, she paid André a thousand francs to leave Angers. Leroyer seems not to have begrudged her mother's intrusion, but long afterward she remained in touch with her lover. Thanks to their correspondence—a habit formed early in Leroyer's life—she learned that André studied the law briefly before becoming a theater director in Avignon. In time the unattainable André came to represent an uncomplicated idol inextricably tied to Leroyer's love for the stage, a youthful passion whose memories Leroyer would celebrate in her fictional memoirs.

For Leroyer the memory of André retained a soft, romantic glow; the presence of Mathurin Sourice, however, was much warmer, more immediate, and ultimately more enduring. It is curious how in her long and often detailed accounts of their life together, Leroyer never once mentioned Sourice's first name. On the one hand, he was merely "a respectable man" who managed Leroyer's complicated business affairs and came each day to read her the newspapers.[84] On the other hand, he filled an obvious emotional need left by her mother, coming to Leroyer's attention just two years after she died in 1835.[85] Leroyer's dependence upon him was complete: "I was unable to take a step without him," she confessed to Flaubert on two separate occasions.[86] Whatever the protective distance Leroyer created in her correspondence, though she never married him, Sourice was probably more significant and certainly more cruel to Leroyer than her mother Marie-Catherine.

Sourice was eleven years younger than Leroyer. Jesuit-educated, he trained to be first a priest, then a physician, only to become a Latin tutor to Leroyer's godchildren.[87] When he fell dangerously ill in 1837 without family of his own to care for him, Leroyer stepped in and nursed him back to health. Such generosity soon turned to affection, and the two of them seemed to have fallen in love, at least briefly. Leroyer refused his repeated proposals, she said, because of her scruples about marriage as an institution—her parents had been unhappily married—and because of Sourice's chronic alcoholism—he suffered what Leroyer termed politely "an unhealthy need to drink."[88] Instead, Leroyer bought him a nearby farm for 16,000 francs, so she said, to provide him an independent income. But it is apparent that she also wanted to keep him close to home. This curious arrangement lasted, however contrived, for thirty-five years.

Leroyer confessed their problems to Sand. Evidently in 1849 Sourice fell in love with another woman, Léonie Gautrait, one of Leroyer's household companions. Leroyer had recently hired Gautrait to read aloud and play music for her, but Sourice found the exotic Mexican mestiza to his liking, much to Leroyer's distress.[89] Especially wounding to Leroyer was the lovers' bold request of her to provide Gautrait a dowry so they could marry (after all, she had already established Sourice on his own farm). But Leroyer's selfless generosity had its limits; she refused, despite "an attachment, an affection of twelve years" for Sourice.[90] Bravely she insisted that Léonie leave; and after some devious delaying tactics arranged with the connivance of Leroyer's confessor, Sourice finally resigned himself to a platonic relationship with his patroness.[91] The moral strength of her decision and the physical weakness of his alcoholism, it seems, had combined to save what was left of their commitment to each other.

Leroyer's emotional turmoil in the midst of this crisis is not hard to imagine. She wrote three long letters to Sand about it, and years later she would recount it to Flaubert in comparable though muted detail. Here her romantic idealism was put to the ultimate test and had survived, but barely. Leroyer and Sourice would live out their remaining years of quiet torture together. Until his death in 1872, he continued to visit nearly every evening to read her the newspapers and to discuss her business affairs. Yet Leroyer remained pro-foundly attached to this ne'er-do-well mate. When he almost died from a serious liver ailment in 1867, she appealed passionately for Sand and Flau-bert's sympathy.[92] And when Sourice died of a stroke five years later, Leroyer was inconsolable, losing all sense of time and memory in her grief. At long last, in a gesture of bitter resignation, she ceased to agonize over her loss of religious faith.[93]

Leroyer's ersatz family also dashed her best hopes. The closest members of her household were the children of Leroyer's nanny Modeste Michel: Edouard and Annette. Born in 1829, Annette was apparently Leroyer's favor-ite, "my faithful companion," helping her in countless ways to the end of her life.[94] "A simple girl who serves me well," Annette never married and devoted much of her time and attention to Leroyer.[95] In fact, Leroyer bequeathed the bulk of her estate to Annette in 1888 after a Torterue de Sazilly, her great-nephew, generously turned it down. Hers was devotion nearly equal to Leroyer's, one hardly ever mentioned in the extant correspondence. What disappointments rendered Leroyer so uncharacteristically taciturn about so faithful a relation remains something of a mystery in her extensive personal writing.

Edouard, Leroyer's godchild in 1825, proved to be another story. The object of frequent lamentation, he was apparently bright, "good-hearted," but lazy, selfish, dissolute, and ungrateful.[96] His rare visits to Leroyer usually entailed personal requests for money to pay off his debts.[97] A republican ar-dently opposed to Louis-Napoléon Bonaparte's coup d'état in 1851, Edouard was forced into exile until Leroyer, after years of fretful effort, arranged for his return.[98] Not long afterwards, still without job or trade, Edouard married a working woman, who had to quit when she started having children. The first infant died; but the next one, Marie, became Leroyer's godchild and personal responsibility.[99] In 1860 Edouard fell ill with a meningitis that altered his personality and left him utterly indifferent to his family. In 1861 he was struck again and paralyzed. Unable to recognize anyone, he was now, like his sister, wife, and child, Leroyer's familial charge for the rest of her life.[100]

Toward another relation, Agathe-Julie Gautret de la Moricière, Leroyer felt more kinship than any other.[101] Although Leroyer never indicated her last name, Agathe was a stepniece; that is, the daughter of her mother's daughter by an earlier marriage. Leroyer's mother had taken responsibility for her as a little girl when Agathe's mother died and her father was unwilling to care for her properly. A dwarf with a large head and the small body of a child, Agathe had no marriage prospects, especially after a serious illness at age sixteen rendered her simple-minded and even more deformed. Soon after Leroyer's mother died, Agathe took deathly ill again and nearly fell from a window, an incident that forced Leroyer to request help from the girl's father, who agreed reluctantly to take her back. But he mistreated her, and Agathe fled to a convent, where her care was little better. Except for the expense, Leroyer could hardly justify leaving her there.

Agathe was fortunate enough to have resources of her own. In 1838 she sought legal remedy for the money she inherited from her deceased mother, some 40,000 francs, making it possible for Leroyer to provide for her. Ten years later, however, Agathe began giving away money to an unscrupulous actor, M. Rousseau-Lagrave, who took full advantage of her infatuation with him and then left for America. Agathe had little property left, except for the 800-franc annuity provided by her father on the condition that none of it went to Leroyer, ostensibly out of spite over her assistance with the legal action over Agathe's inheritance. In a fit of despair over Rousseau-Lagrave, Agathe apparently poisoned herself, and at age forty-two she passed away in the same room where Leroyer's mother had died twenty-three years earlier. In the end Leroyer had to acknowledge the close parallels between Agathe and herself. "I envy her fate," she said to Flaubert, because she died with all her illusions intact.[102] Such uncomplicated devotion, Leroyer confessed, was simply too much like her own.[103]

The rest of Leroyer's household consisted of similarly hopeless creatures. "I love those around me, but they are not family; they are kind, but I have no moral support," she confided to Michelet.[104] For example, Pierre Zemiowski was a Polish refugee thanks to the 1830 nationalist uprising in which he had participated as an officer. For years without work, he nonetheless elicited Leroyer's admiration as "a perfectly decent man who is waiting for the opportunity to return home."[105] His elegant manners, deep blue eyes, profound gratitude, and personal devotion to Leroyer won her indulgence. She exclaimed in romantic sympathy, "Here was a second self."[106] Living on a small property nearby—undoubtedly one of Leroyer's—he died after having recovered from bronchitis in 1864. He had been for thirty years Leroyer's brother in all but name.

Leroyer's entourage consisted of many more shadowy figures.[107] Among them were "a devout young woman," an aging and ailing actor, "a very young girl without education," a foundling (Victor Agamemnon) who learned a trade and left for Paris, a penniless cousin who lived with Leroyer for fifteen years before dying of pneumonia, and various imperfect lady friends.[108] The latter members of the household included "a former actress now crazy," a woman of dubious virtue with her natural-born child, and a musician who might have been married to a Parisian banker.[109] Over the years these individuals came and went and occasionally returned for reasons hard to discern in Leroyer's parenthetical remarks. But they all benefited from her generous, sympathetic nature; they all knew that Leroyer closed no doors on needy relations, no matter how distant. They were the only family she had.

Discursively, Leroyer's family was much larger. One might say that it included Flaubert and Sand, her favorite correspondents. Leroyer confided in these prominent authors, even though she never once met them. To Flaubert, for example, she wrote at least sixty-nine letters.[110] Her first concerned *Madame Bovary* in December 1856; her last responded to the news of Sand's death in May 1876. In the intervening nineteen or so years, their correspondence covered many topics, but their common passion for reading and writing prevailed. Flaubert very generously read and critiqued constructively Leroyer's first novel *Cécile*, and Leroyer in turn shrewdly discussed every one of Flaubert's major works. But she did more. Leroyer also revealed much about herself and her family that engaged Flaubert's attention and response. Because of his ironic patience, however different their temperaments and literary values, she soon considered Flaubert an indulgent relation.

It began with Leroyer's flattering judgments of Flaubert's first novel. For her, Emma Bovary was quite simply Leroyer herself, a misunderstood woman in an alien world: "I have lived her life, I have suffered and died with her, for it seemed to me that I had lived in her and that she had died in me!"[111] Contrary to Flaubert's professed views of his craft—"Art ought to rise above such personal matters"—she identified with Emma in an effort to elicit further insight into her own character.[112] Soon her letters recounted a profound emotional and spiritual crisis that for years cried out for Flaubert's sympathetic advice, which he offered and Leroyer of course ignored. After all, what she really needed was his understanding. "You are for me a friend whose soul understands mine," she wrote in 1867. "Telling you about my miseries is a consolation, a necessity."[113] Clearly she sought a kindred soul wherever she could find it, at home or in the mail with Flaubert.

Leroyer's correspondence with George Sand mattered much more to her.[114] As she explained to Flaubert in 1876, "I loved [Madame] Sand like a truly better sister."[115] This familial appropriation occurred throughout her writing; it was a veritable motif in her letters, including those she sent to Sand. Although this correspondence began in 1836, her first extant letter dates only from 1848; her last is from four full years before Sand's death in 1876. Leroyer apparently wrote many more letters than the eighteen surviving in the archives. But what remains reiterates the same themes of identity and relationship that appear in her correspondence with Flaubert. As mentioned earlier, the strongest expression of this impulse was Leroyer's enthusiasm for Sand's *Lélia*, its autobiographical elements in particular: "*Lélia* remains my favorite book," she wrote appreciatively on numerous occasions.[116] Here was another tortured self very much like her own.

In Leroyer's epistolary relations with Sand and Flaubert, there are some critical differences worth noting.[117] Despite Sand's frequent expressions of impatience with Leroyer's unwillingness to resolve her personal crises, the two women revealed much more of themselves than did Leroyer and Flaubert. To Sand, Leroyer gave voice to intimate details that would have been utterly inappropriate in her correspondence with a man. Moreover, Sand represented to Leroyer a figurative Virgin Mary, a deity of confession, consolation, and counsel well suited to women believers.[118] "And yet when you have given so much to humanity, when you have brought wisdom, learning, strength, and consolation to your fellows, when you have created sublime characters, and with the help of your creations you have made everyone better and happier, how can you not be happy?" she wrote admiringly in 1849.[119] Sand the source of divine wisdom was the most frequent and flattering trope in Leroyer's correspondence with the novelist. "For the moment, Madame, you know me better than the priest who hears my confessions, for I speak to him only of practical matters and I have told you of my innermost self."[120]

The best-of-all-women, the greatest heart and intelligence in existence, the writer of magic texts, Sand embodied more than Leroyer's favorite author. She was Leroyer's ideal alter ego, a projection of everything she wanted to see in a successful older sister, perhaps in herself: "Madame, I have lived with you in my heart and in my mind, I recognize you in your works, so congenial are they to my soul which looks for yours in them."[121] Consequently, when Sand died, Leroyer was distraught; and like a member of the family, she worried about the funeral arrangements, hoping that they would be just as Sand wanted them.[122] Four years later, Leroyer consecrated her devotion to Sand in the glowing dedication to *Mémoires d'une provinciale:* "Dear sister in heart and soul . . . you have been my faith and my rule; I saw my soul in yours."[123] Similarly, Leroyer devoted two essays to Sand's work in her collection of literary criticism, *Souvenirs et impressions littéraires.*[124] Sand could do no wrong.

This is not to say that their feelings were entirely symmetrical. Sand's letters to Leroyer are fewer, shorter, and occasionally intemperate in response to Leroyer's endless religious anxiety: "So raise yourself from this prostration, because even if you were very guilty, God the source of all goodness does not want to be doubted or for us to turn inward so much," wrote Sand, obviously irritated.[125] More often than not, however, Sand seemed sympathetic: "However sick and racked by the flu, I wanted to write something, dear friend, to tell you how I commiserate with you to the depths of my heart and how your sorrows distress me."[126] Several of Sand's letters also offer serious advice on religion, politics, and the plight of women that expresses respect if not always affection.[127] Otherwise, unlike the fraternal quality to Flaubert's letters, Sand's correspondence was entirely too personal. It never ventured very far from the intimacy that Leroyer sought in this discursive relationship with an honorary member of her family, with a romantic ideal—ultimately with another self.

Leroyer was less intimate with but much closer to the Mangin brothers, Victor and Evariste, in Nantes. Several times in the 1860s she escaped the cultural backwaters of Angers for a month or more to share the Mangins' enthusiasm for the opera in their hometown.[128] As the editors of *Le Phare de la Loire,* the region's most important newspaper, they published Leroyer's reviews of recent literature and helped her with the copyediting of her manuscripts.[129] Her fourteen extant letters to them, dating from 1860 to 1876, were often businesslike, urging Victor in particular to finish his corrections of a novella, requesting his assistance in locating a house to rent during the theater season, and describing the recent renovations of the opera hall in Angers (the latter account was reprinted in the Mangins' newspaper).[130] On the other hand, Leroyer knew the brothers well, visited with their families, and recounted her many woes to them, though never with the same detail that she provided Flaubert and Sand. Leroyer needed a fictional alter ego, like those the novelists had created for her, through which to relate with other people so personally. However much she had in common with the Mangin brothers, including their staunch republican politics, they offered her no such discursive identity.

Relations as Texts

Besides the people in Leroyer's life, there were the texts she wrote. They preoccupied her every bit as much as the relations with her immediate entourage and her correspondents. The publication of her work, for example, caused no end of frustration and discussion with Flaubert, Sand, and the Mangin brothers.[131] Except for the essays and short stories that appeared in periodicals, all her major works were published at her own expense, including those she provided for in her will.[132] Leroyer's literary legacy owes nearly everything to her own efforts in a world indifferent if not hostile to women's writing. Her identity and agency, her entire existence, seem tightly tied to her self-conscious literary craft as a deliberate discursive practice. In effect, Leroyer's personal correspondence, prose fiction, literary criticism, and history writing defined her relationships.[133]

This truism is most obvious in the many letters Leroyer wrote. She was a passionate correspondent, whose interests ranged from everyday events in Angers to the latest news in the national newspapers. Much depended upon the recipient. Leroyer's letters to Sand and Flaubert, for instance, followed a curious formula: the first paragraph usually reiterated her enduring identification with the narrator or principal character in her favorite novel by the author; the second and longest portion discussed at length the prolonged religious crisis in her emotional life; and the conclusion turned to Leroyer's current reading. The rhetorical pose changed remarkably little. But in her letters to the Mangin brothers, Leroyer appears less anxious to impress or to call on their sympathy for her. That most of their correspondence has been lost may well explain the paucity of telling detail in the Mangin archive. But in her clear, steady handwriting that filled each page, top to bottom, front and back, with her distinct, quaintly anachronistic diction, Leroyer knew well how to address an audience for her particular purposes. Her interlocutors were, in part at least, pretexts for her writing.

The close link that Leroyer saw between experience and language lay in her tendency to read and write autobiographically. Like other romantics, Leroyer firmly believed in literature as self-projection. She got Sand to confess as much in her writing of *Lélia* and in her reading of Leroyer's *Cécile*, though Flaubert stoutly refused to do so in his writing of *Madame Bovary* and in his reading of *Cécile*.[134] Leroyer's own third-person narratives often resorted to the first-person plural *nous,* an inclusive gesture suggesting the interpersonal. In the last sentence of her *Mémoires d'une provinciale*, she wrote, "Let us stop a moment, as this long narrative and intimate drama draw to a close, let us allow the reader's soul to repose with the cheerful picture of this unblemished happiness."[135] Similarly, Leroyer adopted a first-person narrative persona in her first novel *Cécile* that closely resembles, substantively and stylistically, her correspondence with Sand, Flaubert, Michelet, and the Mangin brothers.

Autobiographical elements are apparent wherever Leroyer seems to be speaking in her own voice. In the *Chroniques et légendes,* in the *Souvenirs et impressions littéraires,* and in the long letters habitually inserted into her prose fiction, Leroyer's choice of character and plot is distinctively her own. Throughout her stories and novels there appear superior, artistic figures whose emotional happiness is frustrated by the prejudices of society. Ideal romantic relationships, usually love at first sight, are subject to the obstacles of demanding parents, jealous rivals, or inadvertent misunderstandings. Invariably the narratives end in death or its moral equivalent, withdrawal from the world to a cloister. In the first half of the nineteenth century, these features are typical of sentimental fiction—Leroyer's preferred genre of literary expression—but here they represent more than mindless discursive activity. They are deliberately borrowed in part from the language and literary forms Leroyer lived and still more from her self-conscious intention to craft from her experiential devotions an identity and a sense of agency in the world.

Like many of her contemporaries before 1850, Leroyer explored the creative possibilities of romantic prose fiction. Perhaps the literary form most congenial to her was what D. G. Charlton termed "le roman de l'individu," where "attention is focused upon the experience of the individual less in his relationship to society . . . than in regard to the inner life, the 'existential' dilemma of an intelligent and sensitive personality."[136] Not all written in the first-person, these works often draw on the author's discreet self-disclosure, however much more there is to the practice than the confessional. Analysis of the romantic generation's *Weltschmerz* and its social context played at least as important a role as the proposal of an alternative moral idealism in a world undergoing dramatic historical change since the eighteenth century. But Leroyer blended her expression of the *mal du siècle* with the popular melodramatic imagination that had developed a separate literary tradition on the stage, but that, according to Peter Brooks, had also appeared in the novel.[137] Leroyer's characters were indeed rendered mute emotionally if not discursively in her application of the esthetics and ethics of astonishment in feminine fiction. In her lifetime, the lending libraries of France were filled with this now-disdained literary genre.[138]

Leroyer's longest and most ambitious venture in this vein was her two-volume *Mémoires d'une provinciale,* written and published in the last decade of her long life. It is very much an exercise in autobiographical romance, one dedicated to the memory of George Sand; the death of her closest epistolary confidant four years earlier had deeply moved Leroyer. The novel was set in the region of central-western France that Leroyer knew best, including the towns of Nevers, Clermont, Orléans, Bordeaux, and Nantes. The familiar châteaux of the Loire River valley are evoked by the novel's châteaux de la Chesnaie, de Bois-Castel, de Vernière, and de la Source. Moreover, the *Mémoires'* action takes place between 1825 and 1840, formative years in Leroyer's emotional development, highlighted by her love for the actor Eugène André.

The characters and views expressed in the work have much in common with those found in her copious correspondence. The theme of devotion and its ultimate triumph over social egotism, conjoined with the three female characters who represent three sides to Leroyer's ideal self, is evidence of discursive and personal continuities across genres, from letters to fictional memoirs (and back again). This autobiographical expression was one creative source of "this happiness which was never but a dream for the author." But it also became for her fictional alter egos, figuratively for Leroyer as well, "the sweetest of realities."[139] The author made few critical distinctions between life, literature, and language.

On one level, *Mémoires d'une provinciale* is obviously a romance.[140] It is loosely structured in four unequal parts: the first and longest, entitled "Valérie," takes up the entire first volume. The other sections, also entitled after important characters in the narrative—"Marcie," "Rosine," and "Horace"—share volume 2, which provides a separate pagination for the last part, even though it is as integral to the novel as all the others. As one would expect in so long a work, there are frequent digressions, including descriptions of social life (in Nevers, for example, in "Valérie"), miscellaneous character development (of Jenny in "Rosine"), long explanatory letters (between Horace, Valérie, and Marcie in "Marcie"), and prolonged detours of plot (with the legend of Pâquerette concerning the Abbey of Saint Sulpice, again in "Marcie"). The third-person narrative is interrupted by first-person, epistolary, and dialogic moments, sustained by florid prose, noble truths, and chance turns in plot, all in keeping with eighteenth- and nineteenth-century sentimental and romantic fiction.[141]

At the heart of the story are three women and their relationships to an ideal contending with adversity. The first figure, Valérie de Stenneville, the dutiful, patient, long-suffering wife of a self-indulgent and opinionated count, remains loyal to her husband even after his death; her devotion is sealed by retreat to a convent in order to serve others less fortunate than she. The second woman, Marcie de Villermès, Valérie's naive and sentimental niece and confidant, refuses the profound affection offered by her truly selfless cousin, Maxime de Martignac. Instead, she seeks a more perfect relationship with another love. And the third character, Rosine Bellerive, a passionate and talented orphan, escapes prostitution for a successful career on the stage in Orléans, Nantes, and New York before she finally dies for the sake of her lover's happiness. Rosine's impulsive creativity contrasts sharply with Valérie's religious faith and Marcie's emotional idealism, though all three figures suggest different aspects of Leroyer's better being.

The object of these women's attention is Horace Geraldini, the baron d'Armenfieds, tragically convicted of embezzlement in a complicated affair of honor. An artistic genius, he turns his talents to the theater, where he recovers his noble family's income, which had been lost to unscrupulous bankers and to his insatiable penchant for gambling. In keeping with the women who come to love him, he is a handsome, noble, romantic soul, "a problematic life," in quest of an ideal forever frustrated by circumstances beyond his control.[142] In the course of the narrative, these three women become agents of his rehabilitation in the eyes of society: Valérie rescues him from unjust imprisonment; Marcie clears his name of the embezzlement; and Rosine helps him earn the money he needs to marry. Thanks to these forceful women, Horace is absolved of his crime, reclaims his name, and secures his fortune at long last. In the end he marries his true mate Marcie, whose enduring selflessness reestablishes his family's heritage.

It is not difficult to identify here Leroyer and her relations. Horace is clearly modeled on Eugène André, a character described in the same glowing terms. "Horace's beauty in short embodied the perfection that poets only dreamed of and for which the sculptors and the painters of antiquity have left exquisite models," writes Leroyer. "This was no voice but a soul in search of yours."[143] He possessed to the highest degree the gifts appropriate to a truly romantic hero, the most important of which was his ability to transcend obstacles to human happiness. "His influence reunited all classes, silenced all vanity, and the happiness of being in his presence seemed to transcend all social barriers."[144] And he does so by a superior nature that regards all men with sympathy, but dominates them by the sheer grandeur of its genius. Because of her central role in his life, Marcie defines his essence in two rhetorical questions posed near the end of the narrative: "Wasn't Horace the realization of that earnestly sought ideal so much dreamed of? In short, was he not the very object of the ardent aspirations of a soul opening to light and life?"[145]

Valérie is the sensible Leroyer. Tall, thin, and brown-haired, reminiscent of Auguste Charpentier's famous portrait of George Sand, she has large, black, melancholy eyes like Leroyer. "She had gotten from her father the hatred of despotism, the independent views, the great intellectual pride, and the love for justice. Unswerving in her feelings, she allowed herself to be easily dominated by those she loved."[146] Perhaps the most telling parallel, however, is Valérie's troubled religious devotion, represented here by the sacrament of an unhappy marriage. "Much too attached to her duties even to dream of breaking the ties that she had accepted, she resigned herself to suffering fate without complaint."[147] She, too, regretted not being able to chose freely a spouse after her own heart. "How weak she felt against misfortune, deprived of her confidence and of that unshakable faith in the constancy of the man she loved!"[148] In circumstances largely defined by her noble sentiments and ideas, Valérie feels no less conflicted in her dependence upon moral and intellectual inferiors. As she confesses to Marcie, "My heart [was] overwhelmed by bitterness, my greatest sorrows came to me from those I loved the best."[149] Leroyer could hardly have said truer words about herself.

The blond and blue-eyed Marcie, on the other hand, embodies the idealistic Leroyer, the one who aspired to become a moral Eve. "Marcie felt thus predisposed to providing the world one of those sublime sacrifices that everyone considered insane," the narrative states of this uncompromising individual. "Because her personality had been especially dominated by inspiration and emotion, her reason had always been powerless to enlighten her about the illusions of the heart."[150] What else was happiness to Marcie but the fullest development of her natural talent? "Her whole soul had been moved by the imperious need to seize with hope again life, light, and liberty" right to the end of her days.[151] But when Horace seemed to have abandoned her, she felt

the deep despair and painful sorrow of disappointed love, the most insuffer-
able of all feelings that only loneliness and desolation can bring in their train.
In such a state, Marcie was plunged into the mournful torpor of a life without
goal or purpose. Nevertheless, upon Horace's miraculous return and the
happy prospect of their life together, "she believed in a general regeneration,
assured that truth and justice could never be effaced from the heart of men
where God himself had inscribed them."[152] In Leroyer's fiction and correspondence alike, faith in romantic aspirations ultimately prevails.

The third figure here, Rosine, represents the passionate Leroyer. Both
women felt keenly society's condemnation of their apparent illegitimacy.
"From birth I had been especially unfortunate as a consequence of abandonment and the want of a family," states Rosine candidly. "As it is I was reared in
the guise of an illegitimate child and branded as a bastard."[153] In the midst of
her own religious crisis, God was not a forgiving father but an inexorable
judge of one's sins, including those of one's family passed on from generation
to generation. Salvation, however, was found in art. "For me the exercise of
my art served in lieu of all those advantages; I felt happy and proud conveying
to the crowd the thoughts and feelings that the greatest masters had left in
their immortal creations."[154] In such a context, death no longer frightened
Rosine, or Leroyer; the real mystery of death lay in God's designs that
promised resignation and peace of mind to all impassioned and inspired
believers. Creation was indeed divine.

Independent-minded, superior, yet orphaned and lonely, all three women
enact Leroyer's views of women, love, and marriage. The narrator sets the
tone: "Those deprived of fortune and have neither father nor husband to
defend them are as abandoned as the slave without a master or the worker
without an employer," she explains. "In such circumstances woman is a feeble
being."[155] Woman, it seems, is everywhere a wretched slave to the false
impressions of others, the results of which appear in the application of unjust
laws and the unhappiness ultimately of everyone. Moreover, the situation
only worsens as women grow older. "Middle-aged women no longer have
a place in society. Time sweeps away beauty, talent, and all those frivo-
lous advantages that are admired only in youth. Everything passes and is
eclipsed."[156] Whatever their age, virtuous women who love and suffer for the
sake of others rarely obtain a fair return on their devotions. "God pardons the
repentant creature, but that is not the same with society, which condemns
without appeal all those whose errors and wrongs are nearly always society's
own doing."[157]

Marriage is the source of much misery. Again the narrative emphasizes the unequal relationship between husband and wife guaranteed by religious doctrine, social convention, and the law.[158] In such a situation, marriage can be little more than a market transaction; infidelity is tolerated, even expected. The result is naturally adultery, hypocrisy, and immorality, everything that degrades women. At one point in the memoirs, Marcie exclaims to Valérie,

> Marriage as it exists in our society inspires a lively repugnance in me. Why, I would have to give up my body, my feelings, my will, my thoughts entirely; I would lose the right to all initiative, even that of disposing of my wealth and of keeping my own name, since my existence would no longer be recognized except in that of my husband; I would have to submit, for he would have the right to command and I would have the duty to obey. I ask you, Valérie, is not accepting this situation the suicide of one's heart and the sacrifice of one's whole being unto nothingness?[159]

How sad it is, she concludes, that the sacred role of mother comes at so high a price—the shame and slavery of women.

The remedy for this oppression, the memoirs suggest, lies in remaining true to one's own nature. A magnetic force in life, one's true sentiments are "a resurrection and a life."[160] Nature itself can only have a positive influence on women's physical and moral state. "Besides there are few places that offer shelter from grief and sadness to those who are graced with an active imagination," states the narrator emphatically.[161] Of all the creative arts, it seems, music speaks most directly to such a soul; it is an ideal that brings forgetfulness, a gentle solace for all the suffering and the misery that are inseparable from reality. Like Horace, alone and lost, woman "must live without country, without family, and must find in art her sole consolation."[162] Yet there is more. Women's devotions can also be active agents for good, a major point of Leroyer's fictional memoirs. As the narrator explains, Horace's "noble family, the d'Armenfieds, had recovered its timeless splendor; in the person of its last descendant, it was raised from ruin by the devotion of a woman."[163] Women do make good things happen, if not for themselves, then at least for others.

And they do so by their commitments. In sharp contrast to their lesser rivals for Horace's affection, the three principal characters devote their efforts to one goal, and in the end they succeed. Women incapable of such devotion like Estelle Differmont, a calculating and hard-hearted figure willing to blackmail Horace to arrange her ne'er-do-well brother Jules's marriage to Marcie, ultimately fail. Thus, of Horace, Marcie can say selflessly and without apparent contradiction, "I feel that I will be able to love and to devote myself, to suffer and to die for my beloved, but never will I have the desire or the will to marry him."[164] Centered on this major theme, the many pieces of Leroyer's otherwise discursively written memoirs fit together into a complex whole. Its moral focus on women's enduring virtue serves to bind together the longest and most complete narrative of Leroyer's life, feelings, and views. Her personal devotions provide the memoirs their distinctive literary qualities.

Leroyer wrote other autobiographical romances with similar plots, characters, and themes. Her earliest and probably most successful literary effort, *Cécile*, is also set in western France and concerns troubled relationships between figures resembling Leroyer and members of her informal family. The first-person narrator Arthur de Monthierry and his wife Cécile have two very different temperaments. Confesses Monthierry, "Cécile was simple, spiritual, kind, and rational, while my fiery imagination preferred intellectual idealism to the practical and moderate enjoyment of a heart dominated by reason."[165] Cécile's selfless devotion is sorely tested by Arthur's infatuation with another woman, the self-centered Julia O'Flaerthy, who is married to the comte de Préaubert but also enamored of the duc de Clarencey and an Italian artist, Léonce. The latter figure's suicide, however, leads Julia to sincere repentance and withdrawal to a cloister in Ireland. Only then are Cécile and Arthur reconciled, just before Cécile dies from the unhappiness she selflessly hid for years from her husband. So ends the novella's action, but not its moral message.

Desperately unhappy himself and racked by guilt over his wife's death, Arthur receives a long, final letter from Julia that highlights themes familiar from Leroyer's own correspondence: the ideals of love and faith, the salvation of selfless devotion to others, and the miseries of unrequited emotion. This last point is posed in the form of a rhetorical question: "In fact, what sympathy can there exist between slave and master?"[166] Julia's letter also emphasizes the brevity of life, love, and institutions like marriage. Everything human may be perfect in principle but is nearly always impossible in practice, especially with "the inability of loving exclusively and constantly the same object," except of course the eternal love of God.[167] Finally Julia asks one of Leroyer's unanswerable questions in italics, *"Are not hoping and waiting the only fate of everyone on earth?"*[168]

The frustrations of true love between noble souls appear again in a collection of six thematically related stories, *Les Duranti* (1844). The title tale, "Les

Duranti," illustrates the difficulties that arise from the perfect relationship between cousins Paulette and Gilbert Duranti. Overwhelmed by emotion from his very first encounter with Paulette, the artist Gilbert asks for her hand in marriage from the prejudiced, small-minded father, who flatly refuses. "A painter," it seems, "is not the kin to suit a miser."[169] The two lovers triumph only after Gilbert is tried and acquitted of having deprived Paulette of her inheritance; he then comes into his own lawful inheritance, which is sufficient to support them both. As an artist in love, however, Gilbert possesses even more: "Is not thought man himself? As a result it precedes and makes property possible. It is property in the purest state."[170]

Similar character types and plot structures occur in the other five stories of the collection. They feature sublime figures and their ideal loves who in one way or another prevail literally or figuratively over the petty obstacles to their happiness. In "Zinetta," Zinetta Olinsky the lutist and dancer triumphs with Julien de Marolles the painter and fellow lutist. In "Karrl Sand," a story based on the German nationalist, the hero loves Claire Kauffmann, a poor, honest woman who reveres him long after his execution. In "Les Deux Soeurs," a Napoleonic soldier has two daughters with very different fates: the calculating, ambitious Olympe marries unhappily the wealthy Dermont, while the selfless, modest Clémence marries happily the 1830 revolutionary Gustave Reibel. In "Léona," the title character, a child of nature, finds her future in the Muslim Abull-Hamet-Zégris. And in the suggestive "Souvenirs de Touraine: Rose et Gatien," two poor but pure souls manage to overcome the objections of an avaricious miller who objects to the disgrace of his daughter marrying the son of an impoverished widow. Nothing could be more in keeping with Leroyer's romantic devotions.

The idealist did respond occasionally to a more immediate reality. Painfully aware of her parents' incompatible marriage and the continued use of the guillotine during France's Second Republic, Leroyer attacked a cruel legal system in *Angélique Lagier* (1851). Its preface forthrightly states her intention to offer up "a legal brief in favor of divorce and a passionate protest against the death penalty."[171] The novel wastes no time critiquing the constraints imposed on Frenchwomen: "Condemned by law to a perpetual minority and far from acting in response to her own feelings or her own free will, [woman] submits irresistibly and fatally to the law of necessity and to the rule of a will alien to hers."[172] True to Leroyer's own views, the novel develops accordingly.

The daughter of a miserly bookseller, Angélique Lagier falls madly in love with Berthémy de Montbrun, a young aristocratic officer in Louis XIV's army. When he is apparently killed in battle, Angélique cedes reluctantly to her father's urging to marry the wealthy Armand Noguët de Villiers and move to Paris. Ten years later, however, she discovers that Berthémy was not killed and has returned to find his true love enmeshed in a marriage of convenience: "Unable to foresee the end of a misfortune that she could only escape by her own death or that of M. de Villiers, [Angélique] felt in this respect that her desires and hopes were sins."[173] This tragic conflict between passion and society is resolved by a jealous rival, Arthur de Nérac, who arranges to have his cousin Villiers killed. Despite her obvious virtue, Angélique is implicated, convicted, and executed for the murder.

Leroyer's sympathies are clear. Angélique's faith in God redeems her: "She was to find in heaven the justice that men had denied her on earth."[174] Her faithful lover, convinced of her innocence, devotes the rest of his life to the care of Angélique's two orphaned children and to a religious mission in Mexico, where the three of them escape from the inequity and brutality of the French law. The author's identification with Angélique as the victim of her love and duty seems nearly complete. For instance, they express the same views of woman's limitations in a man's world; they share the same commitment to noble ideals in their relationships; they adore the same Loire valley landscape; they even celebrate the same birthday on 31 October.[175] In its impassioned plot and single-minded characters, this novel is Leroyer's most personal work of ineffable devotion.

Leroyer's penchant for autobiographical romance appears throughout her other publications. Besides the deliberate discursive patterns evident in her more complex, successful efforts—*Angèle, Mémoires d'une provinciale, Cécile,* and *Angélique Lagier*—and in her collections of short stories and novellas—most notably *Les Duranti,* but also *Les Récits d'amour, Les Nouvelles littéraires* (1889), *Luttes du coeur* (1893), and *Groupe de martyres* (n.d.)—the author projected romantic versions of herself, her relations, and her world that deviate remarkably little from the more plaintive accounts in her correspondence. Similarly, Leroyer blurred generic boundaries by incorporating comparable personal fiction into her collections of literary criticism, chronicles, and historical legends—*Souvenirs et impressions littéraires, Chroniques et légendes,* and *Figures historiques et légendaires*—most of which were published or reissued posthumously. The links between life and literature could hardly have been more deliberate.

But Leroyer's literary legacy was brief. Like her life, her work has remained obscure, despite considerable effort and expense to ensure her greater notoriety. She paid the printing expenses, including the 14,000 francs she designated in her will, for every book she wrote. Her correspondence with noted contemporary authors made her known to opinion leaders, such as Flaubert, Sand, and Michelet, as well as Adolphe Thiers and the Mangin brothers in Nantes.[176] Moreover, membership in the Société des Gens de Lettres in 1881 brought her to the attention of many others who would also enter the pantheon of nineteenth-century authors. Nearly every one of her works was advertised in the *Bibliographie de la France,* the nation's most complete annual listing of new titles, and deposited in the Bibliothèque Nationale, France's most prestigious library. Yet Leroyer's writing never reached a large audience.

This fate is still more curious in light of the appraisals that her fiction elicited. "What surprised me and what in my view prevails in your talent," wrote Flaubert, "[are] the poetic ability and the philosophic thought, when [the latter] conforms to the grand eternal moral [of the story]."[177] Similarly, Sand read Leroyer's *Cécile* with interest: "I have found everywhere in it noble sentiments and a serious sensibility. There one sees the reflection of a soul that has suffered much. You will continue to carry with dignity this burden of grief that loving and generous natures cannot throw off. But it is a burden from which good intentions and evidence of a good conscience make possible the ease refused to cold and vain natures."[178] The artistic indivisibility of Leroyer's personae as both author and narrator was also noted by Léon Richer and Maria Deraismes, the women's-rights activists, who sponsored Leroyer for membership in the Société des Gens de Lettres in June 1880. Richer called her a "woman of a delicate and distinguished mind," a judgment to which Deraismes assented in her assessment of "a fine intellect."[179]

Since then, views of Leroyer and her work have been far more critical. Sand and Flaubert expressed their reservations, of course, but their forthright criticism is far from the gratuitous denigration of later commentators. In his 1951 article in Angers's daily newspaper *Le Courrier de l'ouest,* René Gauchet mused condescendingly: "Without genius and without talent, she understood that love and charity do not submit to the law of parsimony. . . . How not to judge life so ugly after having dreamed life so beautiful?"[180] Similarly, Leroyer's entry in Célestin Port's *Dictionnaire historique,* published in 1965, states: "A romantic and charitable lady, author of passionate and unreadable novels, she was more than just peculiar."[181] Finally, the Sand scholar Georges Lubin felt free to ridicule Leroyer as "a provincial type fairly common in the 19th century: educated, intelligent, with advanced ideas for her hometown, constantly scribbling and who was unable to find what she considered a suitable interlocutor in her small city, so she sustained a correspondence with writers in order to be in exchange with them."[182] Leroyer's reputation and writing have aged poorly, for reasons that raise the issues of women's discursive agency in nineteenth-century France.

A century ago Leroyer was more highly regarded than she is today, in part because the literary forms she adopted were more widely accepted than they are now.[183] To her contemporaries, her sentimental fiction was not unusual. Sand herself mastered the genre, though she also took it in new directions. But so did Leroyer and other women writers like her. Autobiographical interests fell into critical disfavor, thanks to the principles promoted by mostly male novelists like Flaubert and the nineteenth-century realists, just as Leroyer was blurring their neat generic boundaries. She artfully incorporated correspondence, fiction, memoir, history, and criticism into her writing in a conscious effort to define herself and her relations with others. In this way, whatever posterity's subsequent views of her work, Leroyer found the most appropriate expression for her commitments—for her devotions, rather—to the romantic ideals that gave her life meaning, purpose, direction, and ultimately strength in the face of adversity.

According to her death certificate, dated Tuesday, 23 October 1888, "Marie Sophie Leroyer de Chantepie, landowner, unmarried, in Angers at eighty-seven years of age, born in Château-Gontier, daughter of the late Robert-Pierre Leroyer de Chantepie and Marie-Catherine-Renée Dupouet, his wife, died at home this morning at ten o'clock."[184] Among the witnesses was Armand Parrot, president of the Académie des Sciences et Belles-Lettres, who was charged by Leroyer's will to have all her literary work reprinted within a year of her death. Apparently Leroyer did not die unexpectedly; the certificate was signed just four hours after her demise. Nor does her body rest alone; she was buried next to members of her surrogate family in Angers's west cemetery, as seems entirely fitting for this figure, so much like the idealistic Angèle de Chavigny, whose devotions put her at odds with many other French provincials.

It remains to be seen in the following chapters to what extent Leroyer's devotions were like the lives and writings of her younger Parisian sisters

Geneviève Bréton and Céline Renooz. Certainly Leroyer's romantic tendencies place her closer in culture and temperament with Bréton. Both of them defined a more or less traditionally gendered discursive identity with few complications of expression or activity to contradict it. Each represented well a relational self in language and comportment that her contemporaries all recognized even if they did not accept it as such. On the other hand, Renooz's incomplete development of a similarly domestic discourse launched her in quest of a utopian vision that Leroyer would have understood and Bréton would have disdained. For this reason alone, it makes sense to examine first Bréton and then Renooz to assess their experience—and more, their writing in relation to it.

Chapter four

❧ "In the Solitude of My Soul": Geneviève Breton

In a diary entry for 26 August 1878, Geneviève Bréton made a curious confession:

> I can't stop myself from thinking, with a little melancholy, that fate could have made of me a very happy man. I have all the tendencies, all the nerves, and in some respects the mental habits of one; my nature transposed into another sex would only be quite natural; and my life would have followed accordingly. As it is, I have applied myself incessantly to subdue a multitude of ideas, inclinations, and opinions that are ill-suited to a woman's character.[1]

These words notwithstanding, Bréton (fig. 7) never considered herself a feminist. "I know that women must remain who they are lest they become monsters or viragoes," she stated emphatically.[2] Far beyond women's issues, she was concerned by relationship and relation—that is, by her family and the diary she kept for more than forty years. Her life and writings focused on close personal ties, first to her brother, to her father, to her fiancé, to her husband, and finally to her eldest son, the author Jean-Louis Vaudoyer. And she did so in the context of her deeply religious nature. Like her writing, it consoled her for the genuine pain that she came to experience. Her faith was a sustaining force in her grief over the betrayals of friends and the deaths of loved ones. Above all, however, Bréton prized her independence of mind, a quality that she saw in men more often than in women and that provided her a special notion of gender in her writing and her commitments to others.

Nowhere is this notion more apparent than on the occasion for Bréton's confession quoted above. Still living at home before her marriage, Bréton participated in the impromptu theatrics that were offered her father on his

Figure 7. Geneviève Bréton-Vaudoyer by Nélie Jacquemart (1868). Oil on canvas (private collection)

sixty-first birthday. Everyone in the household, it seems, was enlisted in the production of *L'Habit vert* (1849), a work by Emile Augier and Alfred de Musset, including Bréton, who chose to play a male character—more than likely the diminutive and hapless painter Henri. Dressed and holding herself like a public figure, she was surprised to discover how well she adapted to her role. After the performance, before she had had a chance to change her clothes, a domestic servant mistook her for a man. "I had an astonishing success," she wrote later that night in her diary. "It was not without some regret that this evening I took off those clothes of liberty, action, and simplicity."[3] Here a self-conscious woman faced both the limitations and the possibilities of gender in nineteenth-century France.

In this expression of herself and her fierce independence, Bréton felt very much alone. She knew well the loneliness of all writers, but even more the solitude of women exploring their uniqueness in a world of bourgeois conformity.[4] In her diary and later in her correspondence, Bréton challenged women's assigned place in Parisian society as sister, daughter, or mother, even though she cherished these relationships, more so with men than with women. Her son-in-law Daniel Halévy once said of her, "Her nature was to make of everything that she loved, including her good fortune, a source of anxiety and torment."[5] It would be more accurate to say: Bréton lived and wrote apart from other women and yet was proud to be one herself. She conceived of and acted on that identity truly "in the solitude of [her] soul."[6]

The Setting

Geneviève Bréton was born in Paris on Wednesday, 7 March 1849, the third of six children—two boys and four girls. This large family was closely associated with the Hachette publishing company, living as they did right next door to its offices and bookstore on the Boulevard Saint-Michel.[7] In 1844 her father Louis had married Zélime Auzat, the stepdaughter of Louis Hachette, his business partner. The other children were not as interested as Geneviève was in the literary side to this family connection; Antoine (born 1845), Catherine (1846), Thérèse (1854), Pauline (1856), and Guillaume (1858) pursued much more conventional activities in their two homes, in Paris and in Le Plessis-Piquet, while Geneviève was enthralled by the lively intellectual and cultural community centered on this important Parisian publisher. She remembered fondly and proudly the visits of *"the flower of letters, arts, and science"* in nineteenth-century Paris.[8] Among them were the writers Alphonse de Lamartine, Victor Cousin, Charles-Augustin Sainte-Beuve, Jules Michelet, Théophile Gautier, Maxime Du Camp, and Sully Prud'homme; the artists Ernest Hébert, Eugène Fromentin, Alexandre Bida, Gustave Doré, and Paul Baudry; the architect Charles Garnier; and the scholars Gaston Paris and Victor Duruy. This remarkable mix of talent met often in the Bréton family drawing room.[9]

Louis Bréton's father had been a wealthy notary whose initial investment in Hachette would make these literary opportunities for Geneviève possible. As a business partner in part because of his command of German and ancient languages, Louis was tolerant, dutiful, hardworking, and good-humored, qualities that earned the respect of his associates as well as his second daughter. He was in fact closer to Geneviève than to his other children; she was his endearing "little one," and he became for her "*the best man in France.*"[10] Together they took especially hard Antoine's death from a painful horse-riding accident in January 1867. The following spring, father and daughter took a trip to Italy in an effort to forget, the first of many other trips like it to Spain and elsewhere in France before her marriage in 1880. Louis Bréton was very nearly Geneviève's second self.

Within certain gendered expectations—"our father, who is [otherwise] so indulgent with us, has some rather rigid notions about 'young ladies'"— Louis actively participated in Geneviève's search for a husband.[11] He proposed and frankly discussed possible suitors with her. Father often consoled daughter in her many disappointing prospects, in the men who unwisely persisted, like Georges Clairin, and in the men who abruptly disappeared, like Henri Regnault and Alfred Vaudoyer (though the latter two did return).[12] Ultimately Geneviève chose for herself twice, each time with Louis's blessings, but not without hearing his reservations on the wisdom of her choices. After his death in August 1883, she would write, "I love him as the personification of everything most elevated and most noble in the world, the incarnation of goodness, impartiality, and gentle gaiety that were peculiar to him, the unconscious and irresistible charm of a supremely good nature."[13] Long afterwards, Geneviève would look for these traits, like Louis's modesty, empathy, and simplicity, in other men.

Zélime, Geneviève's mother, was another figure altogether. She was known by the family, including her husband, as "the Queen Mother," and for good reason.[14] The shrewd manager of two large houses and a family of eight, plus a host of servants, Zélime was strong, practical, and courageous, though she could also be indecisive, suspicious, capricious, and materialistic in her benevolent dictatorship of the Bréton household. Her severity actually focused on observing the social conventions and gender roles appropriate to her aspirations for a better life, much to the more generous-minded and free-spirited daughter's annoyance. Unlike Geneviève's relationship with Louis Bréton, mother and daughter did not have an instinctive understanding of each other. "I love my mother, but I don't pay her much heed," Geneviève wrote candidly. "By my habits and my tastes I do what she absolutely cannot abide; she disdains every kind of mental activity, and I love just that."[15] Zélime permitted Geneviève's independence more out of deference to her indulgent husband than out of any genuine affection for her daughter. Hers was a tough mother-love.

What Zélime objected to most was Geneviève's casual attitudes about her social obligations. For example, she strongly disapproved of her daughter's fiancé Henri Regnault, who as an artist seemed too much of a "workman" to be socially respectable in bourgeois Paris. " 'Geneviève's company,' 'street artists,' that's what she calls artistic talent."[16] And she conceded Geneviève's choice of mate only after some blatant emotional blackmail; if Zélime refused her consent, Regnault promised to go straight to the battlefront to die fighting the Prussians. "The most difficult thing in the world, I'm convinced, is for [a mother] to befriend her daughter," Geneviève had written two years earlier.[17] On at least two occasions, Zélime made a real effort: when Regnault later died a hero at the front and when Geneviève nearly died herself from a serious illness. Well before her daughter had children of her own, the mother's instinct remained mysterious and incomprehensible.[18] A year after Zélime died in 1901, however, Geneviève wrote appreciatively, "I miss her as I would a mother, that is, at every moment and with every event, happy or sad, in life — and she in particular more than others," including, it would seem, her father.[19]

All her life Bréton was on the move. Before her marriage she shuttled regularly between her parents' imposing homes in Paris and Le Plessis-Piquet, just to the south of town, often on the back of her favorite horse Sidi, the Arabian stallion whose fall had killed her brother Antoine. She took many long trips to Italy, Spain, England, Scotland, Switzerland, and the eastern Mediterranean with other members of her family. After her marriage in 1880, she traveled from her own home in Paris on the fashionable avenue de Villiers to her summer home southwest of Paris in Jouy-en-Josas and to many vacation resorts in France—Dieppe, Biarritz, and the Jura mountains. Substantial trips to Bréton's beloved Italy followed when her children had grown up and left home before World War I: "I have a Tuscan and a Florentine soul," she sighed more than once to her son Jean-Louis.[20] In her numerous travelogues and correspondence, Bréton developed a fine sense of place as defined by its artistic and literary culture, especially in Paris, Florence, and Granada, whose creative sensibilities she adored. But she was also moved by nature in her frequent rural retreats to Le Plessis-Piquet (as a daughter) and to Jouy-en-Josas (as a wife and mother). Bréton was a sensitive, restless individual.

After years of disappointment with her choices, she finally married the architect Alfred Vaudoyer on 10 January 1880, a kindred spirit in grief and culture (fig. 8). He had recently been widowed with two young children, Albert (born 1875) and Georges (1877), and wanted very much to remarry. His late wife had been the niece of the noted architectural medievalist Eugène Viollet-le-Duc. There was considerable talent in his own family, many of them prominent architects: his father was Léon Vaudoyer (1803–78), designer of the Conservatoire des Arts et Métiers and the new cathedral at Marseilles, and an influential teacher of architectural history at the Ecole des Beaux Arts. Alfred's son Georges became a pioneer in the construction of publicly subsidized housing (HLMs) and garden cities.[21] Alfred and Geneviève would have three children of their own—Marianne (born 1881), Jean-Louis (1883), and Michel (1885)—whose cultural inclinations followed their parents' interests. A noble, delicate, and artistic figure, Alfred was often impractical, demanding, indecisive, and feckless. All his life he suffered emotional crises and self-doubts, which Bréton described at length in her unpublished diary. At age seventy-one, Alfred died of an unspecified illness in August 1917, just fourteen months before his devoted wife.

There are numerous portraits of Bréton. But the most telling are by her close friend Nélie Jacquemart in 1868 and fiancé Henri Regnault a year earlier. Each one suggests different features of Bréton's character. In Jacquemart's oil painting, she has dark red hair, brown eyes, a long face and nose, and appears introspective, romanesque, perhaps a bit melancholy, as one would expect from Bréton's serious, occasionally morose nature (see fig. 7). "I love everything I'm not like," she confessed to herself in 1876, "happy youth, the sun,

Figure 8. Alfred Vaudoyer (c. 1885). Photograph (private collection)

the paintings of Veronese and Rubens, active lives, healthy and lively spirits, and the 'triumphal' something of nature, the robust and the strong that my poor weakness can only dream of."[22]

Regnault's pencil portrait of Bréton on horseback captures one of her more romantic moments: an almost dreamlike high-spiritedness (fig. 9). She relished the affective features of the plastic arts, literature, travel, and dressage. These almost instinctive proclivities very nearly made Bréton the impassioned amazon that her relations often remarked. The gossip only confirmed her solitary enthusiasms. Years later she wrote to her son Jean-Louis, "At what age does one no longer dream? I dream in the same way other women talk. One is never alone or bored while dreaming. It makes life so rich, so full, so new; reverie is where anything can happen, including every good fortune that life itself cannot provide."[23] All her life, Bréton rode horses to escape into another world of her own making.

An active participant in father's and son's salons that spanned French literary history from romanticism to symbolism, Bréton was a serious reader. Her diary is replete with the names of famous authors and allusions to their work, often in the original languages. Among them are Dante's *Inferno*, Shakespeare's *Midsummer Night's Dream*, *Othello*, and *Hamlet*, Goethe's *Faust*, and the Bible. Bréton's acquaintance with French literature was even more extensive: she quotes Pascal and La Bruyère, and cites La Rochefoucault, Boileau, Joubert, Staël, Chateaubriand, Stendhal, Lamartine, Leconte

Figure 9. Geneviève Bréton-Vaudoyer on horseback by Henri Regnault (1867). Pencil on paper (private collection)

de Lisle, Verlaine, Zola, Bourget, Gide, Proust, Noailles, Colette, among still others. One purpose of her diary was to maintain a record of inspiring passages from her favorite books. A regular reader of *La Revue des deux mondes*, *La Revue de Paris*, *Le Gaulois*, *Le Temps*, and *Le Figaro*, whose articles and reports of literary developments in Paris she would pass on to her eldest son whenever he was traveling, Bréton was extraordinarily well-informed in her literary passions: "What has sustained me the most and alleviated my pain, what has consoled me most in life is *a book*."[24]

Bréton also wrote knowledgeably about art and music. As a young woman, she swooned to renditions of lieder by Charles Gounod, Franz Schubert, and Robert Schumann: "Music for me is a thunderclap, an inexhaustible source of revelation, which is no doubt its power, the terrible vertigo that envelops me, that penetrates as well as possesses me."[25] She poetically likened Hector Berlioz's "Danse des sylphes" to "that agile, serpentine saraband of the fire-flies in an Italian wood."[26] But Bréton often wrote more perceptively about paintings, such as Regnault's portrait of Mme Fouques-Duparc at the 1868 Salon: "The overall effect is ablaze with light."[27] His work, she said, had much in common with the fiery enthusiasm of Eugène Delacroix. Her diary includes a draft essay on the 1874 Salon and whole notebooks dedicated to cultural activities on her travels; her correspondence discusses art seriously with Jean-Louis. Bréton the *amateur d'art* acknowledged her romantic tastes as "the last specimen of the 1830 school," which pervaded much of her capable commentary on the arts.[28]

In good romantic style, Bréton reflects much about herself. At times she confesses to playing the involuntary spectator and judge of a self other than her own.[29] This double consciousness pervades Bréton's adult life and her writing about it. As she remarked, "When one is not dancing, it is quite natural to watch how the others dance."[30] This was particularly true of her self-effacing love; she genuinely believed in the value of unrequited affection.[31] The result was, of course, a poor self-image: "insignificant and plain, always wearing black, buttoned up to the chin like a nun, frail and skinny like the heroine of a novel, silent and sad like Cinderella."[32] When her fiancé died unexpectedly in 1871, Bréton's dual existence, in the world but not of it, grew even more obvious to her. The identification with the deceased was a natural one for literal and figurative widows like her, still nunlike in her mourning clothes. Four years later, Bréton was no less self-conscious: "Oh, . . . dreamer! What have you done with your life? What have you done with your youth, your strength, your passion? You've killed yourself too early, you brash girl . . . and your poor heart still hungers."[33]

Before her marriage to Vaudoyer, Bréton would assess herself in light of Plato's description of woman's three souls—those of head, heart, and womb: "The first governed me only too much, the second has just died, and the third was never born."[34] But in time circumstances would change the direction of Bréton's reflections. Her new family obligations had much to do with it. A few months after their wedding, she considered her husband a cherished ideal, the light and fire of her being, because he represented everything she felt most intensely in life—its need for adoration, tenderness, longing, and passion.[35] She declared herself ready to give up the insistent introspection necessary to her writing. Several times Bréton finished a notebook proclaiming an end to her diary in order to devote more time to her new family responsibilities. She never did.

With the birth of her children, Bréton recalled her divided self in new but recognizable terms. On the one hand, her need to write made her more wife than mother; on the other, her need to nurture made her less of a writer, an identity she was unwilling to forego: "I want [to be] a brave mother with responsibility for three children whose health and happiness must be my only concern—I have no right to indulge myself in what I call excessive sorrows," a resolution broken the very moment she recorded it in her diary.[36] Bréton remained true to her discursive self-respect, the first step toward respect for others and their well-being: "The *principle* is respect for oneself, the only pure, unfailing and faultless rule that's worth the pain incurred for it," whatever it cost her emotionally.[37]

Bréton was a self-conscious woman. "Ah!" she wrote in 1869, "I'm a woman, very much a woman, and I've no wish to be otherwise."[38] She knew that she was destined to marry and raise a family like her sisters Kate, Thérèse, and Pauline. To Bréton, what fate could be more natural? Her reservations arose when she considered the sacrifices it entailed, especially her need for emotional and intellectual space. Here lay the problem. With an indulgent father and a distant mother, Bréton had room to think for herself. A conventional middle-class marriage was not for her, no more so than the male double standards she angrily criticized throughout her diary. Otherwise, Bréton's relationship to others, beginning with her family, defined her identity more subtly than she realized. Bréton generally accepted the traditional gender roles accorded men and women in nineteenth-century France (and elsewhere).[39]

The major theme of her life, however, was an independence of mind and spirit, one that never lost sight of its strong commitments to faith and family. Accordingly, she was much more given to thought than she was to action, resulting in "a great liberty in life," more appropriate to "a man's society, [a] man's conversation, a certain levity in language" than it was to the world of polite society and its women.[40] As her parents well knew, Bréton was willing to fight, if need be, for what she wanted. She acquiesced to no coercion and refused to accept a master of any sort, or so she said bravely at age nineteen.[41] "The principal characteristic of my personality is exaggeration, the exaggeration of feeling, manners, and friendship. . . . I must be passionate about someone or something," be it her family, her cultural interests, or more often her personal writings.[42]

Bréton spoke often of the relation between her independence and her commitment to writing. In reference to Jean-Louis's work, her preference was always for a playful poetry resembling windows open to the world.[43] The freedom of her imagination, as she expressed it in her diary, was more valuable to her than reality itself. On her atypical education, Bréton noted, "It's true that I learned [the English language] with [Stéphane] Mallarmé. When I think about it, I have really had some unusual teachers. Father [Alphonse] Gratry gave me lessons in astronomy; [Ferdinand] Buisseau taught me Latin. These three excellent men helped me with neither English, nor astronomy, nor Latin, but with something else much better than all that: kindness and a truly superior culture of soul and mind."[44] This discursive possibility for something more sustaining than dependence appeared in her relations with others, on which she reflected long and hard in her personal diary.

Bréton's writing, for example, provided her much-needed emotional space in her relations with men. In 1875, after having rejected the attentions of one otherwise sympathetic suitor, Bréton did not believe that she was ready for "this holy mission of being the humblest of mothers rather than the proudest of recluses. Yes, I was proud; it was humiliating for me to love, to humble and abase myself before *a man*. I knew that to love is to suffer."[45] Supplications addressed to *Him* (underscored and the *H* capitalized in her diary) were simply beneath her pride, out of respect less for herself than for the freedom of other women like her. "To be loved *by force!* No, oh, *everything by love, nothing by force*—that's my motto and I shall remain faithful to it."[46]

For this independence of spirit and expression, Bréton paid a high price;

she suffered painful doubts about the wisdom of refusing men's love when she needed it the most. At one point in her diary, she confessed to having doubted her strength and commitment to persist in her cherished ideals.[47] Yet Bréton would ultimately keep faith with her proud resolutions. At the first evidence of her husband's fading affection within months of their happy wedding, the wounded Bréton reiterated in her diary "everything by love, nothing by force."[48] This principle appears in her every personal tie.

Relationships

Like many other women, Bréton expressed a genuine empathy for others. In 1873 she recalled a bon mot attributed to the witty eighteenth-century *salonnière* Mme d'Houdetot: "Someone else drinks the wine, and I'm the one who gets tipsy."[49] To Bréton this quip struck a responsive chord, notwithstanding its off-handed expression. She claimed to have the capacity of a lion for her own suffering and that of a tiny baby for the suffering of others, particularly when she believed herself responsible for it. In her troubled relations with the same suitor mentioned above (Jojotte) she wrote, "My pain, my great inconsolable pain, which neither a possible good fortune nor a longed-for return nor anything in the world will efface, is the thought that *I* Geneviève, a Christian, a virgin, a woman of integrity, that *I was to blame* for dishonoring his soul, this fine soul."[50] On further reflection, however, Bréton realized that her action was not willful and that no one, least of all herself, was responsible for all the world's misery.

"My sisters were right when they named me 'the refuge for sick dogs,'" Bréton wrote amused.[51] She had said as much herself. If she suffered, it was because she had an active conscience, open to the plight of others.[52] In 1878 Bréton recalled the legend of the golden celandine: With the gift of this lovely flower, a fairy grants a dejected shepherd three wishes. His first wish is to laugh as others do, but he is no happier for it. His second wish is to love as others do, only to experience the same disappointment. And so his third wish is that others laugh and love. Only then is the shepherd satisfied because, as Bréton notes, he concerned himself with the happiness and love of people around him.[53] In part born of guilt, this sympathy extended occasionally to unlikely figures, such as the Empress Eugénie upon the death of the prince imperial in 1879. "Why am I happier than she who suffers because of her love, because of her children?" she asked years later as the dutiful wife and mother of a bourgeois family. "Why do I have so much when someone else has so little? My feeling is akin to shame with those less happy than I."[54]

In the face of others' misery, Bréton often felt compelled to define and to justify her profoundly romantic conception of love. She borrowed what she could from the texts of others, like Plato's *The Banquet*, from which she copied long passages, such as on how "[love's] essence is *eternal*."[55] But more frequently Bréton turned inward, to her romantic soul, for the answer she sought: "That's where my literary affinities, my sympathies lie. That's where I rediscover enthusiasm, its excessive train of feelings, apparently beyond all measure perhaps, but still true. . . . It's better to extract from the shabby demands of society a great breath of Freedom, of poetry, before rejuvenating France, the holy insanity of the Ideal and every artistic enthusiasm in all its forms."[56] This perfect notion of love stood in marked contrast to that of the Parisian upper class. Comparing her ideal with Mme Récamier's, the model for much of the French *bonne bourgeoisie*, Bréton denied any resemblance to the beautiful but insensitive Juliette. She had none of the celebrated woman's ferocious vanity, calculated coquetry, charming imprudence, or smiling insincerity. No, the youthful diarist could not bear the responsibility for managing other people's happiness so adroitly, so self-consciously.[57] For the young Bréton, love was everything or it was nothing.

With more experience, Bréton became a little wiser and a little more realistic. She believed, especially after several courtships had turned sour, that emotional happiness lay in solitude and quiet contemplation, which made possible rational, charitable action in the world. But this antidote to disappointed passions Bréton knew to be inadequate. She needed to feel her heart beat; she needed to dream; she needed emotion, too.[58] As more and more members of the romantic generation turned from their original sentiments, Bréton realized that she shared her ideas with fewer and fewer people. "Never has the great *Pan* been so *dead*," she remarked upon hearing the news of Lamartine's demise in 1872.[59] As Charles Garnier remarked to her during a performance of Alfred de Vigny's *Chatteron* at the Théâtre Français, Bréton was the last of the great romantics.[60] "To spiritualize love into an elevated cult, pure and eternal, is still the sole means of giving humankind some dignity, blending as it will [affection] with the *sacred* character of duty, superiority, and *duration*."[61] Very much further from her cherished ideal Bréton would never go: reality for her was just too paltry for words.[62]

In this conviction, Bréton would draw important gender distinctions: men and women loved differently. Copious commentary on the matter, like the books by Jules Michelet (1860) and Alexandre Dumas *fils* (1872), just did not comprehend this simple truth.[63] "I hate everything that tends to debase," responded Bréton indignantly.

> On the contrary, the Disposition of women is to sacrifice the real for the Ideal that is still the essence of love and that has absolutely disappeared from the perspective of these celebrated authors. . . . Love for me is not the search for an Ideal through [other] beings, that is, a successive change of loves, but *more or less the search for an Ideal way of loving*, to search *in oneself* for the Ideal of love, not an Illusion [or] a fever, [it is] a prospective foundation [on which] to base one's home-life, [it is] more than love, [it is] Duty and Devotion.[64]

Of course, there were also some women who did not understand, like the artist Vittoria La Colonna who had been Bréton's rival for the affections of Henri Regnault. Sniped Bréton, "That woman is a Récamier without beauty, a Mme de Staël without genius."[65] Though society women are hostile to true love, they might still recognize the value of true friendship, just as Bréton had known it with older men like Garnier and Alexandre Bida. These latter types at least valued the love of mutual respect.[66]

Because Bréton wrote so much about her relationships and what she wanted from them, it is easy to perceive their psychological implications. Obviously hers was a pre-Freudian conception of love. On several occasions, Bréton likened personal relations to an invisible magnetic fluid, an idea derived from Franz Anton Mesmer and his followers seventy-five years earlier.[67] By this means, Bréton firmly believed, she could protect her fiancé from danger during the Franco-Prussian War. In anticipation of meeting Vaudoyer, her future husband, she wrote, "There had been in my life such curious intuitions, the sort of divinations so peculiar that everything seemed to me fated to come about."[68] Outside this parapsychological context, sexuality took on a crude and vulgar aspect, like male double standards, that often alarmed and offended Bréton's sensibilities. At one point, she found it humiliating to experience the effects of spring just like plants and animals, and she felt insulted by a casual, sensual remark about her portrait in the 1868 Salon.[69]

Repression became a problem. It was particularly evident in her account of a sensuous gypsy dance in Granada, whose "infernal divinity" made her feel faint and short of breath.[70] At times in her diary, Bréton seems frightened by the passion that she and her fiancé had for each other. She confessed to having lost her balance when she was in love and no longer mistress of her will.[71] And her father listened with mixed emotions as she tearfully disavowed her feelings for a man who had left her behind. "Women live very quietly for a long time, but sooner or later their emotions awake," Bréton observed later. "The heart takes its revenge and eventually makes them a slave. . . . Blood, temperament—what do I know? Oh, all that disgusts me to be a woman."[72] Reading Rousseau's *Nouvelle Héloïse* also made her blush.[73]

All her youth, Bréton sought to accommodate the conflicting demands of her physical desires and her romantic ideals. As she put it, "Ashamed of still being an object of love or desire for whomever, I am insulted by life. I want nothing, nothing in the world but to die *in dignity*."[74] This tension continued with all thirty-eight men, by Bréton's count, who courted her more or less seriously. Besides her fiancé and her husband, Georges Duruy was exceptionally attractive: "We all call him 'the golden mug,' which suits well his radiant and manly beauty," she admitted. "But I can't look at those athletic muscles."[75] During her honeymoon, she regrets her lost virginity, justifying to herself the sensual pleasures of marriage by the many pains and sorrows husband and wife still experienced. Only at one moment in her long diary, nearly a year after her wedding to Vaudoyer, did Bréton actually seem to accept and enjoy her sensuality: "There's a certain unspeakable fragrance in a budding passion," she wrote.[76] The rest of the time, however, she alloyed her emotions as much as possible with her old quest for spiritual love, presumably in order to make crude physical reality more palatable to her romantic sensibilities.

This tension was at the heart of Bréton's persistent efforts to define friendship between men and women. Given nature's forces, could there ever be truly disinterested relations outside the family context? Bréton thought she saw an example in the lives of Juliette Récamier and Pierre Simon Ballanche: "They are rare, these documented examples of men whose life is concerned with only the friendship of one woman. . . . It would require too much writing to explain this chivalrous soul, for others to comprehend the incomprehensible: an affection as passionate and as chaste as brotherhood."[77] The death of Bréton's ideal love for Regnault, tragically killed during the Franco-Prussian War, necessitated, she believed, such an ideal friendship with other men, especially with Regnault's companion Georges "Jojotte" Clairin. That she failed in doing so should come as no particular surprise. Like the men who genuinely loved her, Bréton was too passionate an individual to maintain this tenuous balance of heart and head in all her personal relationships.

The model for the men in Bréton's life was her eldest brother Antoine. In January 1867 he was riding Sidi, the handsome Arabian horse given to the family by Louis Hachette, when it slipped on sheer black ice and fell, breaking Antoine's leg as it got up again. Two weeks later he was dead from the accompanying infection. So promising a youth—he was only twenty-two— left his father and sister heartbroken; their grief would take them to Rome, where Bréton began writing her diary. This event marked her for life. Years later she confessed in a letter to Jean-Louis, "The death of a young and healthy being has left me afraid since my brother Antoine died when I was eighteen [sic] years old; since then I have never experienced the thoughtless joy of youth; I have always felt every step threatened; I have always *been afraid*, afraid of life's meanness, afraid of an irreparable blow to those I love. I had lost forever the sense of security, the strength of heedlessness, the antic- ipation of happiness."[78] For his sister, Antoine embodied the best traits she would seek with only partial success in her father, her fiancé, her husband, and finally her eldest son.

Besides Bréton's father, the one man most worthy of Antoine's memory was her fiancé Henri Regnault (1843–71).[79] This flamboyant figure was larger than life—a talented artist trained in the studios of the renowned Louis Lamothe, Dominique Ingres, and the Ecole des Beaux Arts, France's pre- miere art school. At age twenty-four, he won the competition for the Grand Prix de Rome, awarded annually to just one artist in France, which enabled him to study for three years at the Villa Medici in Rome.[80] The son of Victor Regnault, who was a member of the Academy of Sciences, scientist, manufac- turer, and photographer, Henri was well known by prominent contempo- raries: the symbolist poet Stéphane Mallarmé, the orientalist Henry Cazalis, the romantic art critic and poet Théophile Gautier, the composer Camille Saint-Saëns, among others. He developed a passion for painting historical subjects, then scenes from Morocco, because of the coloristic possibilities he saw in their exotic subject matter. According to Gautier, "he did nothing without fire and enthusiasm," embodying "a profound, natural, and requisite originality" as "a first-rate colorist."[81] His artistic career was thus assured when he was killed in January 1871. He was twenty-seven.

From the start, Regnault alternately dazzled and intimidated Bréton by his wit, verve, art, music, azure blue eyes, and bon vivant temperament: "In everything he was an exception."[82] But he represented a fairytale relationship, one celebrated at length in Bréton's diary from 1867 to 1871. It was truly love at first sight, one glorious starry night at the Villa Medici where she met him. He was a genuine Prince Charming, by Bréton's own admission.[83] For six happy months in Paris, their love thrived unspoken, even though Regnault himself was deeply torn between pursuing his art in Italy, Spain, and Morocco, on the one hand, and courting Bréton, the amusing redhead in France, on the other. With difficulty he chose to work. For the next few years, Bréton despaired that he would ever return, especially after a disappointing encounter with him during a trip to Granada. The Franco-Prussian War finally brought Regnault home and made their engagement possible. He had indeed loved her all along, his ambitions and her mother's opposition notwithstanding.

The war also made Bréton miserable again. On 19 January 1871, four years to the day after Bréton's brother had died from his accident, Regnault died a hero at Buzenval, the last major military engagement between French and Prussian armies.[84] She readily admitted that Regnault was another Antoine in both life and death: "Henri, Antoine, my brother, my betrothed," she wrote in her grief. "I seemed to see him transported to a bloodstained bed just as I had seen Antoine once before."[85] For a long time, Bréton struggled to regain her composure, a process complicated by her troubled relations with Regnault's closest friend Jojotte. But a turning point in Bréton's grief eventually arrived with the painful reconstruction of her identity apart from Regnault's memory. In 1872 she asked herself,

> What is this need therefore of saying to someone who feels: *I am suffering?* And is it not quite natural, is it not a need of Affection to bring our good or bad impressions to a being similar to us and capable of responding? Why this need? Why not be content with a symbol? Why this necessity for a sensitive confidant, man or woman, intelligent or inert? Is it not to descend? The soul, the Pain should have the strength to live with itself, only to count on *itself,* to give itself another self! but to count on another. *Allein* [sic], this word is without charm; it is not without either merit or virtue.[86]

Consequently, when Regnault's father Victor died seven years to the day after Henri, Bréton stoically recognized the loss of the last living link to her beloved fiancé.[87]

Bréton's confidant for most of this emotional turmoil was Nélie Jacquemart. She was a close friend whom Bréton first met at the Villa Medici in May 1867, actually the same day as her first meeting with Regnault. For the next four years, Bréton and Jacquemart developed a special bond that initially helped Bréton in her troubled relationship with the artist. Jacquemart's own wit and artistic talent attracted Bréton's attention and sympathy nearly on a daily basis, such that Bréton's diary refers frequently to "this profound attachment . . . our devoted friendship."[88] Jacquemart's portrait of Bréton for the 1868 Paris Salon marked the high point of a relationship that arose from an almost instinctive knowledge of what would please the other. Unknowingly they even came to dress alike for various balls and theatrical performances. But important differences in temperament, especially with Jacquemart's social ambitions and passionate outbursts, made their continued relations increasingly difficult. After Jacquemart turned her affections elsewhere, hurt feelings slid quickly into mutual dislike. Bréton remarked in her diary, "It's not my friendship with Nel that has disappeared, it's *Friendship* itself."[89]

This loss was hard for Bréton to take. There are shades here of the strained relations with her mother. Despite the Queen Mother's contempt for Jacquemart—she was too much of an artist—Zélime would have approved of Jacquemart's choice of husband, the banker Edouard André, whose artistic interests and fabulous wealth made possible the purchase of the Abbaye de Chaâlis near Ermenonville and the construction of a sumptuous hôtel, now the Jacquemart-André museum on the Boulevard Haussmann in Paris. As a result, Bréton accused her friend of betraying their youthful ideals: "She failed to understand the elevated sense of life."[90] Bréton attributed her confidant's betrayal to jealousy. Apparently, as an artist Jacquemart had felt a special kinship with Bréton's fiancé, an unrecognized and unrequited affinity worthy of a misdirected revenge.[91] "In the face of my profound misery," Bréton wrote of Jacquemart after Regnault's death, "[she] could neither open her arms nor shed a tear nor find one tender memory to temper her disdain. She could not understand the sincerity of my *real* [voice]."[92] In the light of Bréton's selfless nobility of sentiment, this friendship was fated to fade.

A comparable, troubled relation came with Georges Clairin.[93] Affectionately known as Jojotte—a name suggestive of a child's toy—Clairin was Regnault's closest friend. They first met at the Ecole des Beaux Arts in 1861 and lived together in Tangier, where Regnault's artistic interests had taken him and where Clairin was posted as a foreign-service attaché. When Regnault became engaged to Bréton two years later, in 1870, the affable Jojotte readily befriended his friend's fiancée, swearing solemnly to honor Bréton as his own wife-to-be. Consequently, Regnault's sudden death threw these two unlikely young people together in their common grief. True to his word, Jojotte consoled Bréton the best he could, and she in turn felt obliged to help him. In time, because of their mutual interest in art as well as Regnault, Jojotte assumed for Bréton the role of a surrogate fiancé, an assumption she resisted with considerable difficulty. Jojotte was so much like Regnault, it was hard for Bréton to distinguish them in her lingering grief and need for consolation. She was torn between remaining loyal to her ideal love and transferring it to another man who seemed to share it with her.

Bréton's first response to the gossip about her new suitor so soon after her fiancé's death was outrage: "How can anyone dare to defile by suspicion and innuendo the sacred affection I feel for you?" she confronted Jojotte.[94] She recognized that as Henri's oldest friend, his rights were truly inviolable. After all, he had been the first to find Regnault's body in an unmarked military coffin at the Père Lachaise cemetery, and he had selflessly visited Bréton nearly every day thereafter. As she put it, Jojotte was Regnault's "brother, his best friend."[95] Jojotte's departure for Versailles a month later left her feeling abandoned. The three of them had pledged an eternal union, she remembered sadly.[96] Despite his generous offer of a more enduring affection, however, Bréton stayed true to her grief and her ideal; she decided to make of Jojotte a true friend, like Ballanche had been to Juliette Récamier. She even nicknamed him Ballanche in her diary: "This affection is like a viaticum to my heart; it does not restore [my heart] to health but it lets [my heart] die [feeling] less desperate; it enlightens by a kind reflection of faith and peace."[97] As such, Jojotte remained an important figure in her life.

But Jojotte had other things in mind. He continued his appeal for Bréton's affections. "This poor invalid to whom I can give neither money nor happiness nor talent, who offers me such dangerous consolations, such influences uncongenial to my mental habits, what infinite charity do I not owe him all the same!" Bréton wrote more than a year later, torn by the conflicting emotions she felt over his courtship.[98] She resolved to end the relationship by the letter she apparently never sent in June 1873.[99] His overt sensuality simply revolted her. "I am beginning to understand. He is *no good*, [he is] not worthy of me or of [Regnault's] memory," she concluded.[100] A serious illness and a very slow, painful recovery began the emotional healing process. At long last, in 1875, Bréton seemed to have assessed him accurately: here was a man capable of inspiring selfless devotion only in others.[101] She had less ironic, much harsher words for Jojotte's philandering before she finally gave up all illusions about him in 1878. In the meantime, she bade a sad farewell to her "fine impossible dream, Edenic fruit, fleeting bird, too rare a flower, *friendship.*"[102]

The unhappy end to Bréton's relationship with Jojotte, and more, to her sacred dispassionate ideal, also marked Bréton's emotional liberation from Regnault. Along the way she had received advice that only now made sense to her from two friends, Marie Astrue and Alexandre Bida. This odd couple was another model for Bréton to consider. Marie married a much older man after a deeply disappointing love, and suggested to the grieving younger woman a superior sort of resignation, a deliberately chosen abnegation.[103] For Bréton the real secret to Marie's happiness in a marriage that seemed to blend perfectly both heart and head was work—hard work to attain her ideals and to resolve her inner turmoil. Although, like Jacquemart, Marie would later grow profoundly jealous of Bréton, her example was an inspiration that temporarily assuaged her pain.

Bréton's avuncular confidant, the talented painter and book illustrator Alexandre Bida, provided inspiration of another sort: wisdom in the face of adversity. "How well he knows the unfailing route to the soul," Bréton remarked early in her diary.[104] "He understands me perfectly, incomparably. Undemonstrative in his friendship, truly devoted, [he] will always be there, like an angel of mercy, to support me, compassionate and steadfast in times of anguish."[105] In turn Bréton offered advice and consolation of her own before Bida married Marie. "I feel that we speak the same language, that he is really the father to my mind and intelligence; we see with the same eyes, hope in God with the same faith, judge men with the same indulgence. . . . I find again with him my belief in friendship, my confidence, nearly my youth."[106] In part thanks to Bida, after years of grief and disappointment, Bréton was ready to consider marriage once again.

Les Vaudoyer

Alfred Vaudoyer was a natural choice for Bréton's husband; he had suffered emotionally more than possibly any other man she had met. Her innate empathy made him all the more attractive. After all, suffering attracted her more than anything else, as she had remarked years earlier, in men even more than in women.[107] So when Vaudoyer and Bréton met for the first time at a mutual friend's home in January 1879, not long after Bréton had finally settled matters with Jojotte, her destiny seemed decided. "My God!" she exclaimed a few days later, "is it possible that very soon now perhaps my fate will change, will rest in an affection that seems likely to me, acceptable and charming, that appeals to me, to someone otherwise so hostile to strangers?"[108] There were premonitions of trouble apparent in Vaudoyer's bizarre behavior and in the information gathered by her youngest brother Guillaume about his emotional instability. But Bréton discounted them. "No, his is a distracted spirit that nothing can focus. . . . It's a pleasure for me to hear him speak, even if he says crazy or bizarre things."[109] The possibilities seemed all too real.

Vaudoyer's sorrows arising from his wife's untimely death appealed to Bréton's need to console. Sharing her sorrow from a comparable experience with her fiancé, she felt an immense and profound pity for this poor man in such personal pain, truly a kindred soul to her own.[110] Bréton did not need her brother to tell her that Vaudoyer lacked the will to assure her happiness. That seemed all too obvious. "And yet, yet if he extended his hand to me, I would place it in mine without hesitating an instant, this womanlike nature, this wounded refinement, these gifts for analyzing oneself, and of originality, this perfect taste, in sum this truly extraordinary solace."[111] Then quite unexpectedly Vaudoyer informed the entire Bréton household of his intention not to marry anyone in the foreseeable future, dashing Bréton's immediate hopes for an engagement. Vaudoyer disappeared from her life altogether, except for his odd, occasional inquiries about her from various people they both knew. Suddenly the possibilities no longer seemed so real.

Eight months later, Vaudoyer reappeared. Bréton cautiously noted this implausible event in a postscript to her diary on 2 December 1879. Five days later they were engaged. "Ah! so I have found myself again, I the true Geneviève," Bréton exclaimed breathlessly. " 'Oh Fortune, add a golden nail to your wheel.' I belong to someone. I have a love. I am so *happy*. . . . This sweet reality melds duties with tenderness."[112] Bréton's great joy survived the guarded concerns of the family about her fiancé, the shrewd negotiations over her dowry, the hurried arrangements for their wedding, and the expression of her own lingering sadness. She discounted her instinctive reticence in light of her anticipation of tending to a delicate and tenderhearted man as both a wife and a mother.[113] Above all, understanding would prevail, she felt, even though Bréton also expressed reservations about the wedding ceremony: "Yes, this public possession has something about it that revolts and wounds me," she lamented, especially one before two thousand invited guests.[114] Nevertheless, they were married on 10 January 1880, a bitterly cold day in Paris, and left immediately on their honeymoon for warmer climes in Algeria.

Theirs was a sadder-but-wiser marriage. Bréton mused soberly on the evening after the wedding how long suffering had matured them both. Her faith in his love was unshakable. After years of misery, such a subdued happiness, without anticipation, seemed entirely appropriate.[115] Although this assessment is hardly effusive, it did square with the reality of their experiences in life.

> The unusual and touching effort of two dreamers, in love with the impossible, who want to make their ideal love a reality, who will not allow themselves a deceptive delirium or a passionate illusion, who in one year, in ten years, in twenty years want their love to be the same. . . . We are preparing ourselves . . . to walk together, to make ourselves better for each other, probably to struggle, possibly to suffer. . . . I've found my way and I'm walking along it full of so profound and so silent a joy to be alive that it takes my breath away and nearly frightens me.[116]

Vaudoyer, Bréton believed, had a cultivated nature very much like her own, however little he seemed to resemble her brother Antoine, her father Louis, or her fiancé Regnault. In his many lucid moments, the character of her dear companion in life remained everything to her, because his best qualities seemed both noble and sensitive. The two of them had the same habits of mind and taste; Bréton detected in him absolutely nothing mean, narrow, vulgar, or unworthy of her.[117]

Otherwise reserved and melancholy, her beloved "Sylvio" was a passionate man. Initially Bréton felt deep ambivalence about their sexual relations. During their honeymoon in Algeria, she noted nostalgically in her diary, "Dear virginity, oh, innocent companion. . . . farewell, never again will I be yours."[118] But Bréton located her happiness elsewhere in a family life of her own. She longed for children, a house full of noise, of laughter, of life. Imagine the elation she felt in April when she learned that she was expecting a child: "Yes, *three months,* for three months the world's strangest and most solemn mystery has begun to work in me."[119] Bréton's pregnancy provided the solace she needed in her occasionally troubled relations with her temperamental spouse.

Vaudoyer's personality disorders were manifest early in their relationship—before their betrothal, again on their honeymoon, and then increasingly often during the first years of their marriage, especially in the winter months. As Bréton described the problem, "He suffers troubling crises as one suffers from a raging toothache or neuralgia, crises where he is obsessed by a mad, false, painful, and unchanging idea that nothing can conjure away, that leads to reproaches, that makes him unjust, like a delirium . . . an imaginary misery, the worst of all, since it has neither reality, nor truth, nor form, nor name, nor reason."[120] At first the crises were followed the next day by sincere apologies and marks of tenderness. He was at least aware of his behavior, leading Bréton to believe that as a loving wife she could cure it herself. Vaudoyer's troubles indeed seemed tied to their marriage: he worried about his inability to ensure her happiness, to meet his family responsibilities, to earn an income worthy of Bréton's handsome dowry—in short, to overcome the social distance between them. Although these concerns were considerable, they were certainly not insurmountable.

Vaudoyer's spending habits made his problems worse. Even by Parisian standards, the family lived very comfortably, thanks to the foresight of others.[121] Bréton's father had provided a dowry of two million francs, which he placed in a separate trust for safe keeping—essentially from Vaudoyer, who brought much less property of his own to the marriage.[122] What money Vaudoyer had he used unwisely to build an expensive house on the avenue de Villiers in Paris, for which he paid 20 percent more than its appraised value, according to Bréton years later. His income from architecture, about fifteen thousand francs a year, was insufficient to sustain a spendthrift's feelings of inadequacy. Money rapidly became and for a long time remained an issue in their marriage, at times forcing Bréton to sell precious family heirlooms: "I've sold my dreams for cash," she wrote sadly in 1901.[123]

Meanwhile, the violence of Vaudoyer's crises increased, and Bréton despaired of ever finding a cure for her husband's episodes. His malady, she finally realized, was too deeply ingrained in his character.[124] After her first child was born in November 1880, her inclination was to seek solace in motherhood. She swore on her little Marianne's golden head that she would no longer derive her happiness from just one unstable person.[125] Her desperate resolution was no help to Vaudoyer, of course; and it was no solution to other difficulties, such as the anger that Vaudoyer's eldest son directed at his new stepmother. It seemed to her that she would die from the misery caused by a deluded husband and a rebellious stepchild, primarily because Vaudoyer was incapable of punishing his recalcitrant son.[126] When Vaudoyer's first mother-in-law Mme Viollet-le-Duc also despaired over his utterly unruly children, he had another crisis. This episode was very nearly the last straw for Bréton until they finally agreed to send the boys to a nearby boarding school.[127]

Bréton was not entirely free of emotional crises of her own. In 1885 Vaudoyer became infatuated with an unidentified Madame X, who had been invited to Bréton's sister Pauline's wedding ball over Bréton's stout protestations. "The role of Donna Elvira [in Mozart's *Don Giovanni*] suits me the least of all," she lamented. "I cannot continue to live this way."[128] Bréton hoped that it was nothing more than a flirtation, but she was badly shaken by the obvious attraction Madame X had for Vaudoyer, one he did not bother to hide. At stake was Bréton's longstanding equilibrium between physical and spiritual love. "He's enamored with my body and my beauty," she realized, but "he no longer respects my heart or my feelings. How shameful is such a life!"[129] In this instance, Bréton's troubled Roman Catholic faith could not sustain her emotionally; were Vaudoyer to go any further, she would seriously consider a separation. Bréton was relieved to learn later that there was actually nothing to it.

Vaudoyer's activities strongly suggest a bipolar syndrome.[130] At one moment he felt invincible, such as when he decided to quit architecture for bookbinding and then painting, all the while frenetically spending far more than he made. At another moment he felt utterly incapable, such as during his crises of paranoic self-abasement and exculpation. There never seemed to be a stable medium. Whatever his mood, either manic or depressive, he never burned the candle at just one end.[131] Husband and wife were the proverbial grasshopper and ant in Aesop's fable rewritten by La Fontaine, an unaccustomed role for Bréton, who noted wanly, "The grasshopper of the Bréton family, I'm the farsighted ant here, wisdom itself."[132] This asymmetry remained for the rest of their lives together, however much it cost the idealistic Bréton. There would be no change in either Vaudoyer's erratic behavior or Bréton's long-suffering. Eventually, she blamed it all, somewhat unfairly, on a childish, self-indulgent temperament. During Vaudoyer's serious illness in 1912, she had exhausted all sympathy and reported to Jean-Louis that Vaudoyer was throwing yet another impossible temper tantrum.[133] Their pain knew no end.

In all fairness to Bréton, she may have been right. For many years she observed and analyzed Vaudoyer as the complex product of a wretched family. His every whim had been indulged, she claimed, by miserable parents. Vaudoyer's father had met an unhappily married woman who had long been separated from her husband. Living together, the lovers apparently defied social convention until her divorce. But the children from the woman's failed marriage found the domestic trauma too much to bear, Bréton reported in 1881: one child killed himself, another blamed Vaudoyer for his unhappiness, and the last died tragically in childbirth. The only child of this union, Alfred, Bréton's husband-to-be, felt orphaned when his mother died and his father remarried two years later, at which point Alfred himself married. In three years, he was a widower with troubled children of his own. "Sometimes I think there is here some hereditary factor, probably on his mother's side," Bréton concluded, "like a reflection of his happy childhood that was both indulged and painfully tormented."[134] Bréton saw the same pattern at work again in Vaudoyer's indulgent behavior toward his eldest son Albert. She resolved to do better by her own children.

Marianne was Bréton's firstborn. She arrived on 3 November 1880 with a dimple in her left cheek, the only obvious feature in common with the father. The less obvious features that Marianne inherited from her mother developed only in time, especially her rebellious nature. Otherwise, mother and daughter were very different people. Marianne never tortured herself with useless fantasies, Bréton reported years later, nor did she express very much curiosity or imagination.[135] Much to the mother's chagrin, Marianne married very young, at age seventeen, to the philosophical freethinker and historian Daniel Halévy. The deeply religious Bréton took it personally; she blamed herself for her daughter's choice.[136] Marianne's marriage was the source of much concern; the ideologically minded Halévy often upset Bréton, for instance, when he refused to have his son Sonny (Léon) baptized. Bréton decided that Marianne was not to blame for her ideas or for the distance between them. "But as for him," she wrote angrily of Halévy, "a thinker, a man, as for him he neglects everything that he owes to me; I gave him what was truly most dear to me." Bréton tried to bite her tongue for the sake of her daughter's happiness. The two of them were in love, she told herself; they were happy, they were young, nothing else really mattered.[137]

Like Marianne, Bréton's youngest child Michel did not live up to her expectations. He was born on 29 August 1885 after a long, hard labor. Much to Vaudoyer's dismay, she had preferred a girl, because girls, she thought, were easier to raise. Michel of all the children was most like his father. "Chimérique," she called him in 1912, because of his improbable business schemes.[138] "[Michel] goes about all that utterly unmindful, without any sense of reality," in the hopes of supporting his wife Charlotte and the child they were expecting before the outbreak of World War I.[139] But on 6 September 1914, this improbable figure of Balzacian proportions was killed by an artillery shell at Villiers-Saint-Georges near Provins during the battle of the Marne: "I've waited so long for this pain that it doesn't surprise me," wrote Bréton two weeks later. "I can only think of Charlotte" and the awful responsibility of breaking the news to her.[140] Bréton remembered all too well how she felt forty-three years earlier when Regnault was killed. In her son's death, Bréton now felt closer to her daughter-in-law, her sister in pain and sorrow, Michel's legacy to his grieving mother.[141]

Consequently, Bréton's second child Jean-Louis became her closest familial (and discursive) relation (fig. 10). Born 10 September 1883, he was more like her than either Marianne or Michel. Her emotional dependence upon him grew rapidly after her daughter married Halévy and her other son started behaving like his father. More than Bréton's beloved brother Antoine and her indulgent father Louis, he represented a confidant to whom she often turned for advice and reassurance, a consolation for her many domestic difficulties. In one of her earliest letters to him, she wrote, "Good evening my Jean-Louis, good evening my joy, good evening my life."[142] At times, Bréton's letters made Jean-Louis her alter ego. He led the life that she only dreamed of as a youth.[143] More to the point, she confessed in 1912, "I especially think of you, Jean-Louis, in your heart and in your nature, your intelligence, in some way the joy and recompense of my life, the last bit of good luck—and who succeeded."[144] Jean-Louis was a second self to relieve Bréton's agonizing solitude.

This special bond between mother and son was strengthened considerably by Jean-Louis's interest in writing. It is no accident that he became the author of many art books, travelogues, and novels.[145] Bréton left little to chance in Jean-Louis's professional development. With her warm encouragement, his cultural sensibilities became very much like her own in art, travel, and literature. At one point she actually likened him to Regnault and sent to him in Florence, her favorite Italian city, a postcard of Regnault's portrait of Mme la comtesse de Barck, as if to remind Jean-Louis of the great promise the two young talents shared with each other. She took obvious pride in his accomplishments, for years keeping a scrapbook of and about his publications. "I

Figure 10. Jean-Louis Vaudoyer by Albert Besnard (1932). Oil on canvas
(© Musées de la Ville de Paris / cliché Joffre)

want all the happiness for my children, and when I see this happiness threatened, nothing more is left me," wrote the mother in Bréton. "So *work* to make me happy."[146] In time, however, her correspondence with Jean-Louis tended to more practical matters, such as the latest literary news from Paris, reflecting their very similar cast of mind and temperament. Their relationship, like Bréton's identity and agency in the world, became virtually inseparable from their writing.

Relations as Texts

Bréton's diary was truly her first love.[147] The thirty-three somber, leather-bound notebooks of varying sizes that she used for her writing are now worn and yellow with age, their musty-smelling pages covered with Bréton's hurried scrawl in black ink. Occasional smudges and second thoughts, often written in pencil, betray a nervous need to capture the moment and movement of her thoughts. Apparently for similar reasons, Bréton inserted dried flowers, picture postcards, newspaper clippings, and additional written pages. But as much as 10 percent of the diary was torn or scratched out, probably to guard precious secrets from curious eyes, at least until she decided that portions of her work should be published. For years after her sister Kate had surreptitiously read their contents, Bréton kept her notebooks securely under lock and key. Their straps have since been cut, undoubtedly by less discreet relatives.

Bréton's writing flowed unceasingly. She was constantly adding and revising portions of the first nine notebooks, the ones devoted to her relationship with Regnault, which she had identified for publication. Although she did not complete the revision herself, Bréton left explicit instructions to her son as to what she wanted done. "All this was copied and collected," the diarist wrote in an undated note to Jean-Louis, "not to speak of me, but to make known an unrecognized side to Henri Regnault—his young and charming affirmations, the tender and sensitive qualities of his soul—since only the inspired painter and military hero are still remembered."[148] Bréton's ostensible purpose in her project was to focus on her fiancé—to leave a memoir of the man, not the diary of a woman.

Accordingly, the diarist formulated a plan for the published version. It would begin with the lovers' first encounter in Rome at the Villa Medici in 1867 and end with Regnault's tragic death at Buzenval just west of Paris four years later. Bréton began the revision herself, disassembling the first note-book, rewriting it and having it typed, marking entries in the second note-book for similar treatment, rewriting selected entries in two other notebooks, and finally culling and having typed the correspondence that she wanted to include in the published diary. Her conception had its own integrity, deliber-ately structured by the diarist to resemble a historical novel, with a beginning, a middle, and an end, not unlike the fiction she read: Germaine de Staël's *Corinne* (1807), Victor Hugo's *Notre Dame de Paris* (1831), Stendhal's *Le Rouge et le noir* (1830), and other novels from the romantic period.[149]

The remainder of her diary underwent no such transformation. It was clearly more a piece of herself and therefore seemed inappropriate to publish. Bréton understood just how personal her persona, and those of other women like her, could become in a lifetime of journal writing. In 1914 she wrote Jean-Louis of her respect for one such voice: she was reading Marie Bida's diary before her marriage to Alexandre.[150] Bréton also recognized the distinctively feminine *I* in letters she read by Julie de Lespinasse and Bettina von Arnim. "Everyone in life has a novel," she noted early on in her diary. "It's only a matter of understanding it. I've understood mine all too well."[151] Years later she reread her diary in an effort to redefine her regrets, especially in her initial reticence with Regnault, recalling painfully "useless doubts" like the timeless fable of the princess and the rose petal.[152] Publishing these notebooks without careful revision would have been a betrayal of her discursive identity.

In her diary Bréton was a self-conscious woman writer. She discussed, for example, the personal implications in the writing of others, such as the flatter-ing letter she received from the accomplished writer Emile Caro. There was in it, she said critically, a worldly flattery that she knew better than any other woman.[153] A few years later, Bréton would recount the story of the monk captivated for a century by the singing of a nightingale: "An eternal story of distracted souls' dreams that a tiny imperious melody liberates and capti-vates. . . . The idea is so fine that one could make a delightful little gothic tale of it. Alas, many realities and worries have led me from the enchanted forest and I am suffering, such that I hasten to jump back in."[154]

Reading one's writing here promises the same self-discovery as writing itself. Consequently, when Bréton returned to her diary entries on her trou-bled friendship with Jojotte, the more resolute and self-assured young woman noted, "Now I've come to terms with it, I'm calm and like a stone with indifference. But when I reread what I've written, then I see how my heart tried to settle down, this heart that was so invincibly young and enthusiastic, that despair had filled full with madness, visions, and impossible illusions."[155] For Bréton there was no question that language became experience. Nothing was more obvious.

This truism arises frequently in Bréton's diary. Not long after she first met Vaudoyer at Henriette Escalier's in 1879, Bréton recalled her account of a sympathetic stranger encountered on a tramway, as if the diary itself had been a literary premonition of their relationship. When she learned that despite their plans Vaudoyer would fail to appear at Henriette's a few days later, Bréton borrowed a writer's metaphor: "So there's a story stopped in the second chapter, what a shame!"[156] Her life needed a text to give it form. Nowhere in Bréton's diary is her personal experience more discursive than in the folios written three days before her wedding. In reality marriage was to start everything, promise everything, renew everything. Its joy and wisdom, like its difficulties and struggles, would always preoccupy her heart, and as a result there would always be a need to keep a journal.[157] Bréton simply could not live without writing.

The journal is remarkable as both a literary work and a historical document. Its immediacy and poetic grace are most apparent in the portions that Bréton framed deliberately before her death and that her granddaughter Daphné Doublet-Vaudoyer had published in 1985.[158] Besides the charming romance of Bréton and Regnault, as mentioned earlier, the earliest notebooks portray the colorful cultural life of Second Empire Paris and the dramatic events of the Franco-Prussian War (July 1870–February 1871), the Third Republic's origins (September 1870), the Paris siege (September 1870–January 1871), and the Paris Commune (March–May 1871).[159] The diarist was an acute observer of the world around her as well as a talented writer with a gift for language, qualities reflected nearly everywhere in the text.

From July 1871 onward, the twenty-four other notebooks continue Bréton's personal story through her anxious relations with Jojotte, Vaudoyer, her children, and their families, including accounts of the long trips she took in Europe and the many art works she loved. Gradually, as Bréton matured, her diary grows less lyrical and more mundane; it reflects her more immediate, emotional concerns; historical events like the various political crises of the Third Republic, from General MacMahon via Alfred Dreyfus to Georges

Clemenceau, elicit no attention.[160] Her interests eventually turn from the journal to correspondence, where her family mattered most. The diary thins out and ends by 1908.

Bréton's letter writing was not a late development.[161] Her self-conscious correspondence actually began in the same year as her diary. From 1867 to 1871, the letters were literally indistinguishable from the diary, using much the same language on the same topics; namely, Bréton's relations with her family and her fiancé. All thirteen letters to and from Regnault, for example, take on the same sacred, affective quality as the early notebooks that Bréton wanted published. Years later, she told Jean-Louis, "I alone can still read these yellowed and effaced pages, because I know them by heart, even though they were written nearly forty years ago and I only read them again after thirty years. . . . For ten years I cried a lot over these poor little letters that had been all my life for those ten years. I cried a lot these last few days in recopying them. They are so beautiful that I don't think I have the right to conceal the heart that is revealed only there."[162] When Bréton formally turned the letters over to her eldest son, she reflected on what they said about Regnault; after all, the published diary was intended to focus more on him than on her. But, she knew, the letters continued to speak directly of her own life.

Bréton's correspondence with Jean-Louis is much more substantial. She wrote at least 556 letters to him, sent with increasing frequency between 1898 and 1915. In turn Jean-Louis sent at least 400 of his own to her in the same period. As he grew older and left home, they kept in touch by mail before the widespread use of the telephone. But as the anxious mother, Bréton felt compelled to write more often; their correspondence simply meant more to her. "Your letters are my joy," she wrote in 1912, primarily because she found so little happiness with other members of the family.[163] Such emotional compensation went hand in hand with the genuine affection they felt for each other and the many interests they shared. "When you are traveling, you write me such long beautiful letters," rejoiced Bréton, "and we are less apart than when you are so close by without writing."[164] Letters in hand, she followed him step by step on his trips to Italy, vicariously reliving her own visits to Florence, Venice, and Rome. Such a pleasure was worth tracing.[165]

Bréton's letters were thus more than transcribed conversation or psychic displacement. Their larger import is suggested by Bréton's declining interest in her diary. Contrary to the correspondence with Regnault, not one of the letters between mother and son was transcribed or noted in Bréton's journal.

It is clear that their correspondence came to serve the same emotional and discursive function as the diary, and ultimately replaced it. Her personal journal waned as their epistolary relationship waxed. At times their correspondence became little more than a diary for two in transit. "I got your letter," she wrote in 1902, "a real letter where you tell me your true life."[166] Bréton had been doing nothing less herself, and only she could say as much to him. "No one but me would dare tell you that."[167] A closer examination of her letters certainly lends credence to so bold a claim.

There is one tension in the letters' implicit narrative; it is Bréton's difficult transition from mothering to mentoring. Throughout the correspondence, she is coping with the empty nest. Her children were old enough to be on their own and she needed to develop a new role: "It's sad having neither mother nor daughter nor granddaughter to kiss on this first day of the year," she lamented in 1898.[168] Later that year, she bemoaned Marianne's plans to marry Halévy. The preparations made her very sad, and she wrote Jean-Louis to elicit his sympathy, especially with Michel's departure for the year and Albert's preoccupations with his health.[169] Other family concerns, as discussed earlier, would follow or continue. Bréton found it equally impossible to give up her maternal admonitions for Jean-Louis to prepare a career commensurate with the family's cultural and social status. "I'm sending you to England," she wrote, obviously annoyed when she suspected that her son was loafing. "I'm making a big monetary sacrifice, you know, why? Have you asked yourself that? So that you will learn a language that much later will benefit your career in the arts."[170]

For Bréton the shaping of Jean-Louis's life resembled the shaping of a text, and she did not hesitate to advise her son about the professional implications of his personal relations. Choose a well-read girlfriend, she urged him in all seriousness. "I won't let your emotional concerns become an impediment to work as you say. On the contrary, work is an ambition and a goal. I want you to have a varied, substantive, and refined knowledge in literature."[171] Intermixed with the good sense wrought by experience and wisdom, such as Bréton's shrewd response to Jean-Louis's early work, in each letter there was all the nonsense that only a parent can write: "I will try to console myself over your noble nose, so much like mine, that's been harmed by a pimple."[172] Of such admixtures letters and diaries are made, and Bréton's were certainly no exception to the rule.

Bréton was self-conscious about the discursive elements of her correspondence. She urged her son to adopt her mania for journals and letters. The missive, Bréton stated, was a model for all good writing. She had said as much to a friend: the journalist and literary *salonnière* Augustine Bulteau had remarked on the delight she took as a writer in thinking of a particular reader, who later told her how pleased he was by her work. It was just like correspondence, Bréton mused.[173] But she warned that letters could be too personal, such as those that the young Bettina von Arnim sent to the aging Goethe. As she had noted back in 1870, they expressed a shameless diaristic admiration of the great author: "What does such love by letter mean to a man seventy or eighty years old, apparently?"[174] Moreover, the travel postcard genre had taught Bréton to put on a brave face for her friends back in Paris when she actually felt lonely and unloved on a trip to Florence. She knew what epistolary conventions required.[175]

Other deliberate letter writing appears at crucial turning points in Bréton's life. Most important occasions are marked by correspondence. In 1873 Elisabeth Paris wrote tellingly to Marie Bida about the need for Bréton to let go of the past and get on with living again in the present. Bréton transcribed the letter in its entirety directly into the journal, as if the diarist could not have said it better.[176] Similarly, Bréton broke most decisively with Jojotte by letter. Long afterwards she continued to report all her correspondence, like the curious letter from Regnault's father tearfully imploring her not to cry: "My God, what does all this mean?" she asked.[177] All the more significant then is the absence of her correspondence with Jean-Louis from her diary, perhaps because the diary no longer served her discursive purposes. By then other forms of writing preoccupied her.

One other genre that Bréton explored tentatively is the novel. Among her papers is the sketch of a fictional narrative based in part on her romance with Regnault and in part on her expertise with personal writing. After earlier sections set in Italy and Brittany, part 4 is a "mélange of narrative, letters, a journal fragment." Clearly the work was intended to be a literary transcription of Bréton's diary. The male protagonist Daniel resembles Regnault, "an artist [with] a sensible, nuanced and easy appearance," who falls in love with Gertrude, "a more resolute and reflective philosopher's daughter," much like Bréton and her father.[178] There is little plot other than vague references to various adventures, the story of a kiss, a musical episode, and a crisis that results in Daniel's and Gertrude's decision to separate. Besides selections from Gertrude's diary, the narrative draws on fragments of Daniel's diary, which captures a romanticized voice in love with Gertrude but is frustrated by her enduring commitment to another man, Oliuto. Most of the fragment, however, is given to Daniel's evocations during Gertrude's performance of Chopin's "Marche funèbre": "Chopin is one of us, and our soul influenced him. He was nervous and sick like us. He sang of the century's suffering, and all the beats of his heart had their echo in ours."[179] Nothing could be more in the spirit of the journal Bréton devoted to Regnault's singing at the Villa Medici back in June 1867.

Bréton also tried her hand at travelogues. Sections of her diary offer well-informed impressions of Italy and Spain. Underlying each description is Bréton's association of travel with freedom from social and gender conventions, like her metaphor of the water in the Trevi fountain and her account of riding horseback in the Bois de Boulogne near Paris: "Those who haven't galloped across open fields wouldn't understand. It's freedom, fantasy, *unreality*, a sense of dominance," that only a young woman can experience.[180] And in Spain she deliberately rides her horse tandem with Regnault's in order to demonstrate strength and independence in her love for him. This freedom, to be sure, is relative. At times on their travels together, Bréton envies her brazen friend Nélie Jacquemart, "who in leaving everything, leaves nothing, neither mother nor sister nor dog."[181] Travel to Spain, it seems to Bréton, is also more liberating than is travel to Italy, where the conventions of bourgeois society are so much stronger. Otherwise, travel makes for personal revelations of all sorts in Bréton's diary.

Travel is also a discursive occasion. Written on the road, Bréton's diary and correspondence abound with narratives. A chance encounter with a former family servant at the Vatican, for example, brings to Bréton's mind the story of her grandfather and his trip to Rome forty years earlier. Like many other travelers, Bréton recalls appropriate texts, such as Chateaubriand's account of Pauline de Beaumont's glamorous death near the Trinità de' Monti. The most extensively revised portions of Bréton's diary are devoted to her first trips to Italy in 1867 and to Spain in 1870. Here she sets her dramatic meetings with Regnault in a well-crafted travelogue, a fitting literary backdrop to their fairytale romance. Less lyrical than her account of *"that home of restless souls"*[182] in Spain is Bréton's entire notebook written on her trip to Jersey in 1889. Here she notes the weather, the itinerary, the train, the boat, the works of Hugo and Chateaubriand on Brittany and the Channel Islands, the contrasts between English, Breton, and Parisian manners, and the like.

The result is an exercise in structuring a narrative to emphasize the value of travel, to learn more about one's physical and emotional landscape. At least two other notebooks trace subsequent art trips to Italy and are comparable efforts to capture space and time in language.

In each genre Bréton practiced, whether diary, letter, novel, or travelogue, she wrote purposefully, self-consciously, in an effort to mediate experience and give it form. Often this deliberate crafting was moved by deep personal pain, perhaps the primary, though certainly not the only, motivating factor in her writing. In 1881 she noted how her writing captured matters that were no one else's business. She intended to give voice to them only to forget them, as if to fill up a freshly dug grave, she said.[183] Metaphors that Bréton developed for this discursive transformation of experience ranged widely. At one moment her diary resorts to the violence of summer storms in order to capture the emotional turmoil she felt over Regnault's death.[184] At another it turns a fading rose into a symbol of quiet resignation.

> Someone, I don't know who, has put on my little writing table this last rose from Albisbrunnen, a discolored and frail Bengal rose. It is the only young, beautiful, and poetic thing in all that surrounds me. It speaks to me with truly sweet words in the language of angels. Its small pale face turned toward me makes me dream sadly. Thank you, my dear flower, thank you for this last kind, dying smile. . . . By dint of marvels, of sacrifices after a solitary month with an incomparable friend in the absolute oblivion of the future, I have come to build from silence a relative peace of sorts for myself.[185]

Here on a trip with the Bidas to a Swiss mountain resort near Zurich, Bréton reflects on the language that had made possible a special understanding of the self in relation to an unattainable ideal. The wisdom she acquires from this figurative moment is none other than that of a lifetime of writing, a literary discourse at the disposal of a feeling, knowing, self-conscious woman forever in the solitude of her soul.

According to her son-in-law Daniel Halévy, Geneviève Bréton-Vaudoyer died after a long illness on Thursday morning, 17 October 1918. Just as the first modern total war was coming to an end, Bréton succumbed "from a kind of poisoning which her tired condition could not resist."[186] For four months, her temperature had been very high and her condition weakened with each passing day. Home briefly on leave, Jean-Louis had apparently mistaken her composure for a deep sleep and returned to his military post. But only five minutes later, Marianne entered her mother's room to find her dead. The remaining members of her family—Michel had died in 1914, Vaudoyer in 1917—gathered to bury her near her home in Jouy-en-Josas just four days later. As Halévy noted, "She wore herself out; she had a conflicted personality, but life had not been entirely unpleasant for her; she was much loved; she loved much; she suffered blows, was bruised, and wounded in a hundred ways . . . but she received much. . . . Her life had been full and complete."[187]

In the solitude of her life and writing, Geneviève Bréton was perhaps no more privileged than were her older provincial sister Marie Leroyer and her Parisian contemporary Céline Renooz. Bréton's self-fashioning certainly resembled Leroyer's in its very conservative expression, in literary forms considered most appropriate to women in nineteenth-century France: the private relations of diary and letter transformed from deeply personal relationships of family and loves. In fact, out of their deliberately chosen gender roles, however much Bréton and Leroyer contested them in their work, came a distinct, discursive identity and discreet agency that it made possible. Renooz, on the other hand, failed in this endeavor. Instead, she chose to express herself and to act very differently, more overtly and more contentiously, in ways and for reasons that require elaboration. The instructive contrast between Bréton and Leroyer, on the one hand, and Renooz, on the other, will be obvious in the next chapter.

Chapter five

❧ Destiny Made Manifest: Céline Renooz

Céline Renooz felt the control of destiny nearly all her life. In "Une révéla-tion" (1888), she recalled "reading the book by Helvétius, *[De] l'homme*, for no other reason than curiosity. Nevertheless, all at once the question of human origins came to me, and I suddenly perceived the solution to this prob-lem. The unexpected revelation was instantaneous, and in several minutes it aroused in me such a multitude of ideas that since then I have needed several years to develop them."[1] As a force beyond her own, destiny drew Renooz to study first the interconnectedness of evolution, embryology, and physics, then the relationship of all knowledge in science, religion, and history. At the center of her epistemology was the intuitive power of every woman like her to apprehend, to seize upon the truth of complex issues as a whole. More than a mere cognitive faculty, this female intuition was the source of society's moral redemption, which would return women to their rightful place at the head of a new cosmic order. Renooz's self-assumed mission was to promote this insight into the feminine nature of the physical universe and its manner of shaping our lives directly.

These sweeping ideas came to Renooz insistently. At the Bibliothèque Nationale in Paris on a hot summer afternoon in June 1878, she was struck by a new train of thought while reading Helvétius's *De l'homme* (1772), as she said, and Holbach's *Système de la nature* (1770). She wrote years later, "I don't know what synthetic work occurred in my mind" at the time.[2] She left the library in a daze that lasted the entire trip to Suresnes, on the west side of Paris, where she was visiting her daughters. "It was only when I got off the train . . . that my latent ideas took a startling form, which fascinated me and thrust me into a new world."[3] For the next week, in a room facing east from

Mount Valérien, inspired by the regenerating force of the sun, Renooz outlined her theory on the origins of humankind and much of her subsequent work in science. "Everything was illuminated in my mind at the time; wherever I turned, I perceived *the Truth*."[4]

In this way Renooz defined a lifetime of relations. She committed her remarkable independence of mind and spirit to writing and teaching, acts of assertion far beyond the mere framing of an identity as a knowing and feeling self. Renooz was thus more than a self-conscious woman in her memoirs and correspondence. Besides science she published and lectured extensively on religion, history, and feminism, confronting the considerable hostility to her ideas the best way she knew, by confrontation. In the process, her relationships with family and friends were often as strained as they were with professional foes. Renooz would broach no opposition to her sacred cause to write and to act on what she believed, for what she believed to be the truth of a higher order. It was her fate, she wrote, to persevere right to the end, as the *prédestinée* in her unpublished autobiography *de la femme cachée*.

At the heart of Renooz's visionary endeavors, however, lay serious problems. Her personal life was fraught with disappointment and conflict, first with her mother and eldest brother, then with her feckless husband. As Renooz developed her scientific interests, she struggled to support herself and her four sick children. These difficult circumstances contributed to her persecution complex that ultimately made for an unstable and unreliable discursive identity.[5] Renooz never completed her memoirs, and for good reason. She turned her creative energies instead to the construction of another, more active self. The result was an overt, combative public persona, the mirror image in fact of the discreet agency and resistance that most self-conscious women expressed in modern France. But Renooz's ardent quest in her manifold autobiographical writings remained very much the same with her many, more restrained contemporaries: the language of experience still played a leading role.

The Setting

Céline Renooz was born Tuesday, 7 January 1840, in Liège, one of Belgium's most prominent cities. Her ancestors were actually of Celtic stock and had migrated two generations earlier from the French town of Besançon. Originally the family spelled its name Renoz, but Céline later added an extra *o*, in

Figure 11. Emmanuel Nicolas Joseph Antoine Renoz, after an earlier portrait, by Céline Renooz-Muro? (c. 1855). Ink on paper (Document BHVP)

order to distinguish herself from a sister-in-law, Céline Renoz-Borgnet, even though doing so complicated the proper pronunciation of her name. Most Anglo-Saxons tended to make the French *oo* into the longer vowel sound *ou*. She also dropped her husband's Spanish surname, Muro, not long after their separation. As she explained it, Renooz wanted no association with a nationality whose women did not take themselves seriously.[6] In the smallest details of her life, including the birthday she claimed to share with Jeanne d'Arc, Renooz was "an unusual story."[7]

Her father, Emmanuel Nicolas Joseph Antoine Renoz (1800–1856), was a native Liègeois who had studied law in Paris before returning home to participate in the 1830 revolution.[8] A political liberal influenced by Voltaire and Saint-Simon, he headed the contingent of Belgian exiles in Paris seeking to secure their country's independence from Austria. By then his wealthy family had lost most of its substantial landholdings, forcing him to take up work as a notary. He was elected five times to the Liège city council and appointed *échevin,* or marshal, in a professional capacity after the 1848 revolution had brought his Liberal Party to power. When he died unexpectedly in 1856, the local bishop refused to bury him; so with much pomp and ceremony, the mayor of Liège officiated instead. Renooz greatly admired her father (fig. 11), "the handsome Renoz" as he was known by his contemporaries, for his public achievements, of course, but also for his broad-minded generosity and indulgence toward her, the youngest of his many children.[9]

Renooz was less well disposed toward her mother, Marie Marguerite Louise Maugé (1800–1870), whom Renoz had met while studying law. Years later the daughter would write, "Her family belonged to that Parisian middle class where ideas are unexalted, instruction undeveloped, and the education of women distorted by prejudice," such as an unshakable belief in the natural superiority of Parisian manners and mores.[10] Mme Renoz detested Liège. Accustomed to getting her way, she unilaterally decided matters for her children, like Renooz's marriage with a Spanish engineering student, Angel Muro, without her knowledge. Matters were not any easier for the daughter forty years younger than the mother.[11] The distance between them appears clearly in the coolness of their correspondence. According to a letter from Renooz's brother Fernand, Mme Renoz was evidently a tiresome sort: "Mama is always pretty much the same, complaining a lot about her loneliness and being bored to everyone's disgust about it."[12] The mother died Christmas Day 1870 in Anvers, without much comment from Renooz, who could not attend the funeral because of the Franco-Prussian War.

Renooz's parents were married in Paris on 23 November 1830. Two of their seven children, unnamed, died in infancy. The eldest surviving child, Ernest, attempted to make his fortune in the United States. Edouard was the black sheep, his whereabouts unknown. The eternal optimist, Fernand, was closest in age and affection to Renooz, even though he moved to London to become a dramatist. Renooz's only sister Léontine was a conventional woman married to the artist Louis Tinant; she was nine years older and served as Renooz's surrogate mother during her long visits to Neuilly, on the western edge of Paris, where the Tinants made their home. Plausibly because of the differences in age and temperament among the siblings, Renooz was left alone to read in the garden at home and to make the most of her education, first in a German school for girls, then for two years in a Roman Catholic pension, Les

Dames de l'Instruction Chrétienne. Her parents supplemented her schooling for five years with private tutors in piano, mathematics, French, English, and literature, resulting in Renooz's schoolgirl notebook on the history of Western classics from Homer onward.[13]

Renooz had fond memories of her large, comfortable home in Liège, a former convent that provided ample space for the family's different personalities. In an effort to re-create her beloved Parisian comfort, Renooz's mother actually had a separate apartment for herself on the second floor. Between language and music lessons, Renooz enjoyed her father's large library, whose books she took on her rural retreats to nearby Froidment: "It was here that my finest childhood days were spent," she wrote nostalgically. "There I was in the midst of Nature, such as our phylogenetic ancestors must have been, without social conventions to hinder them, enjoying the greatest liberty."[14] Otherwise left to herself by an indifferent mother and a busy, indulgent father, the youthful Renooz gathered fruit, picked flowers, and played games very much on her own. Her self-sufficiency developed very early.

In 1859 Renooz married Angel Muro (1840–97). After his studies at the University of Liège and the Ecole des Mines in Paris, he worked briefly as an engineer with the Periere firm in Bordeaux. But as the son of a prominent banker, Victor Muro in Madrid, he soon became involved in anti-Carlist politics as a journalist and party official before Spain's 1868 liberal revolution. An agricultural and commercial reformer widely known for his efforts to improve food distribution in the Spanish countryside, he died before having achieved very much more.[15] According to Renooz, he was proud, expansive, and independent, but also vain, self-indulgent, and prodigal, not at all intellectually inclined and thus never entirely compatible with her. The mismatched couple had three daughters—Cocette (born 1860), Irene (1861), and Marthe (1869)—and one son—Emmanuel (born 1863); all of them bore endearing nicknames—Zita, Tita or Lily, Marie, and Quiqui or Manolo, respectively. This painfully fragile family remained more or less intact until Muro and Renooz separated in 1875.

During her marriage, Renooz lived on the road. She had spent her first nineteen years in Liège, except for a year in Paris with the Tinants (1856–57). From 1859 onward, however, "I moved frequently during my married life."[16] Three years in Paris (1859–62), one in Bordeaux (1862), and another two in Paris (1862–64) preceded the family's move to Madrid for five years, a stay interrupted by regular visits to the beach in Bilbao and to be with relatives in

Paris: "These changes in language, family, and ideas made me strangely ill at ease," Renooz wrote later; the malaise was compounded by still more moves to Bilbao (1869–71), Seville (1871–72), and back to Madrid (1872–75).[17] But no matter where the Muro family settled, boredom overtook Renooz during the long evenings she spent alone at home.[18] Vacations to San Lucas, Cordova, Cadiz, and Malaga were unavailing, and she felt all too keenly the legal and social constraints of her unhappy marriage in a foreign land. Consequently, in 1875 she left her husband and the loneliness that his peripatetic life had created for her. For the next fifty-three years Renooz made her home in Paris.

"During the whole time of my intellectual exile in Spain," she explained years later, "I continued to devote myself to serious study." Her move to Paris with her four children was in effect a continuation of her scientific interests, which were to culminate in the epiphany in the Bibliothèque Nationale in 1878. "I know not what cerebral fermentation had occurred in me under the intense southern sun. Grafted onto quite special physiological and hereditary circumstances, this condition led me to some surprising ideas."[19] First at 19 rue de Lille (1875–95), then at 9 rue de la Tour in Passy (1895–1928), with occasional vacations to summer leases in Suresne and Meudon, Renooz secured a physical if not exactly an emotional home in France's capital city (fig. 12). Her active intellectual life there, like her freedom from a disastrous marriage, brought Renooz none of the spiritual comfort she had felt in her hometown of Liège. She remained a Liègeoise in her profound dislike for Paris and its unjustifiable pretensions to intellectual superiority. For Renooz the French generally were close-minded, and she relished the opportunity to attend conferences elsewhere. When she was saluted by a stranger on the streets of Leyden—"as one must have formerly greeted a Goddess," she remarked—"No such thing would have occurred in France."[20]

Much of Renooz's personality can be read in her face. A lithographic portrait of her appears opposite the title page to Henry Carnoy's study of her life and work in 1902.[21] There, with unadorned hair and unpretentious dress, Renooz looks precisely as she wanted the world to see her: spare, intense, determined, and serious. But she was also proud, voluble, ambitious, combative, prophetic, and self-confident. Renooz remarked, for instance, how pleased she was to have a head the same size as a man's. At one of her conferences in 1903, a stenographer complained about the rapidity of her speech, making it almost impossible to record her entire talk. This torrent of words reflects an

Figure 12. Céline Renooz-Muro's home, 9, rue de la Tour, Paris (1998). Photograph (private collection)

effort to encompass as much as possible of her position and at the same time to address every conceivable objection to it. As Dr. Jules Gérard wrote in a letter to her in 1891, "With you one never has the last word, not out of obstinacy but out of sincere conviction."[22] Her aspiration was to create a vision of new possibilities transcending the profound limitations of modern scientific knowledge. "I hope to replace the Ecole d'Anthropologie," Renooz proclaimed proudly to Dr. Gérard Encausse.[23] Whether or not she succeeded, the attempt was worth sacrificing everything, perhaps even her sanity.

Renooz saw herself prophetically. Her vocation, as she put it, was too important to permit petty indulgences, even though the mundane details of life sometimes mattered to her. For instance, one aspect of Renooz's love for nature had absolutely no larger significance: "I adore gardening, I missed my real calling—I was born to live out in nature and to devote myself to work in the fields."[24] Most of the time, however, Renooz was less earthy, more otherworldly, much more given to philosophic reflection that verged on the spiritual: "There is something within that tells me that I'm not *of the world*, and when I find myself caught up in it, I suffer."[25] Throughout her memoirs, there is at work a self-conscious conflation of the prophetic and the actual, of the religious and the feminist, indeed of the mythic and the self. Her history of religions was nothing less than "the memory . . . of my race."[26] Otherwise she disliked introspection. Only toward the end of her life, when there remained so much left to do, was she forced to reassess her project. Poverty, old age, illhealth, apparent failure—in short the revenge of physical reality—gave her pause. "I am truly wounded by life," she wrote.[27]

Until then Renooz lived inspired. "A curious coincidence!" she remarked just before World War I, "while [Frédéric-Auguste] Bartholdi was carving his gigantic statue of *Liberty Lighting the World*, a woman was beginning the gigantic work that would enlighten science."[28] Such grandiosity came frequently to her, most often in the midst of adversity, in the face of opposition to her life's work when she needed reassurance. In the midst of her doubts, she took immense satisfaction in thinking that she was in possession of the truth. Without it there could be no progress in the natural sciences.[29] At such moments Renooz far exceeded the bounds of normal personal pride, likening the significance of her doctrine to that of the Roman Catholic Church. After all, she was merely responding to an immediate need, an external source of inspiration compelling her to discover and to speak. "It seemed to me that the enormous power of thought that had overwhelmed me and made me see so clearly into all the mysteries of nature was a moral force, which I was commanded to use in order to save the old world."[30]

Renooz's purpose was nothing less than humankind's redemption. At her most grandiloquent megalomania, Renooz would proclaim herself a savior: "Yes, I had a great mission to accomplish, I have indeed understood since [the publication of Jules Michelet's *Bible de l'humanité* (1864)] that the knowledge given to me was a sacred trust. It is one I had to spread among men in order to save them from their moral misery, from their life of falsehood and error, in order to defeat their pride, to give them back happiness by making them virtuous."[31] She also noted the apparent coincidence of her birth date with that of Jesus, according to the reformed Gregorian calendar, and she remarked the anagram of her family name in the French spelling of the prophet Zerubbabel and the mother of Immanuel (in Isaiah 7:14); her first name was derived from Archangel Michael's celestial home, meaning the daughter of heaven.[32] "Reading thus between the lines of the altered texts [in the Bible], finding all my own ideas in the great cry of pain in the psalms by a woman — *the female prophet David* — (the sex of the prophets [has] been changed), searching for myself how deliverance would be accomplished, I realized one day that all the predictions made in antiquity about such matters corresponded to my work."[33]

On the other hand, Renooz feared failure and all its many personal consequences. Enemies were everywhere, their threats seemed all too real, they justified the title she gave to the last section of her memoirs: "Persécution — Dévastation (1896–1908)." For long periods, Renooz was susceptible to profound paranoid suspicions. In 1893, for example, she became uneasy about giving conferences at home, she said, because stories were circulating about her activities there; reports questioned her sanity and the morality of her work.[34] Renooz's self-proclaimed role as prophet contributed to her insecurity. Even an advertisement, such as for Hachette's two-volume history of art, expressed a direct attack on her; Benvenuto Cellini's famous statue of Perseus holding the severed head of Medusa represented to Renooz man's mythic murder of woman in the Napoleonic Code, but also science's decapitation of her.[35] When the city of Paris refused to buy her books for its public-library collections, she remarked half-seriously, "The censors have already forbidden my books in Russia, here I am condemned by the city of Paris. Now the only thing lacking is for me to be excommunicated by the Pope."[36]

Renooz saw parallels between her life and that of Louise of Saxony, the princess whose scandalous affair with her children's music tutor was the talk of Europe before World War I. Underscoring the passages of particular interest to her, Renooz clipped and preserved Louise's memoirs when the Parisian daily newspaper *Le Matin* published them in September 1911.[37] The melodramatic installments were intended to exonerate the princess of her marital infidelity by revealing her personal miseries at court in Dresden. What Renooz apparently found significant in this tawdry tale was the persecution Louise experienced at the hands of her royal relatives: "I was like a cuckoo in a nest of sparrows, or like the sole person of artistic or original taste in the midst of a conventional middle-class family," explained the princess in a section marked by Renooz for her specific underlinings: "I had forgotten that *originality and imagination are the only unpardonable sins.* I was reminded of it. In retrospect, I confess now that I had to make trouble and create a scandal, because *I did not consider myself satisfied merely with being a princess.* Each indication of *my independent mind* was received with *anger* and gasps."[38] Evidently in her expressions of frustrated pride and fearful insecurity, Louise spoke directly to Renooz, whose emotional need to explain herself was no less intense or conflicted than that of the princess.

These personal preoccupations, however, did not always interfere with Renooz's sympathies for other people in misery. As a matter of principle, she was a convinced vegetarian and pacifist: she understood how uncongenial military service was to another pacifist, Henri Dupont, who had been called up for training in 1890.[39] Such occasional empathy is partially redeeming for someone otherwise so sharply focused on her work. "Actually . . . I'm rather pleased about it," she wrote to Louis Ranvier in 1895.[40] Renooz's vision and its promotion were consolations, as she herself admitted toward the end of her memoirs; the greatest consolation for her would have been to succeed.[41] Late in life, right into the 1920s, she was still sending brochures and publications to public officials, still selling books on consignment through bookstores, still writing the history of religion, still giving conferences to promote her ideas to a small circle of devotees. "My material life is very difficult, I am alone, [there is] no one to help me and [I am] often deprived of the most ordinary things," she wrote to Blanche Fournet after World War I, because she had given everything she possessed toward the achievement of her vision.[42]

Despite Renooz's later protestations that she never read—to free her work, she said, from the errant ideas of others—she was for many years an omnivorous reader. As a youth, Renooz studied nearly all the canonical works of Western literature. For decades thereafter, her reading continued in Lamartine, Renan, and Jules Simon, as well as Goethe, Cervantes, and Byron. The woman question caught her attention early on, including the debate between Jules Michelet and Jenny d'Héricourt, while the novels of Balzac appealed to her especially in their depiction of the long-suffering woman.[43] Ludwig Büchner and Jacob Moleschott disappointed Renooz by their rejection of the historical and scientific implications of ancient religions. In natural history, Renooz also engaged Buffon, Cuvier, Darwin, Haeckel, and the members of the Société Botanique de France, whose meetings she attended from 1878 to 1886. Among the arts and humanities, Renooz had her strong preferences: "I love music—great music—Meyerbeer, Beethoven, Mozart—and I go to the Opera. I love philosophy and all that goes into the search for truth. I love Nature, its calm, its silence, and the great dreaming state to which it urges me."[44]

Notwithstanding Renooz's obvious emotional instability, a major theme in her life and work is the movement beyond commitment and independence to concerted action. Her discursive identity was insufficient in itself; her ideas had to be propagated tirelessly. So Renooz divided the section of her memoirs entitled "Ma vocation scientifique" into two parts, one devoted to its formation (1878–90) and the other to its propagation (1890 onward). All her professional life, she experienced "an immense desire to promote," organizing conferences on behalf of her work, raising the money needed to publish it, and soliciting the cooperation of others to spread the word.[45] What was left of her modest dowry and inheritance after separating from Muro, Renooz devoted to the *Revue scientifique des femmes* in 1887.[46] Already in 1893, not long after beginning her memoirs, she felt the pinch of her single-minded activity, fleeing her frigid apartment to attend a meeting of the Alliance des Savants et des Philanthropes at a friend's home in order to get warm.[47] For years she requested money from friends and supporters and deliberately cut corners on inessentials like her appearance, whose shabbiness surprised her when she noticed it one day reflected in a storefront window.[48] Whatever her many personal problems, Renooz had an aptitude for work right to the end of her busy life of ambitious destiny.[49] Her experiential and discursive relations deserve closer study in themselves.

Relationships

Renooz's passion was invested in her mission; she had little left for anyone but her immediate family. Consequently, her notion of love appears almost ruthless in its focus on bloodless abstractions. Her memoirs speak often of animal magnetism and extrasensory presentiment, neoromantic anachronisms of Mesmer's magnetic fluids carried right into the twentieth century. At various moments, she claims hypnotic powers over other people, such as her husband Angel early in their marriage. She also claims to have hypnotized Louis Pasteur during an award ceremony in order to make him cry and to disrupt the proceedings in his honor, which she felt he did not deserve.[50] Renooz's *magnétisme télépathique,* however, was no substitute for the sentiments of everyday life.[51] Other than perhaps an unnamed Frenchman in Malaga, no man, not even her husband, moved her to think of love as anything but a diversion from her vocation. Sex was strictly a male matter, marriage a distortion of woman's true calling.

Renooz was more forgiving toward her girlhood friends in Liège. In her correspondence with the Dandely sisters Adèle and Mathilde, Eveline Simons, Emilie Alexander, and Félicie Wavrens, for instance, Renooz expressed the depth and range of her youthful affections.[52] These friendships were the closest she was to have until the birth of her children decades later. A touching letter from Adèle, written on the eve of the latter's wedding, suggests Renooz's reluctant acceptance of an asymmetrical relation between spouses: "Be indulgent to your big Coco who can't even imagine that someone was ever able to love [another]," Adèle wrote her friend, confessing to a marriage of convenience on her part.[53] Apparently for Renooz, the bond between friends meant more than the one between spouses, an emotional projection originating from painful personal experience of her own.

Renooz's marriage to Angel Muro brought her no happiness. They first met in December 1857 and continued to see each other for a year, off and on, until Muro decided to seek her hand in marriage. Without the protection of her wise father, Renooz was married off by her distant mother, who did not bother to check Muro's background. Renooz's oldest brother Ernest negotiated her dowry, agreeing to pay Muro's gambling debts out of her marriage portion, without either her knowledge or her consent. Renooz greeted her wedding day with little apparent enthusiasm: "Finally June 18 arrived," she wrote years later.[54] Within eighteen months Muro had already found a mistress, a servant girl from Dijon, who earned two hundred francs a month for her trouble.[55] Such arrangements soon became a habit, paid from the income on Renooz's dowry of fifty thousand francs.[56] Also to Renooz's chagrin, the restless Muro moved their young family frequently from place to place, often wherever his political sympathies secured him jobs during decidedly unsettled times in Spain. Differences in temperament and cultural mores forced Renooz to cut her ties with Muro in 1875. They visited and corresponded occasionally for five years, after which they lost touch. In October 1897 Renooz was surprised to learn in the Paris newspapers of her husband's death.[57]

If Renooz's marriage to Muro ultimately resulted only in material for her work—she stated that her husband's irrational temper was the basis for her book on comparative psychology—her relationship to their children was much more important:[58] "The two big interests of my life have been my science and my children—the rest for me is secondary."[59] This concern appeared clearly in her memoirs, even though it is difficult to ascertain precisely when her children were born or what they did. More important to Renooz was their emotional presence. She felt keenly each one of their untimely deaths to tuberculosis. One after another, they left her bereft of immediate family support. The tenor of their correspondence expresses the depths of her affection as they fell ill and died, despite the formal conventions of her letters. A month after her last child passed away, she wrote a friend tearfully, "In my heart there is a great moral pain right next to a mother's deep sorrow."[60] She felt truly alone.

Renooz's firstborn child Cocette, or Zita, was the first to die. She had been just two weeks shy of her twenty-sixth birthday in April 1886 when Renooz wrote her own brother Fernand with the unhappy news. Otherwise, Zita had no particular place in Renooz's memoirs, which occasionally confused her with her youngest sister Marie. She is a shadowy figure, much like her younger brother Manolo. However sad Renooz became upon his death at age twenty-seven in 1890, she kept little of their correspondence and noted nothing about him other than his work at the French Ministry of Finance. Renooz's relative silence about her eldest daughter and only son suggests an emotional distance that narrowed briefly in her anxiety for them during their illnesses and in her profound grief for them some time afterwards. Their deaths gave Renooz pause.

Renooz paused still longer for her second child Irene, or Lily, who also suffered from tuberculosis. Renooz interrupted work on the *Revue scientifique des femmes* in 1889 so she could nurse her daughter in the peace and quiet of Meudon for nearly a year before she finally died. The physicians, both male and female, were again no help, leading Renooz to reconsider the efficacy of medicine and to ponder the health problems of women generally. Undoubtedly more akin to Renooz intellectually, Lily had faced death without the consolation of religion. Later, when the mother read Marie Bashkirtseff's journal, the daughter came immediately to mind: "If my poor Lily had written, she would have sounded like that," Renooz noted. "There was no dark side to her, she was moral and physical perfection itself."[61] In her courage and intellect, like the outlandish Bashkirtseff, Lily was another Céline Renooz.

Renooz's most important family relationship, however, was with her youngest daughter Marie. This attachment developed in part from their life together in Paris; Marie lived most of her forty-one years with Renooz. The furthest Marie moved away from her mother was to Nancy. For nine years, from 1892 to 1902, she worked as a tutor for the Lazare Dreyfus family nearby in Passy and used her small income to help support Renooz until this child, too, fell ill with TB. Despite their manifest poverty, mother and daughter retreated to Perpignan, where Marie's care was better. A brief recovery enabled her to do translation work for a Paris fashion magazine. Then her illness recurred and forced her to waste away at home for two years, to die quietly in 1910: "There's a fatality about my work," Renooz exclaimed in deep despair.[62] The receipt of more than two hundred letters was no consolation for the loss of her last material and emotional support. "She was half of my life and I was half of hers. . . . All her life had been full of devotion and work. We struggled with everything thanks to unfortunate circumstances. How accustomed she became to self-denial, to sacrifice"—just like Renooz herself.[63]

Renooz did have a substitute family; it consisted of the loyal and like-minded members of the Société Néosophique, the association she founded for the promotion and publication of her ideas. It was a logical outgrowth of Renooz's principal Parisian income-generating activity as director of a conference hall, an activity she began upon her arrival in Paris from Madrid.[64] First at the rue du Bac (1875–77), where she arranged the speaking engagements of others, then at the rue des Capucins, where she began promoting her own ideas, Renooz came into contact with a host of Parisian intellectuals and politicians like Alfred Naquet, Edouard Lockroy, Camille Flammarion, Léon Richer, Henri de Lapommeraye, Alfred Madier de Montjau, Pascal Duprat, and Maria Deraismes, among others. Eventually she expanded her pedagogical activities to include the Universités Populaires, the Ecole d'Enseignement Supérieur Libre, and then her own Ecole des Néosophiques. "The lecture," she realized, served "to tell the book, the spoken newspaper article," for both prophecy and profit at more than a hundred conferences of her own.[65] As early as 1893, Renooz began receiving money from devoted followers, like Blanche Fournet, who paid a hundred francs to publish the Néosophes' first conferences.[66] The society itself was formally organized and established on 30 June 1897.

The Société Néosophique began with thirty members. Like Renooz, most of them were intrigued by the possibilities of "a rational and nonempirical science."[67] Léon de Rosny, Dr. Broëns de Charleroi, Dr. Verrier, M. G. Eloffe, Mme Resséquier, Mlle Gertrude Dullay, Mme Urban da Castro, Mme de Marsy, Mme Louise Rieville, Mme Vidal, Mme Dorel, and M. Renhas, more or less obscure figures listed in the association's monthly *Bulletin*, constituted the inner core. They met nearly once a week at Renooz's home until 1898, when their growing numbers moved to the Salle de la Nouvelle Encyclopédie on the rue de Rennes and the Salle Rudy on the rue Caumartin. By 1901 the society had more than a hundred dues-paying members. But over the course of the next twenty years, divergent interests forced the group to reconstitute under various names for purposes different from those stated boldly in the association's founding principles: "A Society is founded in order to work for the intellectual and moral awakening of humanity by the study of Nature's laws and their application to human life."[68]

By 1927, under the impetus of another generation of generous benefactors, the Société Néosophique reappeared. Renooz remained as before the *présidente en perpétuité*, but other members took up leadership responsibilities, such as Aléxis Métois, Robert Chochon, Louise Chapel, and Lucie Lecomte, who were listed in the new bulletin.[69] "Neosophy is the Wisdom that results from the knowledge of Nature's laws as formulated in *La Nouvelle Science*," explained Renooz in a blurb on the cover to her brochure *La Science et l'empirisme*.[70] The Néosophes' three principles were nothing less than "Respect for the truth. Respect for woman. Moral courage."[71] In short, Renooz's family of kindred spirits gathered regularly to hear their prophet speak and to promote her work by raising the money for its publication. Renooz could never have established closer personal bonds, based on a common vision, than this loosely knit group who would ultimately arrange her funeral and honor her memory by printing the last volume to her history of Western religions.

Renooz certainly needed the support of family and friends in her struggle with Mathias Duval (1844–1907, fig. 13). For much of her professional life,

Figure 13. Mathias Duval in *Journal de l'anatomie et de la physiologie* (1907). Photograph (Cliché Bibliothèque Nationale de France)

Renooz was obsessed by this man and what he came to represent for her. A professor in the Paris faculty of medicine and honored member of several scientific associations, Duval was an influential figure in the French scientific community. Early on, Renooz had sought out his good opinion of her work. When she visited his office in 1885, however, he made the mistake of offering his candid assessment of her *L'Origine des animaux.*[72] He had critiqued it sharply in a public lecture; and when she confronted him for an explanation, he responded curtly with a series of pointed questions. Had she consulted any botanists? What evidence did she have for the analogies she developed in the book? Impatient with Renooz's extended answers, Duval rudely cut short her visit. From that point onward, Renooz explained, the persecution of her work began in earnest.[73]

A few years later, she approached again *le prophète du Darwinisme*, as Duval was known by his students, to invite him to her public lecture at the Sorbonne. This time his exasperated response was still more blunt: "I have already told you, what you are doing is mentally deranged."[74] From then on, Renooz suspected Duval's malevolent role in nearly every one of her professional misfortunes, such as the presence of hecklers at her conferences and the unwillingness of publishers to consider her work. She was convinced that at best Duval was behind a conspiracy of silence about her scientific theories; at worst he was the source of all evil in her life. "Certain newspaper articles have said that I'm a shrew speaking ill of everyone. Thus speaks the conscience of Duval, foreseeing everything that one could have said of him, if it came to that. He played for me the same role that [Ferdinand] Esterhazy played for [Alfred] Dreyfus."[75] Eventually Duval symbolized to Renooz the unrelenting resistance of the scientific establishment to her ideas. If she failed in her mission, it was because of the community of prejudice that he represented. Her memoirs devoted an entire chapter to him.

In the face of Duval's overwhelming credentials and the power they gave him in the world of science, Renooz persevered, because she felt that his advocacy of Darwinism was nothing less than the promotion of brutality. This man bore a terrible responsibility for his opposition to her ideas. He served his personal interest at the expense of humanity's enlightenment, salvation, and happiness, as she saw them.[76] When he finally died in 1907, Renooz wrote her own necrology of him in her memoirs: "By his colossal struggle against Woman, he embodied the terrifying and satanic figure of the Antichrist, which is not a prophesied or imaginary character but a reality. . . . Duval was *the vandal of science*."[77] Renooz proudly proclaimed the inauguration of a new era. At least seventeen letters from friends congratulated Renooz on her successful struggle to overcome the evils that Duval signified.[78] The new world Renooz and her Société Néosophique envisaged never materialized, of course. What endured, however, was Renooz's memory of this painful relationship, which owed less to her paranoia than it did to her work.[79] Her vision was very nearly her whole life.

Idées Fixes

Renooz's ideas—her entire raison d'être—progressed across three disparate but related fields: evolutionary embryology, scientific epistemology, and visionary feminism. Her earliest interests actually developed in response to Charles Darwin's *The Origin of Species,* translated into French by Clémence Royer in 1862; Renooz's first book, *L'Origine des animaux* (1883), critiqued Darwin's theory of evolution, because she found its method "incompatible with the rigorous demands of science."[80] Instead of tracing the origin of species by the established conventions of natural history—that is, Darwin's approach—Renooz proposed examining evolution in light of recent work in embryology. The results, she felt, were conclusive: "The structures developed by humans and flying animals at the beginning of their evolution are vegetable structures, forms that are faithfully reproduced in the first phases of present-day embryonic life resembling primitive vegetation. But in its slow replication of evolution, the vegetative world is just the *reverse* of that for present-day animal life. In other words, in the vegetative phase of animal gestation, the cephalic extremity is inverted, while the caudal extremity is on top."[81] For Renooz nothing could be more obvious: the vital center of life in the plant is located in its lowest extremities, its roots, while the most important extremity of the human being is the head, which appears upside down in the fully formed fetus. Embryologically, the head develops in the same relation to the body that roots already have to the plant. Renooz thus echoed Ernst Haeckel—ontogeny recapitulates phylogeny both within and across species—but with one critical difference: animals, she believed, appeared only after plants had sufficiently evolved structures for individual animals to imitate in their earliest, embryonic development.[82]

Much later, in 1908, Renooz succinctly summarized her views on the vegetative origins of animal life in a series of newspaper articles written for *La République sociale* in Montpellier: "The differences which exist between plants and animals and which serve to characterize the two kingdoms are those which exist between humans today and humans in the embryonic, that is, primitive state. The transitory stages through which the embryo passes in order to develop the features that characterize the newborn animal are those that primitive vegetation traversed in order to resemble the features which characterize present-day animals."[83] Evidence for this special relationship between plant and animal life, Renooz asserted, can be found everywhere, including the remarkable peace humans feel in the woods, as opposed to the

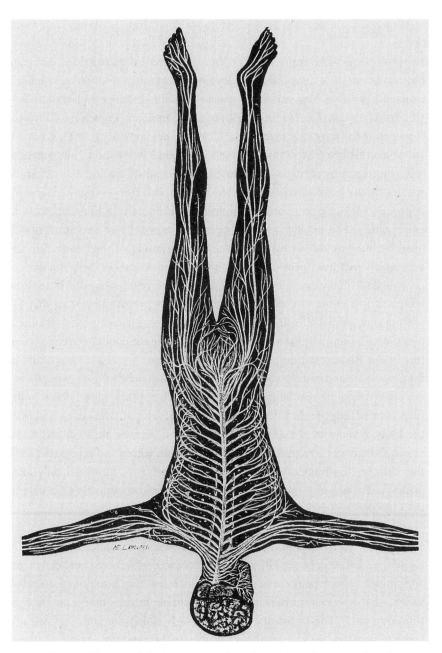

Figure 14. Direction de l'arbre nerveux observée dans la station renversée de la vie embryonnnaire, by H. E. Langlois, in C. Renooz, *L'Origine végétale de l'homme et des animaux aériens* (1905). Lithograph (Document BHVP)

profound anxiety they experience in the ocean. The close ties between flora and fauna were also evident materially: "Protoplasm [in animals] is the same as that of former vegetable species, because it contains the initial biochemistry of all life."[84] Consequently, for Renooz the "great problem" of science was to rewrite its account of human evolution based on the "natural laws" of vegetable life.

One significance of this argument, based on creative analogy drawn from biology (fig. 14), is Renooz's rejection of a principal feature to Darwin's theory: the differentiation of species by natural selection. "The vegetable origin of animal life leads us back to the fixity of species," she wrote, "but [it also] leads us to the evolution of each species. It shows us that all of them follow their respective evolution, tranquilly, coexisting without conflict with their neighbors and perpetuating across the ages the special characteristics for each one of them."[85] In short, her version of evolution was symbiotic and functional rather than competitive and conflictual. Nature for her was not animals fighting for survival but plants cooperating in harmony. But this quasi-ecological critique of Darwin's theory of the struggle for existence had another significance: Renooz's early anti-Darwinism was at the heart of a new scientific epistemology.

The failure of Darwinians to recognize the obvious—to acknowledge the utility of embryology to the study of evolution—was owed, Renooz felt, to fundamental flaws in the scientific method. Therefore, she argued, the basis of all true scientific knowledge cannot be empiricism, which was the pervasive positivist model for all fields, including literary studies, at the end of the nineteenth century.[86] Rather, science as knowledge must become intuitive; it must adopt a woman's (nonessentialist, Bergsonian) immediate recognition of truth as a formal manner of knowing.[87] Renooz assumed the promotion of this new epistemology as a personal responsibility; hence, her inspiring statement of principles for the journal that she founded in 1888, *La Revue scientifique des femmes:* "Science must be recast in order to show men who they are and what they ought to be. It is to women that this task is entrusted. With the help of the power that even the most obstinate of men recognize in them— intuition—women can bring to the old world the light that will re-create intellectual life."[88] Once science was established on new epistemological foundations, all knowledge, indeed all morality logically derived from it, would ensure a more creative and peaceful existence for everyone.[89]

Renooz understood that science underlay morality—"morality must be the real object of science"—and so she initially focused her attention on rediscovering the scientific laws of the universe.[90] All physical forces, she explained, were not those studied by men using their fatally flawed empiricism; gravity and electromagnetism were in effect illusions. Rather, by her new method, Renooz claimed to have created a truer physics; that is, to have framed "all [natural] laws: the causes of electricity and light, the true cause of gravity, . . . the essence of the *generative Principle*, its intimate connection with our simplest acts, our most secret thoughts, . . . the origin and development of [my] conception of the Divine Principle, . . . [and] the mystery of sexual evolution on which rests [all] *moral law.*"[91] Behind this elaborate physical and metaphysical system, Renooz argued, lay the true prime mover, the great god oxygen, whose irresistible energy infused all animate and inanimate matter:[92] "In our solar system oxygen surpasses all other elements; its impact cannot be exaggerated; it is of such force that it determines the entire physical and physiological disposition of our planetary system."[93] But this fundamental discovery was made possible by the means unique to women, whose intuition redefined knowledge of the universe and reestablished its morality. Without women's thought, there could be no scientific or moral order anywhere.

Perhaps Renooz's most revealing publication about the special epistemological role of women was her brochure *La Science et l'empirisme*, published in 1898. Here she reclaimed for science its original meaning as knowledge in general, rather than its modern definition as a discipline in particular. The earlier, more universal notion of science, Renooz wrote, was most appropriate to orderly, unbiased, abstract thought, with all the certainty of mathematics, the *mathèse* of the ancient world manifested most clearly in the instinctive knowledge of women and children:[94] "Throughout their life women maintain their childhood instincts. Indeed, throughout their exceptional evolution they continue to see clearly the effects of Nature in the same way children do. . . . Thus like children women can disclose spontaneously the truths that they apprehend without even trying."[95] Although the pamphlet was actually intended as a critique of the positivist bible, Ludwig Büchner's *Kraft und Stoff* (*Force and Matter*, 1855), it forthrightly asserted the place that women should have in science and society because of their intuitive grasp of fundamental truths. These truths represented the spirit of the Société Néosophique, outlined on the inside of the pamphlet's front and back covers, which privileged women's mentality, knowledge, evolution, and morality: "To be a Néosophe is to be better and more knowledgeable than others; it is thus a matter of possessing the qualities necessary to work for the regeneration of humanity."[96]

It was a series of small steps in Renooz's thinking that eventually took her all the way from embryology to epistemology to feminism. By the time she began writing her memoirs in 1890, Renooz was already interested in women's issues, especially in higher education and scholarly research. But she was still more concerned with elaborating the feminist vision of universal harmony through a new cosmology of both physical and spiritual forces that she outlined in *La Nouvelle Science* (1890–1920): "Let us hope that the coming generation will take the next step with us, from the old world to the new one that will be based on the ABSOLUTE TRUTH, a great and simple truth like Nature itself, at the heart of which we are born."[97] In its turn, this Saint-Simonian conception rested on yet another, much larger, project tracing the origins of patriarchy in Western society. The establishment of a new cosmology, Renooz asserted, required an understanding of its historical roots reaching back to the ancient world, when, according to J. J. Bachofen, men had usurped women's place as divine agents.[98] This insight led her to write a six-volume study on the original role of women and its displacement in religious practice, arguably her most successful work, *Ere de vérité* (1921–33).

By this circuitous route, too, Renooz's interest in science and religion are linked. Her visionary cosmology is closely tied by natural history to a clear conception of the past. Or as she put it, "for the purpose of creating a NEW WORLD, the inevitable first condition to realize is thus that of regenerating Science in order to give it a new force at the same time that History is being corrected."[99] By reforming the way we know the truth, we can understand the past and the present in order to create a better future. This radical approach was necessary, she felt, because men had falsified the historical records that had once celebrated the divine roles women played as goddesses and priestesses in the ancient world.[100] And so "we will apply ourselves especially to showing all men of good will the works made possible by the female mind. We will try to teach them the *hidden* knowledge [in] the condemned books. We will rescue from oblivion the censored truths, and we will bring to light the fascinating history of the Ancient Mysteries."[101] Such a project was possible if one had the key to knowledge that enabled Renooz to discern in the Bible, for example, what incredible spiritual power women had before men seized control of religion and altered the sacred texts.[102] The new world needed to know this historical erasure of women to re-create a more peaceful, harmonious social order.

In 1908 Renooz outlined her complex history of religion and its basis in feminist reform. Her pamphlet *Evolution de l'idée divine* likened the historical development of divinity to the organic process of maturation. Before the tenth century BCE, when goddesses and priestesses predominated, "theogony was the expression of youthful sentiments. It suddenly appeared in the early stages of humanity's evolution, because it responded to the need of all men, the need to adore Woman." But for the next millennium, a struggle erupted between gods and goddesses. "The second manifestation of the Divine Idea was the source of conflict between men and women, of jealousies, of hatreds that appeared in the adult male in particular." Ultimately the gods won and expelled the goddesses from the Judaeo-Christian pantheon as we now know it. "The third manifestation of the Divine resulted from a benighted mental condition, accompanied by the ardent desire to dominate that in time developed among certain men."[103] With each phase came dramatic changes in social and political institutions as well as religious life, resulting in the subjugation of women and the rewriting of historical records, including the sacred texts, that had documented the former powers of women. "Since *'man changes laws only after having changed gods,'*" Renooz concluded, "social renewal will occur only by reestablishing in the world NATURAL RELIGION, which will re-create the moral life of humanity."[104] This would begin by restoring women to their rightful role as the divine bearers of truth.

Renooz's passionate commitment to feminist action was therefore complemented by an equally passionate exploration of its necessity: to redress the primal injustice done to women's original divinity, which she claimed to have rediscovered and felt compelled to reestablish (notwithstanding the prior claims of the utopian socialists).[105] Accordingly, the end of her life was devoted to explaining and promoting woman's special calling. During a lifetime of creative work, Renooz's ideas had always been moving toward this particular view of woman at the center of a reordered cosmos. Here nature was not red in tooth and claw like a wild jungle, but peaceful and symbiotic like a well-tended garden. Here knowledge was not mere power but social morality. Here woman was not a victimized object, but an active subject in an orderly universe of her own making. This new world owed everything to what women had been and could again become in Renooz's intellectual journey from natural history to feminist utopia.

It took a disaster as monumental as World War I for Renooz to develop a specific utopian vision in keeping with her system. This terrible war, she firmly believed, was the direct result of men having usurped the female pre-rogative in all fields of knowledge and action. "Therefore the preconditions of an enduring peace are first of all the *reestablishment of a moral authority*, which is a corrective for man's brutal instincts. . . , the return of Woman to her natural Right."[106] This authority resembled that which mothers have over their sons, a natural force powerful enough to bring about the union of all races, all nationalities, all beliefs, all truths in the world, and thus to en-sure peace. According to Renooz, *la Matrise* was most likely to be achieved through the establishment of a sacred city, an international center where the representatives of the major states would be guided in their collective deci-sions by the new knowledge that Renooz's work had suggested: "Creators of the Great Work will erect a Sacred City—which will become the Eternal City—because it will be the City of *Redemption*, that is, the one where science has *reappeared*."[107]

In conclusion to this scheme, Renooz proposed a peace treaty and a univer-sal constitution whose implementation she considered "a return to Nature, a return to Truth, a return to Reason."[108] The treaty's twelve articles empha-sized the need to overcome the causes of war, especially in social, ethnic and nationalist rivalries, by urging a reorganization of humanity based on the eternal laws of nature; that is, on the naturally complementary instincts of males and females: women's spiritual force would direct the physical force of men. And so the treaty appended the draft of a universal constitution deter-mined by these principles. Here the welfare of society, the organization of work, the constitution of families, the education of children, and the provi-sion of health care would be structured in the interest of every language, every race, every nationality, based on the absolute truth. *L'Esprit féminin* would ensure the order in Renooz's *Ratiocratie*, which marked the practical culmination of her very particular system of knowledge, belief, and action.

Renooz's system thus brought together her interests in organicism, mysti-cism, history, and women, the guiding principles of her vision. In science, biology became the touchstone of truth, by analogy the model for all fields of knowledge: the secret of human evolution, she believed, lay in the example set by embryology and physiology. Similarly, scientific certitude existed in the intuitive faculties instinctive to women and children, who apprehended phe-nomena naturally, without the falsifying methods of empiricism. There was no rational basis to this assertion; it was obvious to everyone capable of abstraction, whether or not it could be proven experimentally: historical examples demonstrated that such proof was itself epistemologically suspect. Once the records were restored to their original forms, women's science, as both knowledge and morality, promised redemption in Renooz's utopian vision, the product of a lifetime of feminist experience and insight.

One source of interest in Renooz's work is, to be sure, its special place in the history of ideas.[109] It owes much to earlier intellectual movements, such as experimental science, messianic romanticism, and especially utopian socialism, even though her writings often disavowed their most obvious influences. The empirical methods of the physiologist Claude Bernard and the anthropologist Paul Broca, for example, loom large in Renooz's commitment to scientific observation and demonstration. Renooz relied on certain authorities in physiology and sought access to laboratory space at the Sorbonne, thereby placing her work ironically in a French positivist tradition. But also like the poet Alphonse de Lamartine and the philosopher Edgar Quinet before her, Renooz developed a prophetic vision of social justice and spiritual renewal. This Rousseau-like conception of a better world returned a benign, in fact beneficent nature to its rightful place in a society that had been corrupted by men. More in tune with the natural, Renooz believed, women would inspire men to achieve true social harmony, just as Prosper Enfantin, the Saint-Simonian visionary and organizer, had argued they would.

Yet Renooz's work also shares in other, subsequent challenges to the ideologies of positivism and rationalism.[110] Renooz clearly participated in the fin-de-siècle reassessment of experimental science and political liberalism. For her, progress and materialism were pernicious myths. Not having read either the neo-Kantians like Charles Renouvier, syndicalists like Georges Sorel, or the avant-garde like Alfred Jarry—the French counterparts to Nietzsche, Marx, and Freud—Renooz still recognized the limits to reason in the scientific method and the rational individual, the pillars of Western self-confidence and patriarchal hegemony on the eve of the twentieth century. Like the vitalist philosopher Henri Bergson and the mystical nationalist Charles Péguy, Renooz questioned the empirical assumptions of institutional science. In this way Renooz joined many feminist thinkers—Arria Ly and Madeleine Pelletier in particular—in anticipating the postmodern critique of phallogocentrism and its intellectual manifestations. The women's liberation movement in France, as represented by Hélène Cixous, Julia Kristeva, and Luce Irigaray, owes much to such early feminist thought.[111]

Relations as Texts

Within this remarkable synthesis of European ideas, Renooz's real historical interest lies in her complex expression of multiple, often conflicting discourses. Renooz explored a variety of expository forms; all of them came together in her uncompleted memoirs. The conflicted identity revealed here offers the best opportunity to follow these often clashing traces in her work. Despite its forthright chronological organization—the first-person narrative of personal values and identity themes is typical of autobiography as a genre—Renooz's unpublished "Prédestinée: L'Autobiographie de la femme cachée" incorporates the features of several different texts: private diary, personal correspondence, scientific scholarship, polemical journalism, utopian vision, and feminist debate. Examples of these are even attached to the manuscript, where Renooz's retrospective narrative plays off of them.[112] At work in her memoirs is the full range of voices that Renooz adopted, to express her personal vision and, by implication, to give shape and substance to her agency in a hostile world.

Renooz's autobiographical writing is deliberately eclectic. In part, her assemblage is the product of expedient composition. Begun in August 1890 while Renooz was nursing her dying son, the manuscript reflects haste and distraction. Why write out what can be taken directly from original sources? Rusty pins hold in place fragments of Renooz's childhood journal, letters she received and copies of those she sent, articles clipped from scholarly reviews and various newspapers, and pages torn from her other writings. This curious collage suggests Renooz's more ambitious intentions to encompass the whole of her work within the story of her life. The manuscript physically embodies and thereby captures the contrasting discursive practices in Renooz's self-consciously intertextual writing. At one point, citing Albert Kölliker's *Embryologie* (1882), she remarks how "I had only to add some citations here and there from the book . . . in order to lend more authority to my writing."[113] But Renooz had more subversive purposes in mind.

Throughout "Prédestinée" Renooz responds to other texts, most often the ones she attached to her manuscript. For instance, the correspondence she cites is not simply historical documentation that her readers can use, like footnotes, to verify the truth value of her narrative—though Renooz certainly had this purpose in mind, too. Rather, the letters are also sounding boards for her own ideas; they are voices for her to interpret, to correct, or to refute, including the ingenuous letters written by her childhood friends. "In copying my friends' letters," Renooz writes, "I have come to realize that in speaking of me they were continuously praising *my kindness.* That seems to be only an epistolary convention. But, no, in reality kindness was characteristic of the Renoz family, and I take after my father in that. He was the embodiment of kindness itself."[114] For Renooz no correspondence was transparent or innocent. The discursive significance of every missive had to be assessed and contested for the sake of the sacred mission entrusted to her, that only she understood and could express.

Renooz's memoirs also challenge the books they quote. Every scholarly text receives the same critical treatment. Darwin's *The Origin of Species* is only the most obvious manifestation of this habit. There are dozens of others: Ernest Renan's *La Vie de Jésus* (1863), René Descartes's *Discours sur la méthode* (1637), Jules Michelet's *Bible de l'humanité* (1864), Jean-Jacques Rousseau's *Confessions* (1781–88), and more, all by men, of course. But where Renooz found ideas of value, she adopted a less confrontational style despite her contestatory purposes. In reference to Antoine Fabre d'Olivet's *La Langue hébraïque restituée* (1816), a work central to her interpretation of the Old Testament, she remarked parenthetically how she must always read "between the lines with this intuition of mine which enables me to apprehend some things that others do not even see."[115] In time Renooz quoted or cited fewer and fewer books by other authors, because she wanted to free her work from contaminating influences. Renooz found it increasingly burdensome to critique everything that challenged her clearly defined vision: "How petty I find literati, how paltry I find their work, how false are the ideas that science will rectify, and how this eternal glorification of men's force and love tires me!"[116]

Renooz was perhaps the most combative in her accounts of conferences. After 1890, during a period of intellectual activism, she was particularly assiduous in attending and giving public lectures on issues of immediate concern to her. Her memoirs provide deliberately polemical reports of these face-to-face exchanges. In promoting her own ideas, she began "to understand how difficult it is for readers to digest all of my ideas if they are not presented in the form of oral instruction, followed by conversation and discussion."[117] As for the ideas of others, Renooz had few flattering things to say. In March 1892, during a meeting of the Solidarité des Femmes, Marie Pierre openly called on Renooz to document her assertions by references either to recognized authorities or to scientific experimentation. In response to this charge, Renooz wrote, "I am told, 'You don't perform experiments and gather data,' while I do just that. I am told, 'You're engaged in philosophical *speculation*,' while I am fighting precisely that."[118] In this way, Renooz's memoirs become a locus for intense public debate.

But the principal focus of Renooz's "Prédestinée"—and most of her other personal papers—is on the press. More than four boxes of her personal papers are devoted to newspaper clippings on various subjects, most of them concerning her interests in women and their destiny, including articles on divorce, prostitution, and domestic violence. After 1890 Parisian newspapers became her primary source of information and reference. Her memoirs mention more than a dozen different dailies—most often *Le Matin, Le XIXe Siècle, Le Figaro, La Petite République,* and *Le Temps*—whose accounts of her ideas and activities she scrupulously followed. Nearly an obsession, the press offered her the publicity and the medium that she needed for her work, just as it provided her the positions and the discourse that she sought to contest. The polemical edge to her efforts at explanation and justification in her memoirs is obviously derived from the newspapers she read, mimicked, and opposed. Renooz's most important public forum for her ideas was the press; and her memoirs are filled with its rhetorical gestures, with its discursive practices, despite her opposition to everything that the press represented.

When the first story of the Dreyfus Affair appeared in print, for example, Renooz immediately perceived its personal significance. "In reading this I understood right away, from the first article, that this was a devilish intrigue and that this man was not guilty."[119] She then drew explicit parallels between Captain Dreyfus and herself: both were social pariahs and victims of unjust persecutions, she felt. And she wrote the Dreyfus family to offer her assistance.[120] By 1903, in deliberate imitation of Emile Zola's famous open letter originally published in *L'Aurore,* Renooz drew up her own list of accusations. "In the manner of the Dreyfus affair and Zola's manifesto, I too am making public my indictments"—and she identified eleven specific charges against the scholars who had obstructed her mission on behalf of suffering humanity.[121] Renooz never published her list, maybe because she had already adopted the appropriate pose in her memoirs. Either to dispute or to corroborate, Renooz's prose invariably resorts to confrontation.

This clash of voices in Renooz's memoirs appears in another, less overt guise. By 1905, in the face of much opposition, she had despaired of seeing her work accepted, a pessimism reflected in the final pages of her manuscript. For the next eight years, Renooz's autobiography lapses into annual summaries of fruitless activity, frustrated predictions, and extended lamentations. At times the memoirs resemble an appointment diary of her daily routine, her meetings and correspondence, interspersed with angry commentary. Each new year brought forth predictions based on horoscopes acquired from street peddlers and auguries sought from random searches among words in a dictionary. "In order to give myself consolation or hope," Renooz wrote in 1908, "I consult my oracle every month. My mind can make dictionary words speak to it in this intimate conversation."[122] Finally, in November 1913, Renooz's memoirs fall silent; apparently there seemed no point in continuing the discursive combat she had waged for more than twenty-three years.

Renooz did manage to write and publish an autobiography, but she did so under another author's name.[123] In 1902 Renooz agreed to Henry Carnoy's request that he produce a brief intellectual biography of her. A professor at the Lycée Carnot in Paris, Carnoy had been the "author" of many other such portraits. His standard terms included a generous provision for Renooz to participate in the work's composition, effectively allowing her to write it herself, which she did.[124] In its use of extensive quotation, especially from Renooz's previously published article in *La Religion laïque et universelle* (1888), the final product closely resembles her memoirs' themes, style, and organization.[125] The voices in the text are recognizably Renooz's. Fully one-fourth of the sixty-page book was copied from Renooz's other work, much like her longer, unpublished autobiography, to provide a reasonable summary of Renooz's distinctively synthetic vision in science, philosophy, and history up to 1902.

Renooz's interests in natural history were also personal. In her memoirs, she claimed that her work on evolution began during the 1879 international exhibition in Paris. "During our walk through one of the Exposition galleries, my husband brought the anatomy books to my attention," she explained. "I looked at them, [I] examined them, I was captivated by them. They were on histology; it just occurred to me that here was the foundation of all my work, all of the science that I have been reconstituting."[126] Such creative moments underlie her science, based as it was on intuitive insights and analogies drawn from everyday life. Science for her was never less than *connaissance*, the entire universe of interconnected knowledge, as she perceived it.[127] In her work, Renooz often resorted to ad hominem inquiry, which rarely served her interests in debate with other scientists. According to Clémence Royer, a frequent target of Renooz's pointed criticism, "she has defended . . . a hypothesis that everything has been invented by women, that during an early epoch women governed the world, and that Moses himself was a woman."[128] In light of Renooz's reputation, it is easy to understand her allegations that Royer had turned the staff at Marguerite Durand's newspaper *La Fronde* against her work.

It is also easy to understand the development of Renooz's publications in science. Over time her strictly disciplinary research in natural history gave way to much more interdisciplinary, more humanistic concerns derived from Renooz's personal vision. For example, her first book, *L'Origine des animaux* (1883), takes a more or less rigorous scientific approach to a problem in evolution. The same can be said of her second volume, *La Force* (1888), in physics. "At the outset *force* and matter must be defined," she contended forthrightly in the latter book. "We need to know how one comes from the other, what is the mechanism at work in this change of state, what are the causes that give it birth, [and] the effects that result from it."[129] In each case, the table of contents reflects familiar terms, topics, and approaches, like textbooks in their respective fields of inquiry, even though their conclusions proved controversial: animal life evolved from plants, force is incandescent radiation from the sun's combustion, and the earth is gradually gathering heat.[130] Renooz thus uses traditional categories of analysis in order to arrive at her new science:

> This synthesis shows us the relation that exists between all phenomena in the Universe. These are the principles on which detailed studies in each branch of physics can be undertaken. They are also the foundation for biological studies. In order to understand life, the forces prevailing in the Universe that foster new worlds must be known first of all; biological phenomena are just one manifestation of these forces. This is what we have demonstrated in the following books of our *Nouvelle Science*.[131]

Renooz's next volume, *Le Principe générateur de la vie* (1892), sustained this effort to integrate discrete inquiries in the disciplines of physics and biology.

With the publication of *La Psychologie comparée de l'homme et de la femme* in 1898, however, Renooz ventured further into normative issues. Her concerns had clearly shifted from science per se to its social implications as suggested by her personal experience. The analysis in this book, she admits, was based in part on study of her husband's temperamental personality, in part on the mission of the Société Néosophique.[132] It was the first volume of *La Nouvelle Science* subvened by the Néosophes. Its outline moves explicitly from psychology to morality. "The moment where sexual life begins in ontogenetic or phylogenetic evolution—for one is the mirror image of the other—marks the moment when all the psychic disorders in society, that is, in the individuals who make it up, are translated into social facts. This is the origin of evil, violence, falsehood, and injustice."[133] The corrective for this development concerns Renooz here at least as much as its basis in science. Consequently, among other recommendations, Renooz prescribes the moral duties necessary to remedy the evils she sees in modern society—ten commandments for men and another ten for women.[134]

The rest of Renooz's writing follows suit. She ceased work altogether on the other volumes planned for *La Nouvelle Science* in order to revise those she had already written, emphasizing the experiential at the expense of the experimental. "A general rule," she posited in her memoirs, "is to be suspicious of authors who garnish their books with Latin terms, figures, and algebraic formulas intended to dazzle the reader. . . . The more obscure the evidence the more incorrect the conclusions, because truth is always simple and obvious."[135] Renooz's other projects turned to moral and epistemological critiques of positivism as an ideology in both science and society. In 1898 she published *La Science et l'empirisme,* an essay demonstrating that observation and experimentation had not provided the desired results and that it was time to return to the abstract method, the *mathesis,* which was the science of order in ideas and argumentation.[136] Because this instinctive rationalism came naturally to women, Renooz believed, they were the source of true knowledge and morality. "Only woman can *know* and *explain* herself to man."[137] Such a conclusion was clearly based on her own experience.

After 1900 the autobiographical elements to Renooz's expository writing become increasingly obvious. What had been only suggestions in her reliance on self-evident analogies and ad hominem defense of them in her work took on a more deliberate character in Renooz's history of religion.[138] Here she assumed the role of high priestess, redeemer, and goddess of truth and renewal. The history of human thought and morality, her *Ere de vérité,* required six large volumes to trace the origins and development of women in Western religion, the result of which would be Renooz's single-handed restoration of their ancient knowledge and authority. "The source of all truth is the *female Mind*"—that is, her own—Renooz wrote in the introduction to her enormous undertaking.[139] For the next five pages, she summarized all seven volumes, three of them never written, of *La Nouvelle Science*, to highlight the personal intellectual context for her study of religion.

What she sought to accomplish was nothing less than the restitution of women's lost knowledge, "to create a *New Science* which is like knowledge in the ancient world, a synthesis of Nature's laws. Without it the analytic and concrete science of men—without directing ideas—will remain forever sterile."[140] According to Renooz, the first divinities and the leaders of their worship in ancient civilization had been visionary females just like her. This *théogonie* was the source of eternal truth, the secrets of which have been lost in the violent efforts of men to replace it with another of their own making. Consequently, the history of civilization has been in fact the history of a brutal dispossession of Renooz-like women and their natural spirituality. The evidence for this great struggle between the sexes can be read in the scriptures, as reconstituted by the late eighteenth-century Hebraicist Fabre d'Olivet and read by "the new instructor of humanity." Because male leaders were anxious to hide their usurpation of power, Renooz argued, they had the scriptures rewritten, replacing all female deities with Yahweh and all female figures with male prophets. Her sacred mission was to restore these mysteries to their original sense.

The first object of Renooz's attention was a rereading of the Christian scriptures and their fatal mythology. "The New Testament is only the recollection of the story of David, the distorted teaching of Mysteries, the story of Johana attributed in part to Jesus, and the rewriting of her Gospel recalling the antique rule of the female Mind and announcing her resurrection in order to restore the world, such as it had once been, under the moral law of Myriam."[141] But once humanity has learned the true source of wisdom, thanks to Renooz's efforts, it will be transformed. In the next sixty years, she predicted, the atavism of male authority would destroy itself, and women would remake the world in their own image, restoring religion and reconstituting the family. The result Renooz promised in schematic fashion: "peace, calm, happiness. A slackening of sexual activity. The forms of humanity to come: man the animal, woman the spirit." In short, the final chapter of history would be the realization of all her life's work.[142]

In addition to the deeply personal features of Renooz's science and history writing, there was her active involvement in polemical journalism. She never shied from a fight. Her direct participation in the press began with her service as the Paris correspondent for *L'Indépendance belge* for ten months in 1893. For the next fifteen years, Renooz contributed articles to other newspapers on the topics she cared most to discuss, usually on science, religion, and women. Similarly, she kept careful watch on the press, cutting out articles and filing them away for future reference. Most clippings concern accounts and theories of crime, suicide, prostitution, violence, pornography, mental illness, and superstition, suggesting the degeneration of public manners and mores with the supremacy of men and the prevailing ideology of social darwinism. Drawn from many of the same Parisian papers that she cited in her memoirs, but also from more respectable periodicals in literature and science, these themes are entirely consistent with Renooz's own views of society.[143]

One instance of Renooz's personal engagement in the press deserves attention. It concerns her theory of radiant energy, which she felt made climatic conditions at the north and south poles particularly dangerous. In the first volume to *La Nouvelle Science,* Renooz had asserted the primacy of oxygen as a force in the universe.[144] The inordinate consumption of oxygen by the sun in particular made its rays the primary source of physical and spiritual animation on earth. But when the sun's rays hit the earth tangentially, as they do at the poles, the result is a turbulence unmediated by the earth's absorption of their energy. "The consequences of this are that all unfixed objects on this part of the globe must be caught up by the movement caused by tangential radiation and swept by it into the depths of space."[145] The winds at the poles, Renooz warned, preclude any possibility of exploration there. For this reason, Renooz wrote to the editor of *Le Matin* explaining the failure of the polar expedition by balloon undertaken by S.-A. Andrée in 1897; a similar fate, she stated, awaited this Swede's foolhardy imitators.

In light of Renooz's theories, based as they were on her intuitive epistemology, this view made perfect sense. Its expression in the eight newspaper articles she clipped and saved for her memoirs, however, was much less sensible. The published responses to her warning were unequivocally cruel.[146] Several journalists made fun of her, while other writers like the geographer Elysée Réclus flatly contradicted her: "The frightful storms that Nansen [one of Renooz's sources] discussed are no more frightful than other storms in the tropics."[147] But Renooz was unmoved. Her original article, she noted in her memoirs, had been travestied by the press; its scientific language had been deliberately reformulated to make her look absurd. As M. Dautherive, the editor of *Le Matin,* admitted in a letter to Renooz, "It seems impossible to me for a newspaper to clarify such difficult problems. Readers do not possess language as scientific as yours, Madame."[148] Renooz's adversarial practice had to be translated into a less personal language in order to make her views intelligible. In this case, Renooz failed, primarily because she drew no distinction between her ideas and her identity.

Another discursive extension of Renooz's being is her correspondence. She was constantly writing to friends and family, especially late in life, in part because she wanted to keep in touch, in part because she wished to recapture the past, "the letters helping much in recovering lost memories."[149] Apparently much of Renooz's later correspondence was actually written to recall events and ideas to establish a record for posterity. Few if any of Renooz's extant letters to others are original; nearly all of them are copies and re-creations that she made long after the fact. For example, in 1891 she presumably wrote to Célia Schacre about the injuries she sustained while falling down a flight of concrete steps, jamming two fingers of her writing hand and necessitating her daughter's service as a scribe. But the letter to Schacre appears in the same, hurried hand as letters she wrote long before and long after the fall.[150] Only later in life, in the midst of depression, old age, and poverty, did Renooz's handwriting, on increasingly small, odd scraps of paper, change noticeably.

Similarly, the letters to her children read like official documents, closing with impersonal signatures, C. Muro or Céline, never with an affectionate "maman," nickname, or initial. The bulk of Renooz's correspondence concerns invitations to the conferences that she gave and refutations of people's accounts of what they heard there, usually those of the press. One-fourth of her extant correspondence is what she sent, not what she received; and nearly 10 percent of it, almost all dated after 1914, provides no identifiable addressee. Perhaps one-half or more of Renooz's archive is deliberately coordinated with her memoirs and is virtually indistinguishable from it. Such details suggest post hoc reconstitution of Renooz's later papers for the purposes of making them all serve her personal narrative and self-conception.

Renooz tentatively explored two other forms of more or less explicit autobiographical writing: the travelogue and the novel. In 1864, while she was living in Madrid, she wrote a brief essay (later included in her memoirs) on Spanish manners and mores; it noted the cultural differences between Spaniards and Belgians, of course, and their implications in the lives of women.[151] Four years later, she attempted to write a novel entitled *Evariste Lecourier à la recherche d'une croyance*, based on the life of a skeptical young man who falls in love with an Englishwoman. He asks her father for her hand in marriage and receives a positive response, on one condition — that the young man have a religion. So he studies, travels the world, finds all religions in the same state of decadence, and returns to Paris, where he discovers the Natural Religion that will regenerate humanity. This effort was obviously a device for Renooz, in the midst of a deep spiritual crisis, to review religious ideas and to define another of her own. Ideas for two other ventures into prose fiction in 1874, *La Naissance d'une république* about the fall of the Spanish Queen Isabella (1830–1904) and *Le Roman d'un jeune prêtre* about the marriage of a priest, were never developed.[152] Renooz's personal interests in science, religion, and autobiography ultimately prevailed.

In Renooz's mind, these disparate concerns were all of a piece, and her work on them was the manifestation of a force beyond her control. Her destiny was realized in a lifetime of writing and its concomitant commitment, independence, and above all, action. As Hélène Brion stated, Renooz was "an ace in good form to nail you equally well in the natural sciences, prehistory, and ancient history"; in short, she was an "indefatigable feminist."[153] This intimate relationship between Renooz's experience and her ideas was also emphasized in the *Dictionnaire biographique international* by Gilbert Froidure d'Aubigné: "In all her works is found a quality of originality that comes from the fact that she states her own personal views and nothing else. This is why these views are not found anywhere else. It is the most independent manifestation of the female mind."[154] Even the newspaper caricatures of Renooz and her ideas, especially on the vegetable origins of animal life, contributed to her sense of a destiny made manifest.[155]

After a brief illness, Renooz died at home in Paris on Tuesday, 22 February 1928. The devoted members of the association she had founded in 1897, the Société Néosophique, arranged for her body to be cremated at the Père Lachaise cemetery, where "the great Céline Renooz" was honored with a small ceremony, marking the minor cult that had developed before her death.[156] As Renooz instructed in her will, the society saw her last volume into print and transferred her twenty-four boxes of papers to Marie Louise Bouglé. Nearly everything she wrote is now in the Bibliothèque Historique de la Ville de Paris for posterity to read and to learn from her personal experience and her equally personal visionary discourse, notwithstanding the conflicted relations that they represent.

Unlike Marie Leroyer and Geneviève Bréton, Céline Renooz fashioned an assertive, indeed combative public life. Few women have dared to confront their subordination so openly, perhaps so quixotically, with so few concrete results to show for their ardent efforts. But Renooz never considered herself a feminist so much as a scientist, a historian, and a visionary. This latter self-concept was in effect the product of an incomplete discursive self—a self that Leroyer and Bréton developed more fully in their autobiographical writings—projecting instead an otherwise discreet relational identity into her concerted activities on behalf of her ideas. Nevertheless, like Leroyer in writing her novels and Bréton in mentoring her son's literary career, for example, Renooz defined her private being in a variety of personal expressions. The genre mattered little. The process of self-construction, however contradictory the results, remained very much the same for all three women. As the study of their feminist traces suggests in the next chapter, Leroyer, Bréton, and Renooz each in her own way demonstrated a common concern for agency and resistance in language within a patriarchal context.

Chapter six

❧ The Traces of Feminist Consciousness

> Particularly in France, words carry more weight than ideas.
> — George Sand, *Indiana*

What is feminist consciousness? Such a provocative question is impossible to answer to everyone's satisfaction. But Gerda Lerner offers one response that is worth serious consideration. "Feminist consciousness consists [of] (1) . . . the awareness of women that they belong to a subordinate group and that, as members of such a group, they have suffered wrongs; (2) the recognition that their condition of subordination is not natural, but socially determined; (3) the development of a sense of sisterhood; (4) the autonomous definition by women of their goals and strategies for changing their condition; and (5) the development of an alternate vision of the future."[1] In the narrowest sense of this definition, very few women would qualify as feminists. Disputes readily arise over exactly what is women's subordination, its social construction, the nature and utility of sisterhood, the goals and strategies to address women's issues, and of course, the future of and for women. As self-conscious theory and practice, feminism is hotly contested.

In a much broader sense, however, many women are more feminist than they think, including those who eschew the label and decry the women's movement.[2] I want to argue here that Marie Leroyer, Geneviève Bréton, and Céline Renooz are among the latter group. Each of them recognized profound gender inequalities, the arbitrariness of their roles, the special bonds they had with like-minded women, the need to develop priorities and ways to achieve them, and the possibilities of freer lives for themselves and other women. The evidence for this consciousness lies clearly in their relations and their relationships. Each in her own way lived and gave voice to feminism as a historical phenomenon far beyond the confines of a politics per se. Their feminism was instead a deliberate discursive practice based on painful personal experience in a man's world. How they responded to this reality in their writing provides the evidence, the traces rather, of a feminist consciousness.

Avant la lettre

It is ironic that all three women were either indifferent or hostile to the women's movement as they knew it. Leroyer is conspicuous for saying nothing about the organized politics of women's rights, primarily because it received relatively scant public attention before the French Third Republic.[3] The violence of the 1848 revolution and the 1871 Paris Commune were of more immediate concern to Leroyer, despite her sympathies for the Saint-Simonian socialists, like Pierre Leroux, who were among the first to organize on behalf of women's emancipation. "In a word I want for everyone to have her place in the sun," she wrote Gustave Flaubert in 1857.[4] This vague aspiration was shared by Geneviève Bréton, with one critical difference: Bréton knew and disliked those "blind and stupid females" who "clamor for women's rights."[5] She firmly believed that women had other means at their disposal to achieve their interests. "And what masculine power equals that of a woman who *loves* and is *determined?*" Bréton asked rhetorically.[6]

Not even Renooz considered herself a "feminist," as the term developed some time after 1880.[7] Her conversion to concerted action on women's issues had occurred upon reading Jenny d'Héricourt's *La Femme affranchie* (1860) in 1865; and when she moved to Paris ten years later, she became active in various organizations, attending conferences and congresses on well-defined issues of interest to women. "My mind was recovering from the great suffering that I had experienced among men," she noted in 1894. "I understand now that Woman must count on herself alone to make the new world."[8] But Renooz disavowed the most commonly used label for her commitments. "I am not a *Feminist*," she wrote Gustave Hervé in 1911. "I do not want to be associated with those like Séverine and Maria Vérone who are paraded about in the struggle for the political rights of women."[9] Her focus rested on social complementarity and moral harmony, not on political equality and continued conflict. So for Renooz the efforts of a Hubertine Auclert to secure female suffrage was nothing less than a single-minded fanaticism that was demeaning to women, a male politics in drag, that would only lead to more discord for everyone.[10]

This overt antagonism hides more than it reveals. Despite their distance from the women's movement in modern France, all three women were passionate about the matters it addressed—namely, the inequalities of women in public and private life. They thought hard and wrote much about their situations in marriage and the family, in religion, and in politics, because there was far more at stake than their rights and liberty: it was their very identity as women and their dignity as human beings. Leroyer, Bréton, and Renooz defined for themselves positions that in retrospect can indeed be called feminist, even if they disdained the particular configuration that more vocal and more visible commentators have given to various feminisms since the eighteenth century.[11] In the context of their deep commitments, fierce independence, and valiant struggles, then, these women's views, and the consciousness that their writings suggest, clearly deserve closer examination.

Marriage was a major problem for all three of them. Leroyer, for example, never married. As she explained to George Sand in 1849, "According to civil and social laws marriage seemed to me the most unjust, the falsest, the most monstrous of institutions. In accepting it I would have betrayed the truth, my heart, and my conscience. I could never do that."[12] Moreover, religious dogma and the law sharply constricted a woman's physical and emotional being, and were thus major sources of Leroyer's own intense personal misery. The resulting sexual repression was more than she could bear. "The principles by which I was reared made me regard love outside of marriage as a crime. So placed between my beliefs, my feelings, and my convictions, I necessarily suffered frightful struggles. Only God can appreciate and know the moral and physical torture that often reduced me to despair."[13] Whatever the *bien-pensant* social conventions of provincial Angers, notwithstanding her unfulfilled sensuality, Leroyer would never submit to the oppression she saw her own mother endure in an otherwise perfectly unexceptional marriage.

Bréton did marry, but with misgivings that arose long before her wedding and remained with her long afterward. She refused to be sold by her family to a wealthy suitor she could never love; she suspected that Henri Regnault's strong will would not make her happy; and she loathed the infidelity that was more or less expected in bourgeois marriages of convenience. "Alas, a woman's *Happiness* is something more complex and difficult than is thought. Feeling the ridicule of one's husband, seeing the estrangement of everyone else, submitting to continuous nonsense, experiencing *boredom* at every moment, not sharing any of the inclinations of one's partner in life! Is that happiness?"[14] In her case, this premonition of marriage's fleeting bliss proved all too prescient. After ten often difficult years with her husband Alfred Vaudoyer, she remarked bitterly how her own marriage had become "a fool's agreement where I gave everything, where I received nothing."[15] The emotional symmetry in their relations that she had longed for all her adult life simply would never be.

Renooz, too, married, and was clearly the most unhappy of the three women. As she stated in the preface to her memoirs, her interest in the subject came from painful personal experience. Marriage was women's slavery to men, an utter financial and legal dependency disguised by an apparent emotional and spiritual equality. Soon after marrying Angel Muro, she lamented, "I felt that life was going to become a battle, since I had beside me a being who at certain unforeseeable moments became my enemy—*the intimate enemy*—the most dangerous because the wife is delivered up to him without protection."[16] The beneficiaries of this brutal institution were not the wives but the husbands, whose control of women was ensured by law and social convention, as she stated in her *Psychologie comparée de la femme et de l'homme* in 1898: marriage actually ensured men's triumph in the eternal battle of the sexes, which resulted from their fundamentally different natures and had led to the destruction of women's spiritual power.

Renooz spoke at length about her views of marriage in an interview she gave to a reporter for the *Chicago Tribune* in 1922. Based on her concerns with the displacement of women from their original roles in ancient religion, her remarks emphasized the utility of marriage to patriarchal power. "What a terrible mistake! It has warped the whole social fabric, brought about all this confusion of divorce and free love." Instead of a dowry, married women should have a home of their own, and mothers should be supported financially by paternity taxes paid only by men. "If marriage could be arranged on this basis, all the social turmoil would stop of its own accord. Women would inevitably be put back on their pedestal, men would admire them and obey them, society would be organized along lines of peace instead of war, in short . . . a return of the golden age."[17] Renooz believed that marriage was symptomatic of all that was wrong with Western culture and that it could be dramatically improved in a more harmonious society where women once again ruled. After the disaster of World War I, this view made a lot of sense.

A problem closely related to marriage for Leroyer, Bréton, and Renooz was, of course, women's place in the family. Leroyer, for one, was committed to working actively outside the home, despite the many difficulties facing single women, as she explained to Victor Mangin in 1867.[18] She greatly admired the strong independent women she featured prominently in her collection of stories *Figures historiques et légendaires,* such as Queen Berthe, Christine de Pisan, Marie Stuart, and Mesdames de Lafayette and d'Epinay. As she put it, "despite time and oblivion, a part of Christine de Pisan's soul remains for us in her works!"[19] Leroyer's romantic soul was sensitive to the creative spirit, wherever it existed, in men and women alike. As an author herself, Leroyer recognized how valiant were the efforts of women writers to overcome the obstacles to their craft. "In fact for certain superior natures, art is a noble and holy mission, because it serves to make others better and happier," regardless of familial context.[20]

Many times in her letters to Sand and Flaubert, Leroyer expressed a gender conflict in her unconventional household. On the one hand, she was responsible for a large number of needy dependents, just like a man; on the other hand, she felt no larger purpose in life but that responsibility, just like a woman. A matter beyond her control, this painful contradiction made her feel as if she were in a small boat lost at sea without a compass: "I felt utterly lost," she explained to Flaubert.[21] Hence her profound sympathy for the helpless, like Goethe's character Gretchen in *Faust:* "This poor Marguerite subject to an infernal power, is that not the story of all women? All feeble beings are at the mercy of other people's will."[22] Hence, too, Leroyer's infinite capacity for self-pity: "I missed my calling in life; I betrayed my nature; it's not my fault, but that of the milieu where I was born. Probably that's why I'm so unhappy."[23] Ordinarily Leroyer's empathetic understanding extended beyond gender to encompass every suffering creature, but the examples she invariably cited were, like herself, female.

Bréton felt equally torn by gender roles defined for her. When she became engaged to Regnault in October 1870, for instance, this ambivalence became acute. She pledged her troth to a man she truly loved and felt truly loved her, and yet she knew that in marrying him she would lose her precious freedom. Her independence and thus her happiness no longer lay in her own hands but in someone else's, whose interests could never always be hers. "I exercise my free will for the present that still belongs to me," she wrote apprehensively in her diary, adding that "the future . . . will belong to me if I can tie it with this thread, so quickly broken by violent passions, the stronger and more durable bond of deep mutual tenderness and shared trust."[24] She spent much of her engagement trying desperately to reassure herself that Regnault would indeed honor her trust. She pressed him at least twice, face-to-face and in writing, to keep his promise on a matter so vital to her identity.

Regnault's untimely death, however, forced Bréton to reconsider her resolution with other suitors like Jojotte, who repeatedly failed the test. She felt humiliated by the latter's casual sensuality and vain efforts to hide it from her. "Looking him calmly in the face! I see that [Clairin's eyes] evaded mine," she wrote of her disloyal friend long after her passion had cooled. "And I couldn't resist smiling. This time I played the male role. I had the courage to look him in the face; he was the one afraid of letting himself go, of compromising himself by going too far; and I felt the superiority of the one who loves, who gives, over the one who refuses."[25] In this way, however tenuously, she had a control over her gender that was more substantial than cross-dressing and acting a male character in the play performed for her father's sixty-first birthday.

More than either Leroyer or Renooz, perhaps because her diary offered the perfect occasion to do so, Bréton continued to think about gender issues. In 1870, she wrote critically of the women—"so very feminine, white and delicate, tight-waisted and undernourished"—fashionable thirty-five years earlier, whose insubstantial beauty was no longer in style.[26] When the Franco-Prussian War broke out later that summer, Bréton lamented, "What more stupefying existence than a woman's! She can do nothing but talk and talk without acting. It's ridiculous," especially in wartime.[27] In more ordinary times, Bréton loathed most parents' efforts to keep girls and young women utterly ignorant as well as innocent until their marriage. A life devoted exclusively to the family promised little more satisfaction. "Never has domestic life seemed to me so bourgeois and empty," she wrote again in 1870, "this spiritual and intellectual inertia, this annihilation of every ability, this imbecilic slumber."[28] A mother's active participation in her children's education interested Bréton a good deal more, because she could share in their intellectual liberation. And that's exactly what she did with her own Marianne, Jean-Louis, and Michel.

Renooz also recognized the social construction of gender at a young age. When her father died in 1856, she looked forward to inheriting his books, until her brother Ernest claimed them all for himself. "As for you, you will marry," he quipped. "And since every young man has books, your husband will have his library, so you don't need to have your own books, you will have your husband's." To Renooz's pointed question about her marrying a man without any books, Ernest responded, "That's because he won't like to read, in which case you won't need to read either."[29] Renooz was also revolted to hear of the deal her husband Angel had struck with the physician attending her second pregnancy: the charge for delivering a baby boy was 250 francs; the charge for delivering a baby girl was nothing.[30] But the significance of this gratuitous denigration of the female did not move her to indignation until much later. In sharp contrast to the sexist norm was the lesson Renooz immediately drew from the cross-dressing Jane Dieulafoy, the noted photographer and archeologist: "It's when [both men and women] are seen in the same clothes that the difference prevailing between male and female minds becomes obvious," she wrote later in her memoirs.[31]

In response to such hostility, Renooz embraced the solidarity she felt with other women. This affinity remained with her from her schooldays onward. Despite vast cultural differences, she confessed to admiring her female relatives in Spain—her aunts Irene and Vicenta, her stepmother-in-law Valentine, and her sister-in-law Juanita. Renooz also frankly preferred the company of women in her professional work, hence the impulse behind her founding the *Revue scientifique de femmes* in 1888 and the leading role she gave to women for the regeneration of society in her history of religions. Although Renooz was sharply at odds with other women like Clémence Royer, Maria Deraismes, and Pauline Kergomard, she felt instinctively more at ease with them than she did with men. In 1911 she had a lunch with Mme de Bezobrazow that was typical of the lyrical moments Renooz had come to expect with her female colleagues, "in that situation of rest, attention, and intimacy."[32]

In fact nearly all of Renooz's professional activities grew out of such notions of gender. Even though she came to believe that all of humanity would benefit from her work, she learned firsthand of sexism repeatedly and sought to address it directly. Renooz found herself deliberately excluded from the laboratories and the learned societies where she might conduct experiments and communicate her results, all because of her sex. "I wasn't heard *because I was a woman.*"[33] In science, where the institutional authority of men had usurped the moral authority of women, Renooz remarked, the gendered inversion of roles provided the basis for a host of evils epitomized by the Darwinian struggle for survival. Survival of the fittest stood in marked contrast to her vision of a harmonious, symbiotic evolution of separate species.[34] Male science perpetuated the subordination of women by an epistemology that deprecated their manner of knowing intuitively as well as synthetically. Ultimately she hoped her vision—"a reconciliation of men and women as the foundation for renovation"—would overcome the battle of the sexes in science, of course, but also in the society responsible for it.[35]

Sexuality was a problem for all three women.[36] As previously mentioned, Leroyer was tortured by her physical need for a man, on the one hand, and her religious beliefs against extramarital sex, on the other. This problem lay at the heart of her religious crisis and the many letters she sent to Sand and Flaubert in the 1850s and 1860s. Similarly, Bréton found herself deeply ambivalent about the passion she felt as a young woman for Regnault. Although she never had sex with him, she expressed a profound longing for her fiancé that she rarely seems to have felt for her husband Alfred Vaudoyer. She did marry, but it was a sadder, wiser marriage, one entirely in keeping with her anger over the double standards at work in conventional bourgeois relations. As for Renooz, she was indifferent if not hostile to sexuality, which she considered a terrible mistake in evolutionary development that would be resolved when women are finally restored to their original divinity in the new moral order. Accordingly, she declared herself disgusted by the conventions of the wedding night. Like Leroyer and Bréton, Renooz defined a diffident sexual identity, one she always understood as in relationship with others.[37]

The gendered nature of religious belief preoccupied Leroyer, Bréton, and Renooz, too. The institutional presence and power of the Roman Catholic Church in France almost guaranteed critical commentary from these thoughtful women.[38] Leroyer, for example, thanks to her principled aversion to marriage, agonized long and hard over its religious implications. She was a devout Catholic in the romantic tradition of Félicité de Lamennais for much of her life; such faith was as necessary to her as it was to her mother. But Leroyer's conflict with the church over the sacrament of marriage led her to identify with a religious self-castrate from the second century: "Origen had long lived and suffered . . . from a painfully and laboriously charged career," Leroyer wrote of this early church father whose personal sacrifice symbolically resembled her own.[39] Moreover, Origen taught the redemption of both men and women: "Yes, like Origen I believe," she wrote Sand in 1849, "that the final goal is the general rehabilitation not just of men, but of all that exists."[40] Leroyer's kinship with Origen is obvious and was deliberate.

Leroyer's romantic pantheism was put to the test during a religious crisis that lasted more than fifteen years. Although she tended to a sentimental mysticism, including a belief in physical reincarnation and various out-of-body experiences, Leroyer found her defiance of the church's sacraments the source of prolonged hallucinations. Cut off from God by her refusal to confess and take communion, Leroyer feared for her soul. "Right or wrong I believe in confession, in the presence of God in communion. Imagine then my fear!" she exclaimed to Flaubert in 1857.[41] She had no faith in the priest to help her overcome this terrifying problem. When her godson Edouard Michel became paralyzed in 1861, Leroyer reached bottom: "I envy his fate, yes, . . . I envy this intellectual annihilation that leaves one a mere vegetable."[42] Only with the overwhelming loss of her shadow husband Mathurin Source did Leroyer finally release herself from dependence upon the church's control of her religious beliefs. Her release was facilitated by the reactionary politics of Pius IX and the first Vatican Council in 1864, which attacked the European women's movement, among other instances of modernism.

Of the three women under study here, Bréton was undoubtedly the most conventional in her religious practice. She remained a Roman Catholic all her life: "This heavenly joy that's worth everything to me is a great comfort," she remarked in 1870.[43] Like Leroyer, Bréton felt closest to liberal Catholicism, so long as it did not contradict her romantic pantheism and the spiritual freedom of creative souls.[44] She was deeply pained by Regnault's protestant skepticism of Roman Catholic dogma and by her daughter Marianne's refusal to baptize Sonny, her second son. Where Bréton drew her greatest strength as a woman was from the abbé de Lamennais's 1820 translation of Thomas à Kempis's *Imitation of Jesus Christ;* his ideal love in practice was very much her own during the Paris Commune, when she served as a nurse to the wounded *fédérés.*

Bréton had her own religious crisis, however, and it began long before Regnault's death. A full year and a half earlier, she had refused to fulfill her Ascension Day duties.[45] So when she put her faith to the test in January 1871, it failed her; Bréton could not understand how God could have allowed Regnault to die, "such a dreadful sacrilege."[46] "I no longer believe!" she said two days later, not long before she contemplated the *"moral suicide"* of retreating to a religious order—and more:[47] "The deep, horrible, murky green water [of the Seine] attracted me like a [magnet]!"[48] A brief stay at the Convent des Dames de la Retraite in July only compounded the pain she felt, knowing that her abrupt departure from home had deeply wounded her father. For the rest of her life, Bréton would question the church and its dogma; she kept her faith primarily for sentimental reasons: "How difficult it is to break the last bonds of poetry and memory that have tied me to Catholicism. . . . My mind accepts to the furthest extent possible the freedom of thought and scientific progress that no longer understands the language of faith. I am in a moment of moral crisis, my former faith is dead, I no longer pray, I no longer believe in prayer."[49] Bréton found herself too much of a republican to follow the church's conservative turn after the 1848 revolution and its strictures against independent women of her like.[50]

Renooz made a career of her religious views. But she said little about her own faith, primarily because she accepted no other creed than her own. Her father's Voltairian deism and her mother's outright atheism left their marks on her belief. All her adult life Renooz considered herself a freethinker in the mold of Ernest Renan, despite her tendencies to mysticism after 1900.[51] Seeing no ostensible results from her visit to the shrine at Notre Dame de Talence near Bordeaux not long after her marriage to Angel Muro, for instance, she concluded that it was no more than a symbol, "a representation of the living and acting *Woman,* and that's the true Notre Dame, the one who's living."[52] Her experiences with the openly reactionary role of the church in Spain led Renooz to advocate a secular religion of reason and humanity in order to combat intolerance and irrationality. In a letter to Mme Bourdin in 1906, Renooz stated that "the basis for Catholicism" was nothing less than "*the hate* or the fear of Woman."[53] To Cleyre Yvelin that same year, she wrote, "Catholicism's great sin is to have deified man and to have destroyed the Divinity of Woman."[54] The rest of her life was devoted to detailing this view.

A Discursive Presence

At the heart of these women's issues was their personal writing. No discussion of their implicit feminism can ignore these literate efforts to create identity and agency. Leroyer, Bréton, and Renooz were serious writers as well as self-conscious women; in their minds, the two phenomena were inextricably linked. For Leroyer, not to write was to be without life. She told Flaubert in good romantic fashion, "An author ordinarily puts his heart and soul in his work, because that work is himself" (even though she knew that women were authors, too).[55] This identification of author and work was most deliberate in

Leroyer's long, autobiographical letters, to be sure, but can also be seen in the memoirs that she began to write before 1859 and never finished. Although she apparently burned the uncompleted manuscript before she died, Leroyer still felt pleased. As she explained to Flaubert again in 1870, "If the work is long, so much the better; the greatest pleasure of writing is working at it; one wants to finish with it and [yet] one regrets having finished when the last page is written," because one's identity in the text is always evolving with the writing.[56]

Similarly, for Leroyer the act of literary creation was a magical escape to the ideal, a form of therapy often associated with the romantic movement. As she said to Flaubert in 1857, "The work, the love of literature and art, that's what keeps me living! It's my only refuge against grief and boredom!"[57] The link between the ideal and the real, between aspiration and consolation, is deliberate and necessary. "Nevertheless, we write to each other!" she assured Sand following the same lyrical logic. "It's my ultimate happiness, my last illusion. It's the sun's warmth in winter, the rare violets that make us remember and dream of spring. It's both a memory and a hope!"[58] Leroyer never understood, probably because she never wanted to understand, the efforts of literary realists to remove the romantic self from their creation. While Flaubert agonized over his every word in a deliberately impersonal craft, Leroyer continued, as a matter of principle, to write and read her soul into texts.

Leroyer consciously realized a gendered self in literature. Like her poor, simple-minded stepniece Agathe, she could not live without illusion in the midst of her emotional suffering; she needed a powerful antidote for the pain that came from living in a hostile world. Writing for Leroyer was thus a woman's creative cure for a man's cultural curse. "When I think of the repressed, actually the oppressed existence to which I have been condemned," she told Flaubert, "when I see the sad situation where I have been thrown, I am overwhelmed with pity."[59] In writing a review of his *Madame Bovary*, whose title character defined her conflicted existence, Leroyer let inspiration be her guide: "That did me good. I felt myself living again in saying what I think."[60] She always felt better, she said later, when she was writing, living outside herself, fulfilling her duty vicariously in a world of her own making. In response to Flaubert's allegations that her pain was a hysteria common among unmarried women, she wrote, "Yes, I believe that we [women can] desire the impossible, because the possible cannot satisfy us."[61] Consequently, like confession her writing was "a struggle of the will against powerlessness."[62] She was, after all, a woman like any other engaged in a struggle determined by gender.

Bréton's writing was a similar self-conscious effort to define herself as a woman. As they had been for Leroyer, literate activities were for Bréton a necessary pastime, a protection against boredom, an escape from the mundane everyday into the realm of the ideal. Five months into her marriage with Vaudoyer, she wrote, "Writing's exorcism is the sole remedy for the things that haunt you"; it was her lifelong endeavor to create another reality in the face of misery.[63] At times, in fact, there was no other reality; Bréton saw the world self-consciously through texts, both those she wrote and those she read. The letters Regnault wrote while he was at the front, for instance, were for Bréton his very presence. When she learned of Sand's death, she remarked, "This sole, truly passionate, generous, and simple heart spoke a special language more beautiful and still warmer than any other. It knew how to plumb the soul's depths."[64] Sand's books were more than mere amusement; they were a self speaking directly to another as no other author could. "This music truly moves me."[65]

Bréton's own writing was no less distinctive an identity. After her painful break with Jojotte, she wrote of herself as a book: "A new edition of Geneviève has appeared, reviewed and corrected, considerably revised and reduced from all that may be called grand feeling, poetic faith, and generous confidence . . . supplemented by a strong dose of skepticism and what we are accustomed to term common sense."[66] Bréton lived with "an inkstand in the head," in order to record the treasures of her heart in complete solitude.[67] Writing made this loneliness at once possible and bearable, as she discovered after an absence of five weeks from her isolated corner at Le Plessis where "I am writing in my room exactly as I had left it, right next to the same books opened to the same pages. I feel at home again in the order of my usual life, like a dress one has taken off and put back on again."[68] The result was the private space created by her diary that her sister Kate had violated one day, much to Bréton's dismay and anger, by reading it without permission. It was as if Kate sought "to break into a soul."[69]

Bréton's literate life was a gendered space. As a young woman writing alone in her diary, she self-consciously created an ideal alternative to the world controlled first by her family and then by the men in her life. A few months before her engagement to Regnault, she stated, "I've lived in the solitude of my soul for so many years that meditation has given me some notion of a world beyond," which her fiancé would come to represent for her.[70] But Regnault's sudden death left her bereft of that new ideal. A month later, she grimly imagined her marriage to a corpse in his crypt as "a solitude, a marriage without husband, a family without children."[71] For the rest of her life Bréton would seek a balance between the need for privacy to write and the need for family to share her life. Before she met and finally married Vaudoyer, she reflected: "I look back on this whole youth of solitude; my empty hands, my lonely hearth, the broad whiteness of the moonlight made me cry at night. Never had my loneliness been more complete; never had those astonishing first delightful [spring] days been awaited so fiercely to escape the emotional night that enclosed me."[72] The need for kindred spirits aside, Bréton's own family would never displace entirely the discursive space that she reserved for herself far from an alien and hostile world.

Renooz was not particularly self-conscious about her writing. Her occasional reflections about it are overshadowed by what she wanted to say and do. She admitted frankly that her writing was motivated mostly by an enormous need to carry the word.[73] Her mission was everything. Otherwise, in her memoirs especially, Renooz did suggest the same gendered pattern to her literate concerns that Leroyer and Bréton discussed. Years of unhappy marriage with Muro made writing an emotional compensation, too: "The taste for reading and study which solitude had fostered in me nearly became a necessity," she noted, ". . . and that created a great chasm between my husband and me."[74] Her science, as she called her work, helped her forget the emotional pain she suffered with the death of her children, one right after another, of tuberculosis. In this function, writing was no different for Renooz than it was for any other serious author, but the experiential impulse to create seemed to be stronger in her case.

In time Renooz failed to distinguish between her vision and her own being, making all her writing a form of self-discovery. "There are some lives whose history should be written," she remarked proudly in her memoirs, "because there are some lives that are a page from human psychology. The one that I am about to relate here is also a page from the history of modern science."[75] She meant, of course, herself; in Renooz's discursive practice, science and her life were all of a piece. Having invested everything in her work, Renooz still felt misunderstood, perhaps because her efforts bore so little fruit beyond the tomes she wrote and saw into print. "No one in the world has sounded the depths of my being," even when she was in Spain and had not yet undertaken any serious work. "My soul has been a closed book for everyone I've met up to now," necessitating the redaction of her autobiography.[76] She needed it to find herself as much as she did for telling others about her personal discoveries in the process. Ultimately she failed at both tasks.

Renooz was far more comfortable acting than reflecting. Her method of composition without revision suggests as much: she wrote nearly the entire first draft of *La Force* in one sustained sitting. And Renooz undertook her memoirs to demonstrate not only who she was, but also what she had done. More to the point, Renooz saw her work as part of a concerted campaign to redeem humankind, a redemption made possible only by women. As she put it, "All my life I appeared to be doing extraordinary things, and that quite simply because I have always wanted to be *natural*, to be a *true woman*."[77] This effort was preeminently a woman's task, because as Clémence Royer explained in an 1897 letter to Ghénia Avril de Sainte Croix, "She is above all a woman who wants to be a major player," though not in the positive sense that Renooz meant by it.[78] Once Renooz's identity as the redeemer had become firmly established in her mind, all her activities, literary or otherwise, were expressions of her womanhood: "It seemed to me that my fate was . . . to raise human intelligence, to guide it, to rectify it, to pacify men, *to create them*, so to speak, a second time in revealing to them a new moral world."[79]

To what extent, then, were these women actually feminists? Following Gerda Lerner's prescription, I would argue that they certainly saw themselves as members of a subordinate group whose suffering was not of their own making. In each case, these wrongs, especially in their married life, were initially perceived in personal terms and then generalized to all women like themselves. Similarly, they all recognized that their subordination was not a natural but a social phenomenon; physical differences were assumed, but roles in education, for example, which were assigned because of those differences, were certainly not. Leroyer, Bréton, and Renooz also expressed a sense of solidarity with other women in the misery that resulted from rude encounters with the gendered conventions in love relations. However much at odds were their sentiments, they articulated goals and strategies in their writing. Their ideas ranged from Leroyer's phalanstery in Angers and Bréton's focus on her children's education to Renooz's mission to restore women to their original spiritual vocation. Finally, all three women developed views of another life for women in the future, one freer, fuller, and happier than what they endured. In their autobiographical writings and their various traces of feminist consciousness, Leroyer, Bréton, and Renooz were confident that women's future should be nothing like their own painful past.

The similarity of vision among these three women ought not to obscure the differences among them (and with other women in modern France). Had they met each other, they most surely would have disagreed. Both Leroyer the romantic idealist and Bréton the reluctant realist were more discreet in their views than Renooz the self-aggrandizing visionary. Of course, none of them was intellectually inclined or temperamentally suited to sustain with other women a concerted challenge to their patriarchal circumstances. But in her combative paranoia, Renooz was incapable of cooperation with anyone; her trouble in establishing a discursive identity, in completing her memoirs, and in publishing her contradictory work shared in her overt, contentious public life. Most Frenchwomen, Leroyer and Bréton included, could never envisage such a role for themselves. Very few bourgeoises ever overcame their aversion to the socially embarrassing, demeaning spectacles that Renooz created for herself.

Yet in her insistent efforts at self-writing, Renooz had much in common with Leroyer, Bréton, and their like. However sharp the contrast in their outward faces, for all of them, their private world of ink and paper mattered much. Their diaries, letters, memoirs, and other work became a consuming passion and were the result of the same process by which these women defined themselves and their sense of agency. As George Sand suggested in *Indiana*, such personal language prevailed over publicly expressed ideas, often to the mystification of authors and readers alike. From this perspective, these women's ideological differences from one another and from others were resolved in their writing and the selves they attempted thereby to craft forthrightly if not always successfully. In this deliberative gesture, Renooz was hardly exceptional. The results were surprisingly uniform and the consequences even more surprisingly significant historically.

Other indiscreet women certainly shared in the same literate activity. Lesbians and kindred individualists living apart from men wrote of their lives (and occasionally of their loves) to the fascination and dismay of their readers in modern France. Although few writers expressed the provocative self-fashioning apparent in works by Rachilde and Renée Vivien—to name the best known—less extravagant voices dared to defy social convention in their personal narratives. Early in life, George Sand charted a well-documented separate course, inspiring Leroyer among others to strike out on their own. In 1914 Dr. Madeleine Pelletier suggested that young women could avoid "the ugliness of sexuality" by living together; in this way they could also avoid "the solitude that is the great sadness of celibacy," as Pelletier herself knew it.[80] Arria Ly made no secret of her preference to keep company with her mother (in death as in life), while Colette gave eloquent voice to the private world of women more at ease with one another than with men. Clearly women's autobiographical writing assumed various guises no more outrageous than Renooz's, to very much the same purpose.

In short, many writers besides Leroyer, Bréton, and Renooz came to express what Karen Offen terms a "relational feminism."[81] But the particular views of these three women were probably the most pervasive among nineteenth-century French bourgeoises, and they contrast sharply with the more "individualist feminism" that developed in the Anglo-American context. As Offen puts it, "In order to fully comprehend the historical range and possibilities of feminism, we must locate the origins and growth of these ideas within a variety of cultural traditions," such as Leroyer, Bréton, and Renooz experienced them in their own historical setting.[82]

This more inclusive definition of feminism is controversial; it is one rooted in a specific time and place, as opposed to a more exclusive definition based on a universalist and absolute appeal to the transhistorical individual. But the relational character of modern French feminism, at least as these women expressed it, remains firmly and transformationally at odds with culture and society defined by the norms of men. Leroyer, Bréton, and Renooz accepted their sexual difference not as a mark of weakness, but as a source of profound strength. And their self-conscious identity as women, as they gave voice to it in their autobiographical writing, was surely what made this assertion possible.[83]

✌ Conclusion

We need to replace the notion that social power is unified, coherent, and centralized with something like Michel Foucault's concept of power as dispersed constellations of unequal relationships, discursively constituted in social "fields of force." Within these processes and structures, there is room for a concept of human agency as the attempt (at least partially rational) to construct an identity, a life, a set of relationships, a society within certain limits and with language—conceptual language that at once sets boundaries and contains the possibility for negation, resistance, reinterpretation, the play of metaphoric invention and imagination.[1]

The discreet feminism expressed by Marie Leroyer, Geneviève Bréton, and Céline Renooz defines a conceptual language, I think, much like the one that historian Joan Wallach Scott argues for here. Their self-conscious writing made possible an identity and a sense of agency; their deliberate discourse fostered not the organized resistance of the women's movement but the dignity of individuals responsible to themselves and to others with comparable problems. Leroyer, Bréton, and Renooz were all-too-aware of women's issues, most notably in marriage, education, the church, and the law; and they thought seriously about what women could do about them, especially in their relationships with men, with their children, with their faith, and with other women. In their autobiographical writing lies evidence of a feminist consciousness.

Leroyer's, Bréton's, and Renooz's discursive efforts, however, differ from the many different feminisms articulated in nineteenth-century France.[2] Although these three agreed on much—all of them advocated republican politics, a less powerful Roman Catholic Church, a more flexible religious dogma, a greater symmetry in married life, a better education for girls, and a more substantial public role for women—they had many significant differences of perspective, in particular on the women's movement. Leroyer, Bréton, and Renooz might have been Christian feminists like Marie Maugeret if they had been better Catholics; they might have been socialist feminists like Elisabeth Renaud if they had not been so well heeled; they might have been active suffragists like Maria Pognon if they had cared enough about the vote; or they might have been moderate republican feminists like Sarah Monod if they were willing to be more publicly assertive. In one way or another, whatever their strong sympathies for certain positions, none of these women found any of the organized advocates of women's rights congenial enough to support.

Leroyer, Bréton, Renooz, and many other thoughtful women like them were feminist misfits. They fall neatly into no one group, probably because the condition of women in modern France (and elsewhere) was too diverse to be captured by any single reform platform. Class, religion, region, and culture all served to complicate the success (or failure) of a political movement, and that of feminists more than most: their concerns were so numerous, their interests so broad. A bourgeoise was less angry about pay inequities than she was about property rights; a devout Catholic was appalled by the freethinking advocate of birth control; a provincial was more worried about social norms than her Parisian sister; and the literary salonkeeper had more influence than the wealthy but barely literate *rentière*. Diversity made unity difficult if not impossible. In an increasingly differentiated society, partial feminists were most likely to be the vast majority of Frenchwomen.[3]

Distinctions

A fragmented consciousness owes much to women's immediate circumstances. Despite intense literate interests in common, for instance, the worlds of Leroyer, Bréton, and Renooz differed substantially from one another. They varied in wealth—Bréton was by far the richest, Renooz the poorest—though all of them were urban and middle class in what was still very much a country of peasants.[4] They also sustained different religious sentiments—Bréton the idealist was a better Roman Catholic than Leroyer the pantheist, and Renooz the atheist remained a freethinker her entire life. Moreover, Leroyer never married and Renooz left her husband after sixteen awful years. Unlike Leroyer and Renooz who lived for many decades apart from men, Bréton remained faithful to her spouse for thirty-seven years.[5] And temperamentally they viewed themselves and their world differently: Leroyer detested the petty-minded conformity of Angers, Bréton adored the cultural richness of Spain and Italy, and Renooz challenged the scientific community's institutional control of the truth. It is thus not hard to see why they saw women's issues as variously as they did.

Leroyer gave voice to one particular concern: the emotional ideal of sexual relations. More than any of her contemporaries, except perhaps the utopian socialists, Leroyer sought the freer expression of women's passions without the social and religious sanction of marriage. The misery of Gustave Flaubert's Emma Bovary and George Sand's Lélia, she felt, was rooted in the constraints imposed on women's sexuality, such as she felt in her own life, especially in the Roman Catholic milieu of provincial Angers. Leroyer's need for commitments, devotions rather, were outgrowths of her quest to redefine relationships between men and women, preferably in the ennobling virtues of mutual respect and affection. In her writing, women's independence and action were subsumed within this more pressing physical and moral concern, which did not lend itself to overt expression and collective organization to achieve. On the other hand, given the profoundly private nature of this issue, Leroyer's autobiographical relations—her novellas and her correspondence—seemed to her the most appropriate first step toward understanding and then resolving it.

Bréton pursued another issue: the freedom of women's cultural expression. As in Leroyer's case, Bréton's own painful experience also made marriage a concern, but she cared more passionately about the arts—her fiancé's art but above all her writing and that of her son Jean-Louis, an artistic surrogate whose professional development she took as a special charge. Bréton's more traditional views of marriage as a religious sacrament and her hostility to women's rights were rooted less in an innate conservatism than in a passionate conviction about what mattered most in women's lives—namely, the practice and appreciation of the talents that their families made possible. Whatever interfered with the realization of this peculiar patrimony, including prescribed gender roles and religious strictures, she decried and found ways around them. Her spirited personal independence received its clearest expression in the discursive solitude of her diary, not in collective action.

Despite protestations and open conflicts with other feminists, Renooz was far closer than either Leroyer or Bréton to the French women's movement. Renooz's unhappy marriage and her exclusion from the university made her sensitive to the same issues, even though she was indifferent to women's sexuality and generally unmoved by the arts. For her, women's problems suggested a much larger concern: the need to establish a new morality. Accordingly, Renooz put her commitment and independence in the service of concerted action in order to achieve her elaborate vision of another social order. However troubled emotionally, Renooz was intent upon ensuring for women a dominant place in public life—in science, but also in religion and government—just as they had once had in prehistory and early civilizations. So, like Leroyer and Bréton, Renooz was deeply ambivalent about the women's-rights movement, primarily because it seemed beside the point. Political activity was less effective than consciousness-raising, by lecture and publication, about the possibilities for women's leadership in a world of their own making. For this promotional effort, in what she grandiosely considered her destiny, Renooz's writing was the most effective feminism she could fashion.

In the face of the insuperable obstacles to women's rights, these efforts, however earnest, appear very modest. Even the concerted, fully engaged activities of many more women came to little during the Third French Republic, and Leroyer, Bréton, and Renooz were still more ineffectual in their exclusive focus on autobiographical writing. What historical space do these privileged, self-indulgent individuals deserve? What does their example suggest about feminist consciousness in modern France? I want to argue that these particular figures do matter. They developed the conceptual language that Scott considers so essential to women's historical identity, agency, and resistance. Their independence of mind, their commitment to ideals of their own, but primarily their discursive practices in common with other women like them made a difference. For that reason, at least, Leroyer, Bréton, and Renooz merit the same attention as the many other women who endured and wrote about the pain of life in a man's world. Their obscurity makes their accounts revealing. They matter because they were not alone.

In the complex relationship between biography and history, the poignant relations of Leroyer, Bréton, and Renooz suggest how writers together can become historical actors.[6] The voluntaristic element in social processes and institutional settings varies dramatically from period to period and from place to place, of course, necessitating a more detailed analysis of human agency in historical change. Although Leroyer, Bréton, and Renooz did little more than write, they did participate in a much larger development in the women's movement. Their texts are rich evidence of the changes in women's relationship to themselves, to others, and to their world that ultimately brought change to modern French society, its politics, its economy, its culture, and its language. These figures shared in, and as participants they helped promote, the groundswell of concern over the very issues they discussed in their writing. Between the individual and her context there developed a distinctive interaction, a dialogic relationship that, collectively with others, shaped the women's movement in France. The precise nature and function of that historically significant exchange are what deserve more scholarly attention.

As Michelle Perrot has stated recently, women had more important responsibilities than modern French historians first thought. The gendered boundaries between public and private spheres, for instance, blurred in everyday life, especially in literate activities. "A woman in the privacy of her own room can write a book or a newspaper article which will introduce her into public space," Perrot argues, ensuring that "along these moving borders, the relations between men and women are modified, like the figures of an unending ballet."[7] In words or in images, the representations of themselves that women provided to others affected perceptions of gender and the many different social roles women played.[8] Their unpublished correspondence circulated within the family and among friends—their most intimate writing was never entirely just a personal matter. It was a social act, not all that different from the more obvious manifestations of their various activities at work, in church, in the marketplace, as well as in the press.

Even at home, Frenchwomen's private lives had public significance. Besides their household responsibilities—managing the expenses, educating the children, monitoring domestic servants, and the like—women often made personal decisions beyond their husbands' complete control. It is clear, for example, that Leroyer, Bréton, and Renooz all deliberately limited their fertility. Despite high rates of "natural" childbearing—close to one confinement every other year for fifteen years or more of fertile life—Leroyer had no children, Bréton only three, and Renooz four.[9] They did so at great personal sacrifice—that is, by abstaining from sexual relations for extended periods, despite or because of their troubled relationships with men. The admonitions of the church to be fruitful and of various authorities alarmed by France's declining birth rate were unavailing in these women's efforts, and of others like them, to control their own bodies decades before women elsewhere in western Europe did much the same. It is not surprising that all three women wrote, albeit discreetly, about this very important matter.

Equally discreet was women's participation in politics. To be sure, French-women did not vote, much less hold public office, in the nineteenth century. By law they were denied the most basic political rights and duties. This legal exclusion, however, did not prevent women from voicing their political views at home, in the press, and in the books they wrote. Leroyer, Bréton, and Renooz were all enthusiastic republicans. Leroyer was perhaps the most radical in her support of the 1848 *démoc-soc* revolutionaries; and her fiction makes heroes of ardent nationalists like the German Karl Sand. Bréton also sympathized openly with the *fédérés* during her work for an ambulance unit during the Paris Commune, much to the dismay of her family and friends. Although Renooz thought politics irrelevant, she frequently addressed public issues, like the peace settlement for World War I, in her conferences and publications. Prominent politicians were among the many recipients of her letters. Clearly, for most of the modern period, the power of the political pen was not entirely denied to such women.

Similarly, although women had few independent property rights under the Napoleonic Code, they played active roles in the French economy. Women worked and earned wages, most often because they had to; they kept accounts for their family businesses and households; they bought and sold daily at the market; they assumed the financial responsibilities of their absent or deceased husbands; and they had access to the income from the dowries that their parents put in trust for them at marriage. So Leroyer managed the farms she inherited from her father; Bréton controlled the money from her two million-franc dowry; and Renooz invested, somewhat unwisely, the remains of her dowry and inheritance in the bookstore she operated on the rue de Lille. Of course, these middle-class women were privileged in the marketplace and in the law; they had remarkable material and cultural resources at their disposal. But they still had to find ways to pursue their economic self-interest within the imposing constraints on women's public activities. Otherwise, they would have written differently in their diaries, letters, and memoirs.

Despite a reputation for mindless adherence to church doctrine, women's relative independence in religious belief and institutional life is equally evident in modern France.[10] The Roman Catholic Church sharply circumscribed women's lives, making them responsible for original sin, defining the marriage sacrament to men's advantage, controlling their lives quite directly through the confessional, and denying women the same education and leadership roles it accorded men. Nevertheless, the church lost the adherence of believers like Leroyer and Bréton, and it provoked the opposition of free-thinkers like Renooz. After years of worrying about the state of her soul, Leroyer lost her faith altogether when Mathurin Source suddenly died and left her without the moral support she so badly needed. The Roman Catholic God had been too cruel for her to understand, much less worship in her misery. Bréton, too, drifted away from the church in the face of repeated sorrows. Thus each woman adapted Catholic dogma or defined another belief system altogether in order to address her spiritual needs, as Renooz did when she created an elaborate religious vision to explain the historical oppression of women. Religion's social controls on such literate individuals were at best imperfect.

The same may be said of language. Women are born into preexisting discursive practices that obviously serve the interests of men. The very labels and categories that medical and legal experts created in the nineteenth century, for example, had gendered implications: rape was an unpunishable crime of passion, and hysteria the psychosomatic manifestation of a woman's wandering womb.[11] The consequences of these discursive appropriations of knowledge and power left women without protection under the law or from medical quackery. But women had a language of their own to master and to use in their particular interests; it pertained to emotion, idealism, and identity in ways that Leroyer, Bréton, and Renooz's personal writing amply demonstrates. They crafted this deliberate discourse themselves to suggest a distinctive consciousness of women's need for commitment, independence, and action. Whether or not these practices constituted a fully developed conceptual language, they did define a world over which Leroyer, Bréton, and Renooz exercised some control. They created labels and categories of their own that men felt compelled to coopt or to deflect but could not stop or destroy.[12]

In this way modern Frenchwomen like these figures were not entirely powerless. They did realize possibilities within pervasive and profound constraints. Leroyer established an extensive correspondence and created a sizeable body of published work that enabled her to exorcise the demons of her religious doubts and her repressed sexuality. Similarly, Bréton used her diary to define artistic interests in order to live them in her relations with others, especially her fiancé Henri Regnault and her son Jean-Louis Vaudoyer. And Renooz gave expression to her vision of science, religion, and history, ultimately developing a small cult of like-minded individuals who underwrote the costs of her conferences and publications. That none of these women is a household name today is hardly evidence of their failure; like most people in the past, they were in fact much more widely regarded in their own day. Historical obscurity is neither a universal nor an absolute criterion by which to judge the significance of comparable voices; like all reputations, the literary canon is an unreliable gauge of success.

La Femme Auteur

The fact is that these women wrote. The three of them harbored the hope that one day their work would be read and respected. They did so in the face of severe strictures against writing women. According to literary historian Christine Planté, *la femme auteur* was a particularly problematic figure in nineteenth-century France: "By writing and publishing, the woman escaped her assigned role as well as the private, familial space of which she was the mainstay and the essential element."[13] Attitudes toward writing women ranged from fear and hostility—out of concerns about the apparent social disorder they represented—to disdain and indifference—largely because of the "inferior" genres they explored. The need to control women's writing included parental efforts to monitor girls' diaries, a kind of discursive chaperoning equivalent to the extraordinary measures intended to prevent their masturbation. Since then, with a huge female readership and the potential publishing profits it represents, writing women have earned a more positive cachet; favorable images of their activity today obscure the obstacles that women faced less than a hundred years ago.

On the other hand, the challenge posed by literate women must be seen in the context of posterity's initial misappropriation of their writing. In their own day, the power they wielded seemed more relative than real and more cultural than political. Most of what they wrote went unpublished and was most often lost, and what they did publish was ignored and nearly forgotten, like Leroyer's novels and Renooz's science, neither of which is fully represented in France's most complete library, the Bibliothèque Nationale (BN). None of Leroyer's works was ever available outside of France. Bréton's notebooks and letters were preserved only because her better-known son had included them among his personal papers donated to the BN in 1962. More to the point, however, these acts of defiance have elicited much more interest recently. The scholarly attention paid to Leroyer, for instance, has centered on her correspondence with Flaubert, whose stature ensured that her letters would be published. Portions of Bréton's diaries were published by her granddaughter in 1985, an English translation of which appeared in 1994; and Renooz's efforts to create a new scientific epistemology are consistent with current work on gender in the history of science.[14]

Nor is their writing exclusively autobiographical. We do their work a serious disservice in assuming that women can write only about themselves and their immediate experience in life.[15] This is simply not true. Women's imaginative range and intellectual curiosity have no sex, even if the language they use may in fact be gendered. Leroyer's novellas included much material that has no apparent autobiographical element, and her letters did not focus exclusively on personal tribulations. Although she tended to identify with the authors and principal characters of the works she read, Leroyer's criticism also highlighted the high-minded idealism typical of the prose romance as a genre. Similarly, Bréton's extensive travelogues and essays on art made her diaries more than convenient occasions for self-exploration. Their lyrical language alone suggests a deliberate, artful concern to develop the poetic possibilities of her personal reflections. Less interested in language than either Leroyer or Bréton, Renooz worked hard to make sense of natural history, Western religion, and feminist polemic in the context of her vision of a new moral order. Her ideas mattered more to her than her own well-being, and certainly more than her personal self-expression.

How influential this work was, in their own time or later, may be of little import. Even the best-known writers from the past have left minor and seemingly irrelevant texts; many celebrated works contain long stretches of inconsequential material. Not every page of Balzac, Hugo, or Sand is exactly masterful; in light of their propensity for spontaneous, unrevised inspiration, the romantics as a group have aged badly. The romantic features in Leroyer's, Bréton's, and Renooz's writing have suffered accordingly; the sentimental novel practiced by Leroyer, the personal letter favored by Bréton, and the visionary tract written by Renooz are now neglected literary forms. This fact, however, does not mean that they and their authors are no longer worthy of our sustained attention. Understanding the past and its many voices simply requires more sympathetic patience from the present and its own passing concerns. Like personal recollection, historical memory can do better by the past.

These women were more than discursive sites, the apparent mouthpieces of someone else's language.[16] Their texts may have had much in common with those written by other women like them. As Philippe Lejeune has discovered, the personal journal does not vary significantly from instance to instance. Nor does the autobiography, the sentimental novel, or the personal letter. There is a sameness about the forms that Leroyer, Bréton, and Renooz explored; the repetitiveness of Leroyer's plaintive missives to Flaubert, Bréton's journal entries on Vaudoyer's emotional crises, and Renooz's sweeping claims to universal knowledge is painfully obvious. But at the heart of their writing was a conscious rhetorical effort to use words, to craft a text, to state a case for the purposes of moving an audience. They knew what they were about. Their agency lay not in their efforts at mimicry but in their effective command of the discourse at their disposal. Although they were not subjects in the fullest meaning of the term—is anyone truly free to act?—they were not objects in the most demeaning sense either.[17]

This ambiguity of Frenchwomen's discursive practices suggests another side to their subordination. Leroyer, Bréton, and Renooz all recognized the enormous power of men in public and private life. Despite their best efforts, it shaped their writings, providing them themes to develop, conflicts to resolve, and positions to define. But their response to this power was not overtly political, at least not in the traditional sense of the term *politics*. Like most other Frenchwomen, they avoided collective public activity, not just because they believed that such overt individualism contradicted their familial commitments, but because they felt it unnecessary. They sincerely believed that in their writing they were actually doing something about it. Leroyer saw her letters and novellas as ideals for others to embrace; Bréton considered her correspondence and personal journal as models for others to imitate; and Renooz launched her memoirs and visionary science to remake the world. These women thought of themselves not as idle victims but as ardent proponents of greater freedom for women. If their influence was muted in their own day, their historical significance ultimately lies in the present, in the subsequent audience for their ideas, in our recollection of them and their work.[18]

Their writing deserves the attention that historians and theorists are giving to similar women's lives and texts.[19] On the one hand, there is still very much more to learn about writing women; many of the best-known and most-outspoken French activists still await their biographers. Only recently have the likes of Madeleine Pelletier, Hubertine Auclert, and Clémence Royer had monographic studies devoted to them, while the likes of Maria Deraismes,

Marguerite Durand, and Maria Vérone still have not.[20] On the other hand, postmodern theorists are exploring the different approaches scholars and critics can take to the writing of these lives and the framing of their texts. As Barbara Heldt and Linda Wagner-Martin suggest, the power of naming has enabled women to define their experiences in narrative. "What most theoretical issues come down to, finally," writes Wagner-Martin, "is whose story, for whatever reasons, deserves telling? And the corollary to that central question is, who deserves to tell it, using what kind of language or syntax or structure?"[21] Again and again we find that women's efforts to grasp themselves in a narrative violate as well as appropriate men's critical norms. They are all the more of interest for doing so.

Historically, women writers were in good company. Other social marginals created similar literate spaces for themselves. As historians and literary specialists have discovered recently, blacks, workers, immigrants, and homosexuals also left traces of their efforts to define themselves and to develop strategies for survival in a world otherwise meant for others.[22] Their subjective expression and its historical function are little different from those of women in the same circumstances. The self-concept and social comportment of "unmanly" males, for instance, demonstrate the ways in which comparable figures negotiated a modus vivendi with alien cultural constructions of particular groups, some more successfully than others. The anachronistic practice of dueling, like the litigation to forestall the dishonor of divorce by men anxious to prove their virility, suggests the historical implications of comparable texts inscribed against the dominant voices on nineteenth-century France. Discursive agency, it seems, took on many different forms and figures besides women and their autobiographical writing.

As Charles Taylor has argued in another context, "we grasp ourselves in a *narrative.*"[23] The results are more than simply self-understanding; as I have argued here, they are matters of identity, consciousness, agency, and resistance worth historical examination for what they tell us about the women's movement in modern France (and other historical phenomena like it elsewhere). The discreet feminism evident in the texts left by Leroyer, Bréton, and Renooz force us, I believe, to rethink the French quest for equality in difference in the nineteenth and early twentieth century. Apparently it entailed conceptions of gender as much as it did political organization and action. Could it be that the Anglo-American model of feminist consciousness, based as it often is on political equality *tout court*, overlooks the possibility of a distinct French model? Could it be that the modalities of women's subjectivity in liberalism need to be recast from abstract rights in the law to concrete strategies to maximize often conflicting loyalties and interests?[24] In the specific examples provided by Leroyer, Bréton, and Renooz, there is some evidence that women's unpublished writing resembles the distinct forms of associational life in modern French life: its power is mediated more culturally than it is politically.

Frenchwomen in civic organizations, especially in the nineteenth century, seem as much a contradiction as the historical significance of their autobiographical writings. But recent research is showing more and more women at work in such groups and the webs of influence they had in them. Leroyer took a special interest in the reconstruction of the theater in Angers, which brought her in contact with the local Académie des Sciences et Belles Lettres. Bréton was also active in various literary salons, including that of her close friend Augustine Bulteau. And Renooz actually joined a mixed freemason lodge, La Raison Triomphante. The full extent of their participation is difficult to assess, but the time and money at their disposal made it possible, even probable, that they were not passive members. Nor were other women like them idle in the Société des Gens des Lettres, the Société de Saint Vincent de Paul, and the Universités Populaires, among other associations whose purposes provided women appropriate opportunities to assume certain civic responsibilities of their own. Like their quiet participation in *la cité*, women's voices have come to matter.[25]

Were these particular modalities of women's consciousness unique to France? Did modern Frenchwomen follow a singular path, as Mona Ozouf and other historians have argued against the universalist claims of some U.S. scholars?[26] Perhaps. But without more comparative work, these questions are moot.[27] Unsupportable claims to the special case exist in every national history, and the studies of Frenchwomen are no exception. After all, certain facts are telling: women in France received most civil liberties later than did their Anglo-American counterparts. The French also developed very early a pervasively gendered, pronatalist welfare system that addressed some feminist interests, including family allocations and provisions for abandoned mothers and children.[28] Moreover, from its inception in the nineteenth century, the women's movement in France has been ineffective, the apparent pressure of contentious intellectuals. This perception is strengthened by recent claims to the privileged nature of women's being and experience, such as a special affinity for the sacred, with little more than impressionistic evidence to support them. The uniqueness of Frenchwomen is asserted more than it is studied.

The autobiographical writings by Leroyer, Bréton, and Renooz do suggest, however, one peculiarity of Frenchwomen's history. As Priscilla Parkhurst Clark has shown, France has had a striking prediliction for literary culture.[29] Authors, like artists generally, are accorded higher esteem than they are elsewhere in the industrialized West, and the educated command of language often defines social status, economic welfare, and political power.[30] Like the Panthéon, the Académie Française is a very French institution. In such a cultural context, women's discursive practices assume a particular national import that is not apparent from their relative obscurity in manuscript. The presumption of Frenchwomen to write was bitterly contested in the nineteenth century, because their relative success conferred real influence in public affairs. To reframe Christine Planté's argument historically, *la femme auteur* represented more than the defiance of traditional notions of gender; she marked the intrusion of powerfully literate women into the politics of culture.[31]

Whether or not this intrusion was uniquely French, it made possible a telling critique of an imperfect world. The asymmetrical relations between men and women were painfully obvious to my three subjects. They anguished over them at length in their correspondence, journals, memoirs, and other writings. But they also set in opposition to this agonizing reality an ideal of their own, albeit one derived from eighteenth-century sentimentality and nineteenth-century romanticism. However much Leroyer, Bréton, and Renooz were offended by Jean-Jacques Rousseau's hostile views of women's "unnatural" functions, they were attracted by what they took as his suggestion of an emotional equality between men and women, an idea that novelists and poets promoted long afterwards.[32] These women responded to their subordination by taking seriously the possibilities of the companionate relations between husband and wife that had been evolving in middle-class homes since the eighteenth century. In fact, this relational equality developed a life of its own and modified republican ideals, as espoused by Jules Ferry and Eugène Boileau.[33] Patriarchal authority thus faced challenges not just from overt political action; it did so from the personal aspirations that both men and women expressed in their private lives and writings.[34]

A similar deliberate blurring of the public and personal has become a major element in the Mouvement de Libération des Femmes (MLF). As a "new social movement" akin to environmental groups and Women-Church in the United States, the MLF adopted the nonhierarchical organization that was congenial to the activists who had participated in the May 1968 events.[35] Each participant enjoyed roughly the same responsibility to address the needs of the group. Moreover, the process of meeting was at least as important as its results; individual interests, including those ostensibly extraneous to the purposes of the movement, became matters of shared concern. Accordingly, relationships and their expression preoccupied many women in the MLF; they wrote of their lives together and apart from one another with the same vigor and insight that Leroyer, Bréton, and Renooz did about themselves and their relations.[36] In effect, these three precursors to a more diffuse feminist consciousness gave voice to a vital precondition for recent forms of collective action in complex, information-rich societies.[37] For these women at least, the agency for social change lies paradoxically in the language of personal experience.

This particular paradox joins many others in women's history. As Joan Wallach Scott has suggested recently, feminists have only such paradoxes to offer: "In the age of democratic revolutions, 'women' came into being as political outsiders through the discourse of sexual difference. Feminism was a protest against women's political exclusion, but it had to make its claims on behalf of 'women.' . . . This paradox—the need both to accept *and* to refuse 'sexual difference'—was the constitutive condition of feminism as a political movement throughout its long history."[38] Similarly, all women writers had contradictions of their own to live. On the one hand, by their craft they sought to capture on paper the impressions, ideas, and feelings that moved them; on the other, their language failed to fix any of these features of their work. The discourse at their disposal had a life of its own that robbed them of their subjectivity, especially as successive discursive practices erased and rewrote past texts into new ones. But what they wrote was profoundly subversive; it destabilized the universal rhetoric of political rights that excluded women. How much more paradoxical, then, was it to be a writer as well as a feminist: time, gender, and language all seemingly conspired against her very best intentions.

Or maybe they didn't. As Naomi Schor has argued about women's writing, it is subject to an essentialism that is not one.[39] The very process of naming, the placing of a word on human experience, however loose the connection between life and language, suggests an act of self-assertion that is never altogether lost so long as the traces remain. The work of Leroyer, Bréton, and Renooz is neglected but not forgotten; they created self-conscious identities for themselves and others to read and to rewrite in an endless, nearly timeless process of deliberate and deliberative activity. That other women like them were and still are engaged in these efforts ensures that their paradoxes will live on, like the hauntingly poetic phrases offered by Hélène Cixous in my introduction: "Writing is working; being worked; questioning (in) the between (letting oneself be questioned) of same *and of* other without which nothing lives." The past for women in language is in fact no conspiracy but an act of will, if not always on their part then certainly on someone else's like mine, to recall their poignant relations as both literary text and historical experience.[40]

Abbreviations

ADML	Archives Départementales de Maine-et-Loire, Angers
AN	Archives Nationales, Paris
APP	Archives de la Préfecture de Police, Paris
b.	box *(boîte)*
BHVP	Bibliothèque Historique de la Ville de Paris
BMD	Bibliothèque Marguerite Durand, Paris
BMN	Bibliothèque Municipale Médiathèque, Nantes
BN	Bibliothèque Nationale de France, Paris
d.	dossier
f., ff.	folio, folios
FC2	Gustave Flaubert, *Correspondance*, vol. 2, *Juillet 1851–décembre 1858*, ed. Jean Bruneau (Paris: Gallimard, 1980)
FC3	Gustave Flaubert, *Correspondance*, vol. 3, *Janvier 1859–décembre 1868*, ed. Jean Bruneau (Paris: Gallimard, 1991)
GSC	George Sand, *Correspondance*, ed. Georges Lubin (Paris: Garnier, 1964–91). 25 vols.
ISMS	Geneviève Bréton, *"In the Solitude of My Soul": The Diary of Geneviève Bréton, 1867–1871*, ed. James Smith Allen, tr. James Palmes (Carbondale: Southern Illinois UP, 1994)
JLV	Jean-Louis Vaudoyer
NAFr	Nouvelles Acquisitions Françaises
no., nos.	number, numbers
PCR	Papiers Céline Renooz
PUF	Presses Universitaires de France
T.	Tome
vol.	volume

Unless otherwise noted, all translations from the French in the text are the author's; and all punctuation, capitalization, and passages in italics are original to the sources quoted, except where problems with clarity arose.

Notes

Introduction

1. Hélène Cixous, "Sorties," *La Jeune née* (1975), in Hélène Cixous and Catherine Clément, *The Newly Born Woman*, tr. Betsy Wing (Minneapolis: U of Minnesota P, 1986), 86.

2. See Ann Jones, "Writing the Body: Toward an Understanding of 'l'Ecriture Féminine,'" *Feminist Studies* 7, no. 2 (1981): 247–63. Cf. Carolyn Heilbrun, *Writing a Woman's Life* (New York: Norton, 1988).

3. Heilbrun, *Writing a Woman's Life*, 37.

4. See, e.g., ibid., 11–31; and a French equivalent, Tilde A. Sankovitch, *French Women Writers and the Book: Myths of Access and Desire* (Syracuse: Syracuse UP, 1988).

5. See Verena Andermatt Conley, *Writing the Feminine: Hélène Cixous* (Lincoln: U of Nebraska P, 1984), 51–70; *The Cixous Reader*, ed. Susan Sellers (London: Routledge, 1992), xxix–xxxi; and Susan Sellers, *Hélène Cixous: Authorship, Autobiography, and Love* (Cambridge: Polity, 1996), 1–23.

6. For fuller treatment of patriarchy as a historical phenomenon, see Gerda Lerner, *The Creation of Patriarchy* (New York: Oxford UP, 1986), esp. 122–36, 238–42.

7. A useful introduction to *discourse* and *textuality* is Terry Eagleton, *Literary Theory: An Introduction*, 2nd ed. (Minneapolis: U of Minnesota P, 1996), esp. 79–130. However indebted my work is to structuralist theories of language as an autonomous system, I will use the term *writing* here to mean an individual's self-conscious act of crafting a text.

8. For early explorations of Frenchwomen's relations to language, see Marina Yaguello, *Les Mots et les femmes: Essai d'approche sociolinguistique de la condition féminine* (Paris: Payot, 1979); Verena Aebisher, *Les Femmes et le langage: Représentations d'une différence* (Paris: PUF, 1985); and Luce Irigaray, "Représentation et auto-affection du féminin," in *Sexes et genres à travers les langues: Eléments de communication*

sexuée, ed. Luce Irigaray (Paris: Grasset, 1990), 31–82. Cf. *The Women and Language Debate: A Sourcebook,* ed. Camille Roman et al. (New Brunswick: Rutgers UP, 1994).

9. Poststructuralists would question this assertion. Is the writer truly in control of language? Jacques Derrida and his successors would argue that there is nothing "outside the text"; we are all born into language and cannot escape it. Inherent to writing, they contend, is the arbitrary relation between the sign and its referent; language does not refer reliably to anything outside of itself. All binary relations in fact are destabilized by language's operations that have a life and logic all their own. The knowing self is thus a myth, because it is not the conscious individual who speaks but the language that speaks through the individual.

As a historian, I find this position intriguing but problematic. On the one hand, it forces scholars to take language seriously and to consider just how it distorts. Language is neither neutral nor transparent. On the other hand, this challenge to Western metaphysics based on the logos all too easily elides what people actually do outside of language; at least some experience, past and present, escapes its textuality, even as writers try to fix experiential phenomena in words. Conversely, writing still captures at least some kind of experience; the act of writing itself deserves the careful study that historians devote to it—and to its representations of a world so evidently apart from its texts. For more on this issue, see chapter 2.

10. E.g., see the recent survey of the genre by Georges Gusdorf, *Lignes de vie* (Paris: Jacob, 1991), 2 vols. A selected listing of Frenchwomen's published autobiographies, diaries, and letters appears in the bibliography following these notes.

11. Cf. Gerda Lerner, *The Creation of Feminist Consciousness: From the Middle Ages to Eighteen Seventy* (New York: Oxford UP, 1993); and more popularly, Evelyne Sullerot, *Histoire et mythologie de l'amour: Huit siècles d'écrits féminins* (Paris: Club Français du Livre, 1974).

12. Cf. arguments developed in Patricia Meyer Spacks, *The Female Imagination* (New York: Avon, 1975), 405–14; Béatrice Didier, *L'Ecriture-femme* (Paris: PUF, 1981), 5–40; and Joan Elizabeth Cocks, *The Oppositional Imagination: Adventures in the Sexual Domain* (London: Routledge, 1989), 1–22.

13. Cf. the restrictive definition of modern feminism in Nancy Cott, *The Grounding of Modern Feminism* (New Haven: Yale UP, 1987), 4–5: advocacy of the equality of condition, awareness of the social construction of gender, and belief in the solidarity of women. In this sense, very few women in modern France were feminists, not even the strong female figures discussed in Mona Ozouf, *Women's Words: Essay on French Singularity,* tr. Jane Marie Todd (Chicago: U of Chicago P, 1997).

14. Note the definitions proposed by Lerner, *The Creation of Feminist Consciousness,* 14–17, 284–85. It is preferable, for the moment, to speak here of Lerner's *preconditions* for feminist consciousness (232): women's economic independence, con-

trol of their own fertility, education, and social spaces for their exchange with one another.

15. Cf. the first efforts on this problem, Sheila Rowbotham, *Women's Consciousness, Man's World* (London: Penguin, 1973) and Nancy Chodorow, *The Reproduction of Mothering: Psychoanalysis and the Sociology of Gender* (Berkeley: U of California P, 1978); with more recent French assessments of sexual difference, Janine Mossuz-Lavau and Anne de Kervasdoué, *Les Femmes ne sont pas des hommes comme les autres* (Paris: Jacob, 1997) and Catherine Clément and Julia Kristeva, *Le Féminin et le sacré* (Paris: Stock, 1998).

16. Didier, *L'Ecriture-femme*, 19. Cf. the otherness expressed by the working-class actors in E. P. Thompson, *The Making of the English Working Class* (New York: Vintage, 1963), 9—hardly the first or the last scholar to remark this phenomenon among subordinate populations; and Joan Wallach Scott, *Gender and the Politics of History* (New York: Columbia UP, 1988), 68–90.

17. See a similar position developed more fully in Sidonie Smith, *Subjectivity, Identity, and the Body: Women's Autobiographical Practices in the Twentieth Century* (Bloomington: Indiana UP, 1993), 1–23.

18. Simone de Beauvoir, *Le Deuxième Sexe* (Paris: Gallimard, 1949), 2: 13.

19. See Ozouf, *Women's Words*, 229–83. Note the sharp critique offered by Joan Wallach Scott in Bronislaw Baczko et al., "Femmes: une singularité française?" *Le Débat*, no. 87 (1995): 134–39. As I contend in this book, the opposition here is a false one. The peculiarities of the French context have concerned women's historians for some time. Cf. Louise Tilly, "Women's Collective Action and Feminism in France, 1870–1914," in *Class Conflict and Collective Action*, ed. Louise A. Tilly and Charles Tilly (Beverly Hills: Sage, 1981), 207–32; Elisabeth Badinter, *L'Un est l'autre: Des relations entre hommes et femmes* (Paris: Jacob, 1986), 247–337, and Karen Offen, "Defining Feminism: A Comparative Historical Approach," *Signs: Journal of Women in Culture and Society* 14, no. 1 (1988): 119–57.

20. Cf. Steven C. Hause with Anne R. Kenney, *Women's Suffrage and Social Politics in the Third French Republic* (Princeton: Princeton UP, 1984); and Laurence Klejman and Florence Rochefort, *L'Egalité en marche: Le Féminisme sous la troisième République* (Paris: P de la Fondation Nationale des Sciences Politiques, 1989).

21. Cf. the different ways Frenchwomen responded to ideas overtly hostile to feminism, from appropriation in Jean-Marie Aubert, *La Femme: Antiféminisme et christianisme* (Paris: Cerf, Desclée, 1975), to adaptation in Bonnie Smith, *Ladies of the Leisure Class: The Bourgeoises of Northern France in the Nineteenth Century* (Princeton: Princeton UP, 1981), to inversion in Yvonne Turin, *Femmes et religieuses au XIXeme siècle: Le Féminisme "en religion"* (Paris: Nouvelle Cité, 1989).

22. See survey of work on this issue by Claire Goldberg Moses, "Debating the

Present, Writing the Past: 'Feminism' in French History and Historiography," *Radical History Review* 52, no. 1 (1992): 79–94.

23. See Priscilla Parkhurst Clark, *Literary France: The Making of a Culture* (Berkeley: U of California P, 1987).

24. See James Smith Allen, *In the Public Eye: A History of Reading in Modern France, 1800–1940* (Princeton: Princeton UP, 1991), 215–23.

25. See Daniel Brizemur, "Une correspondante de Flaubert: Mlle Leroyer de Chantepie," *Revue hebdomadaire* (18 Oct. 1919): 305–38, reprinted in *Les Amis de Flaubert*, nos. 16 (1960): 3–12, and 17 (1960): 3–10; Françoise Blot-Pautrel, "Marie-Sophie Leroyer de Chantepie: Une femme de lettres romantique en Anjou," in *Les Angevins de la littérature* (Angers: P de l'Université, 1979), 237–50; Hermia Oliver, "Nouveaux aperçus sur Marie-Sophie Leroyer de Chantepie"; *Les Amis de Flaubert*, no. 61 (1982): 4–14; Evelyne Lejeune-Resnick, "Anjou, républicanisme et romantisme: Les Aspirations de Sophie Leroyer," *Annales de Bretagne* 99, no. 4 (1992): 415–22; Martine Reid, "Mademoiselle Leroyer de Chantepie, Tertre-Saint-Laurent, 20, Angers," *Textuel*, no. 27 (1992): 109–21; and James Smith Allen, "A Republic of Romantic Letters: Marie-Sophie Leroyer de Chantepie and her Literary Community, 1836–1878," in *Autour d'un cabinet de lecture*, ed. Graham Falconer (Toronto: Centre d'Etudes Romantiques J. Sablé, 1999), in press. Leroyer often signed her name "Marie-S.," hence its abbreviation to "Marie," used in my book.

26. Marie-Sophie Leroyer de Chantepie, "Madame Cottin," in *Souvenirs et impressions littéraires* (Paris: Perrin, 1892), 130.

27. See James Smith Allen, introduction to *"In the Solitude of My Soul": The Diary of Geneviève Bréton, 1867–1871*, ed. James Smith Allen, tr. James Palmes (Carbondale: Southern Illinois UP, 1994), xv–xxvii.

28. See Henry Carnoy, *Mme C. Renooz et son oeuvre* (Paris: Impr. Maton, 1902); Christine Bard, *Les Filles de Marianne: Histoire des féminismes, 1914–1920* (Paris: Fayard, 1995), 109–16; James Smith Allen, "Science, Religion, and Feminism: The Utopian Signs of Céline Renooz, 1840–1928," in *Worldmaking*, ed. William Pencak (New York: Lang, 1996), 163–84; and, id., "The Language of the Press: Narrative and Ideology in the Memoirs of Céline Renooz, 1890–1913," in *Making the News: Modernity and the Mass Press in Nineteenth-Century France*, ed. Dean de La Motte and Jeannene Pryzblyski (Amherst: U of Massachusetts P, 1999), in press.

29. Cf. discussion of this view—"In their own way, each woman appreciated or embraced a marginal place, reconstituting it as a locally defined center"—in Natalie Zemon Davis, *Women on the Margins: Three Seventeenth-Century Lives* (Cambridge: Harvard UP, 1995), 210.

30. Cf. the social history of private life in *A History of Private Life*, ed. Philippe Ariès and Georges Duby, tr. Arthur Goldhammer (Cambridge: Harvard UP, Belknap, 1987–90), 5 vols.; *Histoire de moeurs*, ed. Jean Poirier (Paris: Gallimard, 1989–91), 3

vols.; and *Ecritures ordinaires*, ed. Daniel Fabre (Paris: Bibliothèque Publique d'Information, Centre Georges Pompidou, 1993).

31. Besides Lerner, *The Creation of Patriarchy* and, id., *The Creation of Feminist Consciousness*, see Cott, *The Grounding of Modern Feminism;* Offen, "Defining Feminism"; and Denise Riley, *"Am I That Name?" Feminism and the Category of "Woman" in History* (Minneapolis: U of Minnesota P, 1988).

32. See excellent surveys of women's history in Joan Wallach Scott, "Survey Articles: Women in History, 2. The Modern Period," *Past and Present*, no. 101 (1983): 141–57; *Writing Women's History*, ed. Michelle Perrot, tr. Felicia Pheasant (Oxford: Blackwell, 1992); *Writing Women's History: International Perspectives*, ed. Karen Offen et al. (Bloomington: Indiana UP, 1991); and Françoise Thébaud, *Sociétés, espaces, temps: Ecrire l'histoire des femmes* (Fontenay-Saint-Cloud: ENS, 1998). Good general histories include *Becoming Visible: Women in European History*, ed. Renate Bridenthal et al., 2nd ed. (Boston: Houghton Mifflin, 1987); Bonnie G. Smith, *Changing Lives: Women in European History since 1700* (Lexington, Mass.: Heath, 1989); and *A History of Women in the West*, ed. Georges Duby and Michelle Perrot, tr. Arthur Goldhammer et al. (Cambridge: Harvard UP, Belknap, 1992–94), 5 vols.

33. E.g., Maïté Albistur and Daniel Armogathe, *Histoire du féminisme français du moyen âge à nos jours* (Paris: Des Femmes, 1977); Claire Goldberg Moses, *French Feminism in the Nineteenth Century* (Albany: State U of New York P, 1984); *Feminisms of the Belle Epoque: A Historical and Literary Anthology*, ed. Jennifer Waelti-Walters and Steven C. Hause (Lincoln: U of Nebraska P, 1994); and Claire Duchen, *Feminism in France from '68 to Mitterrand* (London: Routledge & Kegan Paul, 1986).

34. Cf. work in anthropology, such as *Sexual Meanings: The Cultural Construction of Gender and Sexuality*, ed. Sherry B. Ortner and Harriet Whitehead (Cambridge: Cambridge UP, 1981); and in psychology, such as *Making a Difference: Psychology and the Construction of Gender*, ed. Rachel T. Hare-Mustin and Jeanne Marecek (New Haven: Yale UP, 1990); with work in history, such as Elisabeth Badinter, *The Myth of Motherhood: An Historical View of the Maternal Instinct*, tr. Roger DeGaris (London: Souvenir, 1981); Mary Louise Roberts, *Civilization without Sexes: Reconstructing Gender in Postwar France, 1917–1927* (Chicago: U of Chicago P, 1994); and *Feminism and History*, ed. Joan Wallach Scott (New York: Oxford UP, 1996).

35. See surveys of recent literary theory in *Redrawing the Boundaries: The Transformation of English and American Literary Studies*, ed. Stephen Greenblatt and Giles Gunn (New York: Modern Language Association of America, 1992), esp. 154–208, 251–302, 374–465.

36. Besides Didier, *L'Ecriture-femme*, see Estelle Jellinek, *The Tradition of Women's Autobiography: From Antiquity to the Present* (Boston: Twayne, 1986); and Jacques Lecarme and Elaine Lecarme-Tabone, *L'Autobiographie* (Paris: Colin, 1997), 95–124.

37. E.g., see Roy Pascal, *Design and Truth in Autobiography* (Cambridge: Harvard

UP, 1960); *The Female Autograph: Theory and Practice of Autobiography from the Tenth to the Twentieth Century*, ed. Domna Stanton (Chicago: U of Chicago P, 1987); Françoise Lionnet, *Autobiographical Voices: Race, Gender, Self-Portraiture* (Ithaca: Cornell UP, 1989); and *De/Colonializing the Subject: The Politics of Gender in Women's Autobiography*, ed. Julia Watson and Sidonie Smith (Minneapolis: U of Minnesota P, 1992).

38. See Dominick LaCapra, "Rethinking Intellectual History and Reading Texts," in *Modern European Intellectual History: Reappraisals and New Perspectives*, ed. Dominick LaCapra and Steven L. Kaplan (Ithaca: Cornell UP, 1982), 47–85.

39. E.g., see Nancy Miller, *Subject to Change: Reading Feminist Writing* (New York: Columbia UP, 1988); and a survey of other theorists by Nancy Fraser in her introduction to *Revaluing French Feminism: Critical Essays on Difference, Agency, and Culture*, ed. Nancy Fraser and Sandra Lee Bartky (Bloomington: Indiana UP, 1992), 1–24.

40. Cf. Rosemary Hennessy, *Materialist Feminism and the Politics of Discourse* (New York: Routledge, 1993), 67–99; and Fredric Jameson, *The Prison-House of Language: A Critical Account of Structuralism and Russian Formalism* (Ithaca: Cornell UP, 1972), 101–216.

41. Max Weber, "The Social Psychology of the World Religions," in *From Max Weber: Essays in Sociology*, tr. and ed. H. H. Gerth and C. Wright Mills (New York: Oxford UP, 1946), 280.

42. Cf. Lerner, *The Creation of Feminist Consciousness;* Richard Terdiman, *Discourse/Counter-Discourse: The Theory and Practice of Symbolic Resistance in Nineteenth-Century France* (Ithaca: Cornell UP, 1984); James C. Scott, *Domination and the Arts of Resistance: Hidden Transcripts* (New Haven: Yale UP, 1990); Michel Foucault, *The History of Sexuality*, vol. 1, *An Introduction*, tr. Robert Hurley (New York: Pantheon, 1979), esp. 94–96; and Mikhail Bakhtin, *Rabelais and His World*, tr. Hélène Iswolsky (Cambridge: MIT P, 1968), esp. 152–54.

43. Again women are omitted from serious study in Richard Terdiman, *Past Present: Modernity and the Memory Crisis* (Ithaca: Cornell UP, 1993), notwithstanding a memory crisis in women's history.

44. Cf. James Scott's other work on Southeast Asian peasants: *Weapons of the Weak: Everyday Forms of Peasant Resistance* (New Haven: Yale UP, 1976), and, id., *The Moral Economy of the Peasant: Rebellion and Subsistance in Southeast Asia* (New Haven: Yale UP, 1985).

45. I will use the term *patriarchy* in the same broad sense that Lerner does in her books: a system of ideas and institutions that has historically fostered if not ensured the subordination of women's interests to those of men in both public and private life. See the succinct definition, one derived from an earlier study of the problem, in Lerner, *The Creation of Feminist Consciousness*, 4–6.

46. See Christine Planté, *La Petite Soeur de Balzac: Essai sur la femme-auteur*

(Paris: Seuil, 1989), a thoughtful recasting of Virginia Woolf's influential *A Room of One's Own* (1929) in the French cultural context.

47. Cf. Thérèse Moreau, *Le Sang de l'histoire: Michelet, l'histoire, et l'idée de la femme au XIXe siècle* (Paris: Flammarion, 1982); and Susan Moller Okin, *Women in Western Political Thought* (Princeton: Princeton UP, 1979).

48. See the useful bibliographic survey in James Goodwin, *Autobiography: The Self-Made Text* (New York: Twayne, 1993), 137–57.

49. Pascal Werner, "Préface," *L'Histoire sans qualités*, ed. Christine Dufranctel (Paris: Galilée, 1979), 10.

50. See important assessments of women's power historically: Cécile Dauphin et al., "Women's Culture and Women's Power: An Attempt at Historiography," *Journal of Women's History* 1, no. 1 (1981): 63–107; and Perrot, "Women, Power, and History," in *Writing Women's History*, 160–74. Michelle Perrot has also surveyed the problem most recently for a more popular audience in her *Femmes publiques* (Paris: Textuel, 1997).

51. See Linda Kintz, "Indifferent Criticism: The Deconstructive 'Parole,'" and Jeffner Allen, "An Introduction to Patriarchal Existentialism: A Proposal for a Way Out of Existential Patriarchy," in *The Thinking Muse: Feminism and Modern French Philosophy*, ed. Jeffner Allen and Iris Marion Young (Bloomington: Indiana UP, 1989), 113–35, 71–84, respectively. Cf. Jo-Ann Pilardi, "Feminists Read *The Second Sex*," in *Feminist Interpretations of Simone de Beauvoir*, ed. Margaret A. Simons (University Park: Pennsylvania State UP, 1995), 29–44.

52. I make this assertion fully aware of the real limits to women's freedom of action, the violence against them especially, studied in *De la violence et des femmes*, ed. Cécile Dauphin and Arlette Farge (Paris: Albin Michel, 1997); Michèle Dayras, *Femmes et violences dans le monde*, (Paris: L'Harmattan, 1995); and Georges Vigarello, *Histoire du viol. XVIe–XXe siècle* (Paris: Seuil, 1998).

53. Cf. Gayatri Chakravorty Spivak, "Three Women's Texts and a Critique of Imperialism," *Critical Inquiry* 12, no. 1 (1985): 262–80. Cf., id., "Can the Subaltern Speak?" in *Marxism and the Interpretation of Culture*, ed. Cary Nelson and Lawrence Grossberg (Urbana: U of Illinois P, 1988), 271–313; and Gyan Prakash, "Subaltern Studies in Postcolonial Criticism," *American Historical Review* 99, no. 5 (1994): 1475–90.

54. Cf. the efforts to adapt Freudian theory and practice to women—e.g., Karen Horney, *Feminine Psychology*, ed. Harold Kelman (New York: Norton, 1967), and Juliet Mitchell, *Psychoanalysis and Feminism* (New York: Pantheon, 1974)—with the attempts to modify Lacanian concepts to women, esp. Luce Irigaray, *Speculum de l'autre femme* (Paris: Minuit, 1974); and Julia Kristeva, *La Révolution du langage poétique* (Paris: Seuil, 1974). See also Antoinette Fouque, *Il y a deux sexes: Essais de féminoligie, 1989–1995* (Paris: Des Femmes, 1995), 57–90; and Elisabeth Young-

Bruehl, *Subject to Biography: Psychoanlysis, Feminism, and Writing Women's Lives* (Cambridge: Harvard UP, 1998), 225–52.

55. Cf. *Feminist Literary Theory: A Reader*, ed. Mary Eagleton (Oxford: Blackwell, 1986) with Gisela Bock, "Challenging Dichotomies: Perspectives on Women's History," in *Writing Women's History: International Perspectives*, 1–24; Margaret Homans, "Representation, Reproduction, and Women's Place in Language," in *Bearing the Word: Language and Female Experience in Nineteenth-Century Women's Writings* (Chicago: U of Chicago P, 1986), 1–39; and Nancy Fraser, "The Uses and Abuses of French Discourse Theories for Feminist Politics," in *Revaluing French Feminism*, 177–94.

56. Cf. Sellers, *Hélène Cixous*, 1–24; Rita Felski, *Beyond Feminist Aesthetics: Feminist Literature and Social Change* (Cambridge: Harvard UP, 1989), 1–18, 154–96; Judith Butler, *Gender Trouble: Feminism and the Subversion of Identity* (New York: Routledge, 1990), esp. 1–34, 142–49; and bell hooks, *Talking Back: Thinking Feminist, Thinking Black* (Boston: South End, 1989).

57. Gusdorf, *Lignes de vie*, vol. 1, *Les Ecritures du moi*, 9. Cf. other approaches to discursive liberations in Leo Strauss, *Persecution and the Art of Writing* (Chicago: U of Chicago P, 1988), 22–37; and Peter Stallybrass and Allon White, introduction to *The Politics and Poetics of Transgression* (Ithaca: Cornell UP, 1986).

CHAPTER ONE The Woman Question, Historically Speaking

1. Clémence Royer, "Introduction à la philosophie des femmes," in *Clémence Royer: Philosophe et femme de science*, ed. Geneviève Fraisse (Paris: La Découverte, 1985), 106. Cf. Joy Harvey, *"Almost a Man of Genius": Clémence Royer, Feminism, and Nineteenth-Century Science* (New Brunswick: Rutgers UP, 1997), 52–55.

2. The history of women in the West is well surveyed by *Becoming Visible: Women in European History*, ed. Renate Bridenthal et al., 2nd ed. (Boston: Houghton Mifflin, 1987); Bonnie G. Smith, *Changing Lives: Women in European History since 1700* (Lexington, Mass.: Heath, 1989); and *A History of Women in the West*, ed. Georges Duby and Michelle Perrot, tr. Arthur Goldhammer et al. (Cambridge: Harvard UP, Belknap, 1992), 5 vols. More specifically for the history of Frenchwomen, see Maurice Bardèche, *Histoire des femmes* (Paris: Stock, 1968), 2 vols.; and Alain Decaux, *Histoire des françaises* (Paris: Perrin, 1972), 2 vols. An excellent recent bibliography of important work in the field is in Françoise Thébaud, *Sociétés, espaces, temps: Ecrire l'histoire des femmes* (Fontenay-Saint-Cloud: ENS, 1998), 175–217.

3. See Maïté Albistur and Daniel Armogathe, *Histoire du féminisme français du moyen âge à nos jours* (Paris: Des Femmes, 1977); and Jean Rabaut, *Histoire des féminismes français* (Paris: Stock, 1978). More generally with documents in translation,

see *Women: From the Greeks to the French Revolution* (Stanford: Stanford UP, 1973); *European Women: A Documentary History, 1789–1945*, ed. Eleanor S. Riemer and John C. Fout (New York: Schocken, 1980); and *Women, the Family, and Freedom: The Debate in Documents*, ed. Susan Groag Bell and Karen Offen (Stanford: Stanford UP, 1983), 2 vols. Cf. *Le Grief des femmes: Anthologie des textes féministes du moyen âge à nos jours*, ed. Maïté Albistur and Daniel Armogathe (Paris: Hier & Demain, 1978), 2 vols.

4. See Joan Kelly, "Early Feminist Theory and the *Querelle des femmes*, 1400–1789," *Signs: Journal of Women in Culture and Society*, no. 1 (1982): 4–27.

5. Besides *French Women and the Age of Enlightenment*, ed. Samia I. Spencer (Bloomington: Indiana UP, 1984), see David Williams, "The Politics of Feminism in the French Enlightenment," in *The Varied Patterns: Studies in the Eighteenth Century*, ed. Peter Hughes and David Williams (Toronto: Hakkert, 1971), 331–51; Joan B. Landes, *Women and the Public Sphere in the Age of the French Revolution* (Ithaca: Cornell UP, 1988), 17–89; Margaret C. Jacob, *Living the Enlightenment: Freemasonry and Politics in Eighteenth-Century Europe* (New York: Oxford UP, 1991), 120–42; Dena Goodman, *The Republic of Letters: A Cultural History of the French Enlightenment* (Ithaca: Cornell UP, 1994), 90–135; and Mona Ozouf, *Women's Words: Essay on French Singularity*, tr. Jane Marie Todd (Chicago: U of Chicago P, 1997), 1–44.

6. Landes, *Women and the Public Sphere in the Age of the French Revolution*, 24. Cf. Carolyn Lougee, *Le Paradis des Femmes: Women, Salons, and Social Stratification* (Princeton: Princeton UP, 1976).

7. See Susan Moller Okin, *Women in Western Political Thought* (Princeton: Princeton UP, 1979), 99–194; Christine Fauré, *Democracy without Women: Feminism and the Rise of Liberal Individualism in France*, tr. Claudia Gorbman and John Berks (Bloomington: Indiana UP, 1991), 75–100; and Lieselotte Steinbrügge, *The Moral Sex: Women's Nature in the French Enlightenment*, tr. Pamela E. Selwyn (New York: Oxford UP, 1995).

8. See Ozouf, *Women's Words*, 45–63; Landes, *Women and the Public Sphere*, 93–200; Olwen Hufton, "Women in Revolution, 1789–1796," *Past and Present*, no. 53 (1971): 90–108; id., *Women and the Limits of Citizenship in the French Revolution* (Toronto: U of Toronto P, 1992); Jane Abray, "Feminism in the French Revolution," *American Historical Review* 80, no. 1 (1975): 43–62; Louis Devance, "Le Féminisme pendant la Révolution française," *Annales historiques de la Révolution française*, no. 229 (1977): 341–76; *Women in Revolutionary Paris, 1789–1795*, ed. Darline Gay Levy et al. (Urbana: U of Illinois P, 1979); Harriet B. Applewhite and Darline Gay Levy, "Women, Democracy, and Revolution in Paris, 1789–1794," in *French Women and the Age of Enlightenment*, 64–79; Lynn Hunt, "The Unstable Boundaries of the French Revolution," in *A History of Private Life*, vol. 4, *From the Fires of Revolution to the Great War*, ed. Michelle Perrot, tr. Arthur Goldhammer (Cambridge: Harvard UP,

Belknap, 1990), 13–46; *Rebel Daughters: Women and the French Revolution*, ed. Sara E. Melzer and Leslie W. Rabine (New York: Oxford UP, 1992); and Marilyn Yalom, *Blood Sisters: The French Revolution in Women's Memory* (New York: Basic, 1994).

9. See Joan Wallach Scott, *Only Paradoxes to Offer: French Feminists and the Rights of Man* (Cambridge: Harvard UP, 1996), 19–56.

10. See Jean-François Tetu, "Remarques sur le statut jurdique de la femme au XIXe siècle," in *La Femme au XIXe siècle: Littérature et idéologie*, ed. Roger Bellet (Lyons: PU de Lyon, 1979), 5–17; and *La Famille, la loi, l'état: De la Révolution au Code civil*, ed. Irène Théry and Christian Biet (Paris: Imprimerie Nationale, 1989).

11. Ozouf, *Women's Words*, 64–110; and Madelyn Gutwirth, *The Twilight of the Goddesses: Women and Representation in the French Revolutionary Era* (New Brunswick: Rutgers UP, 1992).

12. Hunt, "The Unstable Boundaries of the French Revolution," 45.

13. A thorough but now dated survey of the woman question is Karen Offen, "The 'Woman Question' as a Social Issue in Nineteenth-Century France: A Bibliographical Essay," *Third Republic/Troisième République*, nos. 3–4 (1977): 238–99. The issues Offen discusses are still relevant. Cf. *Misérable et glorieuse: La Femme du XIX siècle: Les Différentes Positions sociales de la femme*, ed. Jean-Paul Aron (Paris: Fayard, 1980); Priscilla Robertson, *An Experience of Women: Pattern and Change in Nineteenth-Century Europe* (Philadelphia: Temple UP, 1982), 326–42; Christine Planté, *La Petite Soeur de Balzac: Essai sur la femme auteur* (Paris: Seuil, 1989); Anne Martin-Fugier, *La Vie élégante, ou la formation du Tout-Paris, 1815–1848* (Paris: Fayard, 1990); and Geneviève Fraisse, *Reason's Muse: Sexual Difference and the Birth of Democracy*, tr. Jane Marie Todd (Chicago: U of Chicago P, 1994), 1–15, 128–35.

14. See Offen, "The 'Woman Question,'" 291–96; Laure Adler, *À l'aube du féminisme: Les Premières Journalistes, 1830–1850* (Paris: Payot, 1979), 19–73; Claire Goldberg Moses and Leslie Wahl Rabine, *Feminism, Socialism, and French Romanticism* (Bloomington: Indiana UP, 1993), 17–144; and Michèle Riot-Sarcey, *La Démocratie à l'épreuve des femmes: Trois figures critiques du pouvoir 1830–1848* (Paris: Albin Michel, 1994).

15. See Claire Goldberg Moses, *French Feminism in the Nineteenth Century* (Albany: State U of New York P, 1984), 41–60; and Robertson, *An Experience of Women*, 282–300.

16. See Marguerite Thibert, *Le Féminisme dans le socialisme français de 1830 à 1850* (Paris: Giard, 1926); Jehan Ivray, *L'Aventure saint-simonienne et les femmes* (Paris: Alcan, 1928); Maria Teresa Bulciolu, *L'Ecole saint-simonienne et la femme: Notes et documents pour une histoire du rôle de la femme dans la société saint-simonienne* (Pisan: Goliardica, 1980); and Susan K. Grogan, *French Socialism and Sexual Difference: Women and the New Society, 1803–1844* (New York: St. Martin's, 1992).

17. See Marie Cerati, "Elisa Lemonnier," *Femmes extraordinaires* (Paris: Courtille,

1979), 34–85; Claire Démar, *Textes sur l'affranchissement des femmes*, ed. Valentin Pelosse (Paris: Payot, 1976); and Suzanne Voilquin, *Souvenirs d'une fille du peuple, ou la saint-simonienne en Egypte*, ed. Lydia Elhadad (Paris: Maspero, 1978).

18. Claire Démar, "My Law of the Future," in Moses and Rabine, *Feminism, Socialism, and French Romanticism*, 181.

19. See Theodore Zeldin, *France, 1848–1945*, vol. 1, *Ambition, Love and Politics* (Oxford: Clarendon, 1973), 343–62, despite its superficiality; Offen, "The 'Woman Question,'" 273–77; Robertson, *An Experience of Women*, 185–99; and Michelle Perrot, "At Home," in *A History of Private Life*, 4: 341–58.

20. Cf. Jill Harsin, *Policing Prostitution in Nineteenth-Century Paris* (Princeton: Princeton UP, 1985); Alain Corbin, *Women for Hire: Prostitution and Sexuality in France after 1850*, tr. Alan Sheridan (Cambridge: Harvard UP, 1990); and Jacques Termeau, *Maisons closes de province: L'Amour vénal au temps du réglementarisme* (Paris: Cénomane, 1986).

21. See Marilyn J. Boxer, "Socialism Faces Feminism: The Failure of Synthesis in France, 1879–1914," in *Socialist Women*, ed. Marilyn J. Boxer and Jean H. Quataert (Westport: Greenwood, 1978), 75–111; Charles Sowerwine, *Sisters or Citizens? Women and Socialism in France since 1876* (Cambridge: Cambridge UP, 1982); and Patricia Hilden, *Working Women and Socialist Politics in France, 1880–1914: A Regional Study* (Oxford: Oxford UP, 1986).

22. See Jules Puech, *La Vie et oeuvre de Flora Tristan, 1803–1844* (Paris: Rivière, 1925); Dominique Desanti, *Flora Tristan: La Femme révoltée* (Paris: Hachette, 1972); *Un fabuleux destin: Flora Tristan*, ed. Stéphane Michaud (Dijon: PU de Dijon, 1986); and *Flora Tristan: Utopian Feminist*, ed. Paul and Doris Beik (Bloomington: Indiana UP, 1993).

23. Cf. Edith Thomas, *Les Femmes de 1848* (Paris: PUF, 1940); id., *Pauline Roland: Socialisme et féminisme au XIXe siècle* (Paris: Rivière, 1956); and, id., *Louise Michel, ou la Velléda de l'anarchie* (Paris: Gallimard, 1971).

24. Maria Deraismes, *France et progrès* (1873) in *Oeuvres complètes de Maria Deraismes* (Paris: Alcan, 1895), 1: 227. Cf. Patrick Bidelman, *Pariahs Stand Up! The Founding of the Liberal Feminist Movement in France, 1858–1889* (Westport: Greenwood, 1982); and Karen Offen, "Ernest Legouvé and the Doctrine of 'Equality in Difference' for Women: A Case Study of Male Feminism in Nineteenth-Century France," *Journal of Modern History* 58, no. 2 (1986): 452–84. On revolutionary women in the republican tradition, cf. Gay L. Gullickson, *Unruly Women of Paris: Images of the Commune* (Ithaca: Cornell UP, 1996); and David Barry, *Women and Political Insurgency: France in the Mid-Nineteenth Century* (New York: St. Martin's, 1996).

25. See Pierre Rosanvallon, *Le Sacre du citoyen: Histoire du suffrage universel en France* (Paris: Gallimard, 1992), esp. 393–412; and Laure Adler, *Les Femmes politiques* (Paris: Seuil, 1993), despite misspellings and errors of fact.

26. See Thérèse Moreau, *Le Sang de l'histoire: Michelet, l'histoire, et l'idée de la femme au XIXe siècle* (Paris: Flammarion, 1982); Karen Offen, "A Nineteenth-Century French Feminist Rediscovered: Jenny P. D'Héricourt, 1809–1875," *Signs: Journal of Women in Culture and Society* 13, no. 1 (1987): 144–58; and Offen, "The 'Woman Question,'" 257–67.

27. Jan Goldstein, "The Hysteria Diagnosis and the Politics of Anticlericalism in Late Nineteenth-Century France," *Journal of Modern History* 54, no. 2 (1982): 209–39. Cf., id., *Console and Classify: The French Psychiatric Profession in the Nineteenth Century* (Cambridge: Cambridge UP, 1987); and Alain Corbin, "Cries and Whispers," in *A History of Private Life,* 4: 615–67.

28. Francis Ronsin, *La Grève des ventres: Propagande néo-malthusienne et baisse de la natalité française (XIXe–XXe siècles)* (Paris: Aubier Montaigne, 1980); Karen Offen, "Depopulation, Nationalism, and Feminism in Fin-de-Siècle France," *American Historical Review* 89, no. 3 (1984): 648–76; and Ann-Louise Shapiro, "Disordered Bodies/Disorderly Acts: Medical Discourse and the Female Criminal in Nineteenth-Century Paris," in *Gendered Domains: Rethinking Public and Private in Women's History,* ed. Dorothy O. Helly and Susan M. Reverby (Ithaca: Cornell UP, 1992), 123–34.

29. Robertson, *An Experience of Women,* 343–51; and *Feminisms of the Belle Epoque: A Historical and Literary Anthology,* ed. Jennifer Waelti-Walters and Steven C. Hause (Lincoln: U of Nebraska P, 1994).

30. See Offen, "The 'Woman Question,'" 267–73; and Françoise Mayeur, *L'Education des jeunes filles en France au XIXe siècle* (Paris: Hachette, 1979). Arguably the most significant changes are studied in Françoise Mayeur, *L'Enseignement secondaire des jeunes filles sous la troisième République* (Paris: P de la Fondation Nationale des Sciences Politiques, 1977); and Karen Offen, "The Second Sex and the Baccalauréat in Republican France, 1880–1924," *French Historical Studies* 13, no. 2 (1983): 252–86.

31. Madeleine Pelletier, *L'Education féministe des filles* (Paris: Giard and Brière, 1914), 57; and Felicia Gordon, *The Integral Feminist: Madeleine Pelletier, 1874–1939* (Minneapolis: U of Minnesota P, 1991), 122–23.

32. Dorothy McBride Stetson, *Women's Rights in France* (Westport: Greenwood, 1987).

33. Offen, "Ernest Legouvé," 480.

34. See Robertson, *An Experience of Women,* 282–300; and Scott, *Only Paradoxes to Offer,* 57–89.

35. Cf. Mary Louise Roberts, *Civilization without Sexes: Reconstructing Gender in Postwar France, 1917–1927* (Chicago: U of Chicago P, 1994); Margaret Randolph Higonnet et al., *Behind the Lines: Gender and the Two World Wars* (New Haven: Yale UP, 1987); Scott, *Only Paradoxes to Offer,* 90–160; and Steven C. Hause, *Hubertine Auclert: The French Suffragette* (New Haven: Yale UP, 1990).

36. Cf. Claire Duchen, *Feminism in France from May '68 to Mitterrand* (London:

Routledge & Kegan Paul, 1986); *French Feminist Thought: A Reader,* ed. Toril Moi (Oxford: Blackwell, 1987); and Dorothy Kaufmann-McCall, "Politics of Difference: The Women's Movement in France from May 1968 to Mitterrand," *Signs: Journal of Women in Culture and Society* 9, no. 2 (1983): 282–93.

37. Jules Bois, "Les Apôtres femmes du 'féminisme' à Paris," *Le Figaro,* 9 Nov. 1894, in Archives de la Préfecture de Police Ba 1651, d. Le Mouvement féministe. Note that police reports on feminist activities shared the widespread habit of denigrating public women.

38. Cf. Thomas Laqueur, *Making Sex: Body and Gender from the Greeks to Freud* (Cambridge: Harvard UP, 1990), 193–243; and Charles Bernheimer, *Figures of Ill-Repute: Representing Prostitution in Nineteenth-Century France* (Cambridge: Harvard UP, 1989).

39. Cf. Frances Ida Clark, *The Position of Women in Contemporary France* (Westport: Greenwood, 1981); Françoise Thébaud, *Quand nos grand-mères donnaient la vie: La Maternité en France dans l'entre-deux-guerres* (Lyons: PU de Lyon, 1986); and Christine Bard, *Les Filles de Marianne: Histoire des féminismes, 1914–1920* (Paris: Fayard, 1995).

40. Louise A. Tilly, "Women's Collective Action and Feminism in France, 1870–1914," in *Class Conflict and Collective Action,* ed. Louise A. Tilly and Charles Tilly (Beverly Hills: Sage, 1981), 231.

41. See Steven C. Hause with Anne R. Kenney, *Women's Suffrage and Social Politics in the French Third Republic* (Princeton: Princeton UP, 1984), 248–53; and Laurence Klejman and Florence Rochefort, *L'Egalité en marche: Le Féminisme sous la troisième République* (Paris: P de la Fondation Nationale des Sciences Politiques, 1989), 339–44. Cf. Scott, *Only Paradoxes to Offer,* 161–75; Paul Smith, *Feminism and the Third Republic: Women's Political and Civil Rights in France, 1918–1945* (Oxford: Oxford UP, 1996); and more generally, Janine Mossuz-Lavau and Mariette Sineau, *Enquête sur les femmes et la politique en France* (Paris: PUF, 1983).

42. On Frenchwomen and the law, see Robertson, *An Experience of Women,* 275–81; and Offen, "The 'Woman Question,'" 249–57.

43. *Le Code civil.* Textes antérieurs et version actuelle, ed. Jean Veil (Paris: Flammarion, 1988). Cf. Janine Mossuz-Lavau, *Les Lois d'amour: Les Politiques de la sexualité en France de 1950 à nos jours* (Paris: Payot, 1991).

44. Cf. the greater space accorded women in Michelle Perrot, *Femmes publiques* (Paris: Textuel, 1997).

45. Joan Wallach Scott and Louise A. Tilly, *Women, Work, and Family* (New York: Holt, Rinehart & Winston, 1978), 12. Cf. Offen, "The 'Woman Question,'" 277–91; Martine Segalen, *Love and Power in the Peasant Family,* tr. Sarah Matthews (Chicago: U of Chicago P, 1983), 78–111; and Claude Motte and Jean-Pierre Pélissier, "La Binette, l'aiguille et le plumeau: Les Mondes du travail féminin," in *La Société fran-*

çaise: Tradition, transition, transformations, ed. Jacques Dupâquier and Denis Kessler (Paris: Fayard, 1992), 237–342.

46. See, e.g., Scott and Tilly, *Women, Work, and Family;* Theresa M. McBride, *The Domestic Revolution: The Modernization of Household Service in England and France, 1820–1920* (New York: Holmes & Meier, 1976); *Travaux de femmes dans la France du XIXe siècle,* special issue of *Le Mouvement social,* no. 105 (1978); Geneviève Fraisse, *Femmes toutes mains: Essai sur le service domestique* (Paris: Seuil, 1979); Laura S. Strumingher, *Women and the Making of the Working Class: Lyon, 1830–1870* (St. Albans: Eden P, Women's Publications, 1979); James F. McMillan, *Housewife or Harlot: The Place of Women in French Society, 1870–1940* (New York: St. Martin's, 1981); Lorraine Coons, *Women Home Workers in the Parisian Garment Industry, 1860–1915* (New York: Garland, 1991); Judith G. Coffin, *The Politics of Women's Work: The Paris Garment Trades, 1750–1915* (Princeton: Princeton UP, 1995); and Scott, *Gender and the Politics of History,* 93–112, 139–63.

47. Perrot, *Femmes publiques,* 114. Cf. Françoise Parent, *Les Demoiselles de magasins* (Paris: Ouvrières, 1970); Susan D. Bachrach, *Dames Employées: The Feminization of Postal Work in Nineteenth-Century France* (New York: Haworth, 1984); Jo Burr Margadant, *Madame le Professeur: Women Educators in the Third Republic* (Princeton: Princeton UP, 1990); Catherine Rigollet, *Les Conquérantes* (Paris: NiL, 1996); and Catherine Omnès, *Ouvrières parisiennes: Marchés du travail et trajectoires profession-nelles au 20e siècle* (Paris: L'Ecole des Hautes Etudes en Science Sociales, 1997).

48. See Offen, "The 'Woman Question,'" 246–57; and the important work by Etienne Van de Walle, *The Female Population of France in the Nineteenth Century* (Princeton: Princeton UP, 1974); id., "Alone in Europe: The French Fertility Decline until 1850," in *Historical Studies in Changing Fertility,* ed. Charles Tilly (Princeton: Princeton UP, 1978), 257–88; and, id., "Motivation and Technology in the Decline of French Fertility," in *Family and Sexuality in French History,* ed. Robert Wheaton and Tamara Hareven (Philadelphia: U of Pennsylvania P, 1980), 135–78.

49. On preindustrial demographic trends, see Pierre Goubert, *Cent Mille provinciaux au XVIIe siècle: Beauvais et le beauvaisis de 1600 à 1730* (Paris: Flammarion, 1968), 49–108.

50. John C. Hunter, "The Problem of the French Birth Rate on the Eve of World War I," *French Historical Studies* 2, no. 2 (1962): 490–503; Angus McLaren, *Sexuality and Social Order: The Debate over the Fertility of Women and Workers in France, 1770–1920* (New York: Holmes & Meier, 1983), 9–27, 109–83; Robert A. Nye, *Crime, Madness, and Politics in Modern France: The Medical Concept of National Decline* (Princeton: Princeton UP, 1984), 141–43, 166–69; and Joshua H. Cole, "'There Are Only Good Mothers': The Ideological Work of Women's Fertility in Late Nineteenth-Century France," *French Historical Studies* 20, no. 2 (1996): 639–72.

51. See Philippe Ariès, *Histoire des populations françaises et de leurs attitudes devant*

la vie depuis le XVIIIe siècle (Paris: Seuil, 1971), 334; and J. Bourgeois-Pichat, "The General Development of the Population of France since the Eighteenth Century," in *Population and History: Essays in Historical Demography*, ed. D. V. Glass and D. E. C. Eversley (London: Arnold, 1965), app. 2, tables 1a, 1b, 498–99.

52. Cf. the problems, e.g., studied in Rachel G. Fuchs, *Abandoned Children: Found-lings and Child Welfare in Nineteenth-Century France* (Albany: State U of New York P, 1984); id., *Poor and Pregnant in Paris: Strategies for Survival in the Nineteenth Century* (New Brunswick: Rutgers UP, 1992); George Sussman, *Selling Mother's Milk: The Wet-Nursing Business in France, 1715–1914* (Urbana: U of Illinois P, 1982); and *Madame ou mademoiselle? Itinéraires de la solitude féminine, XVIIIe–XXe siècle*, ed. Arlette Farge and Christiane Klapisch-Zuber (Paris: Montalba, 1984).

53. Adeline Duamard, *Les Bourgeois et la bourgeoisie en France depuis 1815* (Paris: Flammarion, 1991), 211–12. Cf. A. D. Tolédano, *La Vie de famille sous la Restauration et la Monarchie de juillet* (Paris: Albin Michel, [1943]); and Margaret Darrow, "French Noblewomen and the New Domesticity, 1750–1850," *Feminist Studies* 5, no. 1 (1979): 41–65.

54. Besides the titles in n. 46, see, e.g., Linda Clark, *Schooling the Daughters of Marianne: Textbooks and the Socialization of Girls in Modern French Primary Schools* (Albany: State U of New York P, 1983); id., "Bringing Feminine Qualities into the Public Sphere: The Third Republic's Appointment of Women Inspectors," in *Gender and the Politics of Social Reform in France, 1870–1914*, ed. Elinor Accampo et al. (Baltimore: Johns Hopkins UP, 1995), 128–56; Isabelle Bricard, *Saintes et pouliches: L'Education des jeunes filles au XIXe siècle* (Paris: Albin Michel, 1985); Marie Françoise Levy, *De mères en filles: L'Education des françaises 1850–1880* (Paris: Calmann-Lévy, 1984); and Marie-Christine Vinson, *L'Education des petites filles chez la comtesse de Ségur* (Lyons: PU de Lyon, 1986).

55. See Yannick Ripa, *Women and Madness: The Incarceration of Women in Nine-teenth-Century France*, tr. Catherine du Peloux Menagé (Minneapolis: U of Minnesota P, 1990), esp. 9–79; and Yvonne Knibiehler and Catherine Fouquet, *La Femme et les médecins: Analyse historique* (Paris: Hachette, 1983), esp. 203–93.

56. Cf. Anne Martin-Fugier, *La Bourgeoise: Femme au temps de Paul Bourget* (Paris: Grasset & Fasquelle, 1983); Bonnie G. Smith, *Ladies of the Leisure Class: The Bourgeoises of Northern France in the Nineteenth Century* (Princeton: Princeton UP, 1981); and the major study by Anne-Marie Sohn, *Chrysalis: Femmes dans la vie privée (XIXe–XXe siècle)* (Paris: La Sorbonne, 1996), 2 vols.

57. E.g., on the ambivalent implications of the 1892 law banning night work for women and children and restricting the hours that they could work, see *Différence des sexes et protection sociale*, ed. Leonora Auslander and Michelle Zancarini-Fournel (Saint-Denis: PUV, 1995), 75–104, 165–82.

58. Fuchs, *Poor and Pregnant in Paris*, 232.

59. Cf. Mary Lynn Stewart, *Women, Work, and the French State: Labour Protection, and Social Patriarchy, 1879–1919* (Kingston, Ont.: McGill-Queen's UP, 1989); and Anne Cova, *Maternité et droits des femmes en France, XIXe–XXe siècles* (Paris: Anthropos, 1997).

60. Maria Pognon, "La Loi néfaste de 1892," *La Fronde* 3, no. 743 (1899) in *Women, the Family, and Freedom*, 2: 212.

61. Besides the important work on autobiography cited in chapter 2, nn. 4, 7, 13, 29, 30, 35, 36, 42, 44, 45, 51, and 52, see the useful bibliographic essay at the end of James Goodwin, *Autobiography: The Self-Made Text* (New York: Twayne, 1993), 137–57.

62. Major studies of French autobiography in particular include P. Mansell Jones, *French Introspectives from Montaigne to André Gide* (Cambridge: Cambridge UP, 1937); Jeffrey Mehlman, *A Structural Study of Autobiography: Proust, Leiris, Sartre, Lévi-Strauss* (Ithaca: Cornell UP, 1974); Huntington Williams, *Rousseau and the Romantic Autobiography* (Oxford: Oxford UP, 1983); Germaine Brée, *Narcissus Absconditus: The Problematic Art of Autobiography in Contemporary France* (Oxford: Clarendon, 1978); Michael Sheringham, *French Autobiography: Devices and Desires* (Oxford: Clarendon, 1993); and the special issue of the *Revue d'histoire littéraire de la France* (1975).

63. See Marilyn Yalom, "Women's Autobiography in French, 1793–1939: A Select Bibliography," *French Literary Series* 2 (1985): 197–205. Studies of women's autobiographies generally are just being published. Besides the theorists and/or critics cited in the introduction, nn. 17, 36, 37, and in chapter 2, nn. 2, 5, 28, 33, 35, 39, 40, 41, 50, and 52, see *Woman's Autobiography: Essays in Criticism*, ed. Estelle Jellinek (Bloomington: Indiana UP, 1980); Leigh Gilmore, *Autobiographics: A Feminist Theory of Women's Self-Representation* (Ithaca: Cornell UP, 1994); and the special issues of *Woman's Studies International Forum* (1987) and *Michigan Quarterly Review* (1987).

64. See Germaine Brée, "George Sand and the Fictions of Autobiography," *Nineteenth-Century French Studies* 4 (1976): 438–49; Lucienne Frappier-Mazur, "Nostalgie, dédoublement et écriture dans *Histoire de ma vie*," *Nineteenth-Century French Studies* 17, nos. 3 and 4 (1989): 265–75; and Sara Murphy, "Refusing to Confess: George Sand's *Histoire de ma vie* and the Novelization of Autobiographical Discourse," in *Correspondances: Studies in Literature, History, and the Arts in Nineteenth-Century France*, ed. Keith Busby (Amsterdam: Rodopi, 1992), 157–64.

65. See chapter 2, n. 10.

66. Elizabeth C. Goldsmith, "Giving Weight to Words: Madame de Sévigné's Letters to Her Daughter," in *The Female Autograph: Theory and Practice of Autobiography from the Tenth to the Twentieth Century*, ed. Domna C. Stanton (Chicago: U of Chicago P, 1987), 98. On recent research on the letter, see *Écrire-publier-lire: Les Correspondances: Problématique et économie d'un genre littéraire*, Actes du Colloque International, ed. Jean-Louis Bonnat et al. (Nantes: U de Nantes, 1983); *La Correspon-*

dance: Les Usages de la lettre au 19e siècle, ed. Roger Chartier (Paris: Fayard, 1991); *Les Facultés des lettres: Recherches récentes sur l'épistolaire français et québecois*, ed. Benoît Melançon and Pierre Popovic (Montreal: U de Montréal, 1993); *Expériences limites de l'épistolaire: Lettres d'exil, d'enfermement, de folie*, Actes du Colloque de Caen (Paris: Champion, 1993); *La Lettre à la croisée de l'individuel et du social*, ed. Mireille Bossis (Paris: Kimé, 1994); and Cécile Dauphin et al., *Ces bonnes lettres: Une correspondance familiale au XIXe siècle* (Paris: Albin Michel, 1995).

67. Note the important role men played until just recently in editing and publishing women's autobiographies, memoirs, letters, and diaries, as noted in the selective checklists included in the research bibliography at the end of this book.

68. On the letter specifically as a literary form, see Janet Gurkin Altman, *Epistolarity: Approaches to a Form* (Columbus: Ohio State UP, 1982); *La Correspondance: Edition, fonction, et signification* (Toulouse: U de Provence, 1984); *Les Correspondances inédites*, ed. A. Françon and Claude Goyard (Paris: Economica, 1984); J. L. Cornille, *L'Amour des lettres ou le contrat déchiré* (Mannheim: Mana, 1985); *Des mots et des images pour correspondre*, Actes du Colloque (Nantes: U de Nantes, 1986); Vincent Kaufmann, *L'Equivoque épistolaire* (Paris: Minuit, 1990); Alain Viala, "Littérature épistolaire," *Le Grand Atlas des littératures*, ed. Gilles Quinsat et al. (Paris: Encyclopédie Universalis, 1990), 50–51; and the special issues of *Revue des sciences humaines* (1984), *Yale French Studies* (1986), and *Textuel* (1992).

69. On this genre in France, see Albert J. Salvan, "Private Journals in French Literature," *American Legion of Honor Magazine* 25 (1954): 201–14; David Bryant, "Revolution and Introspection: The Appearance of the Private Diary in France," *European Studies* 8 (Apr. 1978): 259–72; and Philippe Lejeune, in *Le Moi des demoiselles: Enquête sur le journal de jeune fille* (Paris: Seuil, 1993).

70. See Cheryl Cline, *Women's Diaries, Journals, and Letters: An Annotated Bibliography* (New York: Garland, 1989), even though it is already outdated.

71. Lejeune, *Le Moi des demoiselles*, 20.

72. See Isabelle Eberhardt, *Lettres et journaliers*, ed. Eglal Errera (Paris: J'ai Lu, 1987).

73. On the diary as a genre, see Michèle Leleu, *Les Journaux intimes* (Paris: PUF, 1952); Alain Girard, *Le Journal intime* (Paris: PUF, 1963); Béatrice Didier, *Le Journal intime* (Paris: PUF, 1976); *Le Journal intime et ses formes littéraires*, Actes du Colloque de Septembre 1975, ed. Victor Del Litto (Geneva: Droz, 1978); and Gérard Genette, "Le Journal, l'anti-journal," *Poétique*, no. 47 (1981): 315–22.

74. See interesting discussions of George Sand the epistolary writer in autobiography and diary, in *Ecrire-publier-lire*, 146–238, 375–408.

75. On the generic transgression of autobiographical writings generally, see Emile Henriot, *Epistoliers et mémorialistes* (Paris: La Nouvelle Revue Critique, 1931); *Les Récits de vie: Théorie et pratique*, ed. Jean Poiret et al. (Paris: PUF, 1983); Paul Kirby,

Narrative and the Self (Bloomington: Indiana UP, 1991); Jean-Pierre Albert, "Ecritures domestiques," *Ecritures ordinaires*, ed. Daniel Fabre (Paris: Bibliothèque d'Information, Centre Georges Pompidou, 1993), 37–94; and *Le Récit d'enfance: Enfance et écriture*, Actes du Colloque de NVL/CRALEJ, Bordeaux, Oct. 1992 (Bordeaux: Sorbier, 1993).

76. Joan DeJean, *Tender Geographies: Women and the Origins of the Novel in France* (New York: Columbia UP, 1991), 5. Studies of women and the novel are too numerous to cite, but most relevant here are Michel Mercier, *Le Roman féminin* (Paris: PUF, 1976); Béatrice Didier, *L'Ecriture-femme* (Paris: PUF, 1981); *The Voyage In: Fictions of Female Development*, ed. Elizabeth Abel et al. (Hanover: UP of New England, 1983); and *Redefining Autobiography in Twentieth-Century Women's Fiction*, ed. Janice Morgan and Colette Hall (New York: Garland, 1991).

77. On women writers in the eighteenth century, see *French Women and the Age of Enlightenment*, 197–241.

78. Georges Sand, *Lélia*, ed. Béatrice Didier (Meyland: L'Aurore, 1987), 1: 224. Cf. Eileen Boyd Sivert, "*Lélia* and Feminism," *Yale French Studies* 62 (1981): 45–66.

CHAPTER TWO   Variations on the Feminine *I*

1. Nancy K. Miller, *Bequest and Betrayal: Memoirs of a Parent's Death* (New York: Oxford UP, 1996), x.

2. Nancy K. Miller, *Subject to Change: Reading Feminist Writing* (New York: Columbia UP, 1988), 8. Cf. the perspective of Jennifer Waelti-Walters, *Feminist Novelists of the Belle Epoque: Love as a Lifestyle* (Bloomington: Indiana UP, 1990).

3. This point is not to deny the usefulness of genre as a tool of critical analysis. Cf. Paul Hernadi, *Beyond Genre: New Directions in Literary Classification* (Ithaca: Cornell UP, 1972), 152–85; Jacques Derrida, "La Loi du genre," *Glyph* 7 (1980): 176–201; and Adena Rosmarin, *The Power of Genre* (Minneapolis: U of Minnesota P, 1985), 3–51.

4. Georges May, *L'Autobiographie* (Paris: PUF, 1979), 208–15. Cf. extended treatments of this problem in Georges Gusdorf, *Lignes de vie* (Paris: Jacob, 1991), 2 vols.; and Peter Gay, *The Bourgeois Experience: Victoria to Freud* (New York: Oxford UP, 1984–86; Norton, 1993–95), 4 vols.

5. Cf. this approach with Carolyn Heilbrun, *Writing a Woman's Life* (New York: Norton, 1988).

6. Cf. Thelma Jurgrau, "Critical Introduction," in George Sand, *Story of My Life*, ed. Thelma Jurgrau, collective tr. (Albany: State U of New York P, 1991), 7–30; Michel Beaujour, "Autobiographie et autoportrait," *Poétique*, no. 32 (1977): 442–58; and Naomi Schor, *George Sand and Idealism* (New York: Columbia UP, 1993), 157–84.

7. Note Philippe Lejeune's discontinued project to publish biannual bibliographies of autobiographical writings and studies just in French; clearly there were too many titles to record for a comprehensive listing. See *Bibliographie des études en langue*

française sur la littérature personnelle et les récits de vie, ed. Philippe Lejeune (Paris: Cahiers de Sémiotique Textuelle 3, U de Paris X, 1984–90), 4 vols.

8. Note that Miller considers the complex relationship between gender and genre from the perspective of the reader rather than from that of the writer. See Miller, *Subject to Change*, 102–21, a position influenced by Jonathan Culler, "Reading as a Woman," in *On Deconstruction: Theory and Criticism after Structuralism* (Ithaca: Cornell UP, 1982), 43–64.

9. The bulk of the known correspondence appertaining to Marie-Sophie Leroyer de Chantepie (hereafter Leroyer) is found in the Bibliothèque Nationale (hereafter BN), Nouvelles Acquisitions Françaises, MS 23825 (ff. 208–389), most of which appears in *Flaubert: Correspondance*, vol. 2, *Juillet 1851–décembre 1858* (hereafter *FC2*); and vol. 3, *Janvier 1859–décembre 1868* (hereafter *FC3*), ed. Jean Bruneau (Paris: Gallimard, 1980–91). But other important collections of her letters exist in the Bibliothèque Historique de la Ville de Paris (hereafter BHVP), Fonds George Sand G. 4404–575 (ff. 199–248); BHVP, Fonds Jules Michelet, Tome 11 (ff. 137–46); and the Bibliothèque Municipale Médiathèque, Nantes, MS 2942.

10. Leroyer to George Sand, 3 Jan. 1856, BHVP, Fonds Sand G. 4404–575, f. 237.

11. See ibid.; Leroyer to Gustave Flaubert, 18 Dec. 1856 and 26 Feb. 1857, in *FC2*, 654–55, 684–87; and Leroyer to Jules Michelet, 12 Aug. 1859, in BHVP, Fonds Michelet, T. 11, ff. 137–38.

12. A list of Leroyer's major publications is found in the bibliography.

13. On the autobiographical uses of third-person narratives, see Michel Butor, "L'Usage des pronoms dans le roman," in *Essais sur le roman* (Paris: Minuit, 1960), 73–88; and Philippe Lejeune, "Autobiography in the Third Person," in *On Autobiography*, ed. Paul John Eakin, tr. Katherine Leary (Minneapolis: U of Minnesota P, 1989), 31–52.

14. Leroyer, *Mémoires d'une provinciale* (Paris: Dentu, 1880), 1: 1.

15. See Leroyer, *Mémoires d'une provinciale*, 1: 371–404; 2: 85–100, 298–310; id., "Arthur de Monthierry," in *Nouvelles littéraires* (Paris: Perrin, 1889), 51–53, 105–36; and, id., *Une vengeance judiciaire* (Paris: Perrin, 1888), 260–66, a subsequent edition of *Angélique Lagier*, whose second volume has been lost at the BN.

16. See Leroyer to Flaubert, 26 Sept. 1857, in *FC2*, 766.

17. Leroyer, *Chroniques et légendes* (Château-Gontier: Bézier, 1870), iii.

18. Geneviève Bréton's personal papers, her letters and diary notebooks, are included with those of her son Jean-Louis Vaudoyer, maintained but as yet uncatalogued in the BN. Most of the first nine notebooks of her diary appeared in Bréton, *Journal, 1867–1871*, ed. Daphné Doublet-Vaudoyer (Paris: Ramsay, 1985) and a more complete rendition in Bréton, *"In the Solitude of My Soul": The Diary of Geneviève Bréton, 1867–1871*, ed. James Smith Allen, tr. James Palmes (Carbondale: Southern Illinois UP, 1994) (hereafter *ISMS*).

19. Bréton, 25 Feb. 1868, *ISMS*, 42; *Journal*, 64.

20. Bréton, 7 Feb. 1871, *ISMS*, 174–75; *Journal*, 214–15.

21. Bréton, 18 Nov. 1870, *ISMS*, 141–42; *Journal*, 174.

22. The twenty-four boxes of the personal papers appertaining to Céline Renooz (hereafter Renooz)—containing her extensive correspondence, memoirs, and newspaper clippings—as well as most of her publications in natural history, embryology, the history of religion, and feminist theory are maintained in the BHVP, Fonds Marie Louise Bouglé, Papiers Céline Renooz (hereafter PCR). The papers are indexed in Maïté Albistur, *Catalogue des archives Marie Louise Bouglé* (Paris: BHVP, 1982), photocopied typescript. I list her most important publications in the bibliography.

23. Renooz, "Une révélation," *La Religion laïque et universelle* (15 May 1888): 268.

24. Renooz, "Prédestinée: L'Autobiographie de la femme cachée," BHVP, Fonds Bouglé, PCR, b. 16, f. 2.

25. Renooz, *Ere de vérité*, vol. 6, *Le Monde moderne* (Paris: Giard, 1933), 738.

26. Gerda Lerner, *The Creation of Feminist Consciousness: From the Middle Ages to Eighteen Seventy* (New York: Oxford UP, 1993).

27. Cf. Jean Larnac, *Histoire de la littérature féminine* (Paris: Kra, 1929), which perpetuates the tradition of trivializing all women's writing as merely autobiographical.

28. See succinct statement of this problem in Shari Benstock, "The Female Self-Engendered: Autobiographical Writing and Theories of Selfhood," *Women's Studies* 20, no. 1 (1991): 5–14.

29. Note the emphasis on the particular lawlessness of the genre in John Pilling, *Autobiography and Imagination: Studies in Self-Scrutiny* (London: Routledge & Kegan Paul, 1981), 1–2.

30. Philippe Lejeune, *L'Autobiographie en France* (Paris: Colin, 1971), 14.

31. Cf. Lejeune, *On Autobiography*, 3–30, 119–39.

32. Lejeune's definition also works badly with poststructuralist writing like Jacques Laurent's *Les Bêtises* (Paris: Club Français du Livre, 1971), a provocative combination of fiction, essay, diary, questionnaire, encyclopedia article, critical commentary, and much else.

33. A telling critique of male autobiographical norms is Susan Stanford Friedman, "Women's Autobiographical Selves: Theory and Practice," in *The Private Self: Theory and Practice of Women's Autobiographical Writing*, ed. Shari Benstock (Chapel Hill: U of North Carolina P, 1987), 34–62. Cf. *These Modern Women: Autobiographical Essays from the Twenties*, ed. Elaine Showalter (New York: Feminist P / City U of New York, 1989), 33–133.

34. See useful survey of this issue, among others, in *Feminist Issues in Literary Scholarship*, ed. Shari Benstock (Bloomington: Indiana UP, 1987).

35. E.g., Shoshana Felman, *What Does a Woman Want? Reading and Sexual Difference* (Baltimore: Johns Hopkins UP, 1993), 1–19, 121–51, 156–57 n. 17. Some theorists would contend that all autobiographical texts, not just those by women, lack referen-

tiality. See Jean Starobinski, "Le Style de l'autobiographie," *Poétique*, no. 3 (1970): 257–65; Paul de Man, "Autobiography as De-facement," *Modern Language Notes* 94, no. 5 (1979): 919–30; and Serge Doubrovsky, "Autobiographie / vérité / psycho-analyse," in *Autobiographiques: De Corneille à Sartre* (Paris: PUF, 1988), 61–79.

36. Shari Benstock, introduction to *The Private Self*, 15. Cf. this perspective with that of an older tradition (of autobiography as a distinct literary genre) represented by Henri Peyre, *Literature and Sincerity* (New Haven: Yale UP, 1963); Lionel Trilling, *Sincerity and Authenticity* (Cambridge: Harvard UP, 1972); and Lionel Gossman, "The Innocent Art of Confession and Reverie," *Daedalus* 3 (1978): 59–78. As for the older historical tradition (of autobiography as a historical document), it is well repre-sented by Georg Dilthey's student Georg Misch, *Geschichte der Autobiographie* (Bern: Francke, 1949–50; Frankfurt: Schulte-Bulmke, 1955–69), 4 vols.; and more accessibly in Karl Joachim Weintraub, *The Value of the Individual: Self and Circumstance in Autobiography* (Chicago: U of Chicago P, 1978). Of course, the poststructuralist critique of these traditions has significantly undermined such critical and scholarly confidence in the form.

37. See Roland Barthes, "The Death of the Author," in *Image / Music / Text*, tr. Stephen Heath (London: Fontana, 1977), 142–48; Jacques Lacan, *The Language of the Self: The Function of Language in Psychoanalysis*, ed. and tr. Anthony Wilden (Bal-timore: Johns Hopkins UP, 1969); Michel Foucault, "What Is an Author?" in *Textual Strategies: Perspectives in Post-Structuralist Criticism*, ed. Josué Harari (Ithaca: Cornell UP, 1979), 141–60; and more generally, Jonathan Culler, *Structuralist Poetics: Struc-turalism, Linguistics, and the Study of Literature* (Ithaca: Cornell UP, 1975).

38. See surveys of French feminist theory and criticism in Michelle Richman, "Sex and Signs: The Language of French Feminist Criticism," *Language and Style* 14, no. 1 (1980): 62–80; Elissa D. Gelfand and Virginia Thorndike Hules, *French Feminist Criticism: Women, Language, and Literature: An Annotated Bibliography* (New York: Garland, 1985); and Toril Moi, *Sexual / Textual Politics: Feminist Literary Theory* (New York: Routledge, 1988).

39. See *The Female Autograph: Theory and Practice of Autobiography from the Tenth to the Twentieth Century*, ed. Domna Stanton (Chicago: U of Chicago P, 1987). Cf. the feminist critique of universal subjectivity in women's autobiographical writings sum-marized in Shari Benstock, "Authorizing the Autobiographical," in *The Private Self*, 10–33.

40. Miller, "Arachnologies: The Woman, the Text, and the Critic," in *Subject to Change*, 80–81. Note the strategic change in the title of her essay on Frenchwomen's autobiography—from "Women's Autobiography in France: For a Dialectics of Iden-tification," in *Women and Language in Literature and Society*, ed. Sally McConnell-Ginet et al. (New York: Praeger, 1980), 258–73; to "Writing Fictions: Women's Autobiography in France," in *Subject to Change*, 47–64—primarily in order to empha-

size the writer's creative agency, even though she does not pursue this theme with any specific texts, as I do here.

41. Sidonie Smith, *A Poetics of Women's Autobiography: Marginality and the Fictions of Self-Representation* (Bloomington: Indiana UP, 1987), 7. Cf. Janice Morgan, "Subject to Subject/Voice to Voice: Twentieth-Century Autobiographical Fiction by Women Writers," in *Gender and Genre in Literature: Redefining Autobiography in Twentieth-Century Women's Fiction,* ed. Janice Morgan and Colette T. Hall (New York: Garland, 1991), 3–19.

42. See more developed statements of this position in Paul John Eakin, *Fictions in Autobiography: Studies in the Art of Self-Invention* (Princeton: Princeton UP, 1985), 181–278; and more recently, id., *Touching the World: Reference in Autobiography* (Princeton: Princeton UP, 1992).

43. Cf. John E. Toews, "Intellectual History after the Lingusitic Turn: The Autonomy of Meaning and the Irreducibility of Experience," *American Historical Review* 92, no. 4 (1987): 879–907; Joan Wallach Scott, "The Evidence of Experience," *Questions of Evidence: Proof, Practice, and Persuasion across the Disciplines,* ed. James Chandler et al. (Chicago: U of Chicago P, 1994), 363–87, 397–400; and Dori Laub and Shoshana Felman, *Testimony: Crisis of Witnessing in Literature, Psychology, and History* (New York: Routledge, 1992).

44. James Olney, *Metaphors of the Self: The Meaning of Autobiography* (Princeton: Princeton UP, 1972), 34. Cf., id., "Autobiography and the Cultural Moment: A Thematic, Historical, and Bibliographic Introduction," and Georges Gusdorf, "Conditions and Limits of Autobiography," both in *Autobiography: Essays Theoretical and Critical,* ed. James Olney (Princeton: Princeton UP, 1980), 3–27, 28–48, respectively.

45. Eakin, *Fictions in Autobiography,* 192. Cf. Janet Varner Gunn, *Autobiography: Towards a Poetics of Experience* (Philadelphia: U of Pennsylvania P, 1982); Paul Jay, *Being in the Text: Self-Representation from Wordsworth to Roland Barthes* (Ithaca: Cornell UP, 1984); and most recently, Jacques Lecarme and Elaine Lecarme-Tabone, *L'Autobiographie* (Paris: Colin, 1997).

46. Ernst Cassirer, *An Essay on Man: An Introduction to a Philosophy of Human Culture* (New Haven: Yale UP, 1944), 24.

47. Ibid., 134.

48. Michael Bleich, *Subjective Criticism* (Baltimore: Johns Hopkins UP, 1977), 44. Cf. Suzanne K. Langer, *Philosophy in a New Key: A Study in the Symbolism of Reason, Rite, and Art,* 3rd ed. (Cambridge: Harvard UP, 1969); and, id., *Feeling and Form: A Theory of Art Developed from "Philosophy in a New Key"* (London: Routledge & Kegan Paul, 1967).

49. Paul Ricoeur, *Oneself as Another,* tr. Kathleen Blamey (Chicago: U of Chicago P, 1992), esp. 1–26, 113–68. Though highly technical, this work lays the hermeneutical foundations for the approach I take to women's autobiographical writings. Cf.

the aesthetics of existence and being, argued in John Dewey, *Art as Experience* (New York: Capricorn, 1934), esp. 3–19, 58–81.

50. See also Françoise Lionnet, *Autobiographical Voices: Race, Gender, Self-Portraiture* (Ithaca: Cornell UP, 1989), esp. 3–28; Julia Watson and Sidonie Smith, "De / Colonization and the Politics of Discourse in Women's Autobiographical Practices," introduction to *De / Colonizing the Subject: The Politics of Gender in Women's Autobiography,* ed. Julia Watson and Sidonie Smith (Minneapolis: U of Minnesota P, 1992), xiii–xxxi; and more recently, Sidonie Smith, *Subjectivity, Identity, and the Body: Women's Autobiographical Practices in the Twentieth Century* (Bloomington: Indiana UP, 1993).

51. Elizabeth W. Bruss, *Autobiographical Acts: The Changing Situation of a Literary Genre* (Baltimore: Johns Hopkins UP, 1976), 4. Cf. Jean Rousset, *Le Lecteur intime de Balzac au journal* (Paris: Corti, 1986), 141–218; and reflections on comparable autobiographical acts in another medium, Linda Haverty Rugg, *Picturing Ourselves: Photography and Autobiography* (Chicago: U of Chicago P, 1997), 1–27.

52. Bella Brodzki and Celeste Schenk, introduction to *Life / Lines: Theorizing Women's Autobiography,* ed. Bella Brodzki and Celeste Schenk (Ithaca: Cornell UP, 1988), 12–13. Cf. similar perspectives taken in Susan Groag Bell and Marilyn Yalom, introduction to *Revealing Lives: Autobiography, Biography, and Gender,* ed. Susan Groag Bell and Marilyn Yalom (Albany: State U of New York P, 1992), 1–11; the Personal Narratives Group, "Origins," in *Interpreting Women's Lives: Feminist Theory and Personal Narratives* (Bloomington: Indiana UP, 1989), 3–15; and Rita Felski, *Beyond Feminist Aesthetics: Feminist Literature and Social Change* (Cambridge: Harvard UP, 1989), 86–121.

53. See also Caren Kaplan, "Resisting Autobiography: Out-Law Genres and Transnational Feminist Subjects," in *De / Colonizing the Subject,* 115–38.

54. Cf. Francis Jacques, *Difference and Subjectivity: Dialogue and Personal Identity,* tr. Andrew Rothwell (New Haven: Yale UP, 1991); Charles Taylor, *Sources of the Self: The Making of the Modern Identity* (Cambridge: Harvard UP, 1989); Mikhail Bakhtin, *Rabelais and His World,* tr. Hélène Iswolsky (Cambridge: MIT P, 1968); and Michel Foucault, *The History of Sexuality,* vol. 1, *An Introduction,* tr. Robert Hurley (New York: Pantheon, 1979).

55. Foucault, *History of Sexuality,* 95–96.

56. Denise Riley, *"Am I That Name?" Feminism and the Category of "Women" in History* (Minneapolis: U of Minnesota P, 1988); Françoise Thébaud, *Sociétés, espaces, temps: Ecrire l'histoire des femmes* (Fontenay-Saint-Cloud: ENS, [1998]); Kathleen Canning, "Feminist History after the Linguistic Turn: Historicizing Discourse and Experience," *Signs: Journal of Women in Culture and Society* 19, no. 2 (1994): 368–404; and Mari Jo Buhle, *Feminism and Its Discontents: A Century of Struggle with Psychoanalysis* (Cambridge: Harvard UP, 1998), 351–58.

57. Tyler Stovall, *Paris Noir: African-Americans in the City of Light* (Boston: Houghton Mifflin, 1996); Vernon A. Rosario II, *The Erotic Imagination: French Histories of Perversity* (New York: Oxford UP, 1997); Jann Matlock, *Scenes of Seduction: Prostitution, Hysteria, and Reading Difference in Nineteenth-Century France* (New York: Columbia UP, 1994); and Gyan Prakash, "Subaltern Studies in Postcolonial Criticism," *American Historical Review* 99, no. 5 (1994): 1475–90.

58. Note comparable reassessments of individual agency in *Constructions of the Self*, ed. George Levine (New Brunswick: Rutgers UP, 1992); Paul Smith, *Discerning the Subject* (Minneapolis: U of Minnesota P, 1988); and more tentatively, *Critical Encounters: Reference and Responsibility in Deconstructive Writing*, ed. Cathy Caruth and Deborah Esch (New Brunswick: Rutgers UP, 1995).

CHAPTER THREE   A Provincial's Devotions

1. Marie-Sophie Leroyer de Chantepie (hereafter Leroyer), *Angèle, ou le dévouement filial* (Tours: Mame, 1860), 140. This title appeared in the publisher's "Bibliothèque des Ecoles Chrétiennes, approuvée par Msr. l'Archevêque de Tours." Leroyer often signed her name "Marie-S.," hence its abbreviation to "Marie," used in my book.

2. Ibid., 5.

3. Ibid., 6.

4. See birth certificate in Archives Nationales (hereafter AN) 454 AP 253 Société des Gens de Lettres, d. Leroyer de Chantepie, f. 1; and Leroyer, *Chroniques et légendes* (Château-Gontier: Bézier, 1870), 1–4.

5. Letter from Leroyer to Gustave Flaubert, 17 Jul. 1858, in *Flaubert: Correspondance*, vol. 2, *Juillet 1851–décembre 1858*, ed. Jean Bruneau (Paris: Gallimard, 1980) (hereafter *FC2*), 823.

6. See discussion of France's revolutionary experiment with divorce in Roderick Phillips, *Putting Asunder: A History of Divorce in Western Society* (Cambridge: Cambridge UP, 1988), 256–76; and Francis Ronsin, *Le Contrat sentimental: Débats sur le mariage, l'amour, le divorce, de l'Ancien Régime à la Restauration* (Paris: Aubier, 1990).

7. Leroyer to George Sand, 28 Jan. 1849, in Bibliothèque Historique de la Ville de Paris (hereafter BHVP), Fonds George Sand, G. 4404–575, f. 205r.

8. Ibid.

9. Leroyer to Flaubert, 11 Aug. 1857, in *FC2*, 754; and 15 Apr. 1872, in Bibliothèque Nationale, Nouvelles Acquisitions Françaises (hereafter BN, NAFr) MS 23825 (microfilm 1375), f. 383.

10. Leroyer to Flaubert, 15 Apr. 1872, in BN, NAFr MS 23825, f. 383r.

11. Leroyer to Flaubert, 28 Mar. 1857, in *FC2*, 695.

12. See Leroyer to Flaubert, 11 Aug. 1857, in *FC2*, 754; and 14 Oct. 1859, in *Flaubert: Correspondance*, vol. 3, *Janvier 1859–décembre 1868*, ed. Jean Bruneau (Paris: Gallimard, 1991) (hereafter *FC3*), 49.

13. Leroyer to Sand, 3 Jan. 1856, in BHVP, Fonds Sand, G. 4404–575, f. 237v.

14. Leroyer to Flaubert, 28 Mar. 1857, in *FC2*, 694. See also Leroyer to Sand, 28 Jan. 1849, in BHVP, Fonds Sand, G. 4404–575, f. 205r.

15. See entries on the Leroyer de Chantepie family in Célestin Port, *Dictionnaire historique, géographique, et biographique de Maine et Loire et de l'ancienne province d'Anjou,* rev. ed. (Angers: Siraudeau, 1965), 2: 360–61.

16. See Leroyer to Flaubert, 28 Mar. 1857, in *FC2*, 694; Archives Départementales de Maine-et-Loire (hereafter ADML), 4O 52, Testament: Marie-Sophie Leroyer de Chantepie, certified 14 Dec. 1888; and ADML, 3Q 1765, Inventaire après décès: Marie-Sophie Leroyer de Chantepie, certified 23 Apr. 1889.

17. Leroyer, *Chroniques et légendes,* 19–21.

18. Ibid., 2.

19. See the progress report on her chronicle in Leroyer to Victor Mangin, 7 Jul. 1860, in Bibliothèque Municipale Médiathèque de Nantes (hereafter BMN), MS 2942. On Leroyer's region, see *Histoire des pays de la Loire: Orléans, Touraine, Anjou, Maine,* ed. François Lebrun (Toulouse: Privat, 1972).

20. On the history of Angers in particular, see *Histoire d'Angers,* ed. François Lebrun (Toulouse: Privat, 1975); and François Lebrun, *Les Hommes et la mort en Anjou aux XVIIe et XVIIIe siècles: Essai de démographie et de psychologie historiques* (Paris: Flammarion, 1975).

21. See, e.g., George H. Forsyth Jr., *The Church of St. Martin at Angers: The Architectural History of the Site from the Roman Empire to the French Revolution* (Princeton: Princeton UP, 1953); and Claire Giraud-Labalte, *The Apocalypse Tapestry,* tr. Angela Moyon (Angers: Caisse Nationale des Monuments Historiques et des Sites, 1986).

22. Leroyer, *Figures historiques et légendaires* (Paris: Perrin, n.d.), 31.

23. See Evelyne Lejeune-Resnick, "Anjou, républicanisme et romantisme: Les Aspirations de Sophie Leroyer," *Annales de Bretagne* 99, no. 4 (1992): 415–22. Cf. Leroyer's naive letters to Sand on the Paris Commune, in BHVP, Fonds Sand, G. 699–838, ff. 242–50.

24. Leroyer to Flaubert, 15 Mar. 1861, in *FC3*, 149.

25. Leroyer to Flaubert, 15 Jan. 1866, in *FC3*, 477; 13 Jun. 1866, in *FC3*, 506; and 11 May 1867, in *FC3*, 640. Cf. her analysis of continuing clerical influence in Angers discussed in Leroyer to V. Mangin, 7 Jul. 1867, in BMN, MS 2942.

26. Leroyer, *Mémoires d'une provinciale* (Paris: Dentu, 1880), 1: 1.

27. Leroyer to Flaubert, 26 Nov. 1869, in BN, NAFr MS 23825, f. 378. Cf. her "ideal" hours spent in Tours, expressed in Leroyer to Flaubert, 8 Sept. 1862, in *FC3*, 245.

28. Leroyer, *Chroniques et légendes,* 1.

29. ADML, 3Q 1765 Inventaire après décès: Leroyer.

30. Leroyer to Flaubert, 22 Jan. 1859, in *FC3*, 8.

31. Leroyer, *Chroniques et légendes,* 19–21.

32. Leroyer to Jules Michelet, 16 Sept. 1859, in BHVP, Fonds Jules Michelet, tome 11, f. 144r.

33. Ibid., f. 143v.

34. ADML, 3Q 1255, case no. 10: Leroyer de Chantepie, Marie-Sophie. For comparisons of middle-class family budgets in the late nineteenth century, see Marguerite Perrot, *Le Mode de vie des familles bourgeoises, 1873–1953* (Paris: P de la Fondation Nationale des Sciences Politiques, 1982), 168, table 12.

35. See Adeline Daumard, *Les Bourgeois et la bourgeoisie en France depuis 1815* (Paris: Flammarion, 1991), 71–72; and Georges Dupeux, *La Société française, 1789–1970* (Paris: Colin, 1972), 113–14.

36. Leroyer to Sand, 28 Jan. 1849, in BHVP, Fonds Sand, G. 4404–575, f. 205r.

37. See Leroyer to Flaubert, 28 Mar. 1857, in *FC2,* 694; and 23 May 1859, in *FC3,* 29.

38. Leroyer to Flaubert, 11 Mar. 1859, in *FC3,* 20.

39. Leroyer to Michelet, 12 Aug. 1859, in BHVP, Fonds Michelet, T. 11, f. 138r.

40. See Leroyer to Flaubert, 22 Dec. 1867, in *FC3,* 715; 13 Apr. 1868, in *FC3,* 742; 10 Jan. 1870, in BN, NAFr MS 23825, f. 380; and 10 Jul. 1870, in BN, NAFr MS 23825, f. 382. Note the assistance of another hand in writing Leroyer to V. Mangin, 26 Sept. 1867, in BMN, MS 2942.

41. Leroyer to Michelet, 12 Aug. 1859, in BHVP, Fonds Michelet, T. 11, f. 138r. Note the profound ambivalence of ordinary individuals like Leroyer toward the church and its doctrines suggested in Theodore Zeldin, "The Conflicts of Moralities: Confession, Sin and Pleasure in the Nineteenth Century," in *Conflicts in French Society: Anticlericalism, Education and Morals in the Nineteenth Century: Essays* (London: Allen & Unwin, 1970), 13–50.

42. Leroyer to Sand, 28 Jan. 1849, in BHVP, Fonds Sand, G. 4404–575, f. 205v.

43. Leroyer to Flaubert, 30 Jun. 1857, in *FC2,* 738.

44. See, e.g., Leroyer to Flaubert, 23 May 1857, in *FC2,* 723. Cf. literary developments discussed in F. W. J. Hemmings, *Culture and Society in France 1848–1898: Dissidents and Philistines* (London: Batsford, 1971), 77–120.

45. Leroyer to Flaubert, 10 Nov. 1857, in *FC2,* 777.

46. Leroyer to Flaubert, 21 Dec. 1857, in *FC2,* 789.

47. See René Gauchet, "Au temps du romantisme: Une angevine extravagante et débonnaire: Marie-Sophie Leroyer de Chantepie," *Le Courrier de l'ouest,* 31 Oct. 1951, 4.

48. Cf. Achille Ouvré's woodcut of Leroyer in *Oeuvres complètes illustrées de Gustave Flaubert: Correspondance,* vol. 2, *1853–1863,* ed. René Descharmes (Paris: Librairie de France, 1923), 329.

49. At the bottom of the painting, upside down to the viewer, read the words,

"God and the immortality of the soul are the only two realities. If they did not exist, there would be nothing, for the rest is nothing."

50. See Leroyer to Flaubert, 28 Mar. 1857, in *FC2*, 694; 10 Nov. 1857, in *FC2*, 778; and 21 Dec. 1857, in *FC2*, 789.

51. Leroyer to Flaubert, 10 Nov. 1857, in *FC2*, 777, 776.

52. Leroyer, *Récits d'amour* (Paris: Didier, Perrin, 1890), 83.

53. See Leroyer to Flaubert, 10 Nov. 1857, in *FC2*, 776; and 13 Mar. 1858, in *FC2*, 801.

54. Leroyer to Flaubert, 3 Jul. 1872, in BN, NAFr MS 23825, f. 385.

55. Leroyer, *Chroniques et légendes*, 1.

56. See Leroyer to Sand, 28 Jan. 1849, in BHVP, Fonds Sand, G. 4404–575, f. 203r; and 3 Jan. 1856, in BHVP, Fonds Sand, G. 4404–575, f. 235r.

57. Leroyer to Flaubert, 22 Jan. 1858, in *FC2*, 792. But see also, e.g., Leroyer to Flaubert, 22 Jan. 1859, in *FC3*, 9; 11 Mar. 1859, in *FC3*, 20; 7 Mar. 1860, in *FC3*, 78; 3 Apr. 1860, in *FC3*, 85; and passim. Note Sand's own tendency to identify with Lélia assumed in André Maurois, *Lélia: The Life of George Sand*, tr. Gerard Hopkins (New York: Harper, 1953), 147–58, seconded by Sand herself to Leroyer, 21 Aug. 1856 in *George Sand: Correspondance*, ed. Georges Lubin (Paris: Garnier, 1964–91) (hereafter *GSC*), vol. 3, *Juillet 1835–avril 1837*, 539: "where I have put more of myself than in any other book." Cf. Isabelle Hoog Naginski, *George Sand: Writing for Her Life* (New Brunswick: Rutgers UP, 1991), 105–37.

58. Leroyer to Michelet, 12 Aug. 1859, in BHVP, Fonds Michelet, T. 11, f. 137r.; and Leroyer to Flaubert, 18 Dec. 1856, in *FC2*, 654.

59. Leroyer to Flaubert, 22 Jan. 1858, in *FC2*, 792.

60. Leroyer to Flaubert, 6 Jun. 1867, in *FC3*, 648.

61. Leroyer to Flaubert, 13 Apr. 1868, in *FC3*, 743. Cf. Sand to Leroyer, 12 Feb. 1860, in *GSC*, vol. 15, *Juillet 1858–juin 1860*, 695–96.

62. Mona Ozouf, *Women's Words: Essay on French Singularity*, tr. Jane Marie Todd (Chicago: U of Chicago P, 1997), 130.

63. Leroyer to Flaubert, 23 Oct. 1860, in *FC3*, 122–23.

64. Leroyer to Michelet, 2 Sept. 1859, in BHVP, Fonds Michelet, T. 11, f. 139r.

65. Leroyer to Michelet, 16 Sept. 1859, in BHVP, Fonds Michelet, T. 11, f. 143r.

66. Leroyer to Flaubert, 28 Mar. 1857, in *FC2*, 695.

67. Leroyer to Flaubert, 23 Oct. 1860, in *FC3*, 122.

68. Leroyer to Flaubert, 5 Sept. 1858, in *FC2*, 834.

69. Leroyer to V. Mangin, 26 Sept. 1867, in BMN, MS 2942.

70. Leroyer to V. Mangin, 9 Jul. 1867, in BMN, MS 2942.

71. See Leroyer to V. Mangin, 9 Jul. 1867, in BMN, MS 2941; and Leroyer to Flaubert, 10 Jul. 1868, in *FC3*, 773–75.

72. Leroyer to Flaubert, 23 May 1857, in *FC2*, 723.

73. Ibid., 724.

74. Leroyer to Flaubert, 11 Aug. 1857, in *FC2*, 755.

75. Leroyer to Flaubert, 6 Jun. 1867, in *FC3*, 649.

76. Leroyer to Flaubert, 22 Jan. 1859, in *FC3*, 8.

77. Leroyer to Sand, 28 Jan. 1849, in BHVP, Fonds Sand, G. 4404–575, f. 206v.

78. Leroyer, *Souvenirs et impressions littéraires* (Paris: Perrin, 1892), 209–21.

79. See Leroyer to Flaubert, 11 Aug. 1857, in *FC2*, 754–55; and, id., 10 Jul. 1868, in *FC3*, 776.

80. Leroyer to Flaubert, 28 Mar. 1857, in *FC2*, 695.

81. Leroyer to Flaubert, 26 Sept. 1857, in *FC2*, 764.

82. Leroyer to Flaubert, 28 Jul. 1868, in *FC3*, 781–82.

83. Leroyer to Sand, 8 Sept. 1849, in BHVP, Fonds Sand, G. 4404–575, f. 208r.

84. Leroyer to Flaubert, 11 Aug. 1857, in *FC2*, 754. Sourice's first name in listed in the Angers death registry, ADML no. 216, 15 May 1872.

85. Leroyer to Sand, 5 Nov. 1849, in BHVP, Fonds Sand, G. 4404–575, ff. 221r.–225v.; and Leroyer to Flaubert, 21 Jan. 1867, in *FC3*, 596.

86. Leroyer to Flaubert, 21 Jan. 1867, in *FC3*, 596; and 10 May 1867, in *FC3*, 639.

87. Leroyer to Flaubert, 11 May 1867, in *FC3*, 639.

88. Ibid.

89. Leroyer to Sand, 28 Jan. 1849, in BHVP, Fonds Sand, G. 4404–575, ff. 203r.–207v.; and 8 Sept. 1849, in BHVP, Fonds Sand, G. 4404–575, ff. 208r.–218v.

90. Leroyer to Sand, 5 Nov. 1849, BHVP, Fonds Sand, G. 4404–575, f. 224v.

91. Leroyer to Sand, 3 Oct. 1849, in BHVP, Fonds Sand, G. 4404–575, ff. 218r.–20v.; and 23 Nov. 1849, in BHVP, Fonds Sand, G. 4404–575, ff. 226r.–27v.

92. Leroyer to Sand, 21 Jan. 1867, in BHVP, Fonds Sand, G. 4404–575, ff. 239v.–40r.; and Leroyer to Flaubert, 21 Jan. 1867, in *FC3*, 596–97.

93. Leroyer to Flaubert, 3 Jul. 1872, in BN, NAFr MS 23825, f. 385.

94. Leroyer to Flaubert, 15 Mar. 1861, in *FC3*, 148.

95. Leroyer to Michelet, 16 Sept. 1859, in BHVP, Fonds Michelet, T. 11, f. 144r.

96. Leroyer to Flaubert, 11 Aug. 1857, in *FC2*, 754.

97. Leroyer to Sand, 8 Sept. 1849, in BHVP, Fonds Sand, G. 4404–575, f. 210v.

98. See Leroyer to Flaubert, 28 Mar. 1857, in *FC2*, 695; and 15 Mar. 1861, in *FC3*, 148. On Leroyer's political efforts on Edouard's behalf, see Sand to Leroyer, 2 Jun. 1852, in *GSC*, vol. 11, *Avril 1852–juin 1853*, 199–200.

99. Leroyer to Flaubert, 5 Sept. 1858, in *FC2*, 833; and 15 Mar. 1861, in *FC3*, 149.

100. Ibid.; Leroyer to Sand, 21 Jan. 1867, in BHVP, Fonds Sand, G. 4404–575, f. 241–42.; and Leroyer to Michelet, 16 Sept. 1859, in BHVP, Fonds Michelet, T. 11, f. 144r. Cf. Leroyer to V. Mangin, 7 Jul. 1860, in BMN, MS 2942.

101. See Leroyer to Flaubert, 17 Jul. 1858, in *FC2*, 823–26. Leroyer does not mention Agathe's family name, but it appears in the Angers death registry, ADML no. 274, 18 May 1858.

102. Leroyer to Flaubert, 12 Sept. 1858, in *FC2*, 835.

103. Leroyer to Michelet, 16 Sept. 1859, in BHVP, Fonds Michelet, T. 11, ff. 144v.–145r.

104. Ibid.

105. Ibid., 144v. Leroyer refers to Zemiowski as M. Pierre, but his family name appears in the Angers death registry for Agathe-Julie Gautret de la Moricière, ADML no. 274, 18 May 1858.

106. Leroyer to Flaubert, 20 Mar. 1863, in *FC3*, 312.

107. Leroyer surveys her household at various times in her correspondence. See especially Leroyer to Michelet, 16 Sept. 1859, in BHVP, Fonds Michelet, T. 11, ff. 143r.–146v.; Leroyer to Sand, 29 Jan. 1849, in BHVP, Fonds Sand, G. 4404–575, ff. 206r.–v.; and Leroyer to Flaubert, 11 Aug. 1857, in *FC2*, 754–55.

108. Leroyer to Michelet, 16 Sept. 1859, in BHVP, Fonds Michelet, T. 11, ff. 144v, 144r.

109. Ibid., f. 144v.

110. This correspondence is the subject of Daniel Brizemur, "Une correspondante de Flaubert: Mlle Leroyer de Chantepie," *Revue hebdomadaire* (18 Oct. 1919): 305–38, reprinted in *Les Amis de Flaubert*, nos. 16–17 (1960): 3–12, 3–10; and Hermia Oliver, "Nouveaux aperçus sur Marie-Sophie Leroyer de Chantepie," *Les Amis de Flaubert*, no. 61 (1982): 4–14. For more about the disposition of Leroyer's correspondence, see the letters she wrote to Ernest Commanville after Flaubert's death, now in the Collection Spoelberch de Lovenjoul in the Bibliothèque Mazarine of the Institut de France, discussed in Jean Bruneau's note in *FC2*, 1332–33, despite errors, as in nearly all previous works on Leroyer.

111. Leroyer to Flaubert, 26 Feb. 1857, in *FC2*, 686.

112. Flaubert to Leroyer, 18 Mar. [1857], in *FC2*, 691.

113. Leroyer to Flaubert, 10 May 1867, in *FC3*, 639.

114. See discussion of Leroyer's correspondence with both Sand and Flaubert in Martine Reid, "Mademoiselle Leroyer de Chantepie, Tertre-Saint-Laurent, 20, Angers," *Textuel*, no. 27 (1992): 109–21, though she omits consideration of the manuscript materials and thus miscounts the actual number of letters Leroyer sent to Flaubert.

115. Leroyer to Flaubert, 15 Jun. 1876, in BN, NAFr MS 23825, f. 387.

116. See, e.g., Leroyer, *Souvenirs et impressions littéraires*, 190; Leroyer to Sand, 28 Jan. 1849, in BHVP, Fonds Sand, G. 4404–575, f. 203r.; and Leroyer to Flaubert, 22 Jan. 1858, in *FC2*, 792. Cf. the views of *Lélia* as a feminist text: Eileen Boyd Sivert, "*Lélia* and Feminism," *Yale French Studies* 62 (1981): 45–66; and Naomi Schor, *George Sand and Idealism* (New York: Columbia UP, 1993), 55–68.

117. Note the tension here between the public and the private in Leroyer's correspondence, as suggested by Roger Chartier and Jean Hébrard, "Entre public et privé: La Correspondance, une écriture ordinaire," in *La Correspondance: Les usages de la lettre au XIXe siècle*, ed. Roger Chartier (Paris: Fayard, 1991), 451–56. On the one

hand, her letters to Flaubert take on a formulaic quality, not unlike that described by Cécile Dauphin, "Les Manuels épistolaires au XIXe siècle," ibid., 209–72; on the other hand, her letters to Sand seem to foster an intimacy discussed by Anne Martin-Fugier, "Les Lettres célibataires," ibid., 407–26.

118. Cf. Stéphane Michaud, *Muse et madone: Visages de la femme de la Révolution française aux apparitions de Lourdes* (Paris: Seuil, 1985), 168–69.

119. Leroyer to Sand, 28 Jan. 1849, in BHVP, Fonds Sand, G. 4404–575, f. 207r.

120. Leroyer to Sand, 8 Sept. 1849, in BHVP, Fonds Sand, G. 4404–572, f. 213v.

121. Leroyer to Sand, 23 Nov. 1849, in BHVP, Fonds Sand, G. 4404–572, f. 226r.

122. See Leroyer to Flaubert, 15 Jun. 1876, in BN, NAFr MS 23825, ff. 387–88.

123. Leroyer, *Mémoires d'une provinciale*, 1: v.

124. Leroyer, "George Sand," in *Souvenirs et impressions littéraires*, 185–92; and, id., "Le Compagnon du tour de France de George Sand," ibid., 255–62.

125. Sand to Leroyer, 21 Feb. 1860, in *GSC* 15: 696.

126. Sand to Leroyer, 20 May 1872, in *GSC*, vol. 23, *Avril 1872–mars 1874*, 86.

127. Sand to Leroyer, 4 Jan. 1873, in *GSC* 23: 375–76; 6 Mar. 1872, in *GSC*, vol. 22, *Avril 1870–mars 1872*, 756–57; 21 Aug. 1836, in *GSC* 3: 539–40; and 28 Aug. 1842, in *GSC* vol. 5, *Avril 1840–décembre 1842*, 756–59.

128. See, e.g., Leroyer to V. Mangin, 4 Jun. 1862, in BMN, MS 2942.

129. E.g., Leroyer to V. Mangin, 10 Mar. 1865, in BMN, MS 2942.

130. See Leroyer to V. Mangin, 8 and 17 Nov. 1865, in BMN, MS 2942.

131. E.g., Leroyer to Flaubert, 12 Sept. 1858, in *FC2*, 834; and Leroyer to V. Mangin, 10 Mar. 1865, in BMN, MS 2942.

132. Leroyer to Michelet, 16 Sept. 1859, in BHVP, Fonds Michelet, T. 11, f. 145v.

133. The only previous effort to take Leroyer's work seriously is Françoise Blot-Pautrel, "Marie-Sophie Leroyer de Chantepie: Une femme de lettres romantique en Anjou," in *Les Angevins de la littérature* (Angers: P de l'Université, 1979), 237–50.

134. Sand to Leroyer, 12 Aug. 1836, in *GSC* 3: 539; and Flaubert to Leroyer, 18 Mar. 1857, in *FC2*, 691.

135. Leroyer, *Mémoires d'une provinciale*, 2: 187.

136. D. G. Charlton, "Prose Fiction," in *The French Romantics*, ed. D. G. Charlton (Cambridge: Cambridge UP, 1984), 1: 168.

137. Peter Brooks, *The Melodramatic Imagination: Balzac, Henry James, Melodrama, and the Mode of Excess* (New Haven: Yale UP, 1976), 24–80.

138. Cf. Jules Larnac, *Histoire de la littérature féminine en France* (Paris: Kra, 1929); John S. Wood, *Sondages, 1830–1848: Romanciers français secondaires* (Toronto: U of Toronto P, 1965); and James Smith Allen, *Popular French Romanticism: Authors, Readers, and Books in the Nineteenth Century* (Syracuse: Syracuse UP, 1981), 141–45.

139. Leroyer, *Mémoires d'une provinciale*, 2: 187. Cf. the perspective of Schor, *George Sand and Idealism*, 55–132.

140. I use the term *romance* in the generally accepted sense of works "which are relatively free of the more restrictive aspects of realistic verisimilitude and which are expressive of profound or transcendent or idealistic truths," per C. Hugh Holman, *A Handbook to Literature*, 4th ed. (Indianapolis: Bobbs-Merrill, 1980), 387.

141. See, e.g., Michel Mercier, *Le Roman féminin* (Paris: PUF, 1976), 87–114; Joan Hinde Stewart, *Gynographs: French Novels by Women of the Late Eighteenth Century* (Lincoln: U of Nebraska P, 1993), 1–23, 199–206; and David J. Denby, *Sentimental Narrative and the Social Order in France, 1760–1820* (Cambridge: Cambridge UP, 1994), 71–94.

142. Leroyer, *Mémoires d'une provinciale*, 2, pt. 2: 40.

143. Ibid., 1: 15.

144. Ibid., 1: 125.

145. Ibid., 2, pt. 1: 137.

146. Ibid., 1: 31.

147. Ibid., 1: 57.

148. Ibid., 1: 197.

149. Ibid., 1: 373.

150. Ibid., 1: 36–37.

151. Ibid., 2, pt. 1: 159.

152. Ibid., 2, pt. 1: 261.

153. Ibid., 2, pt. 1: 298.

154. Ibid., 2, pt. 1: 310.

155. Ibid., 1: 76.

156. Ibid., 1: 371.

157. Ibid., 1, pt. 1: 371–72.

158. Ibid., 1: 57.

159. Ibid., 2, pt. 1: 85.

160. Ibid., 1: 117.

161. Ibid., 1: 57.

162. Ibid., 1: 156.

163. Ibid., 2, pt. 2: 187.

164. Ibid., 2, pt. 1: 85–86.

165. Leroyer, "Arthur de Monthierry," in *Nouvelles littéraires* (Paris: Perrin, 1889), 17. Note that the original edition of Leroyer's *Cécile* is not in the BN and does not appear to be available at any other public collection in France (or elsewhere). Nor is it listed in the annual editions of the *Bibliographie de la France*, the most complete catalog of new titles published in France since 1810. But the novel was apparently retitled "Arthur de Monthierry" and included in Leroyer's posthumously published collection of stories and novellas *Nouvelles littéraires*. In response to Leroyer's *Cécile*, Flaubert describes precisely the characters, the narrative frame, and certain sentences

that appear in "Arthur de Monthierry." See Flaubert to Leroyer, 18 May 1857, in *FC2*, 719–20.

166. Leroyer, "Arthur de Monthierry," 125.

167. Ibid., 136.

168. Ibid., 147.

169. Leroyer, "Les Duranti," in *Les Duranti* (Paris: Souverain, 1844), 2: 7.

170. Ibid., 1: 125.

171. Leroyer, *Angélique Lagier* (n.p., 1851), 1: i–ii. Note that the second volume of this title has disappeared from the BN, so one must consult the second edition under a different title, *Une vengeance judiciaire*, for citations to the second half of the novel.

172. Leroyer, *Angélique Lagier*, 1: 4.

173. Ibid., 1: 176.

174. Leroyer, *Une vengeance judiciaire*, 2: 258.

175. Leroyer, *Angélique Lagier*, 1: 78.

176. See Leroyer to Adolphe Thiers, [1876], in Papiers Adolphe Thiers, BN, NAF MS 20622, vol. 28: ff. 304–5; and Leroyer to Victor and Evariste Mangin, in BMN, MS 2492.

177. Flaubert to Leroyer, 18 May [1857], in *FC2*, 719.

178. Sand to Leroyer, 7 Feb. 1843, in *GSC*, vol. 6 *1843–juin 1845*, 33–34.

179. Inscriptions on Leroyer's official letter of application in AN, 454 AP 253 Société des Gens de Lettres, d. Leroyer, f. 2.

180. Gauchet, "Au temps du romantisme," 4. See also Brizemur, "Une correspondante."

181. Port, *Dictionnaire historique*, 2: 361.

182. Note by Georges Lubin in *GSC*, 3: 883. Cf. Oliver, "Nouveaux aperçus."

183. Cf. Schor, *George Sand and Idealism*, 23–54.

184. ADML, Etat civil: Décès, 1888, no. 537, f. 92r.

CHAPTER FOUR "In the Solitude of My Soul"

1. Geneviève Bréton (hereafter Bréton), 26 Aug. 1878, carnet no. 16, f. 127v. Bibliothèque National (hereafter BN), Fonds Jean-Louis Vaudoyer (uncataloged).

2. Ibid.

3. Ibid.

4. Note discussion of the self-conscious French bourgeoisie in Adeline Daumard, *Les Bourgeois et la bourgeoisie en France depuis 1815* (Paris: Flammarion, 1991), 27–68.

5. Daniel Halévy, *L'Europe brisée: Journal et lettres, 1914–1918*, ed. Sébastien Laurent (Paris: Fallois, 1998), 269. Note Halévy's generally accurate but ungenerous assessment of his mother-in-law, ibid., 270–71.

6. Bréton, 22 Jul. 1870, in *"In the Solitude of My Soul": The Diary of Geneviève*

Bréton, 1867–1871, ed. James Smith Allen, tr. James Palmes (Carbondale: Southern Illinois UP, 1994) (hereafter *ISMS*), 102; id., *Journal, 1867–1871*, ed. Daphné Doublet-Vaudoyer (Paris: Ramsay, 1985), 127. Discrepancies between the French and English editions of Bréton's first nine notebooks, especially in dates, are owed to omissions and errors in transcription in the French version. All references here are to the more complete English version and to the French edition wherever appropriate.

7. The Boulevard Saint-Michel was one of the newest additions to Paris during the Second Empire. See David H. Pinkney, *Napoleon III and the Building of Paris* (Princeton: Princeton UP, 1958), 57. Cf. David P. Jordan, *Transforming Paris: The Life and Labors of Baron Haussmann* (Chicago: U of Chicago P, 1995).

8. Bréton, 9 Mar. 1869, in *ISMS*, 69; *Journal*, 92.

9. See Jean Mistler, *La Librairie Hachette de 1826 à nos jours* (Paris: Hachette, 1964), 81–102, passim, and 398–99; James Harding, *Artistes Pompiers: French Academic Art in the Nineteenth Century* (London: Academy, 1979), 7–30; and Roger Williams, *The World of Napoleon III, 1851–1870* (New York: Free P, 1965), 113–31, 173–235.

10. Bréton, 12 Jun. and 7 Jul. 1867, in *ISMS*, 7, 9; *Journal*, 26, 29.

11. Bréton, Jul.-Oct. 1867, document found in carnet no. 1, f. 2v., the source of Bréton, 30 Oct. 1867, in *ISMS*, 23; *Journal*, 43.

12. Bréton, 27 Mar. 1875, carnet no. 10 ter, f. 1v.

13. Bréton, 19 Aug. 1883, carnet no. 23, f. 22r.–v.

14. E.g., Bréton, 7 Jan. 1869, in *ISMS*, 66; 2 Oct. 1870, in *ISMS*, 126; and Jul. 1871, in *ISMS*, 217 esp.; *Journal*, 89, 154, 256.

15. Bréton, May 1868, document found in carnet no. 3, f. 58r.

16. Bréton, 24 Jan. 1877, in carnet no. 18, f. 11v. Such an attitude was increasingly at odds with Parisian middle-class cultural values, according to Daumard, *Les Bourgeois*, 241–53.

17. Bréton, 9 Apr. 1868, in *ISMS*, 49; this passage is incomplete in *Journal*, 70.

18. Bréton, 25 Aug. 1873, in carnet no. 10 bis, pt. 2, f. 41r.

19. Bréton, 4 May 1902, carnet no. 27, f. 14r.

20. Letter from Bréton to Jean-Louis Vaudoyer (hereafter JLV), 30 Sept. 1906, in BN, Fonds Vaudoyer.

21. See Barry Bergdoll, *Les Vaudoyer: Une dynastie d'architectes.* Les Dossiers d'Orsay 45 (Paris: La Réunion des Musées Nationaux, 1991); and on Alfred Vaudoyer's father in particular, see, id., *Léon Vaudoyer: Historicism in the Age of Industry* (Cambridge: MIT P, 1994).

22. Bréton, 2 Jul. 1876, carnet no. 17, f. 98v.

23. Bréton to Jean-Louis, 19 Oct. 1912, in BN, Fonds Vaudoyer.

24. Bréton, 21 Feb. 1877, carnet no. 18, f. 25r.

25. Bréton, 26 Jan. 1873, in carnet no. 11, f. 6v.

26. Bréton, 10 Dec. 1870, in *ISMS*, 149; this passage is incomplete in *Journal*, 181.

27. Bréton, 30 Apr. 1868, in *ISMS*, 52; *Journal*, 73; and, id., 5 Mar. 1872, carnet no. 8, f. 26r.

28. Bréton, 5 Mar. 1872, carnet no. 8, f. 19v. Cf. the changing developments in the arts discussed in Albert Boime, *The Academy and French Painting in the Nineteenth Century* (London: Phaidon, 1971); Gabriel P. Weisberg, *The Realist Tradition: French Painting and Drawing, 1830–1900* (Cleveland: Cleveland Museum of Art, 1980); John Rewald, *The History of Impressionism*, 4th ed. (New York: Museum of Modern Art, 1973); and Michael Fried, *Manet's Modernism, or The Face of Painting in the 1860s* (Chicago: U of Chicago P, 1998).

29. Bréton, 23 Jan. 1868, in *ISMS*, 40; *Journal*, 62.

30. Bréton, 10 May 1878, carnet no. 19, f. 71v.

31. Bréton, 25 Jul. 1870, in *ISMS*, 104; *Journal*, 130.

32. Bréton, 12 Dec. 1870, in *ISMS*, 149; *Journal*, 181.

33. Bréton, 28 Mar. 1875, carnet no. 10 ter, f. 3v.

34. Bréton, 26 Jun. 1875, carnet no. 15, f. 8v.

35. Bréton, 11 Aug. 1880, carnet no. 21, f. 116v.

36. Bréton, 10 Nov. 1880, carnet no. 21, f. 163v.

37. Bréton, 1 Jan. 1882, carnet no. 22, f. 57v.

38. Bréton, 22 Feb. 1869, in *ISMS*, 68; *Journal*, 91.

39. As discussed, e.g., in André Bellessort, *La Société française sous Napoléon III* (Paris: Perrin, 1932), 193–98, 228–35.

40. Bréton, [May 1868], document found in carnet no. 3, f. 57v.

41. Ibid., f. 58v.

42. Ibid., ff. 56v–57r.

43. Bréton to JLV, 14 Nov. 1912, in BN, Fonds Vaudoyer.

44. Bréton to JLV, 13 Aug. 1903, in BN, Fonds Vaudoyer.

45. Bréton, 28 Mar. 1875, carnet no. 10 ter, f. 2v.

46. Bréton, 3 Apr. 1875, carnet no. 10 ter, ff. 11r.–v.

47. Bréton, 3 Apr. 1875, carnet no. 10 ter, f. 14r.

48. Bréton, 19 Apr. 1880, carnet no. 21, f. 60v.

49. Bréton, 3 Aug. 1873, carnet no. 11, f. 83r.

50. Bréton, 6 Apr. 1875, carnet no. 10 ter, ff. 16v.–17r.

51. Bréton, 4 Jul. 1875, carnet no. 15, f. 16v.

52. Bréton, 28 Oct. 1876, carnet no. 17, f. 149v.

53. Bréton, 8 Aug. 1878, carnet no. 19, f. 118r.

54. Bréton, 8 Oct. 1885, carnet no. 24, f. 22v.

55. Bréton, 1877, document found in carnet no. 18, f. 357v.

56. Bréton, 5 Mar. 1872, carnet no. 8, f. 19v.

57. Bréton, 16 Jul. 1872, carnet no. 9, f. 15r.

58. Bréton, 6 Apr. 1878, carnet no. 19, f. 54r.

59. Bréton, 1 Oct. 1872, carnet no. 9, f. 2v.

60. Bréton, 3 Feb. 1877, carnet no. 18, f. 17r.

61. Bréton, 31 Mar. 1875, carnet no. 10 ter, f. 6v.

62. Bréton, 2 Aug. 1876, carnet no. 17, f. 114r.

63. See Jules Michelet, *La Femme* (Paris: Hachette, 1860); and Alexandre Dumas *fils, L'Homme-femme: Réponse à M. Henri d'Ideville* (Paris: Michel Lévy, 1872).

64. Bréton, 10 Aug. 1872, carnet no. 9, ff. 36r.–v., 38v.

65. Bréton, 26 Aug. 1872, carnet no. 9, f. 55r. Cf. the achievements of Marcello in Ghislain de Diesbach, *La Double Vie de la duchesse Colonna, 1835–1879: La Chimère bleue* (Paris: Perrin, 1988); and those of another apparent rival for Regnault's attention, one of his studio models, Gérard Gefen, *Augusta Holmès, l'outrancière* (Paris: Belfond, 1987).

66. Bréton, 3 Jan. 1877, carnet no. 18, f. 2r.

67. Cf. Bréton, 14 Nov. 1869 in *ISMS,* 79; May 1870, ibid., 91; *Journal,* 100, 116; and Robert Darnton, *Mesmerism and the End of the Enlightenment in France* (Cambridge: Harvard UP, 1968), 126–59.

68. Bréton, 2 Jan. 1879, carnet no. 20, ff. 5v.–6r.

69. Bréton, 4 Apr. 1868, in *ISMS,* 47; 19 May 1868, ibid., 53; *Journal,* 68, 73.

70. Bréton, May 1870, in *ISMS,* 90; *Journal,* 115.

71. Bréton, May 1870, in *ISMS,* 92; *Journal,* 117.

72. Bréton, 27 May 1872, carnet no. 8, f. 39v.

73. Bréton, 17 Jun. 1868, in *ISMS,* 54; *Journal,* 74.

74. Bréton, 26 Jul. 1872, carnet no. 9, f. 30r.

75. Bréton, 18 Aug. 1878, carnet no. 19, f. 123r.

76. Bréton, 7 Dec. 1880, carnet no. 21, f. 177r.

77. Bréton, 16 Jul. 1872, carnet no. 9, ff. 13v.–14r.

78. Bréton to JLV, 4 Sept. 1910, in BN, Fonds Vaudoyer.

79. See *Henri Regnault, 1843–1871: 16 octobre 1991–5 janvier 1992,* ed. Sophie de Juvigny (Saint-Cloud: Musée Municipal, 1991); Henri Cazalis, *Henri Regnault, sa vie et son oeuvre* (Paris: Lemerre, 1872); Philip Gilbert Hamerton, "Henri Regnault," *Modern Frenchmen: Five Biographies* (Boston: Roberts Bros., 1878), 346–422; and Henri Regnault, *Correspondance,* ed. Arthur Duparc (Paris: Charpentier, 1872).

80. On this important prize, see Philippe Grunchec, *Le Grand Prix de peinture: Les Concours des Prix de Rome de 1797 à 1863* (Paris: Ecole Nationale Supérieure des Beaux Arts, 1983); and Harding, *Artistes Pompiers,* 99, 121–22.

81. Théophile Gautier, "Notice" in *Oeuvres d'Henri Regnault exposées à l'Ecole des Beaux Arts* ([Paris]: Impr. Claye, [1872]), 6, 18, 24.

82. Bréton, 21 Nov. 1867, document found in carnet no. 2, f. 6r.

83. Bréton, 10 Jul. 1867, document found in carnet no. 1, f. 4.

84. See Georges Clairin's account of Regnault's death in André Beaunier, *Les*

Souvenirs d'un peintre (Paris: Fasquelle, 1906), 195–97; and Bréton, *ISMS*, 172–74. On the battle of Buzenval, see Michael Howard, *The Franco-Prussian War: The German Invasion of France, 1870–1871* (New York: Collier, 1961), 365–66, passim.

85. Bréton, 9 Mar. 1871 in *ISMS*, 185; Oct. 1870, ibid., 133; a portion of this passage does not appear in *Journal*, 224, 163.

86. Bréton, Jul. 1872, carnet no. 9, f. 4r.

87. Bréton, 22 Jan. 1878, carnet no. 19, f. 15v.

88. Bréton, 4 Jan. 1869, in *ISMS*, 66; a portion of this passage does not appear in *Journal*, 89.

89. Bréton, 25 Mar. 1871, in *ISMS*, 188; this passage does not appear in *Journal*, 227.

90. Bréton, 20 Jun. 1871, in *ISMS*, 210; *Journal*, 249.

91. Ibid., 211; *Journal*, 250.

92. Ibid.; *Journal*, 249.

93. See Beaunier, *Les Souvenirs d'un peintre;* and a reproduction of Clairin's best-known work, his celebrated portrait of Sarah Bernhardt in the Petit Palais Museum, in Michelle Perrot, *Femmes publiques* (Paris: Textuel, 1997), 27.

94. Bréton, 21 Jul. 1871, in *ISMS*, 221; *Journal*, 261.

95. Bréton, 18 Feb. 1871, in *ISMS*, 184; *Journal*, 223.

96. Bréton, 11 Mar. 1871, in *ISMS*, 186; this passage does not appear in *Journal*, 225.

97. Bréton, 26 Oct. 1872, carnet no. 10, f. 34r.

98. Bréton, 20 Dec. 1872, carnet no. 10, f. 30v.

99. Bréton, 18 Jun. 1873, carnet no. 11, ff. 60v.–61r.

100. Bréton, 16 Sept. 1873, carnet no. 10 bis, f. 42r.

101. Bréton, 28 Jun. 1875, carnet no. 15, f. 10r.

102. Bréton, 18 Jun. 1873, carnet no. 11, f. 61r.

103. Bréton, 3 Oct. 1876, carnet no. 17, f. 141v.

104. Bréton, 23 Jun. 1870, in *ISMS*, 97; *Journal*, 122.

105. Bréton, 16 Feb. 1871, in *ISMS*, 183; *Journal*, 222.

106. Bréton, 10 Jul. 1875, carnet no. 15, f. 23r.

107. Bréton, 4 Jul. 1875, carnet no. 15, f. 16v.

108. Bréton, 8 Jan. 1879, carnet no. 20, f. 10r.

109. Bréton, 24 Jan. 1879, carnet no. 20, ff. 18v.–19r.

110. Bréton, 8 Feb. 1879, carnet no. 20, f. 25v.

111. Ibid., f. 27v.

112. Bréton, 7 Dec. 1879, carnet no. 20, ff. 180v., 181r.

113. Ibid., f. 182r.

114. Bréton, 28 Dec. 1879, carnet no. 20, f. 191r.

115. Bréton, 10 Jan. 1880, in *ISMS*, 226; *Journal*, 267.

116. Bréton, Dec. 1879, document found in carnet no. 20, f. 389r.

117. Bréton, 1 Jan. 1883, carnet no. 23, f. 2r.

118. Bréton, 20 Jan. 1880, carnet no. 21, f. 11v.

119. Bréton, 26 Apr. 1880, carnet no. 21, f. 63v.

120. Bréton, 8 Sept. 1880, carnet no. 21, ff. 130v., 131v.–132r.

121. By Marguerite Perrot's definition, they ranked among the "familles riches" in her *Le Mode de vie des familles bourgeoises, 1873–1953* (Paris: P de la Fondation Nationale des Sciences Politiques, 1982), 167, table 12.

122. For information about the Vaudoyer family's property, see Bréton, 25 Jan. 1890, carnet no. 26, ff. 14v.–15v. Such a fortune easily places the Vaudoyers among the top 1 percent of the French population, according to data offered by Daumard, *Les Bourgeois,* 83–83, 90.

123. Bréton, 2 Dec. 1901, carnet no. 27, f. 12v. Note how little material possessions are otherwise mentioned in Bréton's diaries (or the autobiographical writings of Leroyer and Renooz), in contrast to the bourgeois women discussed in Leora Auslander, *Taste and Power: Furnishing Modern France* (Berkeley: U of California P, 1996), 277–96.

124. Bréton, 28 Jan. 1881, carnet no. 22, f. 5r.

125. Bréton, 10 Nov. 1880, carnet no. 21, f. 163v.–64r.

126. Bréton, Sept. 1881, carnet no. 22, f. 53r.

127. Bréton, 8 Sept. 1885, carnet no. 24, f. 15r.

128. Bréton, 23 Apr. 1885, carnet no. 23, f. 54r.

129. Ibid., f. 55r.

130. On this common condition, see George Winokur et al., *Manic-Depressive Illness* (St. Louis: Mosby, 1969); and its historical context, Annelise Mangue, *L'Identité masculine en crise: Au tournant du siècle, 1871–1914* (Paris: Rivages, 1987).

131. Bréton, 25 Jan. 1890, carnet no. 26, f. 15v.

132. Ibid., f. 16r.

133. Bréton to JLV, 27 Dec. 1912, in BN, Fonds Vaudoyer.

134. Bréton, 28 Jan. 1881, carnet no. 22, f. 5r.

135. Bréton to JLV, 16 Aug. 1903, BN, Fonds Vaudoyer.

136. Bréton to JLV, 13 Sept. 1906, BN, Fonds Vaudoyer. One of Charles Péguy's collaborators on the *Cahiers de la quinzaine,* author of studies devoted to Nietzsche, Michelet, and Proudhon, Daniel Halévy (1872–1962) was a prominent intellectual, prolific journalist, and imposing historian of the French Third Republic.

137. Bréton, 1 Feb. 1903, carnet no. 27, f. 29r.–v.

138. Bréton to JLV, 23 Aug. 1912, in BN, Fonds Vaudoyer.

139. Bréton to JLV, 16 Apr. 1913, in BN, Fonds Vaudoyer.

140. Bréton to JLV, 19 Sept. 1914, in BN, Fonds Vaudoyer.

141. Bréton to JLV, 13 Nov. 1914, in BN, Fonds Vaudoyer. Note the self-conscious

parallels between her wartime experiences, exploring the battlefield where Regnault died in 1871 and exploring another one where Michel died forty-three years later. Cf. Bréton, 9 Mar. 1871, *ISMS*, 185–86, *Journal*, 224–25; and Halévy, *L'Europe brisée*, 46–47.

142. Bréton to JLV, 19 Sept. 1909, in BN, Fonds Vaudoyer.

143. Bréton to JLV, 11 Oct. 1907, in BN, Fonds Vaudoyer.

144. Bréton to JLV, 16 Sept. 1912, in BN, Fonds Vaudoyer.

145. There is no sustained, published scholarship on Jean-Louis Vaudoyer (1883–1963), despite his prominent place in French letters and culture in the first half of this century. A member of the Académie Française for his contributions to prose fiction, art criticism, and travel literature, he was at various times director of the Comédie Française and the Musée Carnavalet. See, e.g. Jean-Louis Vaudoyer, *Poésies* (Paris: Calmann-Lévy, 1913); id., *La Bien-aimée* (Paris: Calmann-Lévy, 1909); id., *Italie retrouvée* (Paris: Hachette, 1950); and, id., *Les Peintres provençaux de Nicolas Froment à Paul Cézanne* (Paris: La Jeune Parque, 1947). Cf. Mario Maurin, "Jean-Louis Vaudoyer, romancier," *Contrepoint*, 29 (1979): 83–99.

146. Bréton to JLV, 16 May 1910, in BN, Fonds Vaudoyer.

147. Note where Bréton's diary fits within the many thematic issues discussed by Philippe Lejeune, *Le Moi des demoiselles: Enquête sur le journal de jeune fille* (Paris: Seuil, 1993), esp. 448–55. The diaries most like hers are probably [Caroline Brame], *Le Journal intime de Caroline B.*, ed. Michelle Perrot and Georges Ribeill (Paris: Montalba, 1985) and Lucille Le Verrier, *Journal d'une jeune fille second Empire, 1866–1878*, ed. Lionel Mirisch (Paris: Zulma, 1994), both of them by young, wealthy women during the third quarter of the nineteenth century, although Eugénie de Guérin, *Journal* (Paris: Gabalda, 1934) has a comparable cultural interest.

148. Bréton to JLV, no date, Carton Regnault, BN, Fonds Vaudoyer.

149. For discussion of Bréton's reading, see James Smith Allen, introduction to Bréton, *ISMS*, xxiv–xxv.

150. Bréton to JLV, 19 Dec. 1914, in BN, Fonds Vaudoyer.

151. Bréton, 2 Jul. 1868, in *ISMS*, 55; this passage does not appear in *Journal*, 75.

152. Bréton, 20 Sept. 1873, carnet no. 11, f. 90r.–v.

153. Bréton, 26 Jul. 1875, carnet no. 15, f. 31r.

154. Bréton, 29 Jan. 1878, carnet no. 19, f. 19v.

155. Bréton, 3 Nov. 1879, carnet no. 20, f. 163v.

156. Bréton, 2 Jan. 1879, carnet no. 20, f. 6r.–v.

157. Bréton, 7 Jan. 1880, carnet no. 20, f. 194r.

158. Bréton, *Journal, 1867–1871*.

159. Cf. Howard, *The Franco-Prussian War;* Roger L. Williams, *The French Revolution of 1870–1871* (New York: Norton, 1969); Stewart Edwards, *The Paris Commune,*

1871 (New York: Quadrangle, 1971); and Robert Tombs, *The War against Paris, 1871* (Cambridge: Cambridge UP, 1981).

160. For brief surveys of these major events in French political life, see David Thomson, *Democracy in France since 1870*, 5th ed. (London: Oxford UP, 1969), 116–69; Robert D. Anderson, *France, 1870–1914: Politics and Society* (London: Routledge & Kegan Paul, 1977); and Jean-Marie Mayeur and Madeleine Rebérioux, *The Third Republic from its Origins to the Great War, 1871–1914*, tr. J. R. Foster (Cambridge: Cambridge UP, 1984).

161. Note the *pacte épistolaire* marked by a need to maintain contact with loved ones that Bréton develops with her correspondents, as discussed by Cécile Dauphin et al., *Ces bonnes lettres: Une correspondance familiale au XIX siècle* (Paris: Albin Michel, 1995), 131–60. Bréton seems to have chosen deliberately the models for her letters to Henri Regnault (Julie de Lespinasse) and to Jean-Louis (Mme de Sévigné and Mme de Genlis).

162. Bréton to JLV, 2 Sept. 1909, in BN, Fonds Vaudoyer.

163. Bréton to JLV, 19 Oct. 1912, in BN, Fonds Vaudoyer.

164. Bréton to JLV, 11 Apr. 1912, in BN, Fonds Vaudoyer.

165. Bréton to JLV, 30 Dec. 1907, in BN, Fonds Vaudoyer.

166. Bréton to JLV, 3 Jan. 1902, in BN, Fonds Vaudoyer.

167. Bréton to JLV, 31 Mar. 1909, in BN, Fonds Vaudoyer.

168. Bréton to JLV, 1 Jan. 1898, in BN, Fonds Vaudoyer.

169. Bréton to JLV, 8 Sept. 1898, in BN, Fonds Vaudoyer.

170. Bréton to JLV, 1 Jul. 1898, in BN, Fonds Vaudoyer.

171. Bréton to JLV, 30 Aug. 1902, in BN, Fonds Vaudoyer.

172. Bréton to JLV, 29 Jul. 1903, in BN, Fonds Vaudoyer.

173. Bréton to JLV, 30 Sept. 1906, in BN, Fonds Vaudoyer.

174. Bréton, 26 Dec. 1870, in *ISMS*, 156; this passage does not appear in *Journal*, 189.

175. Bréton, 13 Mar. 1873, carnet no. 11, f. 44r.–v.

176. Bréton, 1 Oct. 1873, carnet no. 11, ff. 94r.–96v.

177. Bréton, 4 Sept. 1874, carnet no. 14, f. 21v.

178. Bréton, documents, d. varia, f. 494.

179. Ibid., f. 501.

180. Bréton, 15 Apr. 1868, in *ISMS*, 50; portions of this passage do not appear in *Journal*, 71.

181. Bréton, 21 Apr. 1870, in *ISMS*, 84; *Journal*, 108.

182. Bréton, 23 Jun. 1870, in *ISMS*, 98; *Journal*, 123.

183. Bréton, 13 Aug. 1881, in carnet no. 22, f. 49r.

184. Bréton, 19 Jan. 1873, carnet no. 10, f. 46v.

185. Bréton, 7 and 12 Nov. 1871, carnet no. 8, ff. 16r.–v.

186. Halévy, *L'Europe brisée*, 264.

187. Ibid., 269.

CHAPTER FIVE Destiny Made Manifest

1. Céline Renooz, "Une révélation" (1888), in Céline Renooz (hereafter Renooz) "Prédestinée: L'Autobiographie de la femme cachée," Bibliothèque Historique de la Ville de Paris (hereafter BHVP), Fonds Marie Louise Bouglé, Papiers Céline Renooz (hereafter PCR), b. 16, d. Ma Vocation Scientifique, pt. 5: Le Retour, f. 4.

2. Ibid. There is no apparent connection between the work of Holbach and Helvétius and that of Renooz. She never explained the particular association of ideas that inspired her.

3. Ibid.

4. Ibid., f. 7.

5. On delusional, especially paranoid, disorders similar to Renooz's, see, e.g., *Professional Guide to Diseases*, 4th ed. (Springhouse, Penn.: Springhouse, 1991), 413–15.

6. Renooz to Léon Frédéric, 15 Aug. 1892, in BHVP, Fonds Bouglé, PCR, b. 10, d. 1892, no. 19.

7. Clémence Royer to Ghénia Avril de Sainte Croix, Jun. 1897, in Bibliothèque Marguerite Durand (hereafter BMD), d. Céline Renooz, no. 6. Jeanne d'Arc's birthday is unknown; her politically controversial name-day in France is celebrated on the second Sunday in May.

8. See obituary (untitled) in *La Meuse* (6 May 1856): 4.

9. Renooz, "Prédestinée," b. 16, d. Souvenirs d'enfance, f. 24, carbon typescript.

10. Ibid., f. 16, carbon typescript.

11. Ibid.

12. Fernand Renooz to Renooz, 7 Jun. 1865, in BHVP, Fonds Bouglé, PCR, b. 1, d. 1865, no. 14.

13. Renooz, Cahier littéraire d'enfance, in BHVP, Fonds Bouglé, PCR, b. 20, d. divers.

14. Renooz, "Prédestinée," b. 16, d. Souvenirs d'enfance, f. 34, carbon typescript.

15. On Muro's revolutionary and reformist context, see Raymond Carr, *Spain, 1808–1975*, 2nd ed. (Oxford: Clarendon, 1982), 305–47, 455–63.

16. Renooz, Prédestinée," b. 16, d. Espagne, f. 8.

17. Ibid., f. 3.

18. Ibid., f. 17.

19. Renooz, "Prédestinée," b. 16, d. Retour en France, f. 17.

20. Renooz, "Prédestinée," b. 17, d. 1893, f. 140.

21. Henry Carnoy, *Mme C. Renooz et son oeuvre* (Paris: Impr. Maton, 1902).

22. Dr. Jules Gérard to Renooz, 28 Dec. 1891, in BHVP, Fonds Bouglé, PCR, b. 2, d. 1892, no. 20.

23. Renooz to Dr. Gérard Encausse, 14 Oct. 1891, in BHVP, Fonds Bouglé, PCR, b. 10, d. 1891, no. 15.

24. Renooz, "Prédestinée," b. 16, d. Andalou, f. 180.

25. Renooz, "Prédestinée," b. 17, d. Feu dévovrant, f. 289.

26. Renooz, "Prédestinée," b. 17, d. 1893, f. 76.

27. Renooz to Mme X, no date, in BHVP, Fonds Bouglé, PCR, b. 12, d. 1920, no number.

28. Renooz, "Prédestinée," b. 17, d. Feu, f. 14.

29. Ibid., f. 29.

30. Ibid., f. 43.

31. Ibid., f. 116.

32. Ibid., f. 105.

33. Ibid., f. 103.

34. Ibid., b. 18, d. 1893, f. 198.

35. Ibid., b. 19, d. 1909, f. 41.

36. Ibid., b. 17, d. Feu, f. 421. Cf. the mistaken interest of the Paris police in Renooz, because she had applied for authorization to sponsor a conference by Clémence Royer, in Archives de la Préfecture de Police (hereafter APP) Ba 909, d. Clémence Royer. This official concern in Renooz's activities on 8 March 1877 undoubtedly contributed to her personal fears.

37. See BHVP, Fonds Bouglé, PCR, b. 24, d. Louise de Saxe.

38. Louise de Saxe, "Chapitre 4: Ma 'Belle-famille,' " *Le Matin*, 5 Sept. 1911, ibid.

39. Renooz to Henri Dupont, 2 May and 4 Jun. 1890, in BHVP, Fonds Bouglé, PCR, b. 10, d. 1890, nos. 12, 14.

40. Renooz to Louis Ranvier, 28 Feb. 1895, in BHVP, Fonds Bouglé, PCR, b. 10, d. 1895, no. 23.

41. Renooz to Mme Carlier, 16 Mar. 1910, in BHVP, Fonds Bouglé, PCR, b. 11, d. 1910, no. 12.

42. Renooz to Blanche Fournet, n.d., in BHVP, Fonds Bouglé, PCR, b. 12, d. 1919, no. 29.

43. Renooz, "Prédestinée," b. 16, d. Jeunesse, f. 155.

44. Ibid., d. Espagne, f. 64.

45. Ibid., b. 17, d. Feu, f. 146.

46. Renooz to Léon Giraud, Nov. 1888, in BHVP, Fonds Bouglé, PCR, b. 10, d. 1881, no. 10.

47. Renooz, "Prédestinée," b. 17, d. 1893, f. 15.

48. Ibid., b. 18, d. 1900, f. 102.

49. Ibid., f. 1.

50. Ibid., b. 17, d. Feu, f. 128.

51. Ibid., d. 1893, f. 59.

52. See Renooz's earliest correspondence in BHVP, Fonds Bouglé, PCR, b. 1, d. 1856 and 1857.

53. Adèle Dandely to Renooz, 8 Apr. 1861, in BHVP, Fonds Bouglé, PCR, b. 1, d. 1861, no. 1.

54. Renooz, "Prédestinée," b. 16, d. Souvenirs d'enfance, f. 186.

55. Ibid., f. 64.

56. Ibid., 16, d. Jeunesse, f. 95.

57. Renooz to Fernand Renooz, Oct. 1897, in BHVP, Fonds Bouglé, PCR, b. 10, d. 1897, no. 18.

58. Renooz, "Prédestinée," b. 16, d. Andalou, f. 169.

59. Ibid., b. 17, d. Feu, f. 276.

60. Renooz to Mme Carlier, 16 Mar. 1910, in BHVP, Fonds Bouglé, PCR, b. 11, d. 1910, no. 12.

61. Renooz, "Prédestinée," b. 17, d. Feu, f. 346.

62. Ibid., b. 19, d. 1910, f. 12.

63. Renooz to Mlle Borel, 1 Mar. 1910, in BHVP, Fonds Bouglé, PCR, b. 11, d. 1910, no. 3.

64. Renooz, "Prédestinée," b. 16, d. Retour, f. 35. Cf. Marguerite Guépet, "Céline Renooz, son oeuvre, sa doctrine," BMD MS carbon typescript, 15; and accounts of comparable work discussed in Anne Martin-Fugier, *La Bourgeoise: Femme au temps de Paul Bourget* (Paris: Grasset & Fasquelle, 1983), 36–50; and APP Ba 1651, d. Le Mouvement féminist.

65. Renooz, "Prédestinée," b. 16, d. Retour, f. 35. See Guépet, "Céline Renooz, son oeuvre, sa doctrine."

66. Renooz, "Prédestinée," b. 18, d. 1898, f. 189–90.

67. Dr. Broëns de Charleroi's article in *Le Médecin*, as quoted, ibid., f. 216.

68. Inside covers, *Bulletin mensuel de la Société Néosophique*, no. 1 (1 Jul. 1897) in BHVP, Fonds Bouglé, PCR, b. 20, d. 1897.

69. "Statuts," *L'Ere de vérité*. Bulletin mensuel de la Société Néosophique, n.s. no. 1 (Nov. 1927): 2.

70. Renooz, *La Science et l'empirisme* (Paris: Bibliothèque de la Nouvelle Encyclopédie, 1898), inside back cover.

71. Ibid.

72. Renooz, "Prédestinée," b. 17, d. Feu, f. 78–83. See Mathias Duval, *Le Darwinisme: Leçons professées à l'Ecole d'anthropologie* (Paris: Lehaye & Lecrosnier, 1886).

73. Renooz, "Prédestinée," b. 17, Feu, f. 83. Renooz's professional activities were severely limited by her lack of advanced training, her limited network of colleagues in the university community, and her tactless assault on the gendered nature of much

scientific research. Cf. Joy Harvey, *"Almost a Man of Genius": Clémence Royer, Feminism, and Nineteenth-Century Science* (New Brunswick: Rutgers UP, 1997), 103–21; George Weisz, *The Emergence of Modern Universities in France, 1863–1914* (Princeton: Princeton UP, 1983), 315–40; more generally, Edmée Charrier, *L'Evolution intellectuelle féminine* (Paris: Mechelincle, 1931); and Londa Schiebinger, *Nature's Body: Gender in the Making of Modern Science* (Boston: Beacon, 1993).

74. Renooz, "Prédestinée," b. 17, d. 3me étape, f. 191.

75. Ibid., d. 1893, f. 119.

76. Ibid., f. 6.

77. Ibid., b. 19, d. 1907, fol. 5.

78. Renooz to M. Candargy, 10 Apr. 1907, in BHVP, Fonds Bouglé, PCR, b. 11, d. 1907, n. 11. Cf. Edouard Retterer, "Mathias Duval (1844–1907): Sa vie et son oeuvre," *Journal de l'anatomie et de la physiologie* 43, no. 3 (1907): 241–331.

79. Cf. the brutal assessments by Renooz's contemporaries in Royer to Avril de Sainte Croix: "Cette pauvre folle de Céline Renooz"; and Renooz to M. Vaughan, 10 Oct. 1899, BHVP, Fonds Bouglé, b. 10, d. 1899, no. 15, concerning Paule Mink's having called Renooz "une folle."

80. Céline Renooz, *L'Origine des animaux: Histoire du développement primitif: Nouvelle Théorie de l'évolution réfutant par l'anatomie celle de M. Darwin* (Paris: Baillière, 1883), 1: 5. Cf. Yvette Conry, *L'Introduction du darwinisme en France au XIXe siècle* (Paris: Vrin, 1974), 423–25.

81. Renooz, "Une révélation," *La Religion laïque et universelle* (15 May 1888): 267.

82. Cf. Renooz, *L'Origine des animaux*, 15–16.

83. Renooz, *Le Grand Problème* (Paris: Publications Néosophiques, [1908]), 61–62.

84. Ibid., 7.

85. Renooz, *L'Origine des animaux*, 1: 6. Cf. Conry, *L'Introduction du darwinisme en France*, 259–90.

86. Renooz anticipates the controversy in France sparked by literary historian Ferdinand Brunetière's repudiation of science's positive role in knowledge, society, and morality. Cf. René Wellek, *A History of Modern Criticism, 1750–1950*, vol. 4, *The Later Nineteenth Century* (Cambridge: Cambridge UP, 1983), 58–71; Harry W. Paul, "The Debate over the Bankruptcy of Science in 1895," *French Historical Studies* 5, no. 2 (1968): 299–327; and Renooz, "Prédestinée," b. 17, d. 4me étape, ff. 99–105.

87. Renooz's notion of intuition was not essentialist; she claimed this manner of knowing for children as well as women; in patriarchy, men lost this otherwise innate capacity. Cf. Renooz, "Prédestinée," b. 16, d. Ma Vocation Scientifique, f. 4; with Henri Bergson, *The Creative Mind*, tr. Mabelle L. Andison (New York: Philosophical Library, 1946), 190.

88. Renooz, "Régénération morale par la science," *La Revue scientifique des femmes* 1, no. 2 (1888): 49.

89. Note how this apparently essentialist view of gendered knowledge is itself open to challenge, as recent constructivist feminist theory has argued. See implications of this shift discussed and applied in Judith Butler, *Gender Trouble: Feminism and the Subversion of Identity* (New York: Routledge, 1990); Personal Narratives Group, *Interpreting Women's Lives: Feminist Theory and Personal Narratives* (Minneapolis: U of Minnesota P, 1989); and *Writing Women's History*, ed. Michelle Perrot, tr. Felicia Pheasant (Oxford: Blackwell, 1992).

90. Renooz, *Psychologie comparée de l'homme et la femme* (Paris: Bibliothèque de la Nouvelle Encyclopédie, 1898), 6.

91. Renooz, "Une révélation": 268.

92. See the deification of oxygen in Renooz, "Prédestinée," b. 16, d. Retour en France, f. 39.

93. Renooz, *La Nouvelle Science*, vol. 1, *Les Forces cosmiques: Synthèse des lois de l'univers, l'évolution des astres, principe d'une nouvelle physique*, 3rd ed. (Paris: Librairie Nationale, n.d.), 127–28.

94. On *la mathèse* or "quite simply the science of order," see Renooz to Hubertine Auclert, 22 Aug. 1897, BHVP, Fonds Bouglé, PCR, b. 10, d. 1897, no. 2.

95. Renooz, *La Science et l'empirisme*, 9.

96. Ibid., inside back cover.

97. Renooz, *La Nouvelle Science*, 1: 187. Cf. similar utopian views discussed in Frank E. Manuel, *The Prophets of Paris: Turgot, Condorcet, Saint-Simon, Fourier, and Comte* (Cambridge: Harvard UP, 1962), esp. 1–10; Robert Carlisle, *The Profferred Crown: Saint-Simonianism and the Doctrine of Hope* (Baltimore: Johns Hopkins UP, 1987), 72–88; Jonathan Beecher, *Charles Fourier: The Visionary and His World* (Berkeley: U of California P, 1986), 241–58; and Mary Pickering, *Auguste Comte: An Intellectual Biography*, vol. 1 (Cambridge: Cambridge UP, 1993), 605–90.

98. See Stella Georgoudi, "Bachofen, le matriarcat et le monde antique. Réflexions sur la création d'un mythe," in *Histoire des femmes en occident*, vol. 1, *L'Antiquité*, ed. Pauline Schmitt Pantel (Paris: Plon, 1991), 477–92.

99. Renooz, *Ere de vérité*, vol. 1, *Le Monde primitif* (Paris: Giard, 1921), 5.

100. Johann Jacob Bachofen, *Das Mutterrecht: Eine Untersuchung über die Gynaikokratie der alten Welt* (Stuttgart: Kraus & Hoffmann, 1861) makes a similar argument that Renooz acknowledges. See Renooz to Edouard Lecoq, May 1908, BHVP, Fonds Bouglé, b. 11, d. 1908, no. 18, where she speaks of Blanche Fournet's translation of this work's preface and table of contents for her use, even though Bachofen's work had already been translated into French by 1900. Cf. Gerda Lerner, *The Creation of Patriarchy* (New York: Oxford UP, 1986), 26–27; and Elisabeth Badinter, *L'Un est l'autre: Des relations entre hommes et femmes* (Paris: Jacob, 1986), 69–80, 89–92, 108–18.

101. Renooz, *Ere de vérité*, 1: 13–14.

102. Cf. a comparable critique of Western scripture in Mary Daly, *The Church and*

the Second Sex (Boston: Beacon, 1985), 74–117; the woman biblical redactor studied in *The Book of J*, ed. Harold Bloom and David Rosenberg (New York: Grove Weidenfeld, 1990); and the feminine sources of the sacred in Catherine Clément and Hélène Cixous, *Le Féminin et le sacré* (Paris: Stock, 1998).

103. Renooz, *Evolution de l'idée divine (simple aperçu)* (Paris: Giard & Brière, 1908), 4.

104. Ibid., 55.

105. Despite obvious similarities, Renooz denied any influence of the Saint-Simonians on her work. See Renooz to M. Poignand, 12 Feb. 1902, BHVP, Fonds Bouglé, PCR, b. 10, d. 1902, no. 34, in which she praises the utopian socialists but criticizes their emphasis on economic rather than moral reform.

106. Renooz, *La Paix glorieuse: Nécessité de l'intervention féminine pour assurer la paix future: Edification du monde nouveau par la ratiocratie universelle: Le Nouveau Statut des peuples: Dédié à Monsieur Wilson, président des Etats-Unis* (Paris: Publications Néosophiques, 1917), 4.

107. Ibid., 12.

108. Ibid., 15.

109. For Renooz's intellectual context, see esp. Harry W. Paul, *From Knowledge to Power: The Rise of the Science Empire in France, 1860–1939* (Cambridge: Cambridge UP, 1985); Paul Bénichou, *Le Temps des prophètes: Doctrines de l'âge romantique* (Paris: Gallimard, 1977); and Carlisle, *Profferred Crown.*

110. See William Logue, *From Philosophy to Sociology: The Evolution of French Liberalism, 1870–1914* (DeKalb: Northern Illinois UP, 1983); Roger Shattuck, *The Banquet Years: The Origins of the Avant-Garde in France, 1885 to World War I*, rev. ed. (London: Cape, 1969); H. Stuart Hughes, *The Obstructed Path: French Social Thought in the Years of Desperation, 1930–1965* (New York: Harper & Row, 1968); and Claire Goldberg Moses, *Feminist Thought in Nineteenth-Century France* (Albany: State U of New York P, 1984).

111. See Claire Duchen, *Feminism in France from '68 to Mitterrand* (London: Routledge & Kegan Paul, 1986); *French Feminist Thought: A Reader,* ed. Toril Moi (Oxford: Blackwell, 1987), 1–13, 110–30; and Alice A. Jardine, *Gynesis: Configurations of Woman and Modernity* (Ithaca: Cornell UP, 1985).

112. Note the section headings provided by Maïté Albistur, *Catalogue des archives Marie Louise Bouglé* (Paris: BHVP, 1982): 1. Souvenirs d'enfance et de jeunesse, 1840–1875 (504 folios); 2. Temps intermédiaire entre la vie familiale et la vocation scientifique, 1875–1878 (101 folios); 3. Histoire d'une découverte, 1878–1895: Feu dévorant (512 folios); 4. Histoire d'une découverte, 1896–1900: Persécution, Dévastation (229 folios); 5. 1901–1908 (272 folios); and 6. Mémoires à partir de 1909–1913 (165 folios).

113. Renooz, "Prédestinée," b. 17, d. 1re étape, f. 44.

114. Ibid., b. 16, d. Souvenirs d'enfance, ff. 169–70.

115. Ibid., b. 18, d. 1890, f. 365.

116. Ibid., f. 329.

117. Ibid., f. 377.

118. Ibid., f. 416.

119. Ibid., b. 17, d. 4me étape, f. 97.

120. Renooz to Mme Alfred Dreyfus, 6 Jan. 1895, BHVP, Fonds Bouglé, PCR, b. 10, d. 1895, no. 12; and Renooz to Mme Alfred Dreyfus, 17 Nov. 1898, d. 1898, no. 9.

121. Renooz, "Prédestinée," b. 17, d. 1903, f. 4.

122. Ibid., b. 18, d. 1908, f. 28.

123. Carnoy, *Mme C. Renooz et son oeuvre.*

124. See Renooz to Henry Carnoy, 3 Dec. 1901, in BHVP, Fonds Bouglé, PCR, b. 10, d. 1901, no. 5.

125. Renooz, "Une révélation," 265–69.

126. Renooz, "Prédestinée," b. 16, d. Retour, pt. 5, f. 15.

127. Ibid., b. 17, d. 1893, f. 99.

128. Royer to Avril de Sainte Croix. Royer also attributes Renooz's view of evolution via embryology to Jean-Baptiste-René Robinet, *Considérations philosophiques de la gradation naturelle des formes de l'être, ou essais de la nature qui apprend à faire l'homme* (Paris: Saillant, 1768), a work Renooz seems never to have read. Cf. Harvey, *"Almost a Man of Genius,"* 136, 137–38, 162–63.

129. Renooz, *La Nouvelle Science,* 1: 1.

130. See reviews of *La Force* by fellow Néosophe Gaston d'Hailly in *La Revue des livres nouveaux* (15 Mar. 1890); an anonymous reviewer in *Le Démocrate* (5 Mar. 1890); and an anonymous reviewer in *La Revue Scientifique* (15 Jul. 1895); all in Renooz, "Prédestinée," b. 17, d. 1893, f. 134.

131. Renooz, *La Nouvelle Science,* 1: 187.

132. Renooz, *La Psychologie comparée de l'homme et de la femme, bases scientifiques de la morale,* 2nd ed. (Paris: Société d'Editions Scientifiques, 1901), 1; and, id., "Prédestinée," b. 16, d. Andalou, f. 169.

133. Renooz, *La Psychologie comparée,* 2nd ed., 324.

134. Ibid., 547–48. Cf. views of "l'étrange Mme Céline Renooz" and her ideas in Jules Bois, "Les Apôtres femmes du 'féminisme' à Paris," *Le Figaro,* 9 Nov. 1894, in APP Ba 1651, d. Le Mouvement féministe; and the sustained critique of her *Psychologie comparée* in Théodore Joran, *Autour du féminisme* (Paris: Bibliothèque des "Annales politiques et littéraires," 1906), 129–217.

135. Renooz, "Prédestinée," b. 17, d. Feu, f. 144.

136. Carnoy, *Mme C. Renooz et son oeuvre,* 47.

137. Renooz, "Prédestinée," b. 18, d. 1906, f. 6.

138. See brief interim summary of Renooz's work on the history of religion by a

disciple, Lea Bérard, *La Femme dans les civilisations anciennes d'après le livre de Mme Céline Renooz* (Agen: Foyer Gascon, [1922]).

139. Renooz, *Ere de vérité*, 1: 3. Cf. this perspective with that of Renooz's contemporary Jeanne Deflou, *Le Sexualisme: Critique de la prépondérance et de la mentalité du sexe fort* (Paris: Tallandier, 1906).

140. Renooz, *Ere de vérité*, 1: 5.

141. Ibid., 5: 419.

142. Ibid., 6: 739.

143. Note the increasing importance of the press in French literate life generally discussed in James Smith Allen, *In the Public Eye: A History of Reading in Modern France, 1800–1940* (Princeton: Princeton UP, 1991), 42–43, 52–53, table A.3.

144. Renooz, *La Nouvelle Science*, 1: 127–28.

145. Paraphrased in W. de Fouvielle, "Au Pôle nord: Le Ballon d'Andrée et les courants solaires—La Théorie de Mme C. Renooz—Une expédition impossible," *Le Matin*, 31 Aug. 1900, in Renooz, BHVP, Fonds Bouglé, PCR, d. 20, d. 1900. Cf. Renooz, *La Nouvelle Science*, 1: 106; and Carnoy, *Mme C. Renooz et son oeuvre*, 55.

146. See articles in BHVP, Fonds Bouglé, PCR, b. 20, d. 1900.

147. Elysée Réclus to Renooz, 24 Mar. 1898, in "Prédestinée," b. 18, d. Ostracisme, f. 248. Cf. the original letter, 7 Apr. 1898, BHVP, Fonds Bouglé, PCR, b. 3, d. 1898, no. 48. For more about climatic conditions at the North Pole, see Renooz's source, Fridtjof Nansen, *Vers le pôle*, ed. and tr. Charles Rabot (Paris: Flammarion, [1906]), 158, 171, 421–22; and on S.-A. Andrée's failed expedition and the other weather-related reasons for its failure, see Jeanette Mirsky, *To the North! The Story of Arctic Exploration from the Earliest Times to the Present* (New York: Viking, 1934), 338–43.

148. Letter from M. Dautherive to Renooz, 11 Sept. 1900, in BHVP, Fonds Bouglé, PCR, b. 3, d. 1900, no. 11.

149. Renooz, "Prédestinée," b. 16, d. Espagne, f. 9.

150. Renooz to Célia Schacre, 2 Dec. 1891, in BHVP, Fonds Bouglé, PCR, b. 10, d. 1891, no. 31.

151. Renooz, "Prédestinée," b. 16, d. Espagne, ff. 23–33.

152. Ibid., d. Andalou, ff. 12–13.

153. Hélène Brion, "Céline Renooz," *Encyclopédie féministe*, BMD, MS, 6: f. 81.

154. Gilbert Froidure d'Aubigné, "Renooz (Céline)," in *Dictionnaire biographique international des écrivains, membres des sociétés savantes*, ed. Henry Carnoy (Paris: Librairie Générale et Internationale, 1909), 7.

155. See the cartoons in *Le Français*, 7 Apr. 1902, and in *L'Art de la mode*, 12 Apr. 1902, caricaturing Renooz's views on the vegetable origins of human evolution.

156. See obituary by Louise Chapel, *L'Ere de vérité*, Bulletin mensuel de la Société Néosophique, no. 2 (1928): 1.

CHAPTER SIX The Traces of Feminist Consciousness

1. Gerda Lerner, *The Creation of Feminist Consciousness: From the Middle Ages to Eighteen-Seventy* (New York: Oxford UP, 1993), 274. Cf. recent research in cognitive psychology that rejects such a historical perspective: Jerome Kagan, *Unstable Ideas: Temperament, Cognition, and Self* (Cambridge: Harvard UP, 1989); and the early efforts in clinical and experimental psychology listed in n. 15 of the introduction to this book.

2. Note a more inclusive definition of the term in Karen Offen, "Defining Feminism: A Comparative Historical Approach," *Signs: Journal of Women in Culture and Society* 14, no. 1 (1988): 119–57; and the rejoinders by Ellen Carol DuBois and Nancy F. Cott in "Comment and Reply," *Signs: Journal of Women in Culture and Society* 15, no. 1 (1989): 195–209.

3. See Steven C. Hause with Anne R. Kenney, *Women's Suffrage and Social Politics in the Third French Republic* (Princeton: Princeton UP, 1984), 3–10; and Laurence Klejman and Florence Rochefort, *L'Egalité en marche: Le Féminisme sous la troisième République* (Paris: P de la Fondation Nationale des Sciences Politiques, 1989), 31–44. Women were more likely to be concerned with other issues, according to Louise A. Tilly, "Women's Collective Action and Feminism in France, 1870–1914," in *Class Conflict and Collective Action*, ed. Louise A. Tilly and Charles Tilly (Beverly Hills: Sage, 1981), 207–31.

4. Marie-Sophie Leroyer de Chantepie (hereafter Leroyer) to Gustave Flaubert, 10 Apr. 1857, in *Flaubert: Correspondance*, ed. Jean Bruneau, vol. 2, *Juillet 1851–décembre 1858* (Paris: Gallimard, 1980) (hereafter *FC2*), 704.

5. Geneviève Bréton (hereafter Bréton), 27 Apr. 1869, in *"In the Solitude of My Soul": The Diary of Geneviève Bréton, 1867–1871*, ed. James Smith Allen, tr. James Palmes (Carbondale: Southern Illinois UP, 1994) (hereafter *ISMS*), 73; id., *Journal, 1867–1871*, ed. Daphné Doublet-Vaudoyer (Paris: Ramsay, 1985), 95.

6. Ibid.

7. See Karen Offen, "Sur l'origine des mots 'féminisme' et 'féministe,'" *Revue d'histoire moderne et contemporaine* 34, no. 3 (1987): 492–96.

8. Céline Renooz (hereafter Renooz), "Prédestinée: L'Autobiographie de la femme cachée," in Bibliothèque Historique de la Ville de Paris (hereafter BHVP), Fonds Marie Louise Bouglé, Papiers Céline Renooz (hereafter PCR), b. 17, d. Feu dévorant, f. 221.

9. Renooz to Gustave Hervé, 2 Feb. 1915, in BHVP, Fonds Bouglé, PCR, b. 11, 1911, no. 31.

10. Renooz, "Prédestinée," b. 18, d. 1905, f. 7.

11. See the documents in *Women, the Family, and Freedom: The Debate in Documents*, ed. Susan Groag Bell and Karen M. Offen (Stanford: Stanford UP, 1983), 2

vols., even though the editors deliberately eschew the terms *feminism* and *feminist* throughout.

12. Leroyer to George Sand, 28 Jan. 1849, in BHVP, Fonds George Sand, G. 4404–575, f. 205v.

13. Ibid. Cf. the problem of sexual repression in nineteenth-century France discussed in Antony Copley, *Sexual Moralities in France, 1780–1980: New Ideas on the Family, Divorce, and Homosexuality: An Essay on Moral Change* (London: Routledge, 1989), 79–107.

14. Bréton, Jun. 1873, carnet no. 10 bis, f. 35r.

15. Bréton, 3 Feb. 1890, carnet no. 26, f. 25v.

16. Renooz, "Prédestinée," b. 16, d. Souvenirs de Jeunesse, f. 62.

17. Catherine D. Groth, "On the Wrong Foundation: A Talk with Mme Céline Renooz, Scientist," *Chicago Tribune*, European ed., 27 Mar. 1922, 4, in Renooz, newspaper clippings, in BHVP, Fonds Bouglé, PCR, b. 21, d. 1922. Cf. Renooz, "Union de pensée féministe: La Femme et le mariage," *La Pensée* (25 Aug. 1902): 292–93, ibid.

18. Leroyer to Victor Mangin, 9 Jul. 1867, in Bibliothèque Municipale Médiathèque de Nantes, MS 2942.

19. Leroyer, *Figures historiques et légendaires* (Paris: Perrin, n.d.), 137–38.

20. Leroyer, *Souvenirs et impressions littéraires* (Paris: Perrin, 1892), 207.

21. Leroyer to Flaubert, 20 Mar. 1863, in *Flaubert: Correspondance*, ed. Jean Bruneau, vol. 3, *Janvier 1859–décembre 1868* (Paris: Gallimard, 1991) (hereafter *FC3*), 311.

22. Ibid., 312.

23. Leroyer to Flaubert, 3 Oct. 1859, in *FC3*, 44.

24. Bréton, 3 Oct. 1870, in *ISMS*, 129; *Journal*, 158.

25. Bréton, 16 May 1878, carnet no. 19, ff. 74v.–75r.

26. Bréton, 6 Aug. 1870, in *ISMS*, 105; *Journal*, 131.

27. Bréton, 17 Sept. 1870, in *ISMS*, 119; this passage does not appear in *Journal*, 147.

28. Bréton to Nélie Jacquemart [not sent], 6 Jun. 1870, in document found in carnet no. 4, f. 74r.–v.

29. Renooz, "Prédestinée," b. 16, d. Souvenirs d'enfance, f. 69.

30. Ibid., Souvenirs de Jeunesse, f. 63.

31. Ibid., b. 17, d. Feu, f. 233.

32. Ibid., b. 19, d. 1911, f. 23.

33. Ibid., b. 18, d. 1907, f. 26.

34. Ibid., b. 17, d. Feu, f. 391.

35. Ibid., d. 1893, f. 66.

36. Cf. the different perspectives on the social construction of sexuality in Michel Foucault, *The History of Sexuality*, vol. 1, *Introduction*, tr. Robert Hurley (New York: Pantheon, 1979); *Flora Tristan, George Sand, Pauline Roland: Les Femmes et l'invention*

d'une nouvelle morale, 1830–1848, ed. Stéphane Michaud (Paris: Créaphis, 1994); and Robert Nye, *Masculinity and Male Codes of Honor in Modern France* (New York: Oxford UP, 1993).

37. Cf. the images of women's sexuality in Jennifer Waelti-Walters, *Feminist Novelists of the Belle Epoque: Love as a Lifestyle* (Bloomington: Indiana UP, 1990); Janet Beizer, *Ventriloquized Bodies: Narratives of Hysteria* (Ithaca: Cornell UP, 1994); and Mary Louise Roberts, *Civilization without Sexes: Reconstructing Gender in Postwar France* (Chicago: U of Chicago P, 1994).

38. Cf. Georges Weill, *Histoire du catholicisme libéral en France, 1828–1908* (Paris: Alcan, 1909); Theodore Zeldin, "The Conflict of Moralities: Confession, Sin and Pleasure in the Nineteenth Century," in *Conflicts in French Society: Anticlericalism, Education, and Morals in the Nineteenth Century: Essays,* ed. Theodore Zeldin (London: Allen & Unwin, 1970), 13–50; and Claude Langlois, "Permanence, renouveau et affrontements (1830–1880)," in *Histoire des catholiques en France du XVIe siècle à nos jours,* ed. François Lebrun (Toulouse: Privat, 1980), 291–368.

39. Leroyer, *Figures historiques et légendaires,* 15.

40. Leroyer to Sand, 28 Jan. 1849, in BHVP, Fonds Sand, G. 4404–275, f. 207v.

41. Leroyer to Flaubert, 23 May 1857, in *FC2,* 722.

42. Leroyer to Flaubert, 4 Jul. 1861, in *FC3,* 159.

43. Bréton, 29 Nov. 1870, in *ISMS,* 145; this passage does not appear in *Journal,* 176.

44. Lamennais's *Paroles d'un croyant* (1834) expressed the same sympathy for the poor and the same antipathy for the rich that Bréton (Leroyer and Renooz as well) did after the Paris Commune. See Peter Stearns, *Priest and Revolutionary: Lamennais and the Dilemma of French Catholicism* (New York: Harper & Row, 1967).

45. Bréton, 5 May 1869, in *ISMS,* 74; *Journal,* 96.

46. Bréton, 11 Feb. 1871, in *ISMS,* 180; *Journal,* 219.

47. Bréton, 13 Feb. 1871, in *ISMS,* 181; *Journal,* 220.

48. Bréton, 16 Feb. 1871, in *ISMS,* 182; *Journal,* 221.

49. Bréton, 30 Oct. 1876, carnet no. 17, f. 151r.

50. Cf. views in Norman Ravitch, *The Catholic Church and the French Nation, 1589–1989* (London: Routledge, 1990), 60–90; Philip Spencer, *Politics of Belief in Nineteenth-Century France* (London: Faber & Faber, [1954]), 143–52; and C. S. Phillips, *The Church in France, 1848–1907* (London: SPCK, 1936), 58–73.

51. Cf. Joseph N. Moody, *The Church as Enemy: Anticlericalism in Nineteenth-Century French Literature* (Washington, D.C.: Corpus, 1968).

52. Renooz, "Prédestinée," b. 16, d. Jeunesse, f. 93.

53. Renooz to Mme Bourdin, 10 Oct. 1906, in BHVP, Fonds Bouglé, PCR, b. 11, d. 1906, no. 4.

54. Renooz to Cleyre Yvelin, 19 Apr. 1906, in BHVP, Fonds Bouglé, PCR, b. 11, d. 1906, no. 34.

55. Leroyer to Flaubert, 15 Mar. 1857, in *FC2*, 690.

56. Leroyer to Flaubert, 10 Jul. 1870, in BN, NAFr MS 23825, f. 382.

57. Leroyer to Flaubert, 15 Mar. 1857, in *FC2*, 690.

58. Leroyer to Sand, 27 Jan. 1854, in BHVP, Fonds Sand, G. 4404–575, f. 236v.

59. Leroyer to Flaubert, 13 Jun. 1866, in *FC3*, 506.

60. Leroyer to Flaubert, 23 Apr. 1857, in *FC2*, 705.

61. Leroyer to Flaubert, 11 Mar. 1859, in *FC3*, 19.

62. Leroyer to Flaubert, 18 May 1859, in *FC3*, 23.

63. Bréton, 13 Jun. 1880, document found in carnet no. 21, f. 406r.

64. Bréton, 8 Jun. 1876, carnet no. 16, f. 55v.

65. Bréton, 30 Oct. 1875, carnet no. 16, f. 9r.

66. Bréton, 26 Jun. 1875, carnet no. 15, f. 8r.

67. Bréton, 26 Jul. 1875, carnet no. 15, f. 33r.

68. Bréton, 13 Sept. 1879, carnet no. 20, f. 136r.

69. Bréton, 22 May 1869, in *ISMS*, 75; *Journal*, 97.

70. Bréton, 22 Jul. 1870, in *ISMS*, 102; *Journal*, 127.

71. Bréton, 7 Feb. 1871, in *ISMS*, 175; *Journal*, 216.

72. Bréton, 14 Apr. 1878, carnet no. 19, f. 58r.

73. Renooz, "Prédestinée," b. 17, d. Feu, f. 146.

74. Ibid., b. 16, d. Jeunesse, f. 87.

75. Ibid., b. 17, d. Feu, no folio.

76. Ibid., b. 16, d. Espagne, pt. 4, f. 161.

77. Ibid., pt. 3, f. 45.

78. Clémence Royer to Ghénia Avril de Sainte Croix, Jun. 1897, in BMD, d. Renooz, no. 6.

79. Renooz, "Une révélation," *La Religion laïque et universelle* (15 May 1888): 269.

80. Madeleine Pelletier, *L'Education feministe des filles* (Paris: Giard & Brière, 1914), 67, 71. See also Pelletier's unpublished memoirs in the BHVP Fonds Bouglé, as discussed in Felicia Gordon, *The Integral Feminist: Madeleine Pelletier, 1874–1939* (Minneapolis: U of Minnesota P, 1991); Colette, *Journal intermittent* (Paris: Le Fleuron, 1949); George Sand, *Journal intime* (Paris: Calmann-Lévy, 1926); Arria Ly's personal papers also in the BHVP Fonds Bouglé; and the study by Paul Lorenz, *Sapho 1900: Renée Vivien* (Paris: Juillard, 1977). Cf. Anna Klumpke, *Rosa Bonheur: The Artist's (Auto)biography*, tr. Gretchen van Slyke (Ann Arbor: U of Michigan P, 1998); Isabelle Eberhardt, *Mes Journaliers* (Paris: Les Introuvables, 1985); and Herculine Barbin, *Herculine Barbin, dite Alexina B.*, ed. Michel Foucault (Paris: Gallimard, 1978).

81. Offen, "Defining Feminism," 134–50.

82. Ibid., 152. This point has been made by social anthropologists as long ago as the essays in *Perceiving Women*, ed. Shirley Ardener (London: Malaby, 1975) and by historians as recently as Bronislaw Baczko et al., "Femmes: Une singularité fran-çaise?" *Le Débat*, no. 87 (1995): 118–46, focused on Mona Ozouf, *Women's Words: Essay on French Singularity*, tr. Jane Marie Todd (Chicago: U of Chicago P, 1997). This context is history's contribution to theory.

83. Cf. the more individualist feminism discussed in Waelti-Walters, *Feminist Novelists*, esp. 19–30, 156–82.

Conclusion

1. Joan Wallach Scott, *Gender and the Politics of History* (New York: Columbia UP, 1988), 42. Cf. the more overt manifestations of women's discursive power discussed in David Barry, *Women and Political Insurgency: France in the Mid-Nineteenth Century* (New York: St. Martin's, 1996), esp. 35–104.

2. On the variety of women's-rights organizations and issues, see Steven C. Hause with Anne R. Kenny, *Women's Suffrage and Social Politics in the Third French Republic* (Princeton: Princeton UP, 1984), 3–27; and *Feminisms of the Belle Epoque: A Historical and Literary Anthology*, ed. Jennifer Waelti-Walters and Steven C. Hause (Lincoln: U of Nebraska P, 1994).

3. Relative degrees of feminism are suggested by Evelyn Sullerot, *Histoire de la presse féminine en France: Des origines à 1848* (Paris: Colin, 1966), 164, 189. Using similar sources to another end is Danielle Flamant-Paparatti, *Bien-pensantes, cocodettes et bas-bleus: La Femme bourgeoise à travers la presse féminine et familiale, 1873–1887* (Paris: Denoël, 1984), 185–98.

4. See Eugen Weber, *Peasants into Frenchmen: The Modernization of Rural France, 1870–1914* (Stanford: Stanford UP, 1976).

5. See the useful summary of similar women in Michelle Perrot, "Postface,"in *Madame ou mademoiselle? Itinéraires de la solitude féminine, XVIIIe–XXe siècle*, ed. Arlette Farge and Christiane Klapisch-Zuber (Paris: Montalba, 1984), 297–302.

6. Note a similar point made about comparable figures in the American historical context: Anne Firor Scott, *Making the Invisible Woman Visible* (Urbana: U of Illinois P, 1984), esp. 3–36, 149–58. Cf. Catherine Stimpson, "Female Insubordination and the Text," in *Women in Culture and Politics: A Century of Change*, ed. Judith Friedlander et al. (Bloomington: Indiana UP, 1986), 164–76; and Susan A. Crane, "AHR Forum: Writing the Individual Back into Collective Memory," *American Historical Review* 102, no. 5 (1997): 1372–85.

7. Michelle Perrot, *Femmes publiques* (Paris: Textuel, 1997), 10–11. Cf. the asso-ciational life of women in nineteenth-century France discussed in Evelyne Lejeune-

Resnick, *Femmes et associations, 1830–1880: Vraies démocrates ou dames patronnesses?* (Paris: Publisud, 1991); and *Femmes dans la cité, 1815–1871*, ed. Alain Corbin et al. (Grâne: Créaphis, [1997]).

8. On the varied images of women, not all of their own making, see *Littérature et idéologie: La Femme au dix-neuvième siècle*, ed. Roger Bellet (Lyons: PU de Lyon, 1979); Michèle Sarde, *Regard sur les françaises, Xe–XXe siècles* (Paris: Stock, 1983); Centre de Recherches Littéraires et Historiques, *Visages de la féminité* (Saint-Denis: U de Réunion, 1984); Philippe Perrot, *Le Travail des apparences, ou les transformations du corps féminin, XVIIIe–XIXe siècle* (Paris: Seuil, 1984); and *Das Frauenbild im literarischen Frankreich von Mittelalter bis zur Gegenwart*, ed. Renate Baader (Darmstadt: Wissenschaftliche Buchgesellschaft, 1988).

9. Completely unrestricted fertility does not exist for reasons historical demographers know well, but the largest documented number of children born to an identifiable cohort averages more than twelve (12.3) per woman, among the Hutterites in the United States, c. 1950. See E. A. Wrigley, *History and Population* (New York: McGraw-Hill, 1969), 17. The average for married French women before World War I was between four and five, according to Philippe Ariès, *Histoire des populations françaises et de leurs attitudes devant la vie depuis le XVIIIe siècle* (Paris: Seuil, 1971), 334.

10. See, e.g., Guy Thuillier's queries on prayer in his *L'Imaginaire quotidien au XIXe siècle* (Paris: Economica, 1985), 31–60; Yvonne Turin, *Femmes et religieuses au XIXe siècle: Le Féminisme "en religion"* (Paris: Nouvelle Cité, 1989); and Bonnie G. Smith, *Ladies of the Leisure Class: The Bourgeoises of Northern France in the Nineteenth Century* (Princeton: Princeton UP, 1981), 93–122.

11. See these points discussed at greater length in Ruth Harris, *Murders and Madness: Medicine, Law, and Society in the Fin de Siècle* (Oxford: Clarendon, 1989), 155–207, 285–320.

12. Note a similar project to define a woman's voice, derived from the theoretical positions developed by Hélène Cixous, Luce Irigaray, and Julia Kristeva in France, by Alice Jardine, *Gynesis: Configurations of Woman and Modernity* (Ithaca: Cornell UP, 1985), esp. 13–28.

13. Christine Planté, *La Petite Soeur de Balzac: Essai sur la femme auteur* (Paris: Seuil, 1989), 37. Cf. Béatrice Slama, "Femmes écrivains," in *Misérable et glorieuse: La Femme du XIXe siècle: Les Différentes Positions sociales de la femme*, ed. Jean-Paul Aron (Paris: Fayard, 1980), 213–43; *Femmes de lettres au XIXe siècle: Autour de Louise Colet*, ed. Roger Bellet (Lyons: PU de Lyon, 1982); and Carla Hess, "Reading Signatures: Female Authorship and Revolutionary Law in France, 1750–1850," *Eighteenth-Century Studies* 22 (spring 1989): 469–87.

14. See, e.g., Londa Schiebinger, *Nature's Body: Gender in the Making of Modern Science* (Boston: Beacon, 1993); and more generally, Sandra Harding, *Whose Science? Whose Knowledge?* (Ithaca: Cornell UP, 1991).

15. See the vigorous defense of autobiographical writing generally, not just by women, in Philippe Lejeune, *Pour l'autobiographie: Chroniques* (Paris: Seuil, 1998), 11–25.

16. Note comparable voices of subordinate populations studied by Richard Terdiman, *Discourse/Counter-Discourse: The Theory and Practice of Symbolic Resistance in Nineteenth-Century France* (Ithaca: Cornell UP, 1984); James C. Scott, *Domination and the Arts of Resistance: Hidden Transcripts* (New Haven: Yale UP, 1990); and Gerda Lerner, *The Creation of Feminist Consciousness: From the Middle Ages to Eighteen-Seventy* (New York: Oxford UP, 1993).

17. The implications of denying women voices of their own is evident, I think, in forensic medicine's gendered treatment of female testimony in the investigations of sex crimes in late nineteenth-century France. Male criminologists, it seems, were no more likely to take women's word seriously than some postmodernists are today. See Matt K Matsuda, *The Memory of the Modern* (New York: Oxford UP, 1996), 110–18.

18. Cf. the cultural perspectives on women's issues taken by Geneviève Fraisse, "Feminist Singularity: A Critical Historiography of the History of Feminism in France," in *Writing Women's History*, ed. Michelle Perrot, tr. Felicia Pheasant (Oxford: Blackwell, 1992), 146–59; Mona Ozouf, *Women's Words: Essay on French Singularity*, tr. Jane Marie Todd (Chicago: U of Chicago P, 1997), 229–83; and William M. Reddy, *The Invisible Code: Honor and Sentiment in Postrevolutionary France, 1814–1848* (Berkeley: U of California P, 1997), 228–38.

19. Cf. Cheryl Cline, *Women's Diaries, Journals, and Letters: An Annotated Bibliography* (New York: Garland, 1989); and Peter Gay, *The Bourgeois Experience: Victoria to Freud* (New York: Oxford UP, 1984–86; Norton, 1993–95), 4 vols.

20. See Steven C. Hause, *Hubertine Auclert: The French Suffragette* (New Haven: Yale UP, 1990); Felicia Gordon, *The Integral Feminist: Madeleine Pelletier, 1874–1939* (Cambridge: Polity, 1990); Charles Sowerine and Claude Maignien, *Madeleine Pelletier: Une féministe dans l'arène politique* (Paris: Ouvrières, 1992); and Joy Harvey, *"Almost a Man of Genius": Clémence Royer, Feminism, and Nineteenth-Century Science* (New Brunswick: Rutgers UP, 1997).

21. Linda Wagner-Martin, *Telling Women's Lives: The New Biography* (New Brunswick: Rutgers UP, 1994), 82–83. Cf. "Even if she never sees it published, she has written her own reality and named it herself," Barbara Heldt, *Terrible Perfection: Women in Russian Literature* (Bloomington: Indiana UP, 1987), 102. I thank Michelle DenBeste-Barnett for bringing this source to my attention. See also Elisabeth Young-Bruehl, *Subject to Biography: Psychoanalysis, Feminism, and Writing Women's Lives* (Cambridge: Harvard UP, 1998), 15–25.

22. E.g. Tyler Stovall, *Paris Noir: African-Americans in the City of Light* (Boston: Houghton Mifflin, 1996), 250–62, 286–300; Vernon A. Rosario II, *The Erotic Imagination: French Histories of Perversity* (New York: Oxford UP, 1997), 157–64; Robert A.

Nye, *Masculinity and Male Codes of Honor in Modern France* (New York: Oxford UP, 1993), 172–215; and Reddy, *Invisible Code*, 65–113.

23. Charles Taylor, *Sources of the Self: The Making of the Modern Identity* (Cambridge: Harvard UP, 1989), 47. Cf. the efforts to develop this insight in the special issue, *Narrative Analysis in Social Science*, in *Social Science History* 16, nos. 3 and 4 (1992).

24. Cf. a similar point made in Louise A. Tilly, "Individual Lives and Family Strategies in the French Proletariat," in *Family and Sexuality in French History*, ed. Robert Wheaton and Tamara Hareven (Philadelphia: U of Pennsylvania P, 1980), 201–23; and more generally in Jacques Commaille, *Les Stratégies des femmes: Travail, famille, et politique* (Paris: Découverte, 1993).

25. E.g., LeJeune-Resnick, *Femmes et associations, 1830–1880; Femmes dans la cité, 1815–1871*; Naomi Black, *Social Feminism* (Ithaca: Cornell UP, 1989), 161–239; Sylvie Fayet-Scribe, *Associations féminines et catholicisme: De la charité à l'action sociale, XIXe–XXe siècles* (Paris: Ouvrières, 1990); and Gisèle and Yves Hivert-Messeca, *Comment la franc-maçonnerie vint aux femmes: Deux siècles de franc-maçonnerie d'adoption, féminine et mixte en France, 1740–1940* (Paris: Dervy, 1997), 181–328.

26. Cf. introduction, n. 19; Fraisse, "Feminist Singularity"; Antoinette Fouque, *Il y a deux sexes: Essais de féminologie, 1989–1995* (Paris: Des Femmes, 1995), 57–83; Janine Mossuz-Lavau and Anne de Kervasdoué, *Les Femmes ne sont pas des hommes comme les autres* (Paris: Jacob, 1997); and Catherine Clément and Julia Kristeva, *Le Féminin et le sacré* (Paris: Stock, 1998).

27. *Féminismes et identités nationales*, ed. Yolande Cohen and Françoise Thébaud (Lyon: Programme Rhone-Alpes Recherches en Sciences Humaines, 1998); *Différence des sexes et protection sociale*, ed. Leora Auslander and Michelle Zancarini-Fournel (Saint-Denis: PUV, 1995); and Lelia J. Rupp, *Worlds of Women: The Making of an International Women's Movement* (Princeton: Princeton UP, 1997).

28. See Rachel G. Fuchs, *Abandoned Children: Foundlings and Child Welfare in Nineteenth-Century France* (Albany: State U of New York P, 1984); *Gender and the Politics of Social Reform in France, 1870–1914*, ed. Elinor A. Accampo et al. (Baltimore: Johns Hopkins UP, 1995); and Anne Cova, *Maternité et droits des femmes en France, XIXe–XXe siècles* (Paris: Anthropos, 1997).

29. See Priscilla Parkhurst Clark, *Literary France: The Making of a Literary Culture* (Berkeley: U of California P, 1987).

30. See Pierre Bourdieu, *Language and Symbolic Power*, ed. John B. Thompson, tr. Gino Raymond and Matthew Adamson (Cambridge: Harvard UP, 1991).

31. Planté, *La Petite Soeur de Balzac*. See also Laure Adler, *A l'aube du féminisme: Les Premières Journalistes, 1830–1850* (Paris: Payot, 1979); and Marcelle Marini, "La Place des femmes dans la production culturelle: L'Exemple de la France," in *Histoire des femmes*, vol. 5, *Le XXe Siècle*, ed. Françoise Thébaud (Paris: Plon, 1992), 275–96.

32. Cf. the authors studied in Annie Goldmann, *Rêves d'amour perdus: Les Femmes dans le roman du XIXe siècle* (Paris: Denoël / Gonthier, 1984); and Jann Matlock, *Scenes of Seduction: Prostitution, Hysteria, and Reading Difference in Nineteenth-Century France* (New York: Columbia UP, 1994), 199–280.

33. Anne Martin-Fugier, "The Actors," in *A History of Private Life*, vol. 4, *From the Fires of Revolution to the Great War*, ed. Michelle Perrot, tr. Arthur Goldhammer (Cambridge: Harvard UP, Belknap, 1990), 186–87.

34. Note the ambiguity of Frenchwomen's status before World War I, as suggested by Eugen Weber, *France: Fin de Siècle* (Cambridge: Harvard UP, 1986), 85–99; Edward Berenson, *The Trial of Madame Caillaux* (Berkeley: U of California P, 1992), 89–132; and Marcus Verhagen, "The Poster in *Fin-de-Siècle* Paris: 'That Mobile and Degenerate Art,'" in *Cinema and the Invention of Modern Life*, ed. Leo Charney and Vanessa Schwartz (Berkeley: U of California P, 1995), 103–29.

35. Françoise Picq, *Libération des femmes: Les Années mouvement* (Paris: Seuil, 1993).

36. *French Feminist Thought: A Reader*, ed. Toril Moi (Oxford: Blackwell, 1987), 33–69; and Claire Duchen, *Feminism in France from '68 to Mitterrand* (London: Routledge & Kegan Paul, 1986), 27–47, 103–24.

37. Alberto Melucci, *Nomads of the Present: Social Movements and Individual Needs in Contemporary Society*, ed. John Keane and Paul Mier (London: Hutchinson, 1989); id., *Challenging Codes: Collective Action in an Information Age* (Cambridge: Cambridge UP, 1996); Albert O. Hirschman, *Exit, Voice, and Loyalty* (Cambridge: Harvard UP, 1970); and Joseph M. Jasper, *The Art of Moral Protest: Culture, Biography, and Creativity in Social Movements* (Chicago: U of Chicago P, 1997).

38. Scott, *Only Paradoxes to Offer: French Feminists and the Rights of Man* (Cambridge: Harvard UP, 1996), 3–4.

39. Naomi Schor, *Bad Objects: Essays Popular and Unpopular* (Durham: Duke UP, 1995), 44–60.

40. Cf. the perspectives of Rita Felski, *Beyond Feminist Aesthetics: Feminist Literature and Social Change* (Cambridge: Harvard UP, 1989); Dori Laub and Shoshana Felman, *Testimony: Crisis of Witnessing in Literature, Psychoanalysis, and History* (New York: Routledge, 1992); *Critical Encounters: Reference and Responsibility in Deconstructive Writing*, ed. Cathy Caruth and Deborah Esch (New Brunswick: Rutgers UP, 1995); and *Women Imagine Change: A Global Anthology of Women's Resistance from 1600 BCE to Present*, ed. Eugenia Delamotte et al. (New York: Routledge, 1997).

Bibliography

Archival Materials: Selected

Archives Départementales de Maine-et-Loire, Angers (ADML):
    Etat civil: Actes de naissance et décès
    Inventaires après décès: Dossier Marie-Sophie Leroyer de Chantepie

Archives Nationales, Paris (AN):
    Société des Gens de Lettres: Dossier Marie-Sophie Leroyer de Chantepie

Archives de la Préfecture de Police, Paris (APP):
    Dossier Mouvement féministe
    Dossier Clémence Royer

Bibliothèque Historique de la Ville de Paris, Paris (BHVP):
    Fonds Marie Louise Bouglé: Papiers Céline Renooz
    Fonds George Sand: Letters from Marie-Sophie Leroyer de Chantepie
    Fonds Jules Michelet: Letters from Marie-Sophie Leroyer de Chantepie

Bibliothèque Marguerite Durand, Paris (BMD):
    Hélène Brion, "L'Encyclopédie féministe"
    Dossier Céline Renooz
    Dossier Clémence Royer

Bibliothèque Municipale Médiathèque, Nantes (BMN):
    MS. 2942: Letters from Marie-Sophie Leroyer de Chantepie to Victor and Evariste Mangin

Bibliothèque Nationale de France, Paris (BN):
    Letters (copies) from Marie-Sophie Leroyer de Chantepie to Gustave Flaubert
    Fonds Jean-Louis Vaudoyer: Diary of Geneviève Bréton and Correspondence with Geneviève Bréton-Vaudoyer
    Letter from Marie-Sophie Leroyer de Chantepie to Adolphe Thiers

Collection Spoelberch de Lovenjoul, Institut de France, Paris (CSL):
Letters from Marie-Sophie Leroyer de Chantepie to Ernest Commanville and Gustave Flaubert

Published Works and Letters by Marie-Sophie Leroyer de Chantepie (1844–1991)

Cécile. N.p. [before 1843].

Les Duranti. Paris: Souverain, 1844. 2 vols.

"Laurentia." In Le Livre des feuilletons: Recueil de nouvelles, contes, épisodes, anecdotes, extraits de la presse contemporaine, 299–306. Nancy: Impr. Hinzelin, 1846. Extract from Journal des femmes.

Angélique Lagier. N.p.: n.p., 1851. 2 vols.

Angèle, ou le dévouement filial. Tours: Mame, 1860.

Chroniques et légendes. Château-Gontier: Bézier, 1870.

Mémoires d'une provinciale. Paris: Dentu, 1880. 2 vols.

Une vengeance judiciaire. Paris: Perrin, 1888. Originally published as Angélique Lagier, 1851.

Nouvelles littéraires. Paris: Perrin, 1889. Cécile [n.d.] reprinted here as "Arthur de Monthierry."

Récits d'amour. Paris: Perrin, 1890.

Groupe de martyres. Paris: Perrin, [1891]. A reprint of works previously published in Les Duranti (1844) and Angèle (1860).

Souvenirs et impressions littéraires. Paris: Perrin, 1892.

Luttes du coeur. Paris: Perrin, 1893.

Figures historiques et légendaires. Paris: Perrin, n.d.

Letters in Flaubert: Correspondance, vol. 2: Juillet 1851–décembre 1858 and vol. 3: Janvier 1859–décembre 1868, ed. Jean Bruneau. Paris: Gallimard, 1980–91.

Published Diary by Geneviève Bréton (1867–71)

Journal, 1867–1871, ed. Daphné Doublet-Vaudoyer. Paris: Ramsay, 1985.

"In the Solitude of My Soul": The Diary of Geneviève Bréton, 1867–1871, ed. James Smith Allen, tr. James Palmes. Carbondale: Southern Illinois UP, 1994.

Principal Works by Céline Renooz (1883–1933)

L'Origine des animaux: Histoire du développement primitif: Nouvelle théorie de l'évolution réfutant par l'anatomie celle de M. Darwin, vol. 1. Paris: Baillière, 1883. Subsequent volumes were never written.

"Une révélation," *La Religion laïque et universelle*, 2nd ser., 2nd yr., nos. 57–58 (15 May 1888): 265–69.

"Prédestinée: L'Autobiographie de la femme cachée" [1890–1913, uncompleted MS]. Bibliothèque de la Ville de Paris, Fonds Marie Louise Bouglé, Papiers Céline Renooz, boxes 16–19.

La Nouvelle Science:

Vol. 1: *Les Forces cosmiques: Synthèse des lois de l'univers, l'évolution des astres, principe d'une nouvelle physique*, 3rd ed. Paris: Librairie Nouvelle, n.d. Originally entitled *La Force*, 1890.

Vol. 2: *Les Facteurs de la vie: Les Eléments de l'univers, les familles solaires, la chimie nouvelle, les stades de l'évolution chimique*, 2nd ed. Paris: Rhéa, 1920. Originally entitled *Le Principe générateur de la vie*, 1890.

Vol. 3: *Les Evolutions phylogéniques*, pt. 1: *L'Origine des animaux*; pt. 2: *L'Evolution de l'homme et des animaux: Histoire positive du développement primitif démontrée par le développement embryonnaire*, 1st section. Paris: Vieweg, 1888; pt. 3: *L'Origine végétale de l'homme et des animaux aériens*, 1: *Les Mammifères*, 3rd ed. Paris: Maloine, 1905. Pt. 1 was originally published 1883; pts. 2 and 3 were never completed.

Vol. 4: *La Paléontologie nouvelle*. Never written.

Vol. 5: *Le Dualisme physiologique*. Never written.

Vol. 6: *La Psychologie comparée de l'homme et de la femme, bases scientifiques de la morale*, 2nd ed. Paris: Société d'Editions Scientifiques chez auteur, 1901. Originally published 1898.

La Science et l'empirisme. Paris: Bibliothèque de la Nouvelle Encyclopédie, 1898. Brochure.

Le Grand problème. Articles parus dans la *République sociale* de Marseille en 1908. Paris: Publications Néosophiques, [1908].

Evolution de l'idée divine (simple aperçu). Paris: Giard & Brière, 1908. Brochure.

La Paix glorieuse. Nécessité de l'intervention féminine pour assurer la paix future. Edification du monde nouveau par la ratiocratie: Le Nouveau statut des peuples: Dédié à Monsieur Wilson, président des Etats-Unis. Paris: Publications Néosophiques, 1917. Brochure.

Le Monde nouveau: Projet de réorganisation sociale par la science. Paris: Impr. Lévy, [1919]. Brochure.

Ere de vérité. Histoire de la pensée humaine et de l'évolution morale de l'humanité à travers les âges et chez tous les peuples.

Vol. 1: *Le Monde primitif*. Paris: Giard, 1921.

Vol. 2: *Le Monde ancien*. Paris: Giard, 1924.

Vol. 3: *Le Monde israélite*. Paris: Giard, 1925.

Vol. 4: *Le Monde celtique*. Paris: Giard, 1926.

Vol. 5: *Le Monde chrétien*. Paris: Giard, 1927.
Vol. 6: *Le Monde moderne*. Paris: Giard, 1933.

Newspapers and Journals: Selected

Le Bulletin mensuel de la Société Néosophique (1897)
La Charente (1900)
La Chevauchée (1902)
The Chicago Tribune, European edition (1922)
L'Eclaireur (1901)
L'Ere de vérité. Bulletin de la Société Néosophique (1927–31)
L'Estafette (1900)
Le Figaro (1894)
La Flandre libérale (1900)
Le Français (1902)
La Fronde (1900)
L'Intransigeant (1902)
Le Journal de Bruxelles (1900)
Le Matin (1900, 1911)
Le Médecin (1902)
Le Moniteur du Puy-de-Dôme (1900)
La Patriote (1900)
Le Patriot normand (1902)
La Pensée (1902)
La Petite République socialiste (1900)
La Religion laïque et universelle (1888)
La Revue des deux mondes (1895)
La Revue scientifique des femmes (1888–89)
Le Voltaire (1900)

Published Autobiographies / Memoirs by Frenchwomen: Selected

Abrantès, Laure Junot, duchesse d'. *Mémoires, 1831–1835*. Paris: Mame, 1836.
Adam, Juliette. *Le Roman de mon enfance et de ma jeunesse*. Paris: Lemerre, 1902.
Allart de Méritens, Hortense. *Les Enchantements de Mme Prudence de Saman L'Esbatx*.
    Sceaux: Impr. Dépée, 1872.
——. *Les Nouveaux Enchantements par Mme P. de Saman*. Paris: Michel Lévy frères,
    1873.
——. *Derniers Enchantements . . . par Mme Prudence de Saman*. Paris: Michel Lévy
    frères, 1874.

Barbin, Herculine. *Herculine Barbin, dite Alexina B.*, ed. Michel Foucault. Paris: Gallimard, 1978.

Beauvoir, Simone de. *Mémoires d'une jeune fille rangée*. Paris: Gallimard, 1958.

———. *La Force de l'âge*. Paris: Gallimard, 1960.

———. *La Force des choses*. Paris: Gallimard, 1963.

———. *Une Mort très douce*. Paris: Gallimard, 1964.

Bernhardt, Sarah. *Ma double vie: Mémoires*. Paris: Charpentier, 1923. 2 vols.

Bourignon, Antoinette. *La Vie de dam'lle Antoinette Bourignon, écrite partie par elle-même, partie par une personne de sa connaissance*, ed. Pierre Poiret. Amsterdam: Riewerts & Arents, 1683. 2 vols.

Bouvier, Jeanne. *Mes mémoires, ou 59 années d'activité industrielle, sociale et intellectuelle, 1876–1935*, ed. Daniel Armogathe. Paris: La Découverte / Maspero, 1983.

B[rocher / Brochon], Victorine. *Souvenirs d'une morte vivante*. Paris: Maspero, 1976.

Cappelle-Lafarge, Marie. *Mémoires de Marie Cappelle, veuve Lafarge, écrites par elle même*. Paris: René, 1841–42. 4 vols.

Carles, Emilie. *Une soupe aux herbes sauvages*. Paris: Simoën, 1977.

Cazenove d'Arlens, Constance de. *Deux mois à Paris et à Lyon sous le Consulat: Journal de Mme de Cazenove d'Arlens*. Paris: Picard, 1903.

Clairon, Claire Josèphe-Hippolyte Leris de La Tude, dite Mademoiselle. *Mémoires d'Hippolyte Clairon et réflexions sur l'art dramatique, publiés par elle-même*. Paris: Buisson, an VII [1799].

Colette, Sidonie Gabrielle. *L'Etoile vesper: Souvenirs*. Paris: Milieu du Monde, 1946.

———. *Mes apprentissages: Ce que Claudine n'a pas dit*. Paris: Hachette, 1936.

Crouzet-Benaben, Jeanne Paul. *Souvenir d'une jeune fille bête: Souvenirs autobiographiques d'une des premières agrégées de France*. Paris: Debresse, 1971.

Feuillet, Valérie. *Quelques années de ma vie*. Paris: Calmann-Lévy, 1894.

Gautier, Judith. *Le Collier des jours: Souvenirs de ma vie*. Paris: Juven, 1904.

Guion, Jeanne-Marie Bouvier de La Motte. *La Vie de Mme J. M. B. de La Mothe Guion, écrite par elle-même*, ed. P. Poiret. Cologne: De la Pierre, 1720. 3 vols.

Gyp (Sibylle-Gabrielle Marie-Antoinette de Riquetti de Mirabeau). *Souvenirs d'une petite fille*. Paris: Calmann-Lévy, 1927. 2 vols.

Harpain, Marie-Eustelle. *Recueil des écrits de Marie-Eustelle: Récit de sa vie écrit par elle-même*. La Rochelle: Boulet, 1843.

Jeanne des Anges, Soeur (Jeanne de Belcier). *Soeur Jeanne des Anges, supérieure des Ursulines de Loudun, XVIIe siècle: Autobiographie d'une hystérique possédée*, ed. Gabriel Legué and Gilles de La Tourette. Paris: Aux bureaux du "Progrès médical," 1886.

Klumpke, Anna. *Rosa Bonheur: The Artist's (Auto)biography*, tr. Gretchen van Slyke. Ann Arbor: U of Michigan P, 1997.

Leduc, Violette. *La Bâtarde*. Paris: Gallimard, 1964.

——. *La Folie en tête*. Paris: Gallimard, 1970.

Léo-Lagrange, Madeleine. *La Présent indéfini: Mémoires d'une vie*, ed. Robert Bernard and Albert Ronsin. Orléans: Corsaire, 1998.

Malraux, Clara. *Le Bruit de nos pas*, vol. 1: *Apprendre à vivre;* vol. 2: *Nos Vingt ans;* vol. 3: *Les Combats et les jeux*. Paris: Grasset, 1963, 1966, 1969.

Marie de l'Enfant-Jésus, Mère. *Vie de la Mère Marie de l'Enfant-Jésus, l'une des fondatrices du monastère des Clarisses de Lourdes, écrite par elle-même*. Toulouse: n.p., 1910.

Michel, Louise. *Mémoires de Louise Michel éscrits par elle-même*. NParis: Roy, 1886.

Michelet, Athénaïs Mialaret, Mme Jules. *Mémoires d'une enfant*. Paris: Hachette, 1867.

Montpensier, Anne Marie Louise d'Orléans, duchesse de. *Mémoires*. In *Collection des mémoires relatifs à l'histoire de France*, ed. C. Petitot. Paris: Foucault, 1819–29.

Moreno, Marguerite. *Souvenirs de ma vie*. Paris: Flore, 1948.

Motteville, Françoise Bertaut, dame de. *Mémoires*. In *Collection des mémoires relatifs à l'histoire de France*, ed. C. Petitot. Paris: Foucault, 1819–29.

Noailles, Anna-Elisabeth de Brancovan, comtesse Matthieu de. *Le Livre de ma vie*. Paris: Hachette, 1932.

Pauper, Marceline. *Vie de Marcelline Pauper, de la congrégation des soeurs de la Charité de Nevers, écrite par elle-même*, ed. D. Bouix. Nevers: Impr. Fay, 1871.

Rémusat, Claire-Elisabeth-Jeanne Gravier de Vergennes, comtesse de. *Mémoires de Madame de Rémusat, 1802–1808*, ed. Paul de Rémusat. Paris: Colmann-Lévy, 1880. 3 vols.

Roland de La Platière, Marie-Jeanne Philipon, Mme. *Mémoires*, ed. P. Fauguère. Paris: Hachette, 1864. 2 vols.

Ropars, Jean. *Au pays d'Yvonne: Mémoires d'une paysanne léonarde*. Paris: Payot, 1993.

Rossignol, Elisa. *Une enfance en Alsace, 1907–1918*. Paris: Sand, 1990.

Rouy, Hersilie. *Mémoires d'une aliénée*, ed. Edouard Le Normant des Varannes. Paris: Ollendorff, 1883.

Sand, George. *Histoire de ma vie*. Paris: Lecou & Cadot, 1854–55. 20 vols.

——. *Oeuvres autobiographiques*, ed. Georges Lubin. Paris: Gallimard, 1970. 2 vols.

Staal de Launay, Marguerite-Jeanne Cordier, baronne de. *Mémoires de Mme de Staal, écrits par elle-même*. London: n.p. 1755. 4 vols.

Staël-Holstein, Anne-Louise-Germaine Necker, baronne de. *Mémoires de Madame de Staël (Dix années d'exil)*, ed. le duc de Broglie and le baron de Staël. New ed. Paris: Charpentier, 1861.

Stern, Marie d'Agoult, dite Daniel. *Mes Souvenirs, 1806–1833*. Paris: Calmann-Lévy, 1877.

——. *Mémoires, 1833–1854*, ed. Daniel Ollivier. Paris: Calmann-Lévy, 1927.

Thérèse de l'Enfant-Jésus, Thérèse Martin, Sainte. *Histoire d'une âme, écrite par elle-même*, ed. Mère Agnès de Jésus. Bar-le-Duc: n.p., 1898.

Thérèse de Jésus (Mère Sainte-Thérèse de Jésus, abbesse du Monastère de Sainte-

Claire de Lavaur). *Aimer et souffrir, ou vie de la rde. Mère Sainte-Thérèse de Jésus . . . écrite par elle-même.* Toulouse: Privat, 1884. 2 vols.

Tristan, Flora. *Pérégrinations d'une paria, 1833–1834: Dieu, franchise, liberté.* Paris: Bertrand, 1838. 2 vols.

Vigée-Lebrun, Louise-Elisabeth. *Souvenirs de Mme Louise-Elisabeth Vigée-Lebrun.* Paris: Fournier, 1835–37. 3 vols.

Voilquin, Suzanne. *Mémoires d'une saint-simonienne en Russie, 1839–1846,* ed. Maïté Albistur and Daniel Armogathe. Paris: Des Femmes, 1977.

———. *Souvenirs d'une fille du peuple, ou la saint-simonienne en Egypte, 1834 à 1836, par Madame Suzanne V***.* Paris: Sauzet, 1866.

Weiss, Louise. *Mémoires d'une européenne.* Paris: Plon, 1968–82. 6 vols.

Published Diaries by Frenchwomen: Selected

Ackermann, Louise. *Journal* [1849–69]. In *Mercure de France* (1 May 1927): 524–76.

Aron, Marguerite. *Journal d'une sévrienne.* Paris: Alcan, 1912.

Arvisy, Madeleine d'. *Ce qui passe et ce qui reste: Pages détachées d'un journal de jeunesse* [1901–3]. Paris: Lethielleux, 1907.

Bashkirtseff, Marie. *Cahiers intimes,* ed. Pierre Borel. Paris: Monde Moderne, [1925]. 4 vols.

———. *Journal de Marie Bashkirtseff.* Paris: Charpentier, 1887. 2 vols.

Beauvoir, Simone de. *Journal de guerre: Septembre 1939–janvier 1941.* Paris: Gallimard, 1990.

Bonaparte, Marie. *Cinq cahiers écrits par une petite fille entre sept ans et demi et dix ans et leurs commentaires* [1889–96]. Paris: n.p., 1939–51. 5 vols.

[Brame, Caroline]. *Le Journal intime de Caroline B.,* ed. Michelle Perrot and Georges Ribeill. Paris: Montalba, 1985.

Bréton, Geneviève. *Journal, 1867–1871,* ed. Daphné Doublet-Vaudoyer. Paris: Ramsay, 1985.

Catez, Elisabeth. "Extraits de journal intime [1899–1900]." In Elisabeth Catez, *Ecrits spirituels d'Elisabeth de la Trinité.* Paris: Seuil, 1948.

[Chavent, Marie-Louise]. *Journal et pensées intimes de l'auteur de "La Vierge chrétienne," une des victimes de la catastrophe de St-Gervais, 12 juillet 1892* [1880–85]. Lyons: Delhomme & Briguet, 1894.

Colette, Sidonie Gabrielle. *Journal à rebours, 1938–1940.* Paris: Fayard, 1941.

———. *Journal intermittent* [1915, 1923, 1934, 1941]. Paris: Le Fleuron, 1949.

Curie, Marie. *Journal intime* [1906]. In Eve Curie, *Madame Curie,* 200–206. Paris: Gallimard, 1938.

Delétang, Louise. *Journal d'une ouvrière parisienne pendant la guerre.* Paris: Figuière, [1919].

Desmoulins, Lucille. *Journal, 1788–1793,* ed. Philippe Lejeune. Paris: Cendres, 1995.

Dupouey, Mireille. *Cahiers* [1915–19]. Paris: Cerf, 1945.

Eberhardt, Isabelle. *Mes journaliers.* Paris: Les Introuvables, 1985.

Ernaux, Annie. *Journal du dehors.* Paris: Gallimard, 1993.

Escholier, Marie. *Journal de guerre, 1914–19.* Carcassonne: GARAE/ HESIODE, 1986.

Frémont, Laure. *Journal de Mlle Laure Frémont* [1880], ed. abbé G. Frémont. Besançon: "Femme Contemporaine," 1904.

G., Jeanne. *Journal et correspondance de Jeanne G.* [1895–1900]. Marseilles: Verdot, 1906.

[Geuser, Marie-Antoinette de]. *Notes spirituelles* [1909–17]. In R. Plus, *Consumata.* Toulouse: Apostolat de la Prière, 1932.

Guérin, Eugénie de. *Journal* [1834–41]. Paris: Gabalda, 1934.

Héon-Canonne, Jeanne. *Devant la mort* [1944–45]. Angers: Sirandeau, 1951.

Hugo, Adèle. *Le Journal* [1852–54]. Paris: Lettres Modernes, 1968–71. 3 vols.

La Ferronnays, Pauline de. *Récit d'une soeur: Souvenirs de famille recueillis par Mme Augustus Craven, née La Ferronnays* [1832–48]. Paris: Impr. Claye, 1866. 2 vols.

Lenéru, Marie. *Journal* [1893–1918]. Paris: Crés, 1922. 2 vols.

Leseur, Elisabeth. *Journal d'une enfant* [1877–81]. Paris: De Gigord, 1934.

——. *Journal et pensées de chaque jour* [1899–1906, 1911–14]. Paris: De Gigord, 1917.

Le Verrier, Lucile. *Journal d'une jeune fille second Empire, 1866–1878,* ed. Lionel Mirisch. Paris: Zulma, 1994.

Lombrail, Adeline. *Une belle âme: Notice et souvenirs intimes de Mlle Adeline Lombrail* [1877–90]. Lille: Desclée-De Brouwer, 1913.

Lucie-Christine. *Journal spirituel, 1870–1901.* Paris: Communauté de l'Adoration Réparatrice, 1926.

Manet, Julie. *Journal, 1893–1899.* Paris: Scala, 1987.

Marbeau, Arlette. *Journal spirituel* [1939–46]. Paris: Bloud & Gay, 1951.

Marie ***. *Mon cher petit cahier: Journal d'une jeune ouvrière* [1864–68]. Lyons: Josserand, 1872.

Pau, Marie-Edmée. *Le Journal de Marie-Edmée* [1859–71], ed. Antoine de Latour. Paris: Plon, 1876.

Pomès, Mathilde. *A Rome avec Montherlant* [1947–48]. Paris: Bonne, 1951.

Pozzi, Catherine. *Journal, 1913–1914,* ed. Claire Paulhan. Paris: Ramsay, 1987.

R., Marie-Marguerite. *Un souvenir de la congrégation de Notre-Dame: Marguerite* [1889–99], ed. Henri Joly. Moulins: Crépins-Leblanc, 1908.

Régnier, Paule. "Fragments de journal (1923–47)," *La Table ronde* (November 1951): 30–48.

Saint-Pern, Renée. *Journal de Renée Saint-Pern* [1900–1904]. Angers: Sirandeau, 1906.

Sand, George. *Journal intime* [1834–40]. Paris: Calmann-Lévy, 1926.

Staël, Germaine Necker, baronne de. "Journal de jeunesse," *Occident et cahiers staëliens* 1 (Jun. 1930, Jul. 1931, Oct. 1932): 75–81, 157–60, 235–42.

Thomas, Edith. *Pages de journal 1939–1944: Suivies de journal intime de Monsieur Célestin Costedet*. Paris: Hamy, 1995.

——. *Le Témoin compromis: Mémoires*. Paris: Hamy, 1995.

Tristan, Flora. *Le Tour de France: Journal inédit, 1843–1844*, 2nd ed., ed. Jules Puech. Paris: Maspero, 1980. 2 vols.

Virduzzo, Francine. *Journal, 1958–1974*. Paris: Saint-Germain-des-Prés, 1980.

Weil, Simone. *Journal d'usine* [1934–35]. In Simone Weil, *La Condition ouvrière*, 35–107. Paris: Gallimard, 1951.

Weiler, Amélie. *Journal d'une jeune fille mal dans son siècle, 1840–1859*, ed. Nicolas Stoskopf. Strasbourg: La Nuée Bleue, 1994.

Published Collections of Frenchwomen's Letters: Selected

Aïssé, Mlle. *Lettres de Mlle Aïssé à Mme Calandrini*. Paris: Librairie des Bibliophiles, 1878.

Amécourt, Roger d', ed. *Le Mariage de Mademoiselle de la Verne*. Paris: Perrin, 1987.

Audry, Colette. *Rien au-delà*. Paris: Denoël, 1993.

Bashkirtseff, Marie. *Lettres*. Paris: Charpentier, 1891.

Beaunier, André, ed. *La Comtesse de Lafayette: Correspondance*. Paris: Gallimard, 1942. 2 vols.

Beauvoir, Sylvie Le Bon de, ed. *Lettres à Sartre*. Paris: Gallimard, 1990. 2 vols.

Bonnelle, Mireille, and Alain Caillol. *Lettres en liberté conditionnelle*. Paris: Manya, 1990.

Bourguignon, Jean, ed. *Mémoires, lettres, et papiers de Valérie Masuyer, dame d'honneur de la reine Hortense*. Paris: Plon, 1937.

Breuil, Auguste, ed. *Lettres inédites de Mlle Philipon, Madame Roland . . . de 1772 à 1780*. Paris: Coquebert, 1841. 2 vols.

Bruneau, Jean, ed. *Flaubert: Correspondance*. Paris: Gallimard, 1980–91. Vols. 2 and 3 [with Marie-Sophie Leroyer de Chantepie].

Burns, Marie-Patricia, ed. *Sainte Jeanne-Françoise de Chantal: Correspondance*. Paris: Cerf, 1986–87. 2 vols.

Buchon, J. A. C., ed. *Correspondance inédite de Mme Campan avec la reine Hortense*. Paris: Levavasseur, 1835. 2 vols.

Chancerel, André, ed. *A une amie de province: Lettres de Laure Surville de Balzac, 1831–1837*. Paris: Petits-Fils de Plon & Nourrit, 1932.

Chassagne, Serge, ed. *Une femme d'affaires au XVIIIe siècle: La Correspondance de Madame de Maraise, collaboratrice d'Oberkampf*. Toulouse: Privat, 1981.

Collin, L., ed. *Lettres de Mademoiselle de Montpensier*. Paris: Collin, 1806.

——. *Lettres de Madame la duchesse du Maine et de Madame la marquise de Simiane. . . .* Paris: Collin, an XIII [1805].

———. *Lettres de Mesdames de Scudéry, de Salvan de Saliez, et de Mademoiselle Descartes.* Paris: Collin, 1804.

Cuénin, Micheline, ed. *Lettres et billets* [Marie-Catherine Desjardins, dite Mme de Villedieu]. Paris: La Société d'Etude du XVIIe Siècle, 1975.

Delacour, Marie-Odile, and Jean-René Huleu, eds. *Isabelle Eberhardt: Ecrits intimes: Lettres aux trois hommes les plus aimés.* Paris: Payot, 1991.

Du Barry, Mme la comtesse. *Lettres . . . .* London: n.p., 1779.

Duchêne, Roger, ed. *Madame de Sévigné: Correspondance.* Paris: Gallimard, 1972–78. 3 vols.

Du Fresne de Beaucourt, G., ed. *Etude sur Madame Elisabeth d'après sa correspondance.* Paris: Aubry, 1864.

Duperrey, Annie. *Je vous écris.* Paris: Seuil, 1993.

Falloux, comte de, ed. *Lettres de Madame Swetchine.* Paris: Vaton, 1862. 2 vols.

Fauguère, P., ed. *Lettres de la Mère Agnès Arnauld, abbesse de Port-Royal.* Paris: Duprat, 1858. 2 vols.

Freminville, Bernard de, ed. *Emilie.* Paris: Seuil, 1985.

———, ed. *Marthe.* Paris: Seuil, 1982.

Gacon-Dufour, Mme, ed. *Correspondance inédite de Madame de Châteauroux*, 2nd ed. Paris: Collin, 1807. 2 vols.

Gagnière, A. de, ed. *Marie-Adélaïde de Savoie: Lettres et correspondances.* Paris: Ollendorff, 1897.

Georgel, Pierre, ed. *Correspondance de Léopoldine Hugo.* Paris: Klincksieck, 1976.

Godet, Philippe, ed. *Lettres de Belle de Zuylen à Constant d'Hermenches, 1760–1775.* Paris: Plon, 1909.

Goncourt, Edmond, and Jules de Goncourt, eds. *Sophie Arnould d'après sa correspondance . . . .* Paris: Dentu, 1877.

Guilbert, Yvette. *Mes lettres d'amour.* Paris: Denoël & Steele, 1933.

Jasinski, Béatrice W., ed. *Correspondance générale de Madame de Staël.* Paris: Pauvert, 1962–93. 6 vols.

Lapauze, Henry, ed. *Lettres inédites de Madame de Genlis à son fils adoptif Casimir Baecker, 1802–1830.* Paris: Plon, 1902.

Laplane, Gabriel, ed. *Rachel: Lettres inédites.* Paris: Vigneau, 1947.

Leroy, Pierre-E., and Marcel Loyau, eds. *Mme de Maintainon, Mme de Caylus et Mme de Dangeau: L'Estime et la tendresse: Correspondances intimes.* Paris: Albin Michel, 1998.

Lespinasse, Julie de. *Lettres.* Paris: Garnier, n.d.

Lettres de Sido à Colette. Paris: Des Femmes, 1984.

Louis, Bernadette, ed. *Une correspondance saint-simonienne: Angélique Arnaud et Caroline Simon, 1833–1838.* Paris: Côté-Femmes, 1990.

Lubin, Georges, ed. *Correspondance de George Sand.* Paris: Garnier frères, 1964–91. 25 vols.

Magnieu, E. de, and Henri Prat, eds. *Correspondance inédite de la comtesse de Sabran et du chevalier de Boufflers, 1778–1788*. Paris: Plon, 1875.

Martin-Fugier, Anne, ed. *Les Lettres d'Hélène*. Paris: Hermé, 1986.

Michaud, Stéphane, ed. *Flora Tristan: Lettres*. Paris: Seuil, 1980.

Pélissier, Léon-G., ed. *Le Portefeuille de la comtesse d'Albany, 1806–1824*. Paris: Fontemoing, 1902.

Pichois, Claude, and Robert Forbin, eds. *Colette: Lettres à ses pairs*. Paris: Flammarion, 1973.

Pompadour, Mme la marquise de. *Lettres*. London: Owen, 1776.

Radziwill, Marie de Castellane, princesse Antoine. *Une grande dame d'avant-guerre: Lettres de la princesse Radziwill au général de Robilant, 1889–1914*. Paris: Plon, 1933–34. 4 vols.

Rémusat, Claire de. *Lettres*. Paris: Calmann-Lévy, 1881. 2 vols.

Rey, Françoise, and Remo Forlani. *En toute lettres*. Paris: Ramsay, 1992.

Rivière, Benjamin, ed. *Correspondance intime de Marceline Desbordes-Valmore*. Paris: Lemerre, 1896. 2 vols.

Rochefort, Robert, ed. *Les Lettres de Françoise*. Paris: Beauchesne, 1990.

Sazerac de Limagne, Joséphine. *Journal, pensées et correspondance*. Paris: Le Clere, Reichel, 1874.

Showalter, English, ed. *Madame de Graffigny: Correspondance*. Oxford: Voltaire Foundation, 1985–97. 5 vols.

Sorgue, Mireille. *Lettres à l'amant*. Paris: Albin Michel, 1985.

Souchon, Paul, ed. *Juliette Drouet: Mille et une lettres d'amour à Victor Hugo*. Paris: Gallimard, n.d.

Strich, Marie-José, ed. *La Comtesse de Ségur: Correspondance 1799–1874*. Paris: Scala, 1993.

Thirra, H., ed. *La Marquise de Crenay: Une amie de la reine Hortense*. Paris: Plange, 1898.

Tourtier-Bonazzi, Chantal de, ed. *Correspondance d'Annette de Mackau*. Paris: S.E.V.P.E.N., 1967.

Trabucco, Joseph, ed. *Correspondance: Mme du Deffand à Voltaire*. Paris: Bossard, 1922.

Trébutin, G.-S., ed. *Lettres d'Eugénie de Guérin*, 6th ed. Paris: Didier, 1865.

Studies of Diaries, Letters, and Autobiographies: Selected

Abel, Elizabeth et al., ed. *The Voyage In: Fictions of Female Development*. Hanover: UP of New England, 1983.

Altman, Janet Gurkin. *Epistolarity: Approaches to a Form*. Columbus: Ohio State UP, 1982.

Anderson, Linda. "At the Threshold of the Self: Women and Autobiography." In *Women's Writing: A Challenge to Theory*, ed. Moira Monteith, 54–71. New York: St Martin's, 1986.

Autobiographie. Special issue, *Revue d'histoire littéraire de la France* 75, no. 6 (1975).

Beaujour, Michel. "Autobiographie et autoportrait," *Poétique*, no. 32 (1977): 442–58.

Bell, Susan Groag, and Marilyn Yalom, eds. *Revealing Lives: Autobiography, Biography, and Gender.* Albany: State U of New York P, 1992.

Benstock, Shari. "The Female Self Engendered: Autobiographical Writing and Theories of Selfhood," *Women's Studies* 20, no. 1 (1991): 5–14.

——, ed. *The Private Self: Theory and Practice of Women's Autobiographical Writing.* Chapel Hill: U of North Carolina P, 1987.

Bonnat, Jean-Louis, ed. *Des mots et des images pour correspondre.* Actes du Colloque. Nantes: U de Nantes, 1986.

Bonnat, Jean-Louis et al., eds. *Ecrire-publier-lire: Les Correspondances: Problématique et économie d'un genre littéraire.* Actes du Colloque International. Nantes: U de Nantes, 1983.

Bossis, Mireille, ed. *La Lettre à la croisée de l'individuel et du social.* Paris: Kimé, 1994.

Bossis, Mireille, and Charles Porter, eds. *L'Epistolarité à travers les siècles: Geste de communication et/ou d'écriture.* Colloque. Centre Culturel International de Cerisy la Salle. Stuttgart: Steiner, 1990.

Brée, Germaine. *Narcissus Absconditus: The Problematic Art of Autobiography in Contemporary France.* Zaharoff Lecture for 1977–78. Oxford: Clarendon, 1978.

Brodzki, Bella, and Celeste Schenck, eds. *Life/Lines: Theorizing Women's Autobiography.* Ithaca: Cornell UP, 1988.

Brunet, Manon, and Serge Gagnon, eds. *Discours et pratiques de l'intime.* Quebec: Institut Québécois de Recherche sur la Culture, 1993.

Bruss, Elizabeth W. *Autobiographical Acts: The Changing Situation of a Literary Genre.* Baltimore: Johns Hopkins UP, 1976.

Bryant, David. "Réflexions sur le journal intime," *Bulletin de la Société Néophilologique* 82, no. 1 (1981): 66–74.

——. "Revolution and Introspection: The Appearance of the Private Diary in France," *European Studies* 8 (April 1978): 259–72.

Butor, Michel. "L'Usage des pronoms dans le roman," *Essais sur le roman*, 73–88. Paris: Minuit, 1960.

Chartier, Roger, ed. *La Correspondance: Les Usages de la lettre au 19e siècle.* Paris: Fayard, 1991.

Cline, Cheryl. *Women's Diaries, Journals, and Letters: An Annotated Bibliography.* New York: Garland, 1989.

Cornille, J. L. *L'Amour des lettres, ou le contrat déchiré.* Mannheim: Mana, 1985.

La Correspondance: Edition, fonction, et signification. Actes du Colloque franco-italien, Aix-en-Provence, 5–6 oct. 1983. Toulouse: U de Provence, 1984.

Dauphin, Cécile, et al. *Ces bonnes lettres: Une correspondance familiale au XIXe siècle.* Paris: Albin Michel, 1995.

Del Litto, Vittorio, ed. *Le Journal intime et ses formes littéraires.* Actes du Colloque de septembre 1975. Geneva: Droz, 1978.

Didier, Béatrice. *L'Ecriture-femme.* Paris: PUF, 1981.

———. *Le Journal intime.* Paris: PUF, 1976.

Doubrovsky, Serge. *Autobiographiques: De Corneille à Sartre.* Paris: PUF, 1988.

Duchêne, Roger. "Du destinaire au public, ou les métamorphoses d'une correspondance privée," *Revue d'histoire littéraire de la France* 76, no. 1 (1976): 29–42.

Eakin, Paul John. *Fictions in Autobiography: Studies in the Art of Self-Invention.* Princeton: Princeton UP, 1985.

———. *Touching the World: Reference in Autobiography.* Princeton: Princeton UP, 1992.

Escarpit, Denise, and Bernadette Poulou, eds. *Le Récit d'enfance: Enfance et écriture.* Actes du Colloque de NVL / CRALEJ, Bordeaux, October 1992. [Bordeaux]: Sorbier, 1993.

Expériences limites de l'épistolaire: Lettres d'exile, d'enfermement, de folie. Colloque de Caen. Paris: Champion, 1993.

Françon, André, and Claude Goyard, eds. *Les Correspondances inédites.* Paris: Economica, 1984.

Genette, Gérard. "Le Journal, l'anti-journal," *Poétique,* no. 47 (1981): 315–22.

Gilmore, Leigh. *Autobiographics: A Feminist Theory of Women's Self-Representation.* Ithaca: Cornell UP, 1994.

Girard, Alain. *Le Journal intime.* Paris: PUF, 1963.

Goodwin, James. *Autobiography: The Self-Made Text.* New York: Twayne, 1993.

Gunn, Janet Varner. *Autobiography: Towards a Poetics of Experience.* Philadelphia: U of Pennsylvania P, 1982.

Gusdorf, Georges. "Conditions et limites de l'autobiographie." In *Formen der Selbstdarstellung.* Berlin: Duncker & Humboldt, 1956. A translation is in Olney, 1980: 28–48.

———. *La Découverte de soi.* Paris: PUF, 1948.

———. *Lignes de vie,* vol. 1: *Les Ecritures de moi;* vol. 2: *Auto-bio-graphie.* Paris: Jacob, 1991.

Heilbrun, Carolyn. *Writing a Woman's Life.* New York: Norton, 1988.

Henriot, Emile. *Epistoliers et mémorialistes.* Paris: La Nouvelle Revue Critique, 1931.

Holdenried, M., ed. *Geschriebenes Leben: Autobiographik von Frauen.* Berlin: Schmidt, 1995.

Jay, Paul. *Being in the Text: Self-Representation from Wordsworth to Roland Barthes.* Ithaca: Cornell UP, 1984.

Jelinek, Estelle. *The Tradition of Women's Autobiography: From Antiquity to the Present.* Boston: Twayne, 1986.

——, ed. *Woman's Autobiography: Essays in Criticism.* Bloomington: Indiana UP, 1980.

Jones, P. Mansell. *French Introspectives from Montaigne to André Gide.* Cambridge: Cambridge UP, 1937.

Kaufmann, Vincent. *L'Equivoque épistolaire.* Paris: Minuit, 1990.

Kirby, Paul. *Narrative and the Self.* Bloomington: Indiana UP, 1991.

Laub, Dori, and Shoshana Felman, *Testimony: Crisis of Witnessing in Literature, Psychoanalysis, and History.* New York: Routledge, 1992.

Laurent, Jacques. *Les Bêtises.* Paris: Club Français du Livre, 1971.

Lavelle, Louis. *La Conscience en soi.* Paris: Grasset, 1933.

Lecarme, Jacques, and Elaine Lecarme-Tabone. *L'Autobiographie.* Paris: Colin, 1997.

Lejeune, Philippe, *L'Autobiographie en France.* Paris: Colin, 1971.

——. *Je suis un autre: L'Autobiographie de la littérature aux médias.* Paris: Seuil, 1980.

——. *Le Moi des demoiselles: Enquête sur le journal de jeune fille.* Paris: Seuil, 1993.

——. *Le Pacte autobiographique.* Paris: Seuil, 1975.

——. "Le Pacte autobiographique (2)," *Poétique* 14 (1983): 137–62.

——. *Pour l'autobiographie: Chroniques.* Paris: Seuil, 1998.

——. *La Pratique du journal personnel: Enquête.* Paris: Cahiers de Sémiotique Textuelle 17, U de Paris X, 1990.

——, ed. *Archives autobiographiques.* [Paris]: Cahiers de Sémiotique Textuelle 20, Université de Paris X, 1991.

——, ed. *Bibliographie des études en langue française sur la littérature personnelle et les récits de vie: 1: 1982–1983.* [Paris]: Cahiers de Sémiotique Textuelle 3, U de Paris X, 1984.

——, ed. *Bibliographie des études en langue française sur la littérature personnelle et les récits de vie: 2: 1984–1985.* [Paris]: Cahiers de Sémiotique Textuelle 7, U de Paris X, 1986.

——, ed. *Bibliographie des études en langue française sur la littérature personnelle et les récits de vie: 3: 1986–1987.* [Paris]: Cahiers de Sémiotique Textuelle 13, U de Paris X, 1988.

——, ed. *Bibliographie des études en langue française sur la littérature personnelle et les récits de vie: 4: 1988–1989.* [Paris]: Cahiers de Sémiotique Textuelle 19, U de Paris X, 1990.

——, ed. *"Cher cahier . . . ": Témoignages sur le journal personnel.* Paris: Gallimard, 1990.

Leleu, Michèle. *Les Journaux intimes.* Paris: PUF, 1952.

La Lettre d'amour. Special issue, *Textuel,* no. 24 (1992).

Lettres d'écrivains. Special issue, *Revue des sciences humaines,* no. 195 (1984).

Lionnet, Françoise. *Autobiographical Voices: Race, Gender, Self-Portraiture*. Ithaca: Cornell UP, 1989.

Man, Paul de. "Autobiography as De-facement," *Modern Language Notes* 94, no. 5 (1979): 919–30.

May, Georges. *L'Autobiographie*. Paris: PUF, 1979.

Mehlman, Jeffrey. *A Structural Study of Autobiography: Proust, Leiris, Sartre, Lévi-Strauss*. Ithaca: Cornell UP, 1974.

Melançon, Benoît, and Pierre Popovic, eds. *Les Facultés des lettres: Recherches récentes sur l'épistolaire français et québécois*. Montreal: U de Montréal, 1993.

Men / Women of Letters. Special issue, *Yale French Studies*, no. 71 (1986).

Miller, Nancy K. *Bequest and Betrayal: Memoirs of a Parent's Death*. New York: Oxford UP, 1996.

——. *Subject to Change: Reading Feminist Writing*. New York: Columbia UP, 1988.

——. "Women's Autobiography in France: For a Dialectics of Identification." In *Women and Language in Literature and Society*, ed. Sally McConnell-Ginet et al., 258–73. New York: Praeger, 1980.

Misch, Georg. *Geschichte der Autobiographie*. Bern: Francke, 1949–50; Frankfurt: Schulte-Bulmke, 1955–69. 4 vols.

Morgan, Janice, and Colette Hall, eds. *Redefining Autobiography in Twentieth-Century Women's Fiction*. New York: Garland, 1991.

Olney, James. *Metaphors of the Self: The Meaning of Autobiography*. Princeton: Princeton UP, 1972.

——, ed. *Autobiography: Essays Theoretical and Critical*. Princeton: Princeton UP, 1980.

——, ed. *Studies in Autobiography*. New York: Oxford UP, 1988.

Pascal, Roy. *Design and Truth in Autobiography*. Cambridge: Harvard UP, 1960.

Personal Chronicles: Women's Autobiographical Writings. Special issue, *Women's Studies International Forum* 10, no. 1 (1987).

Personal Narratives Group. *Interpreting Women's Lives: Feminist Theory and Personal Narratives*. Bloomington: Indiana UP, 1989.

Pilling, John. *Autobiography and Imagination: Studies in Self-Scrutiny*. Boston: Routledge & Kegan Paul, 1981.

Poiret, Jean, et al., eds. *Les Récits de vie: Théorie et pratique*. Paris: PUF, 1983.

Rosenblatt, Paul C. *Bitter, Bitter Tears: Nineteenth-Century Diarists and Twentieth-Century Grief Theories*. Minneapolis: U of Minnesota P, 1983.

Rousset, Jean. *Le Lecteur intime de Balzac au journal*. Paris: Corti, 1986.

Rugg, Linda Haverty. *Picturing Ourselves: Photography and Autobiography*. Chicago: U of Chicago P, 1997.

Salvan, Albert J. "Private Journals in French Literature," *American Legion of Honor Magazine* 25 (1954): 201–14.

Sheringham, Michael. *French Autobiography: Devices and Desires.* Oxford: Clarendon, 1993.

Showalter, Elaine. *These Modern Women: Autobiographical Essays from the Twenties.* New York: Feminist P / City U of New York, 1989.

Smith, Sidonie. *A Poetics of Women's Autobiography: Marginality and the Fictions of Self-Representation.* Bloomington: Indiana UP, 1987.

——, ed. *Subjectivity, Identity, and the Body: Women's Autobiographical Practices in the Twentieth Century.* Bloomington: Indiana UP, 1992.

Spengermann, William C. *The Forms of Autobiography: Episodes in the History of a Literary Genre.* New Haven: Yale UP, 1980.

Stanton, Domna, ed. *The Female Autograph: Theory and Practice of Autobiography from the Tenth to the Twentieth Century.* Chicago: U of Chicago P, 1987.

Starobinski, Jean. "Le Style de l'autobiographie," *Poétique,* no. 3 (1970): 257–65.

Viala, Alain. "Littérature épistolaire." In *Le Grand Atlas des littératures,* ed. Gilles Quinsat et al., 50–51. Paris: Encyclopedia Universalis, 1990.

Watson, Julia, and Sidonie Smith, eds. *De/Colonizing the Subject: The Politics of Gender in Women's Autobiography.* Minneapolis: U of Minnesota P, 1992.

Weintraub, Karl Joachim. *The Value of the Individual: Self and Circumstance in Autobiography.* Chicago: U of Chicago P, 1978.

Williams, Huntington. *Rousseau and the Romantic Autobiography.* Oxford: Oxford UP, 1983.

Women and Memory. Special issue, *Michigan Quarterly Review* (1987).

Yalom, Marilyn, ed. "Women's Autobiography in French, 1793–1939: A Select Bibliography," *French Literature Series,* vol. 2, 197–205. Columbia: U of South Carolina P, 1985.

Index

References to illustrations are in italics

Abelard, Peter, 27
abortion, 1920 law against, 25
Abrantès, Laure, duchesse d', 27
Académie des Sciences et Belles-Lettres (Angers), 78, 179
Académie Française, 180
Agamemnon, Victor, 64
agency, 14–15, 171–72; in language, 2, 32–33, 43–47, 167, 181–82
Agoult, Marie d'. *See* Stern, Daniel
Alexander, Emilie, 127
Allart, Hortense, 27
Alliance des Savants et des Philanthropes, 126
Amour, L' (Michelet), 19
André, Edouard, 97
André, Eugène, 60, 70
Andrée, S.–A., 148
Angèle (Leroyer), 48, 76
Angélique Lagier (Leroyer), 35; as autobiographical romance, 76; on death penalty, 75; on divorce, 75; plot of, 75–76; and religion, 76
Angers, 5, 48, 154, 179; Leroyer on, 35, 53–54, 170
Anjou, 5, 50, 54; history of, 53
Arago, Jacques, 56
Arnim, Bettina von, 108, 112

Arnould, Sophie, 27
"Arthur de Monthierry" (Leoyer), 215n. 165
Astruc, Marie. *See* Bida, Marie
Auclert, Hubertine, 4, 20, 153, 177
Augier, Emile, *Habit vert, L'*, 82
Aurore (Paris), 143
autobiographical romance, 69–76
autobiography, 26; agency of, 46; defined, 40; and feminist theory, 41–42; as illocutionary act, 44
Auzat, Zélime. *See* Bréton, Zélime
avenue de Villiers (Paris), 85, 102

Bachofen, J. J., 137
Bakhtin, Mikhail, 45
Ballanche, Pierre Simon, 94
Balzac, Honoré de, 126, 176; *Eugénie Grandet*, 51
Banquet, The (Plato), 92
Barthes, Roland, 41
Bartholdi, Frédéric-Auguste, *Liberty Lighting the World*, 123
Bashkirtseff, Marie, 28, 129
Baudry, Paul, 83
Beauharnais, Hortense de, 27
Beaumont, Pauline de, 113
Beauvoir, Simone de, 4, 15, 28; *Deuxième Sexe, Le*, 21
Benstock, Shari, 41

Library of Congress Cataloging-in-Publication Data

Allen, James Smith.
Poignant relations : three modern French women / James Smith Allen.
    p.   cm.
   Includes bibliographical references and index.
   ISBN 0-8018-6204-3 (alk. paper)
    1. Feminism—France—History—19th century.   2. Women—
France—History—19th century.   3. Leroyer, Marie-Sophie.
4. Bréton, Geneviève, 1848–1918.   5. Renooz, C. (Céline).
I. Title.
HQ1613.A735 2000
305.42′0944—dc21   99-28341
                                                                          CIP